Energy, Transportation & the Environment:

A Statistical Sourcebook and Guide to Government Data

2009 Edition

Energy, Transportation & the Environment:

A Statistical Sourcebook and Guide to Government Data

2009 Edition

Essential Topics Series

Woodside, California

Also from Information Publications

State & Municipal Profiles Series

Almanac of the 50 States

California Cities, Towns & Counties   *Connecticut Municipal Profiles*

Florida Cities, Towns & Counties   *Massachusetts Municipal Profiles*

The New Jersey Municipal Data Book   *North Carolina Ciies, Towns & Counties*

American Profiles Series

Asian Americans: A Statistical Sourcebook and Guide to Government Data
Black Americans: A Statistical Sourcebook and Guide to Government Data
Hispanic Americans: A Statistical Sourcebook and Guide to Government Data

Essential Topics Series

Energy, Transportation & the Environment:
A Statistical Sourcebook and Guide to Government Data

ISBN 978-0-929960-57-9
Energy, Transportation & the Environment:
A Statistical Sourcebook and Guide to Government Data, 2009 Edition

©2009 Information Publications, Inc.
Printed in the United States of America

Information Publications, Inc.
2995 Woodside Rd., Suite 400-182
Woodside, CA 94062-2446

www.informationpublications.com
info@informationpublications.com

Toll Free Phone 877.544.INFO (4636)
Toll Free Fax 877.544.4635

Direct Dial Phone 650.568.6170
Direct Dial Fax 650.568.6150

Table of Contents

Detailed Table of Contents

Chapter 5: Public Transportation   129

Chapter 6: Transportation Safety   157

Introduction

Energy, Transportation & the Environment: A Statistical Sourcebook and Guide to Government Data is an annual reference publication from Information Publications' **Essential Topics Series**, which examines current issues and topics that are particularly relevant. Information on energy, transportation, and the environment is available in a variety of reference sources. This volume pulls together a cross-section of the available information, and serves as a guide to further research.

The overall goal of *Energy, Transportation & the Environment* is to bring together a range of diverse information into a single volume, presented in a clear, comprehensible format. The internet and the increasingly large amount of information available online have changed the face of research. However, finding needed information can be a difficult and time-consuming task, and much of the data available is of questionable reliability. The federal government, through the Bureau of the Census and several other departments, collects a truly staggering amount of data, much of which is available online. However, it is frequently poorly indexed and difficult to find if you do not know exactly what you are looking for.

This volume, then, is not intended as a detailed research tool, but rather as an introduction to the available resources. The goal is to provide a broad cross-section of information, and speed up the reader's ability to find more extensive data on a desired topic. To that end, each of the tables contained in this volume contains a citation that leads back to the original source, and a source guide at the end of the book contains a description of each source used, as well as the type of information each source provides. This volume should serve as a ready-reference source, and a good place to begin any research project.

Another reason for collecting this data on energy, transportation, and the environment in a single volume is that, while each of these three vital topics could fill several books in its own right, in the United States these topics are inextricably linked. A high percentage of America's energy consumption is spent on transportation. The burning of fossil fuels in cars and for electricity production is a major source of pollution and greenhouse gases. The search for alternative sources of energy that will minimize harm to the environment impacts our transportation options. The condition of the environment affects our health. Energy prices are a major factor impacting the economy, and our reliance on oil has important implications for our foreign policy.

Organization

This book is divided into fourteen chapters in four parts:

Each of Parts I–III focuses on a single topic (although as we will see, separating them entirely is not possible, so there will be some overlap between topics). Tables in each chapter present a comprehensive review of available federal government statistical information on a particular aspect of energy, transportation, or the environment. Each table presents pertinent information from the source or sources in a clear, comprehensible fashion. Part IV focuses on economic impact and government funding, which cut across all three subject areas.

The information selected for presentation was chosen for its broad scope and general appeal for a diverse group of readers, all with different needs and interests.

The Sources

Almost all of the information in *Energy, Transportation & the Environment* is either collected directly from or republished by US Government sources (or in several cases, partnerships between private organizations and government departments). In turn, most of the federal information is from either the Department of Energy, Department of Transportation, or the Environmental Protection Agency.

For the chapters on energy, by far the most comprehensive source is the Energy Information Administration's (EIA) annual report (in this edition, the *Annual Energy Review 2007*). This report serves as a clearinghouse for the Department of Energy's other data-collection and reporting programs: the *Annual Energy Review* contains excerpts of the data available in most of these reports, as well as several private sources, in order to present as complete a picture of the state of energy in the United States as possible. It also contains historical time series for most data, in many cases going back over 50 years. Any detailed research into energy should begin with this report. The sources cited in the tables present a logical next step for further information. The EIA also produces several other useful reports, including the *International Energy Annual*, and the *Annual Energy Outlook*, which contains projections for energy statistics through 2030.

The one entirely private organization that supplies energy data for this volume is the oil and gas company BP, which produces the *BP Statistical Review of World Energy for 2008*. Data from that report is used here with permission.

As with energy, statistics for transportation have a single comprehensive source that is the logical place to start any research project. In this case, it is the annual *National Transportation Statistics* report, compiled by the Department of Transportation's Bureau of Transportation Statistics. This report also contains excerpts from many other sources on transportation, and often saves the reader a good deal of time by bringing together data from several different sources in the same table (for example, a table on modes of shipping could contain automobile, airplane, railroad, and pipeline data, all from different sources). *National Transportation Statistics* also collects information from several private organizations, much of which would not be accessible or reproducible otherwise, and time series data that would often require going back to several years' editions of a single report to obtain. The report's sources and citations also contain many good ideas for further research.

Data for the environment is more scattered. The Environmental Protection Agency is the preeminent source for information, but there is no single summary publication like those for energy and transportation. Statistics on the environment are spread out in publications on individual topics, contained under the EPA's primary subject headings (i.e., water, waste, greenhouse gas). Besides the EPA, several other government agences, such as the Department of the Interior's Fish & Wildlife Service and the Department of Agriculture's Natural Resource Conservation Service, also collect information.

One other publication is not used heavily in this volume, but deserves further mention. The *Statistical Abstract of the United States* is the Census Bureau's major annual overview of all the government's publications, and collectively presents a thorough profile of the United States and its population, economy, and government. While most of the *Abstract*'s information on energy, transportation, and the environment is taken from the sources listed above, it also contains information on just about every possible topic, and is a useful place to start any research project, often containing data that is not available elsewhere.

One final note about sources: because of its resources, and the size and scope of its data-collecting apparatus, the federal government is considered the most reliable source of information. For this reason, Information Publications draws as much of its data as possible from federal government sources, and makes no assumptions about the validity, reliability, or motivations behind the presentation of the data. As with any statistical analysis, due care must be taken in its use and interpretation.

The Tables

This section details how the tables have been prepared and presented.

The table number contains the chapter number to the left of the decimal and the location of the table within the chapter to the right of the decimal. Thus (for example), Table 6.04 is the fourth table of Chapter 6.

The table title first presents the general topic of the table, followed by the detail presented about the general topic (e.g., the data is presented by state, mode of transport, energy source, economic sector, etc.), and the years for which data is presented. In most cases, the tables retain the original terms used in the source material to make the book compatible with the original sources.

Along the left margin of each table appears a column of line descriptors. Here, after a general heading, subgroups of the heading are shown. In general, counts and quantities appear first, followed by percentages, rates, per capita amounts, medians, and means.

Wherever available and appropriate, a time series of data is presented in order to provide readers with a historical context for the information. However, readers should be cautioned that the years selected have been chosen from no special knowledge of the subject, nor to make any specific point. The fact that there has been an increase or decrease in a given indicator for the period displayed does not mean that the same trend will continue, or that it represents the continuation of a historical trend. Many apparent changes are merely the result of an agency's redefining its terms: for example, certain sources of energy may be grouped under different types of energy depending on the year, or the agency collecting the data. For this reason, readers are advised to use caution when comparing figures across different time periods or different agencies. In general, information in tables and across each chapter is presented with the oldest, most general information first, followed by newer, more specific information.

The notation "NA" stands for "not available." Although we strive to obtain all available data, there are several reasons for data not being available. Some categories have come into existence (in terms of providing data) fairly recently: for example, some sources of alternative energy only have data available for recent years. Other times, the data was simply not provided in the original source. Finally, the data item simply may not apply for the category given, such as the number of lane-miles of rural roads in Washington, DC, which contains no rural areas.

Table Notes

The bottom of each table contains three key paragraphs: **Source**, **Notes**, and **Units**. The **Source** paragraph lists the source of the data presented in the table. When more than one source was used, the sources are listed in the same order in which the data itself appears in the table. As almost all sources are government publications, the issuing agency is listed as the author. Citations provide the table number (or page number, if table numbers are not available) in the source from which the material was taken. An increasing number of sources are now available only on the internet. For tables pulled exclusively from online sources, the URL is listed as the source, along with the date it was accessed.

The **Notes** paragraph includes pertinent facts about the data. One general note will apply to all tabular data: detail (subgroups) may not add to the total shown, due to either rounding or the fact that only selected subgroups are displayed.

The final paragraph of a table, **Units**, identifies the units used, specifically stating that the quantity is billions of Btu's, thousands of vehicles, dollars spent per capita, etc. Readers are urged to pay special attention to the units when a percent, rate, per capita amount, mean, or median is provided. When dollar amounts are involved, this book uses constant (inflation-adjusted) dollars whenever possible to facilitate comparisons. However, in many cases, figures are only given in current dollars, so readers are advised to check the 'notes' section of the table and proceed with caution in making comparisons between different time periods. If the type of dollars is not explicitly stated or available, the figures are most likely given in current dollars.

Guide to Sources

Energy, Transportation & the Environment also presents a complete guide to sources. Sources are sorted alphabetically by the name of the publication, with the issuing department or group appearing next. Each entry gives a description of the source, in particular how it was used in the present volume and what information it might present for further research, as well as the online location where the data or report can be accessed.

Glossary

This book contains definitions for any specialized terms that are needed to understand the data. The tables contain short, clear definitions with only as much background material as is necessary to make a term understandable in a general sense. However, for many tables, when it is not possible to adequately define a term in the table notes, the glossary provides a full definition and serves as an important tool in using the tables.

Before drawing any conclusions from the data, it is vital to understand the meaning of all terms used in a table. Certain terms require some methodological background in order to accurately understand the material presented. Other terms require some technical expertise: for example, the differences between anthracite and lignite coal, or distillate oil and fuel oil, the details of different methods for treating and managing hazardous waste, or the different products that are considered sources of biomass energy. Agencies all have their own specialized, clearly-defined terms, and different agencies may not necessarily use the terms to mean the same thing. The same data can look quite different when presented in a different set of units or conventions (such as tons of CO_2 equivalent vs tons of emissions for greenhouse gases). In the data tables and glossary, we try to provide enough background information for readers to make sense of the information presented, using our best understanding of the terms and definitions used; however, some terms and concepts may require an expert to provide a full explanation. In this case, readers requiring detailed definitions and an understating of the technical and methodological detail should refer to the source given at the end of each table.

Index

Most key terms from the tables have been indexed. Readers should note that the index provides table numbers as opposed to page numbers. Cross-references are provided whenever they are deemed helpful.

A Suggestion on How to Use This Book

One way to use this book is by locating the subject of general interest in the Table of Contents, and turning to that chapter. While the Table of Contents is detailed enough to narrow a search, and the index can speed access to specific items, sometimes paging through the dozen or so tables in a given field uncovers unexpected information that can prove useful. It is just this type of serendipity that has led to the inclusion of some of the information in this book, and sometimes such an unexpected find can greatly enhance a research project.

Disclaimer

Energy, Transportation & the Environment contains thousands of pieces of information. Every reasonable precaution, along with a good deal of care, was taken in its preparation. Despite our efforts it is possible that some of the information contained in this book may not be accurate. Some errors may be due to errors in the original source materials, others may have been made by the compilers of this volume. An incorrect spelling may occur, a figure may be inverted, or similar mistakes may exist. The compilers, editors, typists, printers and others are all human, and in a work of this magnitude the possibility of error can never be fully eliminated.

The publisher is also aware that some users may apply the data in this book in various remunerative projects. Although we have taken reasonable and responsible measures to insure accuracy, we cannot take responsibility for liability or losses suffered by users of the data. No other guarantees are made or implied.

The publisher assumes no liability for losses incurred by users, and warrants only that diligence and due care were used in the production of this volume.

A Final Word

As this book is updated on an annual basis, questions, comments, and criticisms from users are vital to making informed editorial choices about succeeding editions. If you have a suggestion or comment, be assured that it will be both appreciated and carefully considered. If you should find an error here, please let us know so that it may be corrected. Our goal is to provide accurate, easy to use, statistical compendia that serve our readers' needs. Your help enables us to do our job better. If you know how this book could become more useful to you, please contact us.

The Editors
Information Publications, Inc.
2995 Woodside Road, Suite 400-182
Woodside, CA 94062
www.informationpublications.com
info@informationpublications.com
Toll Free Phone: 877-544-4636
Toll Free Fax: 877-544-4635

Publisher: Eric Weiner
Editors: Beth Ann Allen and Stephen Rauch

Part I: Energy

Chapter 1

Energy Production & Consumption

Chapter 1 Highlights

Chapter 1 contains statistics on energy production and consumption in the United States. Both production and consumption have increased dramatically in the last 50 years (table 1.01, with breakdowns by energy source and economic sector in tables 1.02 and 1.03, respectively). However, it is worth noting that consumption of energy has far outpaced domestic production; the two figures were approximately even in 1955, while energy consumption exceeded domestic production by more than 40% in 2007. Electricity generation, capacity, and consumption (tables 1.05–1.07) and petroleum production and consumption (tables 1.08 and 1.09) deserve special attention.

Energy is also a significant portion of consumer spending, at over $3,500 annually per capita (table 1.04, which also contains a state-by-state breakdown). Both production and consumption are expected to continue to grow in the next 25 years (table 1.29, also see table 1.30 for transportation sector projections).

The vast majority of energy produced and consumed comes from fossil fuels (nearly 85% of consumption in 2007, see table 1.02). The largest single source of fossil fuel energy is petroleum products, over half of which is imported (table 1.08). Most pretroleum consumption comes from the transportation sector, and most of that is motor gasoline (table 1.09). In turn, almost all energy consumed in transportation comes from fossil fuels, with most of that coming from cars (table 1.24). Most households are heated with natural gas or electricity (table 1.21). The Stragetic Pretroleum Reserve, an emergency supply of oil set aside for cases of severe supply interruption, has grown from 107 million barrels in 1980 to almost 700 million barrels in 2007, and contains enough oil to cover the amount of US imports at the current rate for 58 days if the supply suddenly dried up (table 1.11). Most of the United States' estimated oil reserves are located offshore, while most natural gas resources are located in onshore and offshore areas under state jurisdiction (table 1.12).

Transportation sector energy consumption is given in tables 1.24 and 1.26, with a state-by-state breakdown in table 1.25. Of all major modes of transportation, Amtrak has the lowest energy intensity (thus, the highest energy efficiency) per passenger-mile, according to the latest data available. Air travel and passenger cars are comparable, but other 2-axle, 4-wheel vehicles (such as Sport Utility Vehicles) are much more energy-intense (table 1.27). Tables 1.21 and 1.22 give a breakdown of the fuels used for household energy needs.

Readers are also directed to chapter 13, which contains information on energy prices and spending, and chapter 3, which presents energy data for other countries and worldwide.

Table 1.01: Energy Production and Consumption by Source, 1949–2007

	Fossil Fuels		Nuclear Power		Renewable Energy		Total Energy	
	Produced	Consumed	Produced	Consumed	Produced	Consumed	Produced	Consumed
1949	28.748	29.002	0.000	0.000	2.974	2.974	31.722	31.982
1950	32.563	31.632	0.000	0.000	2.978	2.978	35.540	34.616
1955	37.364	37.410	0.000	0.000	2.784	2.784	40.148	40.208
1960	39.869	42.137	0.006	0.006	2.929	2.929	42.804	45.087
1965	47.235	50.577	0.043	0.043	3.398	3.398	50.676	54.017
1970	59.186	63.522	0.239	0.239	4.076	4.076	63.501	67.844
1975	54.733	65.355	1.900	1.900	4.723	4.723	61.357	71.999
1980	59.008	69.826	2.739	2.739	5.485	5.485	67.232	78.122
1985	57.539	66.091	4.076	4.076	6.185	6.185	67.799	76.491
1990	58.560	72.333	6.104	6.104	6.206	6.206	70.870	84.652
1991	57.872	71.880	6.422	6.422	6.238	6.238	70.532	84.607
1992	57.655	73.397	6.479	6.479	5.993	5.993	70.127	85.956
1993	55.822	74.836	6.410	6.410	6.263	6.262	68.495	87.603
1994	58.044	76.258	6.694	6.694	6.155	6.155	70.893	89.260
1995	57.540	77.258	7.075	7.075	6.703	6.705	71.319	91.173
1996	58.387	79.783	7.087	7.087	7.167	7.168	72.641	94.175
1997	58.857	80.874	6.597	6.597	7.180	7.178	72.634	94.765
1998	59.314	81.370	7.068	7.068	6.659	6.657	73.041	95.183
1999	57.614	82.428	7.610	7.610	6.683	6.681	71.907	96.817
2000	57.366	84.733	7.862	7.862	6.262	6.264	71.490	98.975
2001	58.541	82.903	8.033	8.033	5.318	5.316	71.892	96.326
2002	56.894	83.750	8.143	8.143	5.899	5.893	70.936	97.858
2003	56.157	84.078	7.959	7.959	6.149	6.150	70.264	98.209
2004	55.914	85.830	8.222	8.222	6.248	6.261	70.384	100.351
2005	55.056	85.817	8.160	8.160	6.431	6.444	69.647	100.506
2006	55.940	84.658	8.214	8.214	6.872	6.922	71.025	99.856
2007	56.499	86.248	8.415	8.415	6.800	6.830	71.713	101.600

Source: Energy Information Administration, *Annual Energy Review 2006*, table 1.1; *2007*, table 1.1.

Notes: Data for 2007 is preliminary. Some data has been revised since its original publication.

Units: Energy produced in quadrillion Btu.

Table 1.02:   Energy Production and Consumption by Detailed Source, 1995, 2000, and 2007

	1995		2000		2007	
	Produced	Consumed	Produced	Consumed	Produced	Consumed
All Energy	*71.319*	*91.173*	*71.490*	*98.975*	*71.713*	*101.600*
Total Fossil Fuels	57.540	77.258	57.366	84.733	56.499	86.248
Coal	22.130	20.089	22.735	22.580	23.480	22.767
Dry natural gas	19.082	22.671	19.662	23.824	19.817	23.638
Crude oil	13.887	NA	12.358	NA	10.802	NA
Petroleum	NA	34.437	NA	38.264	NA	39.818
Natural gas plant liquids	2.442	NA	2.611	NA	2.400	NA
Nuclear	7.075	7.075	7.862	7.862	8.415	8.415
Total Renewable Energy	6.703	6.705	6.262	6.264	6.800	6.830
Hydroelectric	3.205	3.205	2.811	2.811	2.463	2.463
Geothermal	0.294	0.294	0.317	0.317	0.353	0.353
Solar	0.070	0.070	0.066	0.066	0.080	0.080
Wind	0.033	0.033	0.057	0.057	0.319	0.319
Biomass	3.102	3.104	3.010	3.013	3.584	3.615

Source: Energy Information Administration, *Annual Energy Review 2006*, tables 1.2 and 1.3; *2007*, tables 1.2 and 1.3.

Notes: Data for 2007 is preliminary. Some data has been revised since its original publication.

Units: Energy produced in quadrillion Btu.

Table 1.03:   Energy Consumption by Sector, 1949–2007

	Residential	Commercial	Industrial	Electric Power	Total
1949	5,614	3,661	14,717	4,339	31,982
1950	6,007	3,883	16,233	4,679	34,616
1955	7,303	3,882	19,472	6,461	40,208
1960	9,078	4,589	20,823	8,158	45,087
1965	10,689	5,820	25,075	11,014	54,017
1970	13,798	8,307	29,641	16,259	67,844
1975	14,842	9,466	29,447	20,307	71,999
1980	15,787	10,563	32,077	24,327	78,122
1985	16,088	11,444	28,875	26,132	76,491
1990	17,015	13,333	31,894	30,660	84,652
1991	17,490	13,512	31,485	31,025	84,607
1992	17,427	13,454	32,659	30,893	85,956
1993	18,289	13,836	32,719	32,025	87,603
1994	18,181	14,111	33,606	32,563	89,260
1995	18,578	14,698	34,045	33,621	91,173
1996	19,562	15,181	34,988	34,638	94,175
1997	19,026	15,694	35,288	35,045	94,765
1998	19,021	15,979	34,928	36,385	95,183
1999	19,621	16,384	34,855	37,136	96,817
2000	20,488	17,176	34,757	38,214	98,975
2001	20,106	17,141	32,806	37,366	96,326
2002	20,874	17,367	32,765	38,171	97,858
2003	21,208	17,351	32,650	38,218	98,209
2004	21,178	17,664	33,609	38,876	100,351
2005	21,717	17,875	32,546	39,799	100,506
2006	20,855	17,737	32,404	39,589	99,856
2007	21,753	18,430	32,321	40,567	101,600

Source: Energy Information Administration, *Annual Energy Review 2006*, table 2.1a; *2007*, table 2.1a.

Notes: Total consumption consists of primary energy consumption, electricity retail sales, and system energy losses.
Data for 2007 is preliminary. Some data has been revised since its original publication.

Units: Consumption in trillion Btu.

Table 1.04: Energy Consumption, Spending, and Prices by State, 2005

	Consumption per Capita	Expenditures per Capita	Price
United States	*339.2*	*$3,525*	*$15.66*
Alabama	466.8	3,953	14.28
Alaska	1,193.9	7,806	13.98
Arizona	248.6	2,789	17.78
Arkansas	409.5	3,827	15.15
California	232.3	2,879	17.37
Colorado	305.1	3,137	15.18
Connecticut	258.2	3,571	19.40
Delaware	371.9	3,663	16.25
District of Columbia	327.0	3,496	20.21
Florida	257.3	2,805	17.98
Georgia	348.4	3,554	15.75
Hawaii	263.0	3,943	21.56
Idaho	352.9	3,131	14.13
Illinois	324.0	3,310	14.72
Indiana	464.2	4,041	12.67
Iowa	415.4	4,214	14.31
Kansas	376.4	3,487	14.97
Kentucky	472.3	4,084	13.90
Louisiana	803.7	6,621	13.23
Maine	367.6	4,157	16.21
Maryland	279.1	3,153	17.11
Massachusetts	242.9	3,376	19.37
Michigan	313.3	3,206	14.56
Minnesota	362.2	3,571	14.58
Mississippi	407.6	3,889	15.81
Missouri	330.8	3,426	15.34
Montana	448.2	4,307	14.83
Nebraska	373.4	3,657	14.55

(continued on next page)

Table 1.04: Energy Consumption, Spending, and Prices by State, 2005

	Consumption per Capita	Expenditures per Capita	Price
United States	*339.2*	*$3,525*	*$15.66*
Nevada	302.1	3,523	17.94
New Hampshire	257.4	3,516	18.68
New Jersey	315.2	3,721	16.19
New Mexico	352.3	3,372	16.68
New York	217.0	2,943	18.92
North Carolina	314.8	3,244	16.53
North Dakota	648.1	5,183	11.08
Ohio	356.2	3,656	15.27
Oklahoma	438.6	4,019	14.80
Oregon	301.8	2,955	15.10
Pennsylvania	327.5	3,460	15.69
Rhode Island	213.3	2,915	18.79
South Carolina	398.2	3,717	15.32
South Dakota	350.6	3,710	15.10
Tennessee	390.5	3,645	14.88
Texas	506.0	5,008	14.73
Utah	302.1	2,786	13.69
Vermont	269.5	3,653	18.78
Virginia	345.4	3,468	15.22
Washington	328.3	2,958	14.45
West Virginia	439.7	3,848	13.50
Wisconsin	336.0	3,464	15.22
Wyoming	911.9	7,230	12.93

Source: Energy Information Administration, *Annual Energy Review 2007*, table 1.6.

Notes: Prices and expenditures include taxes where tax data is available.

Units: Consumption per capita in million Btu; expenditure per capita in current 2005 dollars per year; prices in current 2005 dollars per million Btu.

Table 1.05: Electricity Net Generation, Trade, and End Use, 1990–2007

	1990	1995	2000	2007
Net Generation Total	*3,038*	*3,353*	*3,802*	*4,160*
Electric	2,901	3,194	3,638	4,006
Commercial	6	8	8	9
Industrial	131	151	157	145
Net Imports	2	39	34	31
Imports	18	43	49	51
Exports	16	4	15	20
Losses & unaccounted for	203	229	244	299
End Use Total	2,837	3,164	3,592	3,892
Retail sales	2,713	3,013	3,421	3,748
Direct use	125	151	171	144*

Source: Energy Information Administration, *Annual Energy Review 2006*, table 8.1; *2007*, table 8.1.

Notes: 'Losses' includes transmission and distribution losses.
'Direct end use' refers to electricity consumption by the same entity that produced it.
'Retail sales' includes all sales to customers by utilities and other service providers.
Data for 2007 is preliminary.
* Estimate.

Units: Net generation, imports, losses, and end use in billion killowatt-hours.

Table 1.06:   Energy Consumed for Electricity Production by Source, 1990–2007

	1990	1995	2000	2007
Total Consumption	*31,954*	*35,043*	*39,586*	*42,201*
Fossil Fuel Total	21,747	23,473	27,567	29,587
Coal	16,477	17,687	20,411	20,990
Petroleum	1,367	813	1,212	715
Natural gas	3,791	4,840	5,818	7,716
Other gas	112	133	126	166
Nuclear power	6,104	7,075	7,862	8,415
Renewable Energy Total	4,058	4,318	3,995	3,924
Hydroelectric	3,046	3,205	2,811	2,463
Wood biomass	442	480	496	548
Waste biomass	211	316	330	276
Geothermal	326	280	296	312
Solar	4	5	5	6
Wind	29	33	57	319
Net imports	8	134	115	107

Source: Energy Information Administration, *Annual Energy Review 2006*, table 8.4a; *2007*, table 8.4a.

Notes: 'Other gas' includes blast furnace gas, propane gas, and other manufactured and waste gases from fossil fuels.
Data is for electric utilities, independent power producers, commercial plants, and industrial plants.
Data for 2007 is preliminary.

Units: Energy consumed in trillion Btu.

Table 1.07: Net Summer Electrical Capacity, 1950–2007

	Fossil Fuels	Nuclear Power	Renewable Energy	Total
1950	50.0	0.0	19.2	69.2
1960	130.8	0.4	35.9	167.1
1970	265.4	7.0	63.9	336.4
1980	444.1	51.8	82.7	578.6
1985	485.0	79.4	90.8	655.2
1990	527.8	99.6	86.8	734.1
1995	554.2	99.5	93.9	769.5
1996	561.7	100.8	91.7	775.9
1997	564.1	99.7	94.8	778.6
1998	563.9	97.1	94.6	775.9
1999	572.6	97.4	95.3	785.9
2000	598.9	97.9	94.9	811.7
2001	634.9	98.2	95.0	848.3
2002	689.5	98.7	96.1	905.3
2003	731.2	99.2	96.8	948.4
2004	745.4	99.6	96.4	962.9
2005	757.1	100.0	98.7	978.0
2006	761.6	100.3	101.9	986.2
2007	769.0	100.6	106.6	998.8

Source: Energy Information Administration, *Annual Energy Review 2006*, table 8.11a; *2007*, table 8.11a.

Notes: 'Net summer capacity' is defined as the maximum output for a system in a multi-hour test at the time of summer peak demand (June 1 through September 30). This output reflects a reduction in capacity due to electricity use for station service or auxiliaries.

Data prior to 1989 includes only electric utilities; later data includes electric utilities, independent power producers, and commercial and industrial plants. Caution should be used when directly comparing data from before and after 1989.

Data for 2007 is preliminary.

Units: Net summer capacity in million kilowatts.

Table 1.08:   Petroleum Production and Supplies, 1990–2007

	1990	1995	2000	2007
Total Supplies	*16,988*	*17,725*	*19,701*	*20,698*
Production total	8,914	8,322	7,733	6,879
Crude oil	7,355	6,560	5,822	5,103
48 states	5,582	5,076	4,851	4,384
Alaska	1,773	1,484	970	719
Natural gas/Plant liquids	1,559	1,762	1,911	1,776
Net imports	7,161	7,886	10,419	12,040

Source: Energy Information Administration, *Annual Energy Review 2006*, table 5.1; *2007*, table 5.1.

Notes: 'Net imports' equals the value of imports minus exports.
Groups may not add to total.
Data for 2007 is preliminary.

Units: Production, imports, and supplies in thousands of barrels per day.

Table 1.09:   Petroleum Consumption by End-Use Sector, 1990–2007

	1990	1995	2000	2007
Residential Sector total	767	767	897	758
Distillate fuel oil	460	426	424	338
Kerosene	31	36	46	19
Liquefied petroleum gas	276	306	427	401
Commercial Sector total	465	361	383	325
Distillate fuel oil	252	225	230	191
Kerosene	6	11	14	4
Liquefied petroleum gas	49	54	75	71
Motor gasoline	58	10	23	24
Residual fuel oil	100	62	40	34
Industrial Sector total	4,304	4,594	4,903	5,056
Asphalt & road oil	483	486	525	490
Distillate fuel oil	541	532	563	600
Kerosene	6	7	8	8
Liquefied petroleum gas	1,215	1,527	1,720	1,589
Lubricants	84	80	86	70
Motor gasoline	97	105	79	190
Petroleum coke	325	328	361	414
Residual fuel oil	179	147	105	109
Transportation Sector total	10,888	11,668	13,012	14,265
Aviation gasoline	24	21	20	17
Distillate fuel oil	1,722	1,973	2,422	3,048
Jet fuel	1,522	1,514	1,725	1,623
Liquefied petroleum gas	16	13	8	21
Lubricants	80	76	81	66
Motor gasoline	7,080	7,674	8,370	9,076
Residual fuel oil	443	397	386	414
Electric Power Sector total	566	334	505	294
Distillate fuel oil	45	51	82	43
Petroleum coke	14	37	45	77
Residual fuel oil	507	247	378	174

Source: Energy Information Administration, *Annual Energy Review 2006*, tables 5.13a through 5.12d; *2007*, tables 5.13a through 5.13d.

Notes: 'Motor gasoline' refers to finished motor gasoline, and after 1993 also includes ethanol-blended gasoline.
Most data for 2007 is preliminary.

Units: Petroleum consumption in thousands of barrels per day.

Table 1.10: Refinery Capacity and Utilization, 1980–2007

	Number of Operable Refineries	Refinery Capacity	Gross Input	Utilization
1980	319	NA	13,796	75.4%
1985	223	15,671	12,165	77.6
1990	205	15,623	13,610	87.1
1995	175	15,346	14,119	92.0
1996	170	15,239	14,337	94.1
1997	164	15,594	14,838	95.2
1998	163	15,802	15,113	95.6
1999	159	16,282	15,080	92.6
2000	158	16,525	15,299	92.6
2001	155	16,582	15,352	92.6
2002	153	16,744	15,180	90.7
2003	149	16,748	15,508	92.6
2004	149	16,974	15,783	93.0
2005	148	17,196	15,578	90.6
2006	149	17,385	15,602	89.7
2007	149	17,447	15,449	88.5

Source: Energy Information Administration, *Annual Energy Review 2006*, table 5.9; *2007*, table 5.9.

Notes: Operable refineries are as of January 1.
Capacity is the annual average, taken as the weighted average of the monthly capacity data.
Gross input is obtained by taking the sum of the monthly data.
Utilization is obtained by dividing the gross input to distillation units by the annual average capacity.
Data for 2007 is preliminary.

Units: Number of refineries; capacity and input in thousands of barrels per day; utilization as percent of total capacity.

Table 1.11:   Strategic Petroleum Reserve, 1977–2007

	End-of-Year Stocks	% of Crude Oil Stock	% of Total Petroleum Stock	Days of Petroleum Net Imports
1977	7,455	2.1%	0.6%	1
1980	107,800	23.1	7.7	17
1985	493,316	60.6	32.5	115
1990	585,692	64.5	36.1	82
1991	568,508	63.7	35.2	86
1992	574,724	64.4	36.1	83
1993	587,080	63.6	35.6	77
1994	591,670	63.7	35.8	73
1995	591,640	66.1	37.9	75
1996	565,816	66.6	37.5	67
1997	563,429	64.9	36.1	62
1998	571,405	63.8	34.7	59
1999	567,241	66.6	38.0	57
2000	540,678	65.4	36.8	52
2001	550,241	63.8	34.7	50
2002	599,091	68.3	38.7	57
2003	638,388	70.4	40.7	57
2004	675,600	70.3	41.1	56
2005	684,544	67.9	40.3	55
2006	688,605	68.8	40.0	56
2007	696,941	70.9	41.9	58

Source: Energy Information Administration, *Annual Energy Review 2007*, table 5.17.

Notes: The Strategic Petroleum Reserve is a stock of petroleum maintained by the federal government for use during periods of serious shortages and supply interruptions.
'Days of petroleum net imports' is calculated by dividing the total stock in the reserve by the average net amount of petroleum imported each day, to obtain the length of time the reserve could theoretically sustain US import needs if the supply were cut off completely.

Units: Stocks in thousands of barrels; percent of total; days' worth of net imports contained in reserve.

Table 1.12: Recoverable Oil and Natural Gas Estimates, 2006

	Crude Oil	Dry Natural Gas	Natural Gas Liquids
Undiscovered, Conventional	130.16	724.84	7.79
Alaska onshore and state offshore	26.04	126.75	2.23
Alaska federal offshore	26.61	132.06	0.00
48 states onshore and state offshore	18.24	178.21	5.56
48 states federal offshore	59.27	287.82	0.00
Discovered, Conventional	45.54	485.71	18.26
US onshore and state offshore	38.66	454.80	18.26
US federal offshore	6.88	30.91	0.00
Undiscovered, Unconventional	2.13	322.27	3.80
US Total	*177.83*	*1,532.82*	*29.85*
Onshore and state offshore	85.07	1,082.03	29.85
Federal offshore	92.76	450.79	0.00

Source: Energy Information Administration, *Annual Energy Review 2007*, table 4.1.

Notes: 'Federal lands' are owned or under the jurisdiction of the Federal government, excluding Indian and Native lands.
'State offshore' includes shallow water areas near the shoreline, under state jurisdiction.
'Conventional' deposits are discrete subsurface accumulations of crude oil or natural gas with well-defined hydrocarbon/water contacts.
'Unconventional' deposits are geographically extensive and generally lack well-defined hydrocarbon/water contacts.
Estimates are of technically recoverable resources, which refer to those that could be produced using current technology, without reference to economic viability.

Units: Crude oil and natural gas liquids in billion barrels; dry natural gas in trillion cubic feet.

Table 1.13: Crude Oil and Natural Gas Rigs in Operation, 1980–2007

	By Location		By Material		All Rigs
	Onshore	Offshore	Crude Oil	Natural Gas	Total
1980	2,678	231	NA	NA	2,909
1985	1,774	206	NA	NA	1,980
1990	902	108	532	464	1,010
1995	622	101	323	385	723
1996	671	108	306	464	779
1997	821	122	376	564	943
1998	703	123	264	560	827
1999	519	106	128	496	625
2000	778	140	197	720	918
2001	1,003	153	217	939	1,156
2002	717	113	137	691	830
2003	924	108	157	872	1,032
2004	1,095	97	165	1,025	1,192
2005	1,290	93	194	1,186	1,383
2006	1,559	90	274	1,372	1,649
2007	1,695	72	297	1,466	1,768

Source: Energy Information Administration, *Annual Energy Review 2006*, table 4.4; *2007*, table 4.4.

Notes: Data is based on the average of the 52 or 53 consecutive whole weeks that most nearly coincide with the calendar year. Groups may not add to total.

Units: Number of rigs by site and type.

Table 1.14: Natural Gas Production, Trade, Storage, and Consumption, 1950–2007

	Dry Gas Production	Net Imports	Net Withdrawals	Total Consumption
1950	6,022	-26	-54	5,767
1960	12,228	144	-132	11,967
1970	21,014	751	-398	21,139
1980	19,403	936	23	19,877
1985	16,454	894	235	17,281
1990	17,810	1,447	-513	19,174
1995	18,599	2,687	415	22,207
1996	18,854	2,784	2	22,609
1997	18,902	2,837	24	22,737
1998	19,024	2,993	-530	22,246
1999	18,832	3,422	172	22,405
2000	19,182	3,538	829	23,333
2001	19,616	3,604	-1,166	22,239
2002	18,928	3,499	467	23,007
2003	19,099	3,264	-197	22,277
2004	18,591	3,404	-114	22,389
2005	18,051	3,612	52	22,011
2006	18,476	3,462	-436	21,653
2007	19,278	3,793	177	23,055

Source: Energy Information Administration, *Annual Energy Review 2006*, table 6.1; *2007*, table 6.1.

Notes: 'Net imports' equals the amount imported minus amount exported.
'Net withdrawals' equals the amount withdrawn minues amount added.
Negative values indicate greater exports than imports, and greater additions than
    withdrawals, respectively.
Data for 2007 is preliminary.

Units: Petroleum consumption in thousands of barrels per day.

Table 1.15: Fossil Fuel Production on Federally-Run Land, 1980–2007

	Crude Oil	Natual Gas Plant Liquids	Natual Gas	Coal	Fossil Fuels
1980	2.96	0.04	6.01	2.08	11.09
1985	3.64	0.10	5.41	4.04	13.19
1990	2.99	0.19	6.74	6.12	16.05
1995	3.29	0.28	6.96	8.04	18.56
1996	3.46	0.27	7.50	7.56	18.79
1997	3.67	0.28	7.62	7.72	19.29
1998	3.52	0.23	7.27	7.95	18.97
1999	3.65	0.25	7.44	8.73	20.07
2000	4.00	0.33	7.32	9.27	20.92
2001	3.92	0.35	7.17	8.87	20.31
2002	3.76	0.40	6.96	10.51	21.63
2003	2.45	0.38	6.19	9.18	18.19
2004	2.07	0.41	7.59	11.27	21.33
2005	2.55	0.36	6.89	8.78	18.58
2006	2.91	0.31	5.11	9.49	17.82
2007	3.39	0.35	5.89	9.51	19.14

Source: Energy Information Administration, *Annual Energy Review 2006*, table 1.14; *2007*, table 1.14.

Notes: Data for 2000 and earlier refers to the calendar year indicated. Later data refers to the October-September fiscal year (for instance, data for fiscal year 2003 is for October 2002 through September 2003).
Some data has been revised since its original publication.

Units: Production in quadrillion Btu.

Table 1.16: Coal Production and Consumption, Selected Characteristics, 1990–2007

	1990	1995	2000	2007
Production total	*1,029.1*	*1,033.0*	*1,073.6*	*1,145.6*
By Rank				
Bituminous coal	693.2	613.8	574.3	534.9*
Subbituminous coal	244.3	328.0	409.2	530.6*
Lignite	88.1	86.5	85.6	78.5*
Anthracite	3.5	4.7	4.6	1.6*
By Type of Mining				
Underground	424.5	396.2	373.7	351.3*
Surface	604.5	636.7	700.0	794.3*
By Location				
East of the Mississippi	630.2	544.2	507.5	477.2*
West of the Mississippi	398.9	488.7	566.1	668.4*
Consumption total	*904.5*	*962.1*	*1,084.1*	*1,128.8*
By End-use Sector				
Residential	1.3	0.8	0.5	0.3
Commercial	5.4	5.1	3.7	3.0
Industrial	115.2	106.1	94.1	79.2
Electric power	782.6	850.2	985.8	1,046.4

Source: Energy Information Administration, *Annual Energy Review 2006*, tables 7.2 and 7.3; *2007*, tables 7.2 and 7.3.

Notes: Rank of coal is determined by its fixed carbon, volatile matter, heating value, and agglomerating (or caking) properties.

Anthracite, the highest rank, is used primarily for residential and commercial space heating. It is a hard, brittle, and black lustrous coal, often referred to as hard coal.

Bituminous coal (the next rank) is dense, usually black or dark brown, and is used primarily as fuel in steam-electric power generation or heat and power applications in manufacturing and making coke.

Subbituminous coal is used primarily as fuel for steam-electric power generation, and may be dull, dark brown to black, soft and crumbly, or bright, jet black, hard, and relatively strong.

Lignite, the lowest rank of coal, is brownish-black and is used used almost exclusively as fuel for steam-electric power generation.

Most 2007 data is preliminary.

* Estimate.

Units: Coal produced and consumed in millions of short tons (2,000 lbs).

Table 1.17: Nuclear Power Plant Activity, 1960–2007

	Net Generation	% of Total Net Generation	Net Summer Capacity	Capacity Factor	Number of Operable Units
1960	0.5	0.1%	0.4	NA	3
1970	21.8	1.4	7.0	NA	20
1980	251.1	11.0	51.8	56.3%	71
1985	383.7	15.5	79.4	58.0	96
1990	576.9	19.0	99.6	66.0	112
1995	673.4	20.1	99.5	77.4	109
1996	674.7	19.6	100.8	76.2	109
1997	628.6	18.0	99.7	71.1	107
1998	673.7	18.6	97.1	78.2	104
1999	728.3	19.7	97.4	85.3	104
2000	753.9	19.8	97.9	88.1	104
2001	768.8	20.6	98.2	89.4	104
2002	780.1	20.2	98.7	90.3	104
2003	763.7	19.7	99.2	87.9	104
2004	788.5	19.9	99.6	90.1	104
2005	782.0	19.3	100.0	89.3	104
2006	787.2	19.4	100.1	89.9	104
2007	806.5	19.4	100.6	91.5	NA

Source: Energy Information Administration, *Annual Energy Review 2006*, tables 9.1 and 9.2; *2007*, tables 9.1 and 9.2.

Notes: The capacity factor is calculated as the ratio of the actual power generation to the maximum possible generation.
'Operable units' refers to generating units holding full-power licenses at the end of the year in question.
Some 2007 data is preliminary.

Units: Net generation in billion killowatt-hours; net summer capacity in million killowatts; nuclear share and capacity factor as percent of total.

**Table 1.18: Uranium Exploration and
Development Drilling, 1950–2007**

	Holes Drilled			Footage Drilled		
	Exploration	Development	Total	Exploration	Development	Total
1950	NA	NA	NA	0.57	0.21	0.78
1955	NA	NA	NA	5.27	0.76	6.03
1960	7.34	24.40	31.73	1.40	4.21	5.61
1965	6.23	7.33	13.56	1.16	0.95	2.11
1970	43.98	14.87	58.85	17.98	5.55	23.53
1975	34.29	21.6	55.89	15.69	9.73	25.42
1980	39.61	20.19	59.8	19.60	8.59	28.19
1985	2.88	0.77	3.65	1.42	0.34	1.76
1990	1.51	1.91	3.42	0.87	0.81	1.68
1995	0.58	1.73	2.31	0.40	0.95	1.35
2000	*	*	1.55	*	*	1.02
2006	1.47	3.43	4.90	0.82	1.89	2.71
2007	4.35	5.00	9.35	2.20	2.95	5.15

Source: Energy Information Administration, *Annual Energy Review 2006*, table 4.12; *2007*, table 4.12.

Notes: 'Exploration' includes surface drilling in search of new ore deposits or extensions of
            existing deposits, and any drilling at the site of a discovery until a company decides there
            are sufficient reserves to justify commercial explotiation.
            'Development' refers to drilling after commercial exploitation is deemed feasible, to
            determine size, grade, and configuration.
            * Information withheld to avoid disclosure of individual company data.

Units: Holes drilled in thousands; footage drilled in millions of feet.

Table 1.19: Uranium Inventory and Use, 1990–2007

	1990	1995	2000	2007
Overview				
Domestic concentrate production	8.89	6.04	3.96	4.53
Purchased imports	23.70	41.30	44.90	54.10
Export sales	2.00	9.80	13.60	14.80
Electric plant purchases from domestic suppliers	20.50	22.30	24.30	18.50
Loaded into US nuclear reactors	NA	51.10	51.50	47.20
Inventory				
Total Inventory	*129.10*	*72.50*	*111.30*	*111.60*
Domestic suppliers	26.40	13.70	56.50	30.80
Electric plants	102.70	58.70	54.80	80.80
Average Purchase Price				
Purchased imports	$12.55	$10.20	$9.84	$34.18
Domestic purchases	15.70	11.11	11.45	33.13

Source: Energy Information Administration, *Annual Energy Review 2006*, table 9.3; *2007*, table 9.3.

Notes: Uranium concentrate (also called uranium oxide, U_3O_8) is a purified form of uranium used in the generation of fuel rods for nuclear reactors.
Amount of U_3O_8 loaded into reactors does not include fuel rods removed from reactors and later reloaded.

Units: Amounts given in millions of pounds of uranium oxide (U_3O_8); prices given in current dollars.

Table 1.20:   Uranium Reserves and Resources, 2003

	Forward-Cost Category		
	$30 or less	**$50 or less**	**$100 or less**
Reserves			
Total Reserves	*265*	*890*	*1,414*
New Mexico	84	341	566
Wyoming	106	363	582
Texas	6	23	38
Arizona, Colorado, and Utah	45	123	170
Other states	24	40	58
Potential Resources			
Estimated additional resources	2,180	3,310	4,850
Speculative resources	1,310	2,230	3,480

Source: Energy Information Administration, *Annual Energy Review 2007*, table 4.13.

Notes: Forward cost refers to the estimated cost per pound yet to be incurred from the production of uranium from estimated resources, and does not include costs already incurred (e.g., exploration and land acquisition) or taxes.
Figures given here are based on 2003 dollars.
'Other states' includes deposits in California, Idaho, Nebraska, Nevada, North Dakota, Oregon, South Dakota, and Washington.

Units: Reserves and resources in million pounds of uranium oxide (U_3O_8).

Table 1.21:   Households with Selected Appliances, 1978–2005

	1978	1984	1997	2005
Total Households	*77*	*86*	*101*	*111*
By Main Heating Fuel				
Natural gas	55%	55%	53%	52%
Electricity	16	17	29	30
Liquefied petroleum gas	4	5	5	5
Distillate fuel oil	20	12	9	7
Wood	2	7	2	3
By Type of Appliance				
Electric Appliances				
Television	NA	98%	NA	NA
Clothes washer	74%	73	77%	83%
Range top or burners	53	54	60	59
Microwave	8	34	83	88
Clothes dryer	45	46	55	61
Dishwasher	35	38	50	58
Ceiling fan	NA	35	NA	NA
Personal computer	NA	NA	35	68
Gas Appliances				
Range top or burners	48%	47%	39%	40%
Clothes dryer	14	16	16	18
Outdoor grill	6	13	NA	8
Refrigerators				
One	86%	88%	85%	78%
Two or more	14	12	15	22
Air Conditioning				
Central	23%	30%	47%	59%
Individual room units	33	30	25	25
None	44	40	28	16
Portable kerosene heaters	NA	6	2	1

Source: Energy Information Administration, *Annual Energy Review 2006*, table 2.6; *2007*, table 2.6.

Notes: 'Electricity' refers to retail electricity.
Gas appliances use natural gas or liquefied petroleum gases.
Households with both central and room air conditioning units are listed only under 'central.'

Units: Number of total households in millions; percent of total households.

Table 1.22: Fuels Used by Housing Units, by Place of Residence, 2007

	Number of units	Electricity	Gas	Fuel Oil	Kerosene	Coal/ coke	Wood	Solar
Total Housing Units	*128,203*	*128,150*	*93,373*	*23,654*	*702*	*109*	*1,876*	*157*
Occupied units	*110,692*	*110,648*	*77,399*	*9,650*	*586*	*91*	*1,479*	*147*
By Type of Area								
Central Cities	31,602	31,599	24,471	2,721	53	0	48	31
Suburbs	52,062	52,051	35,235	4,870	190	44	553	93
Outside MSA	27,028	26,998	17,694	2,059	343	47	877	22
By Type of Householder								
Black	13,856	13,853	9,582	1,031	101	0	47	5
Hispanic	12,609	12,609	9,212	835	41	0	67	7
Over 65	22,864	22,864	15,850	2,479	124	19	358	50
Below Poverty Threshold	14,157	14,145	9,443	1,240	115	6	213	2
By Housing Tenure								
Owner	75,647	75,608	54,705	6,609	423	86	1,273	128
Renter	35,045	35,040	22,694	3,041	164	5	205	19
By Region								
Northeast	20,392	20,378	15,067	7,584	258	70	300	17
Midwest	25,292	25,272	21,792	721	19	13	343	3
South	40,609	40,600	20,826	1,080	288	3	434	13
West	24,400	24,398	19,715	265	21	6	401	115

Source: US Department of Housing and Human Development, *American Housing Survey 2007*, tables 1-5 and 2-5.

Notes: Figures may not add to total because more than one category may apply to a housing unit. All breakdowns refer to occupied units only.
Characteristics of age, ethnicity, or national origin are based on the householder.

Units: Number of households in thousands.

Table 1.23: Fuel Oil and Kerosene Sales, 1985–2006

	Distillate Fuel Oil	Residual Fuel Oil	Kerosene
1985	2,809	1,048	114
1990	3,120	1,250	43
1995	3,357	804	54
1996	3,472	862	62
1997	3,546	816	66
1998	3,608	961	78
1999	3,756	869	73
2000	3,877	859	67
2001	3,908	888	72
2002	3,871	676	43
2003	4,165	744	55
2004	4,050	767	64
2005	4,120	877	70
2006	4,057	670	54

Source: Energy Information Administration, *Annual Energy Review 2006*, table 5.15; *2007*, table 5.15.

Notes: 'Distillate fuel oil' includes diesel and fuel oils.

Units: Sales in thousands of barrels per day.

Table 1.24: Transportation Sector Energy Consumption, 1990–2007

	1990	1995	2000	2007
Total Consumption	22,420	23,849	26,552	29,096
Primary Consumption total	22,366	23,793	26,492	29,012
Fossil fuels total	22,305	23,678	26,354	28,386
Natural gas	680	724	672	667
Petroleum	21,625	22,954	25,682	27,719
Renewable energy	62	115	138	626
Retail electricity sales	16	17	18	26
Electrical system energy losses	37	39	42	57

Source: Energy Information Administration, *Annual Energy Review 2006*, table 2.1e; *2007*, table 2.1e.

Notes: Total consumption consists of primary energy consumption, electricity retail sales, and system energy losses.
Data for 2007 is preliminary.
Some data has been revised since its original publication.

Units: Consumption in trillion Btu.

Tabel 1.25:   Transportation Sector Energy Consumption by State, 2005

	Natural Gas	Petroleum	Motor Gasoline	Ethanol	Electricity	Total
United States	*626.3*	*27,643.6*	*17,042.5*	*342.0*	*25.7*	*28,352.1*
Alabama	15.6	475.5	321.5	3.5	0.0	491.1
Alaska	2.7	261.2	34.3	0.5	0.0	263.8
Arizona	19.6	514.6	346.4	1.2	0.0	534.2
Arkansas	9.0	280.5	172.9	0.0	0.0	289.5
California	20.6	3,260.9	1,960.2	77.4	2.9	3,290.7
Colorado	13.8	410.3	260.3	8.6	0.1	424.3
Connecticut	3.5	258.1	197.5	13.6	0.6	263.6
Delaware	0.1	72.9	54.4	0.0	0.0	72.9
District of Columbia	0.6	19.1	15.7	0.0	1.1	23.3
Florida	10.5	1,584.5	1,066.1	0.0	0.3	1,596.1
Georgia	6.8	960.4	623.6	0.0	0.6	969.1
Hawaii	0.0	179.4	56.5	0.0	0.0	179.4
Idaho	5.7	117.8	73.7	0.0	0.0	123.5
Illinois	11.3	1,093.7	635.3	38.3	1.8	1,110.8
Indiana	6.9	638.7	393.3	11.5	0.1	645.8
Iowa	11.7	289.9	192.6	10.8	0.0	301.6
Kansas	29.2	229.6	140.3	1.5	0.0	258.8
Kentucky	8.5	468.5	269.9	6.5	0.0	477.0
Louisiana	43.9	674.1	283.8	5.5	0.0	718.1
Maine	0.6	130.6	88.9	0.0	0.0	131.2
Maryland	2.9	450.6	331.6	0.0	1.6	458.7
Massachusetts	2.6	479.9	350.0	0.8	1.4	486.9
Michigan	28.3	777.5	611.2	16.5	0.0	805.9
Minnesota	22.5	510.9	330.5	23.3	0.1	533.7
Mississippi	22.1	335.6	199.3	0.0	0.0	357.8
Missouri	2.7	589.6	389.1	10.7	0.1	592.5
Montana	8.3	109.9	58.0	0.1	0.0	118.2
Nebraska	4.5	168.7	98.5	4.4	0.0	173.2
Nevada	2.8	235.8	138.3	4.5	0.0	238.7
New Hampshire	0.0	104.3	86.3	0.0	0.0	104.4
New Jersey	1.6	972.0	532.4	0.6	1.0	976.8

(continued on next page)

Tabel 1.25: Transportation Sector Energy Consumption by State, 2005

	Natural Gas	Petroleum	Motor Gasoline	Ethanol	Electricity	Total
United States	*626.3*	*27,643.6*	*17,042.5*	*342.0*	*25.7*	*28,352.1*
New Mexico	20.6	199.3	116.2	0.5	0.0	219.9
New York	13.1	1,026.8	703.9	27.6	9.7	1,071.0
North Carolina	4.5	746.8	532.4	9.8	0.0	751.3
North Dakota	13.8	78.4	42.2	1.4	0.0	92.2
Ohio	14.4	1,000.4	637.0	22.3	0.2	1,015.4
Oklahoma	33.1	406.6	226.6	0.0	0.0	439.7
Oregon	7.8	323.0	190.4	2.6	0.2	331.4
Pennsylvania	32.3	994.5	636.0	8.5	3.0	1,036.4
Rhode Island	0.9	61.5	47.5	0.8	0.0	62.4
South Carolina	2.5	425.8	303.9	0.0	0.0	428.3
South Dakota	5.8	82.7	49.4	2.3	0.0	88.5
Tennessee	9.5	637.4	381.5	0.0	0.0	646.9
Texas	85.4	2,643.3	1,421.4	2.4	0.2	2,729.5
Utah	9.5	227.6	125.6	0.2	0.1	237.5
Vermont	0.0	54.2	42.6	0.0	0.0	54.2
Virginia	5.3	776.9	488.2	9.0	0.6	784.1
Washington	9.0	605.4	333.0	2.1	0.0	614.4
West Virginia	21.1	159.9	103.2	1.9	0.0	181.0
Wisconsin	3.8	433.4	310.8	10.7	0.0	437.3
Wyoming	14.8	104.6	38.6	0.0	0.0	119.4

Source: Energy Information Administration, *State Energy Consumption, Prices, and Expenditure Estimates (SEDS)*, 2005 Summaries, table S7.

Notes: 'Motor gasoline' is included under petroleum, but is also shown separately for informational purposes.
Ethanol blended in gasoline is also included under gasoline, but shown separately for informational purposes.
Transportation-related use of natural gas includes the operation of pipelines, as well as gas consumed as vehicle fuel.

Units: Consumption in trillion Btu.

Table 1.26:   Fuel Consumption by Mode of Transportation, 1960–2006

	1960	1970	1980	1990	2000	2005	2006
Air							
Certified carriers							
Jet fuel	1,954	7,857	8,519	12,323	14,845	13,789	13,458
General aviation							
Aviation gasoline	242	551	520	353	333	255	262
Jet fuel	NA	208	766	663	972	1,255	1,289
Highway							
Gasoline, diesel, and other fuels							
Passenger car and motorcycle	41,171	67,879	70,186	69,759	73,275	74,085	NA
Other 2-axle 4-tire	NA	12,313	23,796	35,611	52,939	65,419	NA
Bus	827	820	1,018	895	1,112	1,329	NA
Transit							
Electricity	2,908	2,561	2,446	4,837	5,510	5,954	NA
Motor Fuel							
Diesel	208	271	431	651	786	730	NA
Gasoline and other nondiesel	192	68	11	34	48	58	NA
Compressed natural gas	NA	NA	NA	NA	55	123	NA
Class I Railway							
Distillate/diesel fuel	3,463	3,545	3,904	3,115	3,700	4,098	NA
Amtrak							
Electricity	NA	NA	254	330	350	NA	NA
Distillate/diesel fuel	NA	NA	64	82	76	NA	NA
Water							
Residual fuel oil	3,952	3,774	8,952	6,326	6,410	5,179	NA
Distillate/diesel fuel	787	819	1,478	2,065	2,261	2,006	NA
Gasoline	NA	598	1,052	1,300	1,124	1,261	NA
Pipeline							
Natural gas	347,075	722,166	634,622	659,816	642,210	584,779	NA

Source: Bureau of Transportation Statistics, *National Transportation Statistics 2008*, table 4-5.

Notes: Class I Railroads are the largest class, with annual revenues exceeding $250 million in 1991 dollars (the 2006 rate adjusted for inflation is around $380 million).
The data for some years has been adjusted since its original publication.
Most data for 2006 has not yet been published and is marked as such with an 'NA.'

Units: Fuel consumed (gasoline, diesel, jet, motor, residual, and distillate fuel) in millions of gallons; electricity in millions of kilowatt-hours; natural gas in millions of cubic feet.

Table 1.27: Energy Intensity of Passenger-Transit Modes, 1985–2005

	1985	1990	1995	2000	2004	2005
Air						
Domestic	5,047	4,932	4,382	3,883	3,297	3,182
International	5,103	4,546	4,173	3,833	3,428	3,523
Highway						
Passenger car	4,269	3,811	3,721	3,589	3,509	3,458
Other 2-axle, 4-tire vehicles	4,971	4,539	4,538	4,509	4,452	4,452
Motorcycle	1,896	2,227	2,274	2,273	1,969	1,969
Transit						
Motor bus	3,389	3,723	4,155	4,147	3,572	3,373
Railway						
Amtrak	2,089	2,066	1,838	2,134	NA	NA

Source: Bureau of Transportation Statistics, *National Transportation Statistics 2007*, table 4-20.

Notes: Intensity is given in Btu per passenger-mile, which is calculated by multiplying total Btu consumed (obtained by multiplying total fuel consumed by 135,000 Btu/gallon for air carriers, 125,000 Btu/gallon for highway vehicles, 138,700 Btu/gallon for transit motor buses and Amtrak diesel, and 3,412 Btu/kilowatt-hour for Amtrak electric) by total passenger-miles.

Units: Intensity in Btu per passenger-mile.

Table 1.28: Government Energy Consumption by Agency, 1990–2007

	1990	1995	2000	2007
Total	1,438.0	1,129.3	993.8	1,100.4
Agriculture	9.6	9.0	7.4	6.8
Defense	1,241.7	926.0	779.1	864.6
Energy	43.5	47.3	30.5	32.3
General Services	17.5	13.7	17.6	19.1
Health & Human Services	7.1	6.1	8.0	10.6
Interior	7.4	6.4	7.8	7.5
Justice	7.0	10.2	19.7	34.2
NASA	12.4	12.4	11.1	10.6
Postal Service	30.6	36.2	43.3	45.8
Transportation	19.0	18.7	21.2	5.6
Veterans Affairs	24.9	25.4	27.0	30.1
Other	17.5	17.9	21.0	33.2

Source: Energy Information Administration, *Annual Energy Review 2006*, table 1.11; *2007*, table 1.11.

Notes: Data for 2007 is preliminary.

Units: Consumption in trillion Btu.

Table 1.29:   Projected Energy Production and Consumption, 2006–2030

	2006	2010	2015	2020	2025	2030
Production						
Total Production	*71.41*	*76.17*	*78.96*	*82.21*	*85.53*	*86.56*
Crude oil and lease condensate	10.80	12.76	13.25	13.40	12.99	12.04
Natural gas plant liquids	2.36	2.27	2.29	2.31	2.17	2.11
Dry natural gas	19.04	19.85	20.08	20.24	20.17	20.00
Coal	23.79	23.97	24.48	25.20	26.85	28.63
Nuclear power	8.21	8.31	8.41	9.05	9.50	9.57
Hydroelectric	2.89	2.92	2.99	3.00	3.00	3.00
Biomass	2.94	4.05	5.12	6.42	8.00	8.12
Other renewable	0.88	1.51	1.75	2.00	2.25	2.45
Consumption						
Total Consumption	*99.52*	*103.34*	*107.26*	*110.85*	*114.54*	*118.01*
By Source						
Liquid fuels and other petroleum	40.06	40.46	41.80	42.24	42.70	43.99
Natural gas	22.30	23.93	24.35	24.01	23.60	23.39
Coal	22.50	23.03	24.19	25.87	27.70	29.90
Nuclear power	8.21	8.31	8.41	9.05	9.50	9.57
Hydroelectric	2.89	2.92	2.99	3.00	3.00	3.00
Biomass	2.50	3.01	3.60	4.50	5.40	5.51
Other renewable	0.88	1.51	1.75	2.00	2.20	2.45
By Sector						
All delivered energy	99.52	103.34	107.26	110.85	114.54	118.01
Residential	20.82	22.25	22.56	23.39	24.15	25.01
Commercial	17.91	18.74	20.34	21.98	23.54	24.98
Industrial	32.55	33.32	33.93	34.27	34.93	34.98
Transportation	28.25	29.03	30.42	31.21	31.92	33.04
Electric power	39.68	41.46	43.12	45.21	47.19	49.21

Source: Energy Information Administration, *Annual Energy Outlook 2008 with Projections to 2030*, tables A1 and A2.

Notes: Data for 2006 is from the projection model, and may differ slightly from the official 2006 estimates.
Groups may not add to total.

Units: Projected production and consumption in quadrillion Btu.

Table 1.30: Projected Transportation-Related Energy Use, 2006–2030

	2006	2010	2015	2020	2025	2030
Amount of Travel						
Motor vehicles						
Light-duty vehicles under 8,500 lbs	2,693	2,777	3,058	3,375	3,717	4,069
Commercial light trucks	70	73	81	87	94	101
Freight trucks over 10,000 lbs	235	250	279	304	328	351
Airplanes	994	1,130	1,318	1,457	1,576	1,665
Transport						
Rail	1,656	1,702	1,827	1,932	2,043	2,147
Domestic shipping	619	643	677	701	713	721
Energy Efficiency						
New car	31.1	31.5	34.9	42.0	42.1	42.1
New light truck	23.2	23.7	27.7	31.4	32.2	32.4
New commercial light truck	15.6	15.7	18.1	19.8	20.2	20.2
Freight truck	6.0	6.0	6.2	6.5	6.7	6.8
Aircraft	62.2	63.5	65.3	67.2	68.7	70.0
Energy Use						
Total Energy used	*28.20*	*28.98*	*30.37*	*31.15*	*31.86*	*32.98*
Light-duty vehiclces	16.41	16.52	17.01	17.10	17.11	17.52
Commercial light trucks	0.62	0.62	0.64	0.63	0.63	0.64
Bus	0.26	0.26	0.27	0.27	0.28	0.29
Freight trucks	4.89	5.18	5.60	5.85	6.13	6.44
Passenger rail	0.04	0.05	0.05	0.05	0.05	0.06
Freight rail	0.57	0.58	0.62	0.65	0.69	0.72
Domestic shipping	0.32	0.33	0.34	0.35	0.36	0.36
International shipping	0.78	0.79	0.78	0.79	0.80	0.80
Recreational boats	0.24	0.25	0.26	0.28	0.29	0.30
Air	2.65	2.90	3.29	3.61	3.92	4.22

Source: Energy Information Administration, *Annual Energy Outlook 2008 with Projections to 2030*, table A7.

Notes: Data for 2006 is from the projection model, and may differ slightly from the official 2006 estimates.
Groups may not add to total.
Light-duty vehicles weigh less than 8,500 lbs, commercial light trucks between 8,500 and 10,000 lbs, and freight trucks over 10,000 lbs.

Units: Distance traveled in billions of vehicle-miles for motor vehicles, billions of seat miles for airplanes, and billion ton miles for transport; energy efficiency in miles per gallon for motor vehicles, and seat miles per gallon for airplanes; energy use in quadrillion Btu.

Chapter 2

Alternative Fuels & Renewable Energy

Chapter 2 Highlights

Chapter 2 contains data on Alternative Fuels and Renewable Energy. The number of alternative-fueled vehicles on the road has increased greatly since 1995, with most using liquefied petroleum or some form of natural gas, although ethanol and electricity have both become much more commonplace (table 2.01). There are now over 5,700 alternative fueling stations across the United States (table 2.04 contains details by state and type of station), and production and consumption of ethanol and biodiesel have have risen greatly in recent years (tables 2.05 and 2.10). Where available, prices for alternative fuels are somewhat comparable to gasoline or diesel, but there is a fair amount of regional variation (tables 2.06–2.08). Sales of gasoline-electric hybrid vehicles have increased overall, especially for automobiles, with the greatest number of sales in California (tables 2.02 and 2.03). State governments, as well as the federal government, offer a wide variety of tax and other incentives to encourage use of alternative fuels (over 2,600 total, see table 2.09).

Renewable energy remains a small portion of the US' total energy consumption (table 2.11), but its production is growing (tables 2.12 and 2.13, also see table 1.01). Most electricity generated from renewable sources comes from hydroelectric power (tables 2.12–2.14). Most renewable energy consumed by residential and comercial sectors comes from biomass or wood energy (table 2.15). Sales of photovoltaic (solar) cells have increased dramatically in the last 10 years (table 2.19, also see table 2.18 for information on solar thermal collector sales), and the overall capacity for renewable energy generation (and renewable energy in general) is expected to grow in the next 25 years (tables 2.20 and 2.21). In addition, tables 2.16 and 2.17 contain state-by-state breakdowns of electricity net generation and net summer capacity from renewable energy sources.

Many people are also becoming open to the idea of using alternative fuels in their vehicles. Electricity remained the preferred alternative fuel in 2004, although the preference was not as strong as in 2000. Hydrogen has replaced ethanol as people's second choice. People are concerned over high energy prices, and many would consider buying a hybrid vehicle with better gas mileage, even if the vehicle was much more expensive. People are also open to a variety of proposals to reduce energy use and our dependence on foreign oil (table 2.22).

Table 2.01:   Alternative-Fueled Vehicles on the Road, 1995–2006

	1995		2000		2006	
	Vehicles	Fuel Consumed	Vehicles	Fuel Consumed	Vehicles	Fuel Consumed
All Fuels	*NA*	*3,906,142*	*NA*	*4,744,930*	*NA*	*4,842,577*
Alternative Fuels	246,855	278,121	394,664	324,986	634,562	417,803
Liquefied petroleum	172,806	233,178	181,994	213,012	164,846	173,130
Compressed natural gas	50,218	35,865	100,750	88,478	116,131	172,011
Liquefied natural gas	603	2,821	2,090	7,423	2,798	23,474
M85	18,319	2,122	10,426	614	0	0
M100	386	2,255	0	0	0	0
E85	1,527	195	87,570	12,388	297,099	44,041
E95	136	1,021	4	13	0	0
Electricity	2,860	663	11,830	3,058	53,526	5,104
Hydrogen	0	0	0	0	159	41
Oxygenates	NA	3,628,022	NA	4,413,116	NA	4,164,168
MTBE	NA	2,693,407	NA	3,298,803	NA	435,000
Ethanol in Gasohol	NA	934,615	NA	1,114,313	NA	3,729,168
Biodiesel	NA	NA	NA	6,828	NA	260,606

Source: Energy Information Administration, *Annual Energy Review 2006*, table 10.4; *2007*, table 10.4.

Notes: Oxygenates are substances added to motor gasoline to increase the amount of oxygen in that gasoline blend.
'Electric vehicles' exclude gasoline-electric hybrids.
MTBE = Methyl Tertiary Butyl Ether.
M85 = 85% methanol mixed with 15% gasoline.
M100 = pure methanol.
E85 = 85% ethanol mixed with 15% gasoline.
E95 = 95% ethanol mixed with 5% gasoline.
Data for 2006 is preliminary.

Units: Number of vehicles; fuel consumption in thousands of gasoline-equivalent gallons.

Table 2.02: On-Road and Alternative Fuel and Hybrid Vehicles Made Available by Supplier and Vehicle Type, 2002–2006

	2002	2003	2004	2005	2006
All Vehicles					
Total	*895,984*	*930,538*	*775,638*	*890,281*	*1,234,655*
Automobiles	156,434	126,951	242,130	294,665	514,306
Vans and minivans	262,842	108,329	6,946	8,055	12,470
Pickup trucks	81,323	29,633	60,428	278,096	382,227
SUVs and light duty trucks	377,121	651,379	461,803	305,454	321,104
Heavy duty trucks	724	217	285	146	257
Buses	2,370	1,519	1,816	1,753	1,723
Other	14,825	11,999	1,952	2,042	2,533
Original Equipment Manufacturer					
Total	*894,594*	*929,441*	*774,290*	*889,267*	*1,233,924*
Automobiles	156,354	126,872	241,444	294,113	513,907
Vans and minivans	262,786	108,270	6,896	7,995	12,441
Pickup trucks	80,910	29,392	60,323	277,978	382,135
SUVs and light duty trucks	377,096	651,302	461,604	305,346	321,041
Heavy duty trucks	402	188	258	142	247
Buses	2,178	1,311	1,650	1,639	1,629
Other	14,825	11,999	1,952	2,042	2,524
Converted					
Total	*1,390*	*1,097*	*1,348*	*1,014*	*731*
Automobiles	80	79	686	552	399
Vans and minivans	56	59	50	60	29
Pickup trucks	413	241	105	118	92
SUVs and light duty trucks	25	77	199	108	63
Heavy duty trucks	322	29	27	4	10
Buses	192	208	166	114	94
Other	0	0	0	0	9

Source: Energy Information Administration, *Alternative Fuel and Hybrid Vehicles Made Available 2006*, table S6.

Notes: 'Automobiles' and 'SUVs & light duty trucks' include gasoline-electric hybrids.
'Buses' includes diesel-electric hybrids.
Light duty trucks have a gross vehicle weight rating (GVWR) under 8,500 lbs.
Heavy-duty trucks have a GVWR over 26,000 lbs.

Units: Net generation in billion kilowatt-hours.

Table 2.03: Top 10 States for New Registrations of Gasoline-Electric Hybrid Automobiles, 2006

	State	Registrations
1.	California	52,619
2.	Florida	10,470
3.	Texas	9,632
4.	New York	9,372
5.	Virginia	8,650
6.	Illinois	7,286
7.	Washington	6,970
8.	Pennsylvania	6,948
9.	Massachusetts	6,060
10.	New Jersey	5,673
	United States total	254,545
	Top 10 subtotal	155,979
	% of US total	61.3%

Source: Bureau of Transportation Statistics, *State Transportation Statistics 2007*, table 7-6.

Notes: Data originally from R.L. Polk & Co.

Units: Number of vehicles sold; percent of total.

Table 2.04: Alternative Fueling Stations by State and Type, 2008

	Biodiesel	CNG	Ethanol-85	Electric	Hydrogen	LNG	Propane	Total
United States	*644*	*777*	*1,584*	*435*	*46*	*37*	*2,184*	*5,707*
Alabama	14	3	6	0	0	0	46	69
Alaska	0	1	0	0	0	0	10	11
Arizona	10	41	17	10	1	5	50	134
Arkansas	2	3	5	0	0	0	37	47
California	39	181	10	370	25	27	199	851
Colorado	22	20	45	2	0	0	55	144
Connecticut	1	9	2	3	1	0	16	32
Delaware	3	1	1	0	0	0	3	8
Dist. of Columbia	1	1	3	0	1	0	0	6
Florida	12	15	15	3	2	0	47	94
Georgia	28	18	26	0	0	0	38	110
Hawaii	7	0	0	4	1	0	3	15
Idaho	6	7	4	0	0	1	25	43
Illinois	4	17	185	1	1	0	54	262
Indiana	6	13	110	0	0	0	28	157
Iowa	5	0	94	0	0	0	24	123
Kansas	5	2	23	0	0	0	44	74
Kentucky	1	0	9	0	0	0	13	23
Louisiana	1	5	3	0	0	0	10	19
Maine	5	1	0	0	0	0	8	14
Maryland	7	15	9	0	0	0	15	46
Massachusetts	7	11	1	18	0	0	23	60
Michigan	17	14	55	0	7	0	69	162
Minnesota	1	1	348	0	0	0	30	380
Mississippi	5	0	2	0	0	0	34	41
Missouri	8	7	75	0	1	0	75	166
Montana	4	3	2	0	0	0	31	40
Nebraska	3	2	35	0	0	0	18	58

(continued on next page)

Table 2.04: Alternative Fueling Stations by State and Type, 2008

	Biodiesel	CNG	Ethanol-85	Electric	Hydrogen	LNG	Propane	Total
United States	*644*	*777*	*1,584*	*435*	*46*	*37*	*2,184*	*5,707*
Nevada	14	11	17	0	2	0	28	72
New Hampshire	11	3	1	8	0	0	11	34
New Jersey	0	11	0	0	0	0	10	21
New Mexico	6	9	7	0	0	0	49	71
New York	5	92	14	1	1	0	29	142
North Carolina	66	13	13	0	0	0	44	136
North Dakota	0	4	26	0	0	0	14	44
Ohio	22	9	58	0	0	0	66	155
Oklahoma	6	50	5	0	0	0	68	129
Oregon	36	12	8	9	0	0	29	94
Pennsylvania	5	26	16	0	1	0	63	111
Rhode Island	0	7	0	2	0	0	4	13
South Carolina	73	4	71	0	0	0	20	168
South Dakota	0	0	69	0	0	0	17	86
Tennessee	48	4	21	0	0	0	52	125
Texas	53	17	35	1	0	4	497	607
Utah	7	62	5	0	0	0	22	96
Vermont	2	1	0	2	1	0	5	11
Virginia	13	10	6	1	1	0	21	52
Washington	35	12	11	0	0	0	52	110
West Virginia	1	2	3	0	0	0	7	13
Wisconsin	3	19	107	0	0	0	45	174
Wyoming	14	8	6	0	0	0	26	54

Source: US Department of Energy, Alternative Fuels Data Center (http://www.eere.energy.gov/afdc/fuels/stations_counts.html).

Notes: Station data updated as of August 14, 2008. Accessed August 25, 2008.
CNG = Compressed Natural Gas.
LNG = Liquefied Natural Gas
E85 = 85% ethanol blended with 15% gasoline.

Units: Number of stations.

Table 2.05: Ethanol and Biodiesel Use, 1995–2007

	1995	2000	2003	2005	2006	2007
Ethanol						
Feedstock	200	238	410	570	712	924
Losses and coproducts	86	101	174	241	301	378
Production	32,325	38,627	66,772	92,961	116,294	154,416
Imports	387	116	292	3,234	17,408	10,348
Stocks	2,186	3,400	5,978	5,563	8,760	10,509
Consumption	32,919	39,367	67,286	96,634	130,505	163,002
Biodiesel						
Feedstock	NA	NA	2	12	32	64
Production	NA	NA	338	2,162	5,963	11,691

Source: Energy Information Administration, *Annual Energy Review 2006*, table 10.3; *2007*, table 10.3.

Notes: 'Feedstocks' are the corn and biomass inputs for ethanol production, and the vegetable oil and other biomass used to produce biodiesel.
'Losses and co-products' refers to energy lost in fuel production, and does not include natural gas or electricity energy used in to produce the ethanol or biodiesel.
Stocks are as of the end of the year.
Some data has been changed since the year it was originally published.
Data for 2007 is preliminary.

Units: Feedstocks and losses and coproducts in trillion Btu; production, imports, stocks, and consumption in thousand barrels.

Table 2.06:   Alternative Fuel Prices by Type of Fuel, January–July 2008

	January 2008	April 2008	July 2008	Price Change, January-July 2008
Ethanol (E85)	$2.51	$2.87	$3.27	$0.76
Propane	3.12	3.15	3.14	0.02
Biodiesel				
B20	3.37	3.98	4.66	1.29
B2-B5	3.31	3.99	4.69	1.38
B99-B100	3.69	4.31	4.88	1.19
Compressed natural gas	1.93	2.04	2.34	0.41
Gasoline	2.99	3.43	3.91	0.92
Diesel	3.40	4.14	4.71	1.31

Source: US Department of Energy, Energy Efficiency and Renewable Energy division, *Clean Cities Alternative Fuel Price Report, April 2008*, table 1, *July 2008*, table 1.

Notes: B20 is 20% biodiesel blended with 80% diesel.
B2-B5 is a mix of 2-5% biodiesel and diesel.
B99-B100 is 99-100% biodiesel.
E85 is 85% ethanol and 15% gasoline.

Units: All prices in dollars per gallon, except compressed natural gas, which is in dollars per gasoline gallon equivalent (GGE).

Table 2.07: Energy-Equivalent Prices of Alternative Fuels, July 2007 and 2008

	Gasoline Gallon Equivalents	Diesel Gallon Equivalents	Price per Million Btu
July 2007			
Ethanol (E85)	$3.72	$4.15	$32.21
Propane	3.57	3.98	30.91
Biodiesel			
B20	2.70	3.02	23.43
B2-B5	2.55	2.84	22.09
B99-B100	3.22	3.59	27.89
Compressed natural gas	2.10	2.34	18.18
Gasoline	3.04	3.38	26.25
Diesel	2.65	2.96	22.98
July 2008			
Ethanol (E85)	$4.62	$5.15	$40.00
Propane	4.34	4.84	37.62
Biodiesel			
B20	4.25	4.74	36.86
B2-B5	4.21	4.69	36.48
B99-B100	4.81	5.36	41.68
Compressed natural gas	2.34	2.61	20.29
Gasoline	3.91	4.36	33.90
Diesel	4.22	4.71	36.59

Source: US Department of Energy, Energy Efficiency and Renewable Energy division, *Clean Cities Alternative Fuel Price Report, July 2007*, table 2; *July 2008*, table 2.

Notes: A Gasoline Gallon Equivalent (GGE) is the amount of a fuel that produces the same amount of energy when consumed as a gallon of gasoline. Diesel Gallon Equivalents do the same for diesel fuel.
B20 is 20% biodiesel blended with 80% diesel.
B2-B5 is a mix of 2-5% biodiesel and diesel.
B99-B100 is 99-100% biodiesel.
E85 is 85% ethanol and 15% gasoline.

Units: Prices in dollars per gasoline gallon equivalent, diesel gallon equivalent, and million Btu.

Table 2.08: Alternative Fuel Prices by Region and Type of Fuel, July 2007 and 2008

	National Average	New England	Central Atlantic	Lower Atlantic	Midwest	Gulf Coast	Rocky Mountain	West Coast
July 2007								
B20 Biodiesel	$2.96	$2.98	$3.13	$2.85	$2.81	$2.90	$3.08	$3.07
B2-B5 Biodiesel	2.84	NA	2.97	2.81	2.81	2.90	2.95	3.01
B99-B100 Biodiesel	3.27	NA	3.26	3.41	2.85	3.09	3.52	3.24
Ethanol (E85)	2.63	NA	2.67	2.71	2.61	2.59	2.58	2.72
Compressed natural gas	2.10	2.19	2.12	1.65	1.67	1.80	2.41	2.29
Propane	2.58	2.35	3.59	2.44	2.81	2.04	2.10	2.09
Gasoline	3.03	3.13	2.97	2.87	3.10	2.91	3.09	3.03
Diesel	2.96	3.03	2.96	2.87	2.92	2.85	3.03	3.10
July 2008								
B20 Biodiesel	$4.66	$4.52	$4.49	$4.72	$4.66	$4.60	$4.67	$4.81
B2-B5 Biodiesel	4.69	4.79	4.78	4.66	4.62	4.56	4.91	4.70
B99-B100 Biodiesel	4.88	4.59	4.99	4.60	4.48	4.39	5.35	4.97
Ethanol (E85)	3.27	3.10	3.35	3.53	3.20	3.39	3.10	3.40
Compressed natural gas	2.34	2.96	2.77	2.40	1.95	2.88	1.38	2.91
Propane	3.14	3.14	4.20	4.14	3.15	2.38	2.79	2.96
Gasoline	3.91	4.09	4.06	3.90	3.84	3.85	4.00	4.09
Diesel	4.71	4.86	4.88	4.65	4.58	4.61	4.71	4.83

Source: US Department of Energy, Energy Efficiency and Renewable Energy division, *Clean Cities Alternative Fuel Price Report, July 2007*, table 12; *July 2008*, table 12.

Notes: B20 is 20% biodiesel blended with 80% diesel.
B2-B5 is a mix of 2-5% biodiesel and diesel.
B99-B100 is 99-10% biodiesel.
E85 is 85% ethanol and 15% gasoline.

Units: All prices in dollars per gallon, except compressed natural gas, which is in dollars per gasoline gallon equivalent (GGE).

Table 2.09: Federal and State Incentives for Alternative Fuels, 2008

	Alternative Fuel	Biodiesel	Ethanol	Natural Gas	LPG	Electric	Hydrogen	Total
United States	*175*	*406*	*402*	*316*	*269*	*281*	*253*	*2,609*
Federal Government	*14*	*32*	*27*	*26*	*26*	*17*	*25*	*228*
Alabama	1	2	2	2	2	1	1	11
Alaska	2	1	2	1	1	2	1	12
Arizona	5	6	6	9	10	10	7	56
Arkansas	2	4	4	4	4	3	3	28
California	11	17	15	24	18	30	24	193
Colorado	4	9	9	10	8	6	8	65
Connecticut	4	5	5	7	5	6	6	49
Delaware	1	1	1	2	2	1	1	10
District of Columbia	3	3	3	4	3	3	3	25
Florida	2	11	13	2	2	4	7	52
Georgia	3	7	6	7	3	6	4	42
Hawaii	5	8	11	5	6	6	6	53
Idaho	0	5	4	2	2	1	1	21
Illinois	2	14	12	7	5	7	5	67
Indiana	3	12	17	6	4	4	4	71
Iowa	4	13	17	6	5	8	5	66
Kansas	2	7	10	4	4	2	1	32
Kentucky	3	7	7	6	4	1	1	35
Louisiana	0	3	7	6	4	4	2	33
Maine	3	6	8	5	5	5	4	43
Maryland	1	4	4	1	1	3	1	20
Massachusetts	3	7	7	5	3	3	3	37
Michigan	6	11	9	6	6	5	6	57
Minnesota	3	8	10	4	4	6	4	52
Mississippi	1	2	2	5	3	1	1	17
Missouri	3	7	6	5	4	4	4	41
Montana	2	7	8	4	4	3	2	33
Nebraska	0	3	4	3	3	2	2	19
Nevada	4	4	4	5	5	5	4	38
New Hampshire	1	3	1	1	1	2	1	15
New Jersey	3	4	4	6	5	5	4	42

(continued on next page)

Table 2.09: Federal and State Incentives for Alternative Fuels, 2008

	Alternative Fuel	Biodiesel	Ethanol	Natural Gas	LPG	Electric	Hydrogen	Total
United States	*175*	*406*	*402*	*316*	*269*	*281*	*253*	*2,609*
New Mexico	7	12	10	8	7	7	9	70
New York	8	11	13	16	10	12	12	96
North Carolina	7	16	14	9	9	8	8	93
North Dakota	1	9	9	1	2	1	3	32
Ohio	2	5	4	2	2	2	3	25
Oklahoma	4	8	10	7	7	8	4	50
Oregon	4	13	12	6	5	8	6	74
Pennsylvania	3	5	5	5	3	5	3	38
Rhode Island	2	3	2	4	3	5	3	31
South Carolina	1	10	9	3	4	3	5	44
South Dakota	0	8	9	1	2	0	0	30
Tennessee	5	14	10	8	7	6	5	69
Texas	6	9	9	12	11	8	8	71
Utah	2	2	2	9	7	8	5	40
Vermont	3	5	4	4	3	4	3	37
Virginia	3	9	6	9	7	7	7	55
Washington	4	17	13	9	8	11	6	92
West Virginia	4	4	4	4	4	5	4	30
Wisconsin	8	13	10	8	6	7	8	65
Wyoming	0	0	2	1	0	0	0	4

Source: US Department of Energy, Alternative Fuels Data Center (http://www.afdc.energy.gov/afdc/progs/tech_matrx.php).

Notes: Data is current as of September 18, 2008.
'Alternative' includes all government-designated alternative fuels, including biodiesel, natural gas, liquefied petroleum gas, hydrogen, and electric vehicles.
Laws and incentives that specify a particular fuel are listed under that category instead. Some laws may specify more than one alternative fuel, in which case it would be counted under each specified category. As a result, the sum of the columns may not equal total. Not all categories are shown.
LPG = Liquefied Petroleum Gas.

Units: Number of laws and incentives.

Table 2.10: Biodiesel Production in the United States, 1999–2005

	Million Gallons
1999	0.5
2000	2.0
2001	5.0
2002	15.0
2003	20.0
2004	25.0
2005	75.0

Source: Oak Ridge National Laboratory, *Biomass Energy Data Book*, *1ˢᵗ ed (2006)*, figure 2.9.

Notes: Figures given are estimates.

Units: Estimated production in million gallons.

Table 2.11: Energy Consumption from Renewable and Non-Renewable Sources, 2003–2007

	2003	2004	2005	2006	2007
Renewable Total	*6.150*	*6.261*	*6.444*	*6.922*	*6.830*
Biomass	2.817	3.023	3.154	3.374	3.615
Biofuels	0.414	0.513	0.595	0.795	1.018
Waste	0.401	0.389	0.403	0.407	0.431
Wood	2.002	2.121	2.156	2.172	2.165
Geothermal	0.331	0.341	0.343	0.343	0.353
Hydroelectric	2.825	2.690	2.703	2.869	2.463
Solar	0.064	0.065	0.066	0.072	0.080
Wind	0.115	0.142	0.178	0.264	0.319
Total Consumption	98.209	100.351	100.503	99.861	101.605

Source: Energy Information Administration, *Renewable Energy Consumption and Electricity: Preliminary 2007 Statistics*, table 1.

Notes: 'Wood' includes wood and wood-derived fuels such as black liquor and wood/woodwaste solids and liquids.
'Hydroelectric' includes conventional hydroelectric power.

Units: Energy consumption in quadrillion Btu.

Table 2.12: Electricity Net Generation from Renewable Sources, 1970–2007

	Total Renewable	Hydro-electric	Wood Biomass	Waste Biomass	Geothermal	Solar	Wind	All Electricity
1970	251.8	251.0	0.1	0.2	0.5	NA	NA	1,535.1
1975	306.6	303.2	0.0	0.2	3.2	NA	NA	1,920.8
1980	284.7	279.2	0.3	0.2	5.1	NA	NA	2,289.6
1985	295.0	284.3	0.7	0.6	9.3	0.0	0.0	2,473.0
1990	357.2	292.9	32.5	13.3	15.4	0.4	2.8	3,038.0
1995	384.8	310.8	36.5	20.4	13.4	0.5	3.2	3,353.5
1996	423.0	347.2	36.8	20.9	14.3	0.5	3.2	3,444.2
1997	433.6	356.5	36.9	21.7	14.7	0.5	3.3	3,492.2
1998	400.4	323.3	36.3	22.4	14.8	0.5	3.0	3,620.3
1999	399.0	319.5	37.0	22.6	14.8	0.5	4.5	3,694.8
2000	356.5	275.6	37.6	23.1	14.1	0.5	5.6	3,802.1
2001	287.7	217.0	35.2	14.5	13.7	0.5	6.7	3,736.6
2002	343.4	264.3	38.7	15.0	14.5	0.6	10.4	3,858.5
2003	355.3	275.8	37.5	15.8	14.4	0.5	11.2	3,883.2
2004	351.0	268.4	37.6	15.5	14.8	0.6	14.1	3,970.6
2005	357.5	270.3	38.7	15.5	14.7	0.6	17.8	4,055.4
2006	385.7	289.2	38.6	16.1	14.6	0.5	26.6	4,064.7
2007	351.3	248.3	38.5	16.9	14.8	0.6	32.1	4,159.5

Source: Energy Information Administration, *Annual Energy Review 2006*, table 8.2a; *2007*, table 8.2a.

Notes: Data for 2007 is preliminary.
'Hydroelectric' refers to conventional hydroelectric power.

Units: Net generation in billion kilowatt-hours.

Table 2.13: Electric Net Summer Capacity by Energy Source, 2003–2007

	2003	2004	2005	2006	2007
Total Capacity	*948,446*	*962,942*	*978,020*	*986,215*	*998,837*
Renewable Energy					
Total Renewable	*96,847*	*96,357*	*98,746*	*101,934*	*106,554*
Biomass	**9,628**	**9,711**	**9,802**	**10,100**	**10,313**
Waste	3,758	3,529	3,609	3,727	3,881
Landfill gas	863	859	887	978	1,034
MSW	2,442	2,196	2,167	2,188	2,204
Wood	5,871	6,182	6,193	6,372	6,432
Geothermal	2,133	2,152	2,285	2,274	2,294
Hydroelectric	78,694	77,641	77,541	77,821	77,833
Solar	397	398	411	411	498
Wind	5,995	6,456	8,706	11,329	15,616
Nonrenewable Energy					
Total Nonrenewable	*851,599*	*866,585*	*879,274*	*884,281*	*892,284*

Source: Energy Information Administration, *Renewable Energy Consumption and Electricity: Preliminary 2007 Statistics*, table 4.

Notes: 'MSW' refers to any method whose primary source is municipal solid waste.
'Wood' includes wood and wood-derived fuels such as black liquor and wood/woodwaste solids and liquids.
'Hydroelectric' includes conventional hydroelectric power.

Units: Net summer capacity in megawatts.

Table 2.14: **Electricity Net Generation from Renewable Energy by End-Use Sector and Source, 2003–2007**

	2003	2004	2005	2006	2007
All Sectors					
Total	355,293,119	351,020,900	357,533,995	385,669,799	351,300,592
Biomass	53,341,092	53,073,722	54,160,152	54,758,512	55,400,235
Waste	15,811,993	15,497,303	15,479,005	16,109,652	16,884,973
Landfill gas	5,077,451	5,128,416	5,135,256	5,677,253	6,199,777
MSW biogenic	8,306,065	8,153,230	8,334,720	8,476,478	8,567,940
Wood	37,529,099	37,576,418	38,681,147	38,648,859	38,515,262
Geothermal	14,424,231	14,810,975	14,691,745	14,568,029	14,838,636
Hydroelectric	275,806,329	268,417,308	270,321,255	289,246,416	248,312,395
Solar	534,001	575,155	550,294	507,706	606,082
Wind	11,187,466	14,143,741	17,810,549	26,589,137	32,143,244
Commercial Sector					
Total	1,374,208	1,645,981	1,752,519	1,688,360	1,723,575
Biomass	1,301,963	1,541,014	1,666,483	1,594,915	1,652,569
Waste	1,288,914	1,527,370	1,650,485	1,574,314	1,631,269
Landfill gas	151,801	172,029	210,824	171,979	204,039
MSW biogenic	716,921	945,812	953,591	956,337	969,342
Wood	13,049	13,644	15,998	20,600	21,300
Hydroelectric	72,245	104,967	86,037	93,446	71,005
Industrial Sector					
Total	32,926,242	31,923,522	32,082,295	31,796,137	31,026,204
Biomass	28,703,818	28,675,029	28,886,854	28,897,089	28,757,533
Waste	715,446	839,555	789,325	600,979	644,131
Landfill gas	96,018	120,014	113,082	28,785	29,693
MSW biogenic	35,997	31,333	37,463	33,689	42,025
Wood	27,988,372	27,835,474	28,097,529	28,296,111	28,113,402
Hydroelectric	4,222,424	3,248,493	3,195,441	2,899,048	2,268,671

(continued on next page)

Table 2.14: Electricity Net Generation from Renewable Energy by End-Use Sector and Source, 2003–2007

	2003	2004	2005	2006	2007
Electric Power Sector					
Total	320,992,669	317,451,398	323,699,182	352,185,302	318,550,813
Biomass	23,335,311	22,857,679	23,606,816	24,266,508	24,990,133
Waste	13,807,633	13,130,379	13,039,195	13,934,359	14,609,573
Landfill gas	4,829,632	4,836,372	4,811,350	5,476,488	5,966,044
MSW biogenic	7,553,146	7,176,084	7,343,666	7,486,452	7,556,572
Wood	9,527,678	9,727,300	10,567,621	10,332,148	10,380,560
Geothermal	14,424,231	14,810,975	14,691,745	14,568,029	14,838,636
Hydroelectric	271,511,660	265,063,848	267,039,777	286,253,922	245,972,718
Solar	534,001	575,155	550,294	507,706	606,082
Wind	11,187,466	14,143,741	17,810,549	26,589,137	32,143,244

Source: Energy Information Administration, *Renewable Energy Consumption and Electricity: Preliminary 2007 Statistics*, table 3.

Notes: 'MSW biogenic' includes paper, wood, food, leather, textiles, and yard trimmings form Municipal Solid Waste.
'Wood' includes wood-derived fuels such as black liquor and wood/woodwaste solids and liquids.
'Hydroelectric' includes conventional hydroelectric power.

Units: Net generation in thousand kilowatt-hours.

Table 2.15: **Renewable Energy Consumption by Source and End-Use Sector, 2003–2007**

	2003	2004	2005	2006	2007
All Sectors					
Total	*6.150*	*6.261*	*6.444*	*6.922*	*6.830*
Biomass	2.817	3.023	3.154	3.374	3.615
Biofuels	0.414	0.513	0.595	0.795	1.018
Biodiesel	0.002	0.004	0.012	0.032	0.063
Ethanol	0.238	0.299	0.342	0.462	0.577
Waste	0.401	0.389	0.403	0.407	0.431
Landfill gas	0.141	0.144	0.148	0.150	0.174
MSW biogenic	0.165	0.164	0.168	0.171	0.174
Wood	2.002	2.121	2.156	2.172	2.165
Geothermal	0.331	0.341	0.343	0.343	0.353
Hydroelectric	2.825	2.690	2.703	2.869	2.463
Solar	0.064	0.065	0.066	0.072	0.080
Wind	0.115	0.142	0.178	0.264	0.319
Residential Sector					
Total	*0.471*	*0.483*	*0.527*	*0.495*	*0.556*
Biomass	0.400	0.410	0.450	0.410	0.460
Wood	0.400	0.410	0.450	0.410	0.460
Geothermal	0.013	0.014	0.016	0.018	0.022
Solar	0.058	0.059	0.061	0.067	0.074
Commercial Sector					
Total	*0.113*	*0.118*	*0.119*	*0.117*	*0.119*
Biomass	0.101	0.105	0.105	0.102	0.104
Waste	0.029	0.034	0.034	0.036	0.037
Landfill gas	0.002	0.002	0.003	0.004	0.005
MSW biogenic	0.022	0.025	0.025	0.026	0.025
Wood	0.071	0.070	0.070	0.065	0.065
Geothermal	0.011	0.012	0.014	0.014	0.014
Hydroelectric	0.001	0.001	0.001	0.001	0.001

(continued on next page)

Table 2.15: Renewable Energy Consumption by Source and End-Use Sector, 2003–2007

	2003	2004	2005	2006	2007
Industrial Sector					
Total	*1.731*	*1.861*	*1.884*	*1.999*	*2.025*
Biomass	1.684	1.824	1.848	1.966	1.998
Biofuels	0.178	0.217	0.248	0.311	0.391
Ethanol	0.005	0.006	0.007	0.009	0.012
Waste	0.142	0.132	0.148	0.140	0.151
Landfill gas	0.076	0.075	0.081	0.074	0.089
MSW biogenic	0.005	0.006	0.007	0.006	0.006
Wood	1.363	1.476	1.452	1.515	1.457
Geothermal	0.003	0.004	0.004	0.004	0.005
Transportation Sector					
Total	*0.235*	*0.296*	*0.346*	*0.483*	*0.626*
Biofuels	0.235	0.296	0.346	0.483	0.626
Biodiesel	0.002	0.004	0.012	0.032	0.063
Ethanol	0.233	0.292	0.334	0.451	0.564
Electric Power Sector					
Total	*3.601*	*3.503*	*3.568*	*3.827*	*3.503*
Biomass	0.397	0.388	0.406	0.412	0.427
Waste	0.230	0.223	0.221	0.231	0.243
Landfill gas	0.063	0.066	0.065	0.073	0.080
MSW biogenic	0.138	0.133	0.136	0.139	0.143
Wood	0.167	0.165	0.185	0.182	0.184
Geothermal	0.303	0.311	0.309	0.306	0.312
Hydroelectric	2.781	2.656	2.670	2.839	2.440
Solar	0.005	0.006	0.006	0.005	0.006
Wind	0.115	0.142	0.178	0.264	0.319

Source: Energy Information Administration, *Renewable Energy Consumption and Electricity: Preliminary 2007 Statistics*, table 2.

Notes: Here, biodiesel is primarily derived from soybean oil, and ethanol primarily from corn.
'MSW biogenic' includes paper, wood, food, leather, textiles, and yard trimmings from Municipal Solid Waste.
'Wood' includes wood, wood pellet fuels, and wood-derived fuels such as black liquor and wood/woodwaste solids and liquids.
'Hydroelectric' includes conventional hydroelectric power.

Units: Consumption in quadrillion Btu.

Table 2.16:   Renewable Net Generation by State and Source, 2007

	Landfill Gas/ MSW	Wood	Hydroelectric	Wind	Total
United States	14,767,716	38,515,262	248,312,395	32,143,244	351,300,591
Alabama	3,511	3,834,786	4,584,600	NA	8,439,796
Alaska	NA	NA	1,208,365	7,784	1,222,483
Arizona	23,889	1,798	6,582,545	NA	6,621,734
Arkansas	6,576	1,565,434	3,107,064	NA	4,705,763
California	1,810,118	3,330,403	29,059,757	5,644,272	53,987,474
Colorado	NA	NA	1,731,370	708,291	2,471,522
Connecticut	768,589	29,535	438,275	NA	1,236,400
Delaware	503	NA	NA	NA	503
District of Columbia	NA	NA	NA	NA	NA
Florida	1,846,148	1,924,074	175,042	NA	4,524,323
Georgia	25,807	3,413,571	2,504,532	NA	5,986,026
Hawaii	169,287	NA	105,345	154,947	801,326
Idaho	NA	498,668	8,910,945	177,969	9,587,582
Illinois	655,573	NA	147,157	571,270	1,384,568
Indiana	225,382	NA	439,070	NA	664,451
Iowa	110,808	NA	965,551	2,719,059	3,827,303
Kansas	NA	NA	10,501	1,152,538	1,163,039
Kentucky	93,253	373,763	1,686,342	NA	2,155,313
Louisiana	NA	2,996,010	826,642	NA	3,911,113
Maine	240,727	3,818,824	3,519,405	99,071	7,730,284
Maryland	400,736	214,068	1,660,030	NA	2,274,835
Massachusetts	1,138,266	142,153	1,157,750	NA	2,466,824
Michigan	796,564	1,711,143	1,274,386	2,723	3,786,760
Minnesota	452,194	569,548	509,988	2,466,136	4,004,792
Mississippi	NA	1,491,546	NA	NA	1,496,563
Missouri	15,188	NA	1,141,067	NA	1,164,534
Montana	NA	88,086	9,170,270	485,849	9,744,204
Nebraska	46,184	NA	848,636	217,664	1,127,651
Nevada	NA	NA	1,988,829	NA	3,517,042

(continued on next page)

Table 2.16:   Renewable Net Generation by State and Source, 2007

	Landfill Gas/ MSW	Wood	Hydroelectric	Wind	Total
United States	*14,767,716*	*38,515,262*	*248,312,395*	*32,143,244*	*351,300,591*
New Hampshire	179,317	882,996	1,311,054	NA	2,373,367
New Jersey	830,155	NA	33,541	20,910	994,551
New Mexico	NA	NA	186,703	1,393,239	1,602,702
New York	1,476,048	511,590	25,530,506	839,390	28,365,179
North Carolina	100,921	1,699,079	3,040,887	NA	4,842,021
North Dakota	NA	NA	1,305,393	562,518	1,871,562
Ohio	25,629	345,167	455,232	20,136	862,825
Oklahoma	NA	295,151	2,461,150	1,849,144	4,605,445
Oregon	74,737	935,258	33,375,111	1,142,964	35,581,425
Pennsylvania	1,464,343	609,426	2,322,467	380,784	4,794,908
Rhode Island	150,306	NA	5,029	NA	155,336
South Carolina	108,960	1,754,399	1,735,280	NA	3,598,639
South Dakota	NA	NA	2,442,847	150,018	2,592,865
Tennessee	26,229	444,051	4,928,793	49,937	5,450,612
Texas	241,878	916,981	1,186,635	8,121,835	10,525,871
Utah	14,033	NA	638,102	NA	816,060
Vermont	NA	469,268	1,187,274	10,511	1,667,053
Virginia	668,318	1,828,992	1,328,708	NA	3,851,128
Washington	179,595	978,110	77,634,164	2,170,291	80,994,340
West Virginia	NA	NA	1,238,032	167,588	1,405,620
Wisconsin	397,943	841,217	1,484,426	110,676	2,871,552
Wyoming	NA	NA	727,595	745,729	1,473,325

Source: Energy Information Administration, *Renewable Energy Consumption and Electricity: Preliminary 2007 Statistics*, table 6.

Notes: 'Landfill Gas/MSW' includes landfill gas, as well as paper, paper board, wood, food, leather, textiles, and yard trimmings from Municipal Solid Waste.
'Wood fuels' includes wood and wood-derived fuels such as black liquor and wood/ woodwaste solids and liquids.
'Hydroelectric' includes conventional hydroelectric power.

Units: Net generation in thousand kilowatt-hours.

**Table 2.17: Renewable Net Summer Capacity
by State and Energy Source, 2007**

	Landfill Gas/ MSW	Wood	Hydroelectric	Wind	Total
United States	*3,238*	*6,432*	*77,833*	*15,616*	*106,553*
Alabama	NA	581	3,271	NA	3,852
Alaska	NA	NA	397	3	400
Arizona	4	3	2,720	NA	2,736
Arkansas	5	292	1,389	NA	1,691
California	278	584	10,088	2,318	15,847
Colorado	NA	NA	660	1,064	1,742
Connecticut	170	NA	121	NA	291
Delaware	7	NA	NA	NA	7
District of Columbia	NA	NA	NA	NA	NA
Florida	463	343	55	NA	1,054
Georgia	5	450	2,027	NA	2,526
Hawaii	60	NA	24	64	227
Idaho	NA	75	2,393	75	2,543
Illinois	118	NA	33	541	708
Indiana	40	NA	60	NA	100
Iowa	11	NA	131	1,134	1,280
Kansas	NA	NA	3	363	366
Kentucky	15	43	815	NA	874
Louisiana	NA	318	192	NA	525
Maine	53	620	719	42	1,471
Maryland	126	2	566	NA	693
Massachusetts	264	26	259	NA	557
Michigan	152	210	257	2	620
Minnesota	129	162	175	1,136	1,656
Mississippi	NA	229	NA	NA	229
Missouri	3	NA	552	NA	555
Montana	NA	17	2,614	145	2,776
Nebraska	6	NA	273	73	356
Nevada	NA	NA	1,047	NA	1,324

(continued on next page)

Table 2.17: Renewable Net Summer Capacity by State and Energy Source, 2007

	Landfill Gas/ MSW	Wood	Hydroelectric	Wind	Total
United States	*3,238*	*6,432*	*77,833*	*15,616*	*106,553*
New Hampshire	31	141	494	NA	667
New Jersey	181	NA	5	8	212
New Mexico	NA	NA	82	494	582
New York	325	37	4,307	425	5,093
North Carolina	14	324	1,954	NA	2,292
North Dakota	NA	NA	443	335	788
Ohio	4	64	101	7	175
Oklahoma	16	63	851	594	1,524
Oregon	17	195	8,374	846	9,434
Pennsylvania	359	108	748	293	1,508
Rhode Island	24	NA	4	NA	28
South Carolina	29	220	1,345	NA	1,594
South Dakota	NA	NA	1,516	43	1,559
Tennessee	5	145	2,642	29	2,822
Texas	55	130	680	4,006	4,886
Utah	4	NA	255	NA	292
Vermont	NA	76	309	5	390
Virginia	170	409	671	NA	1,250
Washington	35	345	21,171	1,165	22,718
West Virginia	NA	NA	264	66	330
Wisconsin	62	220	476	53	813
Wyoming	NA	NA	303	287	590

Source: Energy Information Administration, *Renewable Energy Consumption and Electricity: Preliminary 2007 Statistics*, table 8.

Notes: 'Landfill Gas/MSW' includes landfill gas, as well as paper, paper board, wood, food, leather, textiles, and yard trimmings from Municipal Solid Waste.
'Wood fuels' include wood and wood-derived fuels such as black liquor and wood/ woodwaste solids and liquids.
'Hydroelectric' includes conventional hydroelectric power.

Units: Net generation in megawatts.

Table 2.18: Solar Thermal Collector Shipments, by Type, Price, and End-Use, 2006

	Low-Temperature	Medium-Temperature	High-Temperature	All Collectors
Total Shipments	*15,546*	*1,346*	*3,852*	*20,744*
Price per sq ft	$1.95	NA	NA	$5.84
By End Use				
Pool heating	15,225	137	0	15,362
Water heating	10	1,126	0	1,136
Space heating	290	40	0	330
Space cooling	0	3	0	3
Combined space and water heating	21	38	7	66
Process heating	0	0	0	0
Electricity generation	0	2	3,845	3,847
By Market Sector				
Residential	13,906	1,217	0	15,123
Commercial	1,500	120	7	1,626
Industrial	40	2	0	42
Electric utility	0	0	3,845	3,845

Source: Energy Information Administration, *Annual Energy Review 2007*, tables 10.5 and 10.6.

Notes: Low-tempterature collectors operate below 110°F.
Medium-temperature collectors operate between 140°F and 180°F.
High-temperature collectors usually operate over 180°F.
Groups may not add to total.

Units: Shipments in thousand square feet; prices in dollars per square foot.

Table 2.19: Photovoltaic Cell Shipments by Type, End-Use, and Economic Sector, 1995–2006

	1995	2000	2003	2006
Total Shipments	*31,059*	*88,221*	*109,357*	*337,268*
By Type				
Crystalline silicon	29,740	85,155	97,940	233,518
Thin-film silicon	1,266	2,736	10,966	101,766
By End Use				
Communications	5,154	12,269	14,185	6,888
Consumer goods	1,025	2,870	2,995	4,030
Electric generation				
Grid Interactive	4,585	21,713	42,485	274,197
Remote	8,233	14,997	15,025	18,003
Health	776	2,742	2,924	0
Original equipment manufacturers	3,188	12,153	11,334	6,132
Transportation	4,203	12,804	14,143	2,438
Water pumping	2,727	5,644	6,073	2,093
By Market Sector				
Residential	6,272	24,814	23,389	95,815
Commercial	8,100	13,692	32,604	180,852
Government	2,000	4,417	5,538	7,688
Industrial	7,198	28,808	27,951	28,618
Transportation	2,383	5,502	11,089	2,458
Electric utility	3,759	6,298	8,474	3,981
Prices:				
Modules	$4.56	$3.46	$3.17	$3.50
Cells	2.53	2.40	1.86	2.03

Source: Energy Information Administration, *Annual Energy Review 2007*, tables 10.7 and 10.8.

Notes: Photovoltaic modules are assemblies of cells that generate electricity from sunlight using solid-state semiconductor devices with no moving parts.
A 'peak watt' is amount of power a photovoltaic cell or module will produce at standard test conditions (normally 1,000 watts per square meter and 25 degrees Celsius). A 'peak kilowatt' is 1,000 peak watts.
'Grid-interactive' electric generation connects with the electrical distribution system ('the grid'). Remote generation does not, and is typically used at a remote home or other location.

Units: Shipments in peak kilowatts; prices in current dollars per peak watt.

Table 2.20: Projected Renewable Energy Generating Capacty and Generation, 2006–2030

	2006	2010	2015	2020	2025	2030
Electric Power Sector						
Net Summer Capacity	96.34	111.63	117.32	123.62	128.26	132.54
Hydroelectric	76.72	76.73	77.15	77.26	77.26	77.32
Geothermal	2.29	2.50	2.88	3.28	3.77	4.18
Municipal waste	3.39	3.99	3.99	4.02	4.06	4.06
Wood and biomass	2.01	2.20	2.74	4.39	4.84	5.58
Solar thermal	0.40	0.54	0.80	0.82	0.84	0.86
Solar photovoltaic	0.03	0.07	0.14	0.22	0.30	0.39
Wind	11.50	25.61	29.63	33.64	37.18	40.15
Generation	350.62	424.27	469.30	522.35	544.68	557.91
Hydroelectric	285.07	289.47	297.22	298.00	298.09	298.53
Geothermal	14.84	17.52	20.79	23.96	27.84	31.05
Municipal waste	13.46	18.85	18.85	19.08	19.46	19.47
Wood and biomass	10.97	22.98	42.96	77.53	83.30	82.55
Solar thermal	0.49	1.15	1.97	2.04	2.11	2.18
Solar photovoltaic	0.01	0.16	0.32	0.52	0.74	0.96
Wind	25.78	74.13	87.19	101.23	113.14	123.18

(continued on next page)

Table 2.20: Projected Renewable Energy Generating Capacty and Generation, 2006–2030

	2006	2010	2015	2020	2025	2030
End-Use Generators						
Net Summer Capacity	6.00	6.65	8.24	10.85	15.20	16.72
Hydroelectric	0.70	0.70	0.70	0.70	0.70	0.70
Geothermal	0.00	0.00	0.00	0.00	0.00	0.00
Municipal waste	0.35	0.35	0.35	0.35	0.35	0.35
Biomass	4.64	4.89	6.37	8.57	12.21	12.60
Solar photovoltaic	0.27	0.67	0.77	1.13	1.77	2.80
Generation	34.22	37.17	47.88	65.05	94.02	98.19
Hydroelectric	3.24	3.24	3.24	3.24	3.24	3.24
Geothermal	0.00	0.00	0.00	0.00	0.00	0.00
Municipal waste	2.06	2.82	2.82	2.82	2.82	2.82
Biomass	28.44	29.98	40.50	57.00	84.74	86.99
Solar photovoltaic	0.43	1.07	1.25	1.85	2.97	4.76

Source: Energy Information Administration, *Annual Energy Outlook 2008 with Projections to 2030*, table A16.

Notes: 'Electric Power Sector' includes power plants whose primary business is to sell electricity, or electricity and heat, to the public.

'End-use generators' includes power plants in the commercial and industrial sectors, as well as small on-site generating systems in the residential, commercial, and industrial sector that generate power primarily for their own use.

'Solar photovoltaic' does not include off-grid photovoltaic cells.

Data for 2006 is from the projection model, and may differ slightly from the official 2006 estimates.

Units: Net summer capacity in gigawatts; generation in billion kilowatt-hours.

Table 2.21: Projected Renewable Energy Consumption, by Sector and Source, 2006–2030

	2006	2010	2015	2020	2025	2030
Marketed Renewable Energy						
Total Marketed	*6.77*	*8.56*	*10.00*	*11.74*	*13.44*	*13.73*
Residential	0.41	0.44	0.42	0.40	0.39	0.38
Commercial	0.13	0.13	0.13	0.13	0.13	0.13
Industrial	**1.99**	**2.34**	**2.75**	**3.32**	**4.21**	**4.33**
Hydroelectric	0.03	0.03	0.03	0.03	0.03	0.03
Biomass	1.51	1.48	1.57	1.65	1.75	1.83
Transportation	**0.50**	**1.13**	**1.66**	**2.24**	**2.77**	**2.77**
Ethanol in E85	0.00	0.00	0.12	0.64	0.93	0.88
Ethanol in gasoline blending	0.47	1.05	1.22	1.18	1.13	1.13
Biodiesel in distillate blending	0.03	0.08	0.17	0.13	0.14	0.16
Electric power	**3.74**	**4.53**	**5.05**	**5.64**	**5.94**	**6.13**
Hydroelectric	2.86	2.89	2.96	2.97	2.97	2.97
Geothermal	0.31	0.37	0.48	0.58	0.70	0.80
Municipal waste	0.15	0.23	0.23	0.23	0.23	0.23
Biomass	0.16	0.28	0.48	0.82	0.87	0.86
Solar thermal	0.00	0.01	0.02	0.02	0.02	0.02
Solar photovoltaic	0.00	0.00	0.00	0.01	0.01	0.01
Wind	0.26	0.74	0.87	1.02	1.13	1.24
Ethanol, by Source						
Total Ethanol	*0.47*	*1.05*	*1.34*	*1.82*	*2.06*	*2.01*
From corn	0.41	0.95	1.18	1.26	1.26	1.26
From cellulose	0.00	0.01	0.03	0.23	0.58	0.58
Imports	0.06	0.09	0.14	0.31	0.19	0.15

Source: Energy Information Administration, *Annual Energy Outlook 2008 with Projections to 2030*, table A17.

Notes: 'Marketed' energy includes electricity on the electric power grid, and non-electric sources bought and sold in the marketplace.
'Nonmarketed' energy is not bought or sold, either directly or indirectly; totals for nonmarketed energy are not estimated.
Data for 2006 is from the projection model, and may differ slightly from the official 2006 estimates.

Units: Consumption in quadrillion Btu per year.

Table 2.22: Public Opinion about Alternative Energy, 2000, 2004, and 2005

1. Question: Consider a future date when gasoline is no longer available. Which of the following do you think would be the best fuel for use in personal vehicles: electricity, ethanol, or hydrogen?

	2000		2004	
	Best	Worst	Best	Worst
Electricity	52%	15%	41%	21%
Hydrogen	15	27	28	23
Ethanol	21	28	19	28
Don't know	12	30	13	29

2. Question: Suppose that you were going to buy a new vehicle. Would you seriously consider buying a car or SUV that is a gas-electric hybrid, or not? If the hybrid vehicle cost $3,000 more than the standard model of the same vehicle, would you still seriously consider buying it, or not? (asked August 2005)

Response	Percent
Yes, would seriously consider	55%
Even if $3,000 more	45
Not if $3,000 more	9
No, would not	43
No opinion	2

(continued on next page)

Table 2.22: Public Opinion about Alternative Energy, 2000, 2004, and 2005

3. Question: What fuels would you like to see replace gasoline and diesel fuel in the vehicles used in the United States? Anything else? (unaided question, asked September 2005, by type of vehicle owned by respondent)

Response	Total	Small Car	Large Car	Minivan	Pickup/ Van	SUV
Electricity	14%	18%	18%	15%	13%	9%
Hydrogen	14	21	16	15	15	11
Ethanol	11	13	11	11	10	11
Solar	7	6	10	11	10	7
Water	7	6	8	11	3	8
Hybrid fuel/cars	5	9	7	3	7	3
Corn	5	4	6	8	4	4
Vegetable oil	3	3	2	4	4	5
Natural gas	3	2	4	1	3	3
Alcohol	2	4	3	1	3	1
Diesel	2	2	0	2	4	2
Fuel cells (unspecified)	2	3	3	2	1	1
Batteries	2	2	4	1	1	1
Propane	1	2	1	2	4	0
Something environmentally friendly	1	2	3	0	1	1
Anything cheaper/less expensive	1	0	1	2	1	3
Bio-diesel	1	1	0	0	3	0
Cooking oil	1	2	0	0	1	0
Nuclear	1	1	2	0	0	1
Soy/soybeans	1	1	0	1	1	0
Methanol	1	0	1	0	1	0
Wind	1	0	0	0	1	0
Other	11	8	11	12	12	13

(continued on next page)

Table 2.22: Public Opinion about Alternative Energy, 2000, 2004, and 2005

4. Question: Regarding some possible ways of reducing US dependence on imported oil, do you think the following are a good idea or a bad idea? (asked May 2005; aided question)

	Good	Bad	OK/ Can't rate
Require the auto industry to make cars that get better gas mileage	93%	6%	1%
Require the auto industry to make more fuel-efficient cars	90	8	1
Build more solar power facilities	90	6	3
Build more wind-turbine farms to harness wind-generated electricity	87	6	6
Increase funding for renewable energy research	86	9	4
Provide tax credits to people who buy more energy-efficient appliances such as air conditioning, clothes dryers, and water heaters	84	13	3
Promote the development of hydrogen-powered cars	81	8	11
Build more water-powered hydroelectric facilities	81	11	8
Provide tax credits to people who buy cars that get good gas mileage	79	19	2
Promote the use of hydrogen fuel cell technology	71	8	20

Source: National Renewable Energy Laboratory, *Consumer Views on Transportation and Energy, 3rd ed*, Q2.3.8, Q3.1.2, Q4.3.3, Q4.3.5.

Notes: Surveys done by the Opinion Research Corporation for the National Renewable Energy Laboratory (questions 1 and 3), Gallup (question 2), or the Yale Environment Survey (question 4), and are based on approximately 1,000 adults.

Units: Percent of survey respondents giving the stated response to each question.

Chapter 3

International Energy

Chapter 3 Highlights

Chapter 3 provides international data on energy production and consumption. This chapter contains breakdowns of many key energy figures for all the major producers and consumers around the world.

The United States' energy imports (especially for oil and pretroleum products) have risen dramatically, and imports are now the major source for crude oil (table 3.01, also see tables 3.10 and 3.11 for more information on US imports and exports), so the international picture is important to understanding the overall story. (It is also worth noting that the US' two single largest import sources of oil are Canada and Mexico.)

The United States produces around 15% of the world's energy, but accounts for over 20% of world consumption. The Middle East, in contrast, collectively produces around the same amount of energy, but consumes less than 5% of the total (tables 3.02 and 3.03). The US consumes nearly a quarter of the world's oil, despite producing less than 10% (tables 3.06 and 3.07). The major oil producer continues to be the Organization of Petroleum-Exporting Countries (OPEC). In addition to the Middle East and the other OPEC nations, the former USSR is also a major producer (table 3.06). The United States does remain a major generator of electricity (table 3.04) and nuclear power (3.05). In addition to the US, China and Japan are major consumers of energy.

Despite the increased concern over gasoline prices, the United States actually has some of the lowest gas prices in the world (table 3.12). Proved reserves of oil have increased worldwide since 1996, due mostly to increases for South America, Africa, the Middle East, Europe, and Eurasia (table 3.08). The United States and Brazil are the world's leading producers of ethanol, while European countries (especially Germany and France) are the largest biodiesel producers (tables 3.13 and 3.14). Table 3.15 contains international projections for oil supplies and consumption.

Table 3.01: US Energy Imports and Exports, 1970–2007

| | Imports | | | | Exports | | | Net Imports |
	Natural Gas	Petroleum	Total	Coal	Petroleum	Total	Total
1970	0.846	7.470	8.342	1.936	0.549	2.632	5.709
1975	0.978	12.948	14.032	1.761	0.439	2.323	11.709
1980	1.006	14.658	15.796	2.421	1.160	3.695	12.101
1985	0.952	10.609	11.781	2.438	1.657	4.196	7.584
1990	1.551	17.117	18.817	2.772	1.824	4.752	14.065
1995	2.901	18.881	22.262	2.318	1.991	4.511	17.751
2000	3.869	24.532	28.973	1.528	2.154	4.006	24.967
2001	4.068	25.398	30.158	1.265	2.039	3.770	26.386
2002	4.104	24.674	29.408	1.032	2.042	3.668	25.739
2003	4.042	26.219	31.062	1.117	2.151	4.054	27.007
2004	4.365	28.196	33.556	1.253	2.208	4.433	29.110
2005	4.450	29.248	34.721	1.273	2.442	4.561	30.149
2006	4.291	29.168	34.673	1.264	2.751	4.868	29.805
2007	4.717	28.701	34.599	1.507	2.934	5.361	29.238

Source: Energy Information Administration, *Annual Energy Review 2007*, table 1.4.

Notes: Net imports equal imports minus exports; negative values mean greater exports than imports.
Includes trade between the Unites States (50 states and DC) and its territories and possessions.
Data for 2007 is preliminary.

Units: Energy in quadrillion Btu.

Table 3.02:   World Energy Production by Country, 1993–2005

	1993	1997	2001	2005
World Total	*349.36*	*381.49*	*403.19*	*460.14*
North America	91.98	99.17	99.68	98.99
Canada	15.38	17.48	18.25	19.09
Mexico	8.11	9.06	9.54	10.26
United States	68.49	72.63	71.89	69.64
Central & South America	18.83	24.10	26.00	28.36
Brazil	4.10	5.06	6.20	7.71
Colombia	1.99	2.84	3.08	3.38
Venezuela	7.26	9.48	9.23	8.23
Europe	47.13	51.77	51.49	49.13
France	4.84	4.92	5.14	5.10
Germany	5.85	5.57	5.28	5.30
Netherlands	2.98	2.88	2.63	2.71
Norway	7.12	9.59	10.28	10.66
Poland	3.67	3.83	3.08	2.98
United Kingdom	9.42	11.33	11.14	8.73
Eurasia	57.94	50.79	57.94	68.60
Kazakhstan	3.26	2.47	3.69	5.48
Russia	45.01	40.63	44.77	52.72
Ukraine	3.68	3.01	3.08	3.21
Uzbekistan	1.90	2.18	2.65	2.48
Middle East	45.72	51.72	56.16	65.22
Iran	8.83	9.84	10.67	13.01
Iraq	1.21	2.60	5.22	4.11
Kuwait	4.28	4.85	4.81	6.12
Lebanon	0.01	0.01	0.00	0.01
Qatar	1.45	1.90	2.71	3.82
Saudi Arabia	20.11	21.24	20.95	25.51
United Arab Emirates	5.78	6.50	6.59	7.59

(continued on next page)

Table 3.02: World Energy Production by Country, 1993–2005

	1993	1997	2001	2005
World Total	*349.36*	*381.49*	*403.19*	*460.14*
Africa	22.63	26.09	28.01	34.66
Algeria	4.87	5.63	6.26	7.70
Egypt	2.48	2.51	2.68	3.19
Libya	3.17	3.39	3.21	4.00
Nigeria	4.45	4.85	5.45	6.55
South Africa	4.30	5.44	5.62	6.05
Asia & Oceania	65.13	77.84	83.92	115.16
Australia	6.62	8.32	10.26	11.23
China	31.84	37.97	38.48	63.23
India	7.49	9.17	10.29	11.73
Indonesia	6.33	7.41	8.09	9.32
Japan	3.84	4.48	4.38	4.10
Malaysia	2.34	3.01	3.31	3.90
Thailand	0.65	1.13	1.32	1.76

Source: Energy Information Administration, *International Energy Annual 2005*, table F1.

Notes: 'Europe' excludes countries in the former USSR.
Includes production of crude oil, natural gas plant liquids, dry natural gas, coal, and net electricity generation from nuclear power, hydroelectric, wood, waste, geothermal, solar, and wind.
Data for 2005 is preliminary.

Units: Energy production in quadrillion Btu.

Table 3.03:   World Energy Consumption by Country, 1993–2005

	1993	1997	2001	2005
World Total	*353.54*	*381.10*	*402.29*	*462.80*
North America	104.62	113.11	115.57	121.90
Canada	11.69	12.66	12.97	14.31
Mexico	5.31	5.68	6.26	6.88
United States	87.60	94.76	96.33	100.69
Central & South America	16.12	19.44	21.18	23.41
Argentina	2.27	2.47	2.61	2.93
Brazil	6.33	7.86	8.49	9.33
Venezuela	2.29	2.66	3.03	3.14
Europe	75.44	79.74	82.68	86.29
Belgium	2.24	2.60	2.67	2.58
France	9.80	10.36	11.08	11.43
Germany	14.09	14.36	14.62	14.51
Italy	6.86	7.22	7.68	8.07
Netherlands	3.54	3.70	3.93	4.24
Norway	1.71	1.75	1.87	2.09
Poland	3.97	4.08	3.45	3.66
Spain	4.14	4.76	5.87	6.59
Sweden	2.17	2.25	2.35	2.34
Turkey	2.33	2.93	2.89	3.74
United Kingdom	9.58	9.75	9.82	10.01
Eurasia	49.78	39.24	41.20	45.82
Kazakhstan	2.95	1.69	2.01	2.84
Russia	32.31	26.04	27.97	30.29
Ukraine	8.19	6.07	5.64	6.21
Uzbekistan	2.08	1.88	2.03	2.16
Middle East	12.94	15.61	17.95	22.85
Iran	3.48	4.43	5.39	7.26
Saudi Arabia	3.78	4.37	5.14	6.66
United Arab Emirates	1.51	1.77	1.89	2.30

(continued on next page)

Energy, Transportation & the Environment 2009

Table 3.03: World Energy Consumption by Country, 1993–2005

	1993	1997	2001	2005
World Total	*353.54*	*381.10*	*402.29*	*462.80*
Africa	9.97	11.40	12.59	14.43
Egypt	1.51	1.79	2.22	2.75
South Africa	3.74	4.56	4.66	5.04
Asia & Oceania	84.66	102.54	111.12	148.10
Australia	3.88	4.56	5.02	5.49
China	31.32	37.91	39.38	67.09
India	9.29	11.64	13.94	16.20
Indonesia	2.91	3.66	4.46	5.36
Japan	19.24	21.60	22.10	22.57
South Korea	5.39	7.41	8.10	9.28
Malaysia	1.28	1.67	2.11	2.55
Pakistan	1.39	1.69	1.81	2.25
Singapore	1.09	1.45	1.61	2.02
Taiwan	2.43	3.21	3.86	4.50
Thailand	1.68	2.60	2.70	3.63

Source: Energy Information Administration, *International Energy Annual 2005*, table E1.

Notes: 'Europe' excludes countries in the former USSR.
Includes consumption of petroleum products, dry natural gas, coal, and net electricity generation from nuclear power, hydroelectric, wood, waste, geothermal, solar, and wind.
For United States, data also includes consumption of renewable energy not used for electricity generation.
Data for 2005 is preliminary.

Units: Energy consumption in quadrillion Btu.

Table 3.04:   World Electricity Generation by Country and Type, 2005

	Fossil Fuels	Nuclear	Hydroelectric	Alternative	Total Net Generation
World Total	*11,455.3*	*2,625.6*	*2,900.0*	*369.7*	*17,350.6*
North America	3,238.4	879.7	657.7	119.2	4,894.9
Canada	152.2	87.4	359.9	10.0	609.6
Mexico	175.2	10.3	27.5	9.4	222.4
United States	2,910.0	782.0	270.3	99.7	4,062.0
Central and South America	253.3	16.3	613.2	26.0	908.7
Argentina	59.5	6.4	33.9	1.3	101.1
Brazil	34.1	9.9	334.1	18.3	396.4
Chile	23.5	0.0	23.8	0.9	48.2
Colombia	10.5	0.0	39.4	0.5	50.5
Paraguay	0.0	0.0	50.7	0.0	50.7
Venezuela	24.9	0.0	74.3	0.0	99.2
Europe	1,837.7	957.3	539.6	160.1	3,494.7
Austria	21.8	0.0	35.5	3.7	61.0
Belgium	33.0	45.2	0.3	2.4	80.8
Czech Republic	50.8	23.5	2.4	0.7	77.4
Finland	22.0	22.1	13.6	9.3	67.1
France	57.2	429.0	51.2	6.3	543.6
Germany	362.3	154.9	19.4	42.8	579.4
Greece	49.7	0.0	5.0	1.4	56.1
Ireland	22.3	0.0	0.6	1.2	24.1
Italy	231.1	0.0	33.3	14.2	278.5
Netherlands	81.8	3.8	0.1	8.6	94.3
Norway	0.5	0.0	134.4	0.9	135.8
Poland	142.1	0.0	2.2	1.9	146.2
Romania	31.6	5.3	20.0	0.0	56.9
Spain	173.1	54.7	19.4	23.2	270.3
Sweden	3.7	68.6	72.1	8.8	153.2
Turkey	114.8	0.0	39.2	0.3	154.2
United Kingdom	277.5	75.2	4.9	15.0	372.6

(continued on next page)

Table 3.04:   World Electricity Generation by Country and Type, 2005

	Fossil Fuels	Nuclear	Hydroelectric	Alternative	Total Net Generation
World Total	*11,455.3*	*2,625.6*	*2,900.0*	*369.7*	*17,350.6*
Eurasia	843.6	235.8	244.7	3.1	1,327.3
Kazakhstan	56.5	0.0	7.8	0.0	64.2
Russia	588.4	140.2	172.9	2.9	904.4
Ukraine	79.7	83.3	12.4	0.0	175.4
Uzbekistan	39.1	0.0	6.1	0.0	45.2
Middle East	581.7	0.0	21.0	0.0	602.7
Iran	154.4	0.0	15.9	0.0	170.4
Saudi Arabia	165.6	0.0	0.0	0.0	165.6
United Arab Emirates	57.1	0.0	0.0	0.0	57.1
Africa	430.3	12.2	88.7	2.0	533.2
Egypt	89.8	0.0	12.1	0.6	102.5
South Africa	214.9	12.2	0.9	0.3	228.3
Asia & Oceania	4,270.2	524.3	735.3	59.3	5,589.1
Australia	218.4	0.0	15.5	2.8	236.7
China	1,922.1	50.3	397.0	2.4	2,371.8
India	539.2	15.7	99.0	7.7	661.6
Indonesia	103.4	0.0	10.7	6.3	120.3
Japan	645.5	278.4	77.4	23.3	1,024.6
South Korea	222.7	139.4	3.6	0.4	366.2
Malaysia	76.6	0.0	5.7	0.0	82.4
Pakistan	56.9	2.4	30.6	0.0	89.8
Taiwan	164.5	38.0	7.8	0.0	210.3
Thailand	115.7	0.0	5.7	3.1	124.6

Source: Energy Information Administration, *International Energy Annual 2005*, tables 2.6 through 2.8, 6.1, and 6.3.

Notes: 'Europe' excludes countries in the former USSR.
'Alternative' methods of generation include geothermal, solar, wind, wood, and waste.
Data for 2005 is preliminary.

Units: Net generation in billion kilowatt-hours.

Table 3.05: World Nuclear Power by Country, 1997–2006

	1997	2000	2003	2006
World Total	*2,271.3*	*2,449.9*	*2,517.8*	*2,657.3*
North America	716.4	830.9	844.9	888.9
Canada	77.9	69.2	71.1	91.4
Mexico	9.9	7.8	10.0	10.3
United States	628.6	753.9	763.7	787.2
Central and South America	10.5	10.9	20.4	20.9
Argentina	7.5	6.0	7.0	7.2
Brazil	3.0	4.9	13.4	13.8
Europe	902.8	914.9	957.0	955.6
Belgium	45.0	45.7	45.0	44.2
Bulgaria	16.4	17.3	16.0	18.1
Czech Republic	12.5	12.9	24.6	24.7
Finland	19.0	21.4	21.6	21.7
France	375.7	394.4	419.0	427.7
Germany	161.8	161.1	156.8	158.9
Hungary	13.3	13.5	10.5	12.9
Netherlands	2.3	3.7	3.8	3.3
Romania	5.1	5.2	4.5	5.2
Slovakia	10.5	15.7	17.0	17.1
Slovenia	4.8	4.5	5.0	5.3
Spain	52.5	59.1	58.8	57.1
Sweden	66.4	54.5	64.0	63.6
Switzerland	24.1	25.1	26.1	26.4
United Kingdom	93.2	80.8	84.3	69.2

(continued on next page)

Table 3.05: World Nuclear Power by Country, 1997–2006

	1997	2000	2003	2006
World Total	*2,271.3*	*2,449.9*	*2,517.8*	*2,657.3*
Former USSR	192.5	203.4	234.4	240.2
Armenia	1.4	1.8	1.8	2.4
Kazakhstan	0.3	0.0	0.0	0.0
Lithuania	10.9	8.0	14.7	8.7
Russia	104.5	122.5	141.2	144.3
Ukraine	75.4	71.1	76.7	84.8
Africa	**12.6**	**13.0**	**12.7**	**10.1**
South Africa	12.6	13.0	12.7	10.1
Asia and Oceania	**436.5**	**476.8**	**448.4**	**541.5**
China	11.4	15.9	41.7	54.8
India	10.5	14.1	16.4	15.6
Japan	306.2	305.9	228.0	288.9
Pakistan	0.4	0.4	1.8	2.5
South Korea	73.2	103.5	123.2	141.3
Taiwan	34.8	37.0	37.4	38.3

Source: Energy Information Administration, *Annual Energy Review 2007*, table 11.18.

Notes: Groups may not add to total.

Units: Net generation in billion kilowatt-hours.

Table 3.06:   World Oil Production by Country, 1965-2007

	1965	1970	1980	1990	2000	2007
World Total	*31,806*	*48,064*	*62,948*	*65,477*	*74,916*	*81,533*
North America	10,296	13,257	14,063	13,856	13,904	13,665
Canada	920	1,473	1,764	1,965	2,721	3,309
Mexico	362	487	2,129	2,977	3,450	3,477
United States	9,014	11,297	10,170	8,914	7,733	6,879
South and Central America	4,334	4,829	3,747	4,507	6,813	6,633
Argentina	276	399	506	517	819	698
Brazil	96	167	188	650	1,268	1,833
Colombia	203	226	131	446	711	561
Ecuador	8	4	206	292	409	520
Peru	66	75	196	130	100	114
Trinidad & Tobago	135	140	212	150	138	154
Venezuela	3,503	3,754	2,228	2,244	3,239	2,613
Europe & Eurasia	5,652	7,982	15,088	16,106	14,950	17,835
Azerbaijan	NA	NA	NA	254	282	868
Denmark	NA	NA	6	121	363	312
Italy	48	32	35	97	95	122
Kazakhstan	NA	NA	NA	551	744	1,490
Norway	NA	NA	528	1,716	3,346	2,556
Romania	266	284	250	169	131	105
Russia	NA	NA	NA	10,405	6,536	9,978
Turkmenistan	NA	NA	NA	120	144	198
United Kingdom	2	4	1,663	1,918	2,667	1,636
Uzbekistan	NA	NA	NA	69	177	114
Middle East	8,387	13,904	18,882	17,540	23,516	25,176
Iran	1,908	3,848	1,479	3,270	3,818	4,401
Iraq	1,313	1,549	2,658	2,149	2,614	2,145
Kuwait	2,371	3,036	1,757	964	2,206	2,626
Oman	NA	332	285	695	959	718
Qatar	233	363	476	434	757	1,197
Saudi Arabia	2,219	3,851	10,270	7,105	9,491	10,413
Syria	NA	85	158	407	548	394
United Arab Emirates	282	762	1,745	2,283	2,626	2,915
Yemen	NA	NA	NA	182	450	336

(continued on next page)

Table 3.06: World Oil Production by Country, 1965–2007

	1965	1970	1980	1990	2000	2007
World Total	*31,806*	*48,064*	*62,948*	*65,477*	*74,916*	*81,533*
Africa	2,240	6,112	6,225	6,725	7,804	10,318
Algeria	577	1,052	1,139	1,347	1,578	2,000
Angola	13	103	150	475	746	1,723
Cameroon	NA	NA	56	155	88	82
Chad	NA	NA	NA	NA	NA	144
Congo	1	NA	61	156	254	222
Egypt	126	319	580	897	781	710
Equatorial Guinea	NA	NA	NA	NA	91	363
Gabon	25	109	178	270	327	230
Libya	1,220	3,357	1,862	1,424	1,475	1,848
Nigeria	274	1,084	2,059	1,870	2,155	2,356
Sudan	NA	NA	NA	NA	174	457
Tunisia	NA	87	118	96	78	98
Asia Pacific	898	1,979	4,943	6,743	7,928	7,907
Australia	7	176	460	651	809	561
Brunei	80	136	240	152	193	194
China	227	615	2,119	2,774	3,252	3,743
India	62	140	193	732	780	801
Indonesia	486	854	1,577	1,539	1,456	969
Malaysia	1	18	276	634	735	755
Thailand	NA	NA	NA	62	176	309
Vietnam	NA	NA	NA	55	328	340
European Union	707	702	2,277	2,667	3,493	2,394
OECD	10,782	13,922	17,138	18,845	21,521	19,170
OPEC	14,400	23,612	27,399	25,104	32,160	35,204
Non-OPEC	12,549	17,325	23,433	28,807	34,742	33,524
Former USSR	4,858	7,127	12,116	11,566	8,014	12,804

Source: *BP Statistical Review of World Energy, June 2008*, page 8.

Notes: 'OECD' refers to the 30 member countries of the Organization for Economic Cooperation and Development.

'OPEC' refers to 12 nations comprising the Organization of Petroleum-Exporting Countries: Iraq, Indonesia, Iran, Kuwait, Libya, Angola, Algeria, Nigeria, Qatar, Saudi Arabia, the United Arab Emirates, and Venezuela. Non-OPEC estimates exclude countries in the former Soviet Union.

Figures include crude oil, shale oil, oil sands, and natural gas liquids, and exclude fuels from biomass and coal derivatives.

Units: Production in thousands of barrels per day.

Table 3.07: World Oil Consumption by Country, 1965–2007

	1965	1970	1980	1990	2000	2007
World Total	*31,240*	*46,066*	*61,841*	*66,855*	*76,340*	*85,220*
North America	12,941	16,612	20,012	20,206	23,548	25,024
United States	11,522	14,710	17,062	16,988	19,701	20,698
Canada	1,117	1,483	1,915	1,762	1,937	2,303
Mexico	302	419	1,034	1,456	1,910	2,024
South and Central America	1,702	2,201	3,463	3,773	4,907	5,493
Argentina	443	456	476	389	431	492
Brazil	314	534	1,204	1,476	2,056	2,192
Chile	69	98	109	143	238	342
Colombia	73	106	170	209	232	228
Ecuador	14	22	63	92	129	181
Peru	73	97	134	121	155	145
Venezuela	187	211	415	397	496	596
Europe	11,826	18,628	24,389	23,540	19,564	20,100
Austria	110	181	244	223	244	281
Belgium & Luxembourg	335	554	539	509	702	839
Czech Republic	80	140	230	176	169	210
Denmark	204	363	274	185	215	197
Finland	114	213	257	229	224	226
France	1,091	1,904	2,262	1,910	2,007	1,919
Germany	1,746	2,820	3,056	2,708	2,763	2,393
Greece	87	133	248	321	406	443
Hungary	75	120	234	198	145	168
Ireland	48	82	116	92	170	198
Italy	1,017	1,716	1,972	1,932	1,956	1,745
Netherlands	494	722	798	763	897	1,044
Norway	104	167	201	203	201	221
Poland	111	185	353	331	427	532
Portugal	55	92	172	230	324	302
Romania	146	222	374	373	203	229
Russia	NA	NA	NA	5,129	2,583	2,699
Spain	278	552	1,070	1,040	1,452	1,615
Sweden	378	577	498	341	318	364
Switzerland	167	258	268	273	263	243
Turkey	99	153	302	470	677	666
United Kingdom	1,486	2,081	1,672	1,762	1,697	1,696
Uzbekistan	NA	NA	NA	260	138	119

(continued on next page)

Table 3.07: World Oil Consumption by Country, 1965–2007

	1965	1970	1980	1990	2000	2007
World Total	*31,240*	*46,066*	*61,841*	*66,855*	*76,340*	*85,220*
Middle East	957	1,164	2,046	3,484	4,716	6,203
Iran	201	331	625	951	1,301	1,621
Kuwait	104	89	87	109	202	276
Qatar	1	2	12	31	39	95
Saudi Arabia	392	409	599	1,171	1,536	2,154
United Arab Emirates	NA	4	107	248	255	450
Africa	531	725	1,374	1,976	2,458	2,955
Algeria	27	43	121	214	192	270
Egypt	135	120	263	477	564	651
South Africa	119	182	253	355	475	549
Asia Pacific	3,284	6,737	10,557	13,876	21,147	25,444
Australia	350	503	631	694	837	935
Bangladesh	NA	NA	32	39	66	102
China	217	559	1,694	2,323	4,772	7,855
China Hong Kong SAR	41	76	127	131	201	341
India	253	392	643	1,211	2,254	2,748
Indonesia	123	139	410	621	1,064	1,157
Japan	1,726	3,922	4,936	5,304	5,577	5,051
Malaysia	41	57	162	271	441	514
New Zealand	57	83	88	105	134	151
Pakistan	76	92	104	218	373	362
Philippines	85	145	216	234	348	298
Singapore	73	142	181	449	654	917
South Korea	25	163	475	1,038	2,229	2,371
Taiwan	44	105	388	566	1,003	1,123
Thailand	48	103	234	411	725	911
European Union	7,985	12,935	14,806	13,925	14,689	14,861
OECD	23,232	34,387	41,050	41,356	47,672	48,934
Former Soviet Union	3,392	4,940	8,494	8,582	3,623	3,923

Source: *BP Statistical Review of World Energy, June 2008*, page 11.

Notes: 'OECD' refers to the 30 member countries of the Organization for Economic Cooperation and Development.
Consumption of ethanol and biodiesel is also included.

Units: Consumption in thousands of barrels per day.

Table 3.08:   World Proved Oil Reserves, 1980–2007

	1980	1990	2000	2007
World Total	*667.2*	*1,003.2*	*1,104.5*	*1,237.9*
North America	92.5	96.3	68.9	69.3
United States	36.5	33.8	30.4	29.4
Canada	8.7	11.2	18.3	27.7
Mexico	47.2	51.3	20.2	12.2
South and Central America	26.7	71.5	97.9	111.2
Argentina	2.5	1.6	3.0	2.6
Brazil	1.3	4.5	8.5	12.6
Colombia	0.6	2.0	2.0	1.5
Ecuador	1.0	1.4	4.6	4.3
Peru	0.6	0.8	0.9	1.1
Trinidad & Tobago	0.6	0.6	0.9	0.8
Venezuela	19.5	60.1	76.8	87.0
Europe and Eurasia	98.3	80.4	108.5	143.7
Azerbaijan	NA	NA	1.2	7.0
Denmark	0.5	0.6	1.1	1.1
Italy	0.4	0.8	0.9	0.8
Kazakhstan	NA	NA	25.0	39.8
Norway	3.6	8.3	11.4	8.2
Romania	1.1	1.5	1.2	0.5
Russia	NA	NA	59.6	79.4
Turkmenistan	NA	NA	0.5	0.6
United Kingdom	8.4	4.0	4.7	3.6
Uzbekistan	NA	NA	0.6	0.6
Middle East	362.4	659.6	692.9	755.3
Iran	58.3	92.9	99.5	138.4
Iraq	30.0	100.0	112.5	115.0
Kuwait	67.9	97.0	96.5	101.5
Oman	2.5	4.4	5.8	5.6
Qatar	3.6	3.0	13.1	27.4
Saudi Arabia	168.0	260.3	262.8	264.2
Syria	1.5	1.9	2.3	2.5
United Arab Emirates	30.4	98.1	97.8	97.8
Yemen	NA	2.0	2.4	2.8

(continued on next page)

Table 3.08:   World Proved Oil Reserves, 1980–2007

	1980	1990	2000	2007
World Total	667.2	1,003.2	1,104.5	1,237.9
Africa	53.4	58.7	93.4	117.5
Algeria	8.2	9.2	11.3	12.3
Angola	1.4	1.6	6.0	9.0
Chad	NA	NA	0.9	0.9
Congo	0.7	0.8	1.7	1.9
Egypt	2.9	3.5	3.6	4.1
Equatorial Guinea	NA	NA	0.8	1.8
Gabon	0.5	0.9	2.4	2.0
Libya	20.3	22.8	36.0	41.5
Nigeria	16.7	17.1	29.0	36.2
Sudan	NA	0.3	0.6	6.6
Tunisia	2.2	1.7	0.4	0.6
Asia Pacific	33.9	36.6	42.9	40.8
Australia	2.1	3.5	4.9	4.2
Brunei	1.3	1.1	1.2	1.2
China	13.3	16.0	17.9	15.5
India	2.8	5.6	5.3	5.5
Indonesia	11.6	5.4	5.1	4.4
Malaysia	1.8	3.6	4.5	5.4
Thailand	NA	0.3	0.5	0.5
Vietnam	NA	0.2	2.0	3.4
European Union	11.8	8.1	8.8	6.8
OPEC	436.0	767.5	846.5	934.7
Non-OPEC	149.2	172.4	170.4	175.0
Former USSR	82.0	63.3	87.7	128.1

Source: *BP Statistical Review of World Energy, June 2008*, page 6.

Notes: 'OPEC' refers to 12 nations comprising the Organization of Petroleum-Exporting Countries: Iraq, Indonesia, Iran, Kuwait, Libya, Angola, Algeria, Nigeria, Qatar, Saudi Arabia, the United Arab Emirates, and Venezuela.
Non-OPEC estimates exclude countries in the former Soviet Union.
'Proved reserves' refers to quantities that geological information indicates, with a reasonable degree of certainty, could be recovered using existing conditions and methods.

Units: Proved reserves in billion barrels.

Table 3.09:   World Oil Refinery Capacity and Throughput, 1980–2007

	1990		2000		2007	
	Capacity	Throughput	Capacity	Throughput	Capacity	Throughput
World Total	*74,600*	*61,358*	*81,929*	*68,594*	*87,913*	*75,545*
North America	19,195	NA	19,937	NA	20,970	NA
United States	15,680	13,409	16,595	15,067	17,588	15,148
Canada	1,920	1,584	1,861	1,765	1,919	1,869
Mexico	1,595	1,490	1,481	1,363	1,463	1,395
South and Central America	6,009	4,315	6,307	5,337	6,513	5,448
Europe and Eurasia	27,929	22,727	24,837	19,299	25,024	20,829
Middle East	5,214	4,470	6,335	5,430	7,525	6,301
Africa	2,804	2,171	2,872	2,200	3,280	2,470
Asia Pacific	13,449	NA	21,641	NA	24,601	NA
China	2,892	2,153	5,407	4,218	7,511	6,563
Japan	4,324	3,437	5,010	4,145	4,598	3,994
Other Asia Pacific	954	4,885	1,403	8,918	1,451	10,761
European Union	15,213	12,435	15,102	13,762	15,590	13,748
OECD	40,018	34,038	44,006	39,750	44,946	39,783
Former Soviet Union	11,343	9,184	8,301	4,583	8,175	6,039

Source: *BP Statistical Review of World Energy, June 2008*, page 18.

Notes: 'OECD' refers to the 30 member countries of the Organization for Economic Cooperation and Development.
'Throughput' measures input to primary distillation units only.

Units: Consumption and throughput in thousands of barrels per day.

Table 3.10: US Fossil Fuel Imports, Exports, and Net Imports, by Fuel Type, 1990–2007

	1990	1995	2000	2005	2007
All Fossil Fuels					
Imports	$78.23	$62.58	$134.81	$254.44	$301.86
Exports	11.27	8.20	13.28	24.94	35.96
Net imports	66.96	54.38	121.53	229.50	265.89
Coal					
Imports	$0.11	$0.35	$0.38	$1.26	$1.45
Exports	5.53	3.87	2.04	2.97	3.47
Net imports	-5.41	-3.52	-1.66	-1.71	-2.03
Natural Gas					
Imports	$3.64	$4.59	$14.94	$31.19	$26.17
Exports	0.32	0.40	1.00	4.89	4.70
Net imports	3.32	4.19	13.94	26.30	21.48
Crude Oil					
Imports	$53.66	$46.48	$89.88	$161.90	$205.39
Exports	0.17	0.01	0.46	0.53	0.83
Net imports	53.50	46.48	89.41	161.37	204.56
Petroleum Products					
Imports	$20.72	$10.80	$29.38	$59.40	$68.45
Exports	5.19	3.87	9.73	16.42	26.85
Net imports	15.53	6.94	19.65	42.98	41.59

Source: Energy Information Administration, *Annual Energy Review 2006*, tables 3.7 through 3.9; *2007*, tables 3.7 through 3.9.

Notes: Net imports equal imports minus exports; negative values mean greater exports than imports.
'Petroleum product' includes petroleum preparations, liquefied propane and butane, and other mineral fuels.
Most data for 2007 is preliminary.
Natural gas data for 2007 is an estimate.

Units: Imports, exports, and net imports in billions of constant 2000 dollars.

Table 3.11: US Petroleum Imports, Exports, and Net Imports, by Country, 2000 and 2007

	2000			2007		
	Imports	Exports	Net Imports	Imports	Exports	Net Imports
Persian Gulf	2,488	NA	2,483	2,170	NA	2,166
OPEC	5,203	NA	5,181	5,983	NA	5,946
Algeria	NA	NA	225	NA	NA	663
Iraq	620	NA	NA	485	NA	NA
Nigeria	896	NA	896	1,132	NA	1,131
Saudi Arabia	1,572	NA	1,571	1,489	NA	1,487
Venezuela	1,546	NA	1,530	1,362	NA	1,336
Non-OPEC	6,257	NA	5,238	7,456	NA	6,094
Brazil	51	28	NA	202	46	NA
Canada	1,807	110	1,697	2,426	183	2,243
Japan	NA	90	NA	NA	54	NA
Mexico	1,373	358	1,015	1,533	275	1,258
Netherlands	NA	42	NA	NA	75	NA
Spain	NA	40	NA	NA	48	NA
United Kingdom	366	10	356	278	6	272
Virgin Islands/Puerto Rico	NA	10	297	NA	10	336
Total	*11,459*	*1,040*	*10,419*	*13,439*	*1,399*	*12,040*
% of Total imports from OPEC	45.4%	NA	49.7%	44.5%	NA	49.4%
% of Total consumption from net imports	NA	NA	23.6%	NA	NA	28.7%

Source: Energy Information Administration, *Annual Energy Review 2006*, tables 5.4, 5.6, and 5.7; *2007*, tables 5.4, 5.6, and 5.7.

Notes: Net imports equal imports minus exports.
'Petroleum products' include petroleum preparations, liquefied propane and butane, and other mineral fuels.
'OPEC' refers to the nations currently comprising the Organization of Petroleum-Exporting Countries: Iraq, Indonesia, Iran, Kuwait, Libya, Angola, Algeria, Nigeria, Qatar, Saudi Arabia, the United Arab Emirates, and Venezuela.
'Persian Gulf' refers to Bahrain, Iran, Iraq, Kuwait, Qatar, Saudia Arabia, and the United Arab Emirates.
Data is given for the country of origin for crude oil, not the refined product, which may be different.
Data for 2007 is preliminary.

Units: Imports, exports, and net imports in thousands of barrels per day; percent of total given.

Table 3.12: Retail Gasoline Prices for Specified Countries, 2000–2007

	2000	2002	2004	2005	2006	2007
Regular Unleaded						
Australia	$1.94	$1.76	$2.72	$3.23	$3.54	$3.85
Canada	1.86	1.70	2.37	2.89	3.26	3.59
China	NA	1.21	1.48	1.70	2.11	2.29
Germany	3.45	3.67	5.24	5.66	6.03	6.88
Japan	3.65	3.15	3.93	4.28	4.47	4.49
Mexico	2.01	2.24	2.03	2.22	2.31	2.40
South Korea	4.18	3.84	4.51	5.28	5.92	6.21
Taiwan	2.15	1.93	2.46	2.76	3.05	3.20
United States	1.51	1.36	1.88	2.30	2.59	2.80
Premium Unleaded						
France	$3.80	$3.62	$4.99	$5.46	$5.88	$6.60
Italy	3.77	3.74	5.30	5.74	6.10	6.73
South Africa	1.78	1.41	2.58	3.05	3.42	NA
Spain	2.86	2.90	4.09	4.49	4.84	5.36
Thailand	1.38	1.35	1.76	2.25	2.76	3.20
United Kingdom	4.58	4.16	5.56	5.97	6.36	7.13
United States	1.69	1.56	2.07	2.49	2.81	3.03

Source: Energy Information Administration, *Annual Energy Review 2006*, table 11.8; *2007*, table 11.8.

Notes: 'Premium unleaded' is defined as having a Research Octane Number (RON) of 98 in the United States, and 95 elsewhere.
Prices have been converted to US dollars using exchange rates provided by the International Monetary Fund; care should be used when making comparisons due to fluctuations in prices and exchange rates.
Prices given in liters have been converted to gallons using a conversion factor of 3.785412 liters per gallon.

Units: Average yearly price in current dollars per gallon.

Table 3.13: World Ethanol Production, 2005

	Production	% of World Total
World Total	*12,150*	*100%*
United States	4,264	35.1
Brazil	4,227	34.8
China	1,004	8.3
India	449	3.7
France	240	2.0
Russia	198	1.6
Germany	114	0.9
South Africa	103	0.8
Spain	93	0.8
U.K.	92	0.8
Thailand	79	0.7
Ukraine	65	0.5
Canada	61	0.5
Poland	58	0.5
Indonesia	45	0.4
Argentina	44	0.4
Italy	40	0.3
Australia	33	0.3
Saudi Arabia	32	0.3
Japan	30	0.2
Sweden	29	0.2
Pakistan	24	0.2
Philippines	22	0.2
South Korea	17	0.1
Guatemala	17	0.1
Ecuador	14	0.1
Cuba	12	0.1
Mexico	12	0.1
Others	710	5.8

Source: Oak Ridge National Laboratory, *Biomass Energy Data Book,*
1st *ed (2006)*, table 2.5.

Notes: Includes production of all types of ethanol, not just fuel
ethanol.
Not all countries producing ethanol are shown.

Units: Production in million gallons; percent of world total.

Table 3.14   World Biodiesel Capacity, 2002

	Capacity	% of World Total
World Total	*397.05*	*100%*
United States	18.49	4.7
European Union	**357.42**	**90.0**
Austria	8.45	2.1
Belgium	9.51	2.4
Denmark	0.79	0.2
France	101.97	25.7
Germany	165.11	41.6
Italy	63.14	15.9
Spain	2.38	0.6
Sweden	4.49	1.1
United Kingdom	1.59	0.4
Poland	21.13	5.3

Source: Oak Ridge National Laboratory, *Biomass Energy Data Book*, *1ˢᵗ ed (2006)*, table 2.17.

Notes: Poland is not included in the European Union figure, as it was not a member in 2002.

Units: Capacity in million gallons; percent of world total.

Table 3.15:   Projected World Oil Supply and Use, 2006–2030

	2006	2010	2015	2020	2025	2030
Production						
Total Production	*84.66*	*90.40*	*96.70*	*101.80*	*107.14*	*113.31*
OPEC Production	34.90	36.40	39.26	40.87	42.91	46.16
Non-OPEC Production	49.76	54.00	57.44	60.94	64.23	67.15
OPEC Market Share	41.0%	40.3%	40.6%	40.1%	40.0%	40.7%
Conventional Production						
Total Conventional	*81.88*	*85.67*	*90.37*	*93.48*	*96.31*	*99.30*
OPEC	34.30	35.48	38.09	39.45	41.04	43.50
Asia	1.11	1.03	0.99	0.98	0.99	0.94
Middle East	23.21	22.41	23.40	24.09	25.24	27.35
North Africa	3.90	4.28	4.63	4.78	4.84	4.82
West Africa	4.02	5.77	6.88	7.41	7.80	8.23
South America	2.06	1.99	2.20	2.18	2.17	2.16
Non-OPEC						
OECD	19.85	19.69	18.78	18.10	17.48	16.99
United States	7.91	8.84	9.12	9.15	8.84	8.39
Canada	2.00	1.85	1.56	1.32	1.16	1.05
Mexico	3.74	3.37	3.29	3.25	3.24	3.35
European OECD	5.52	4.89	4.05	3.59	3.43	3.39
Australia and New Zealand	0.57	0.62	0.64	0.65	0.66	0.66
Non-OECD	27.73	30.51	33.49	35.94	37.80	38.81
Russia	9.82	10.34	10.60	10.90	11.37	11.69
Other former USSR	2.85	3.77	4.83	5.46	5.88	6.36
China	3.80	3.83	3.87	3.87	3.70	3.53
Other Asia	2.89	2.92	3.22	3.40	3.43	3.17
Middle East (non-OPEC)	1.69	2.00	2.20	2.40	2.70	2.90
Africa	2.49	2.92	3.35	3.83	4.04	3.99
Brazil	1.84	2.40	2.94	3.39	3.65	3.66
Other Central and South America	2.36	2.32	2.49	2.67	3.03	3.51
Unconventional Production						
Total Unconventional	*2.78*	*4.73*	*6.34*	*8.32*	*10.83*	*14.00*
United States	0.34	0.78	1.15	1.53	1.97	2.06
Other North America	1.23	1.91	2.34	2.85	3.41	3.96
European OECD	0.04	0.07	0.10	0.15	0.19	0.26
Middle East	0.00	0.03	0.18	0.31	0.62	1.24
Africa	0.17	0.31	0.36	0.44	0.59	0.83
Central and South America	0.80	1.18	1.45	1.76	2.09	2.51

(continued on next page)

Table 3.15: Projected World Oil Supply and Use, 2006–2030

	2006	2010	2015	2020	2025	2030
Consumption						
Total Consumption	*84.66*	*90.40*	*96.70*	*101.80*	*107.14*	*113.30*
OECD	*49.16*	*49.90*	*51.20*	*51.64*	*52.16*	*53.28*
United States	20.65	20.99	21.59	21.47	21.52	22.11
US Territories	0.38	0.43	0.47	0.51	0.55	0.59
Canada	2.27	2.32	2.34	2.36	2.38	2.40
Mexico	2.06	2.19	2.36	2.61	2.75	2.95
OECD Europe	15.42	15.47	15.63	15.71	15.79	15.86
Japan	5.16	5.18	5.21	5.22	5.24	5.26
South Korea	2.18	2.25	2.47	2.57	2.68	2.81
Australia and New Zealand	1.03	1.07	1.13	1.19	1.25	1.28
Non-OECD	35.51	40.51	45.50	50.16	54.98	60.02
Russia	2.79	2.89	3.03	3.13	3.25	3.32
Other former USSR	2.09	2.26	2.43	2.64	2.79	2.96
China	7.26	9.44	10.55	11.96	13.63	15.69
India	2.49	2.68	3.25	3.62	4.03	4.37
Other non-OECD Asia	6.14	6.67	7.64	8.35	9.08	9.86
Middle East	6.15	7.13	7.79	8.46	9.18	9.84
Africa	2.99	3.36	3.88	4.35	4.62	4.93
Brazil	2.34	2.57	2.87	3.15	3.42	3.68
Other Central and South America	3.26	3.51	4.05	4.51	4.98	5.37
Crude Oil Prices						
Imported low sulfur light crude	$66.02	$74.03	$59.85	$59.70	$64.49	$70.45
Imported crude	59.05	65.18	52.03	51.55	55.68	58.66

Source: Energy Information Administration, *Annual Energy Outlook 2008 with Projections to 2030*, table A20.

Notes: 'Conventional production' includes production of crude oil, natural gas plant liquids, hydrogen and hydrocarbons for refinery feedstocks, alcohol, and refinery grains.
'Unconventional production' includes liquids produced from energy crops, natural gas, coal, oil sands, and shale.
OPEC includes the member nations of Algeria, Angola, Indonesia, Iran, Iraq, Kuwait, Libya, Nigeria, Qatar, Saudi Arabia, the United Arab Emirates, and Venezuela, but does not include Ecuador.
OECD Europe includes the European members of the Organization for Economic Cooperation and Development.
Figures for 2006 are from the projection model, and may differ slightly from the official 2006 estimates.

Units: Production and consumption in millions of barrels per day; prices in 2006 dollars per barrel, market share as percent of total.

Part II: Transportation

Chapter 4

Cars & Driving

Chapter 4 Highlights

Chapter 4 contains data on cars and driving. The United States still owns more cars than any other country, but the rest of the world is catching up; America's share of world car registrations has declined sharply since 1980 (table 4.01). The United States has over 240 million motor vehicle registrations for around 300 million people (table 4.02). Of those vehicles, Sport Utility Vehicles have increased their market share since 1975, mostly at the expense of cars and pickup trucks, despite having lower gas mileage than either one (table 4.04). In recent years, sales of light trucks (including SUVs and pickup trucks) have exceeded sales of new cars (table 4.05).

Miles traveled on US roads have increased, especially for interstate highways in urban areas (table 4.08). In addition to this increase, traffic congestion has gotten much worse, especially in large metropolitan areas, with Los Angeles and San Francisco receiving the worst congestion ratings (tables 4.10 and 4.11). Despite the congestion (or possibly causing it), over three-quarters of Americans still drive themselves to work; only 10% carpool, and fewer use public transportation or other means (tables 4.13 and 4.14).

Fuel efficiency for cars and trucks continues to improve (tables 4.17 and 4.18), but gasoline prices have increased; 2007 marks the first time that prices (when adjusted for inflation) have surpassed the peak from 1980 and 1981 (table 4.20). Readers may also want to compare the estimates for the cost of owning a car in tables 4.15 and 4.16 to the estimates for the annual cost of public transit in table 5.11.

People are concerned about the high price of gas, and many report taking steps to save money. In 2005 nearly 70% reported experiencing financial hardship due to gas prices, nearly double the number who answered the same way in 2000. When asked, most people blamed the higher prices on oil companies or the war in Iraq (table 4.21).

In addition, tables 4.02, 4.03, 4.09, and 4.19 give state-by-state breakdowns of motor vehicle registrations, motor vehicle tax receipts, vehicle-miles traveled, and automobile fuel consumption, respectively.

Table 4.01: World Car Registrations by Country, 1980–2006

	1980	1990	2000	2005	2006
Country					
China	351	1,622	3,750	8,900	11,000
India	NA	2,694	5,150	7,654	8,100
Japan	23,660	34,924	52,437	57,091	57,521
France	18,440	23,010	28,060	30,100	30,400
United Kingdom	15,438	22,528	27,185	30,652	30,920
Germany	23,236	30,695	43,772	46,090	46,570
Canada	10,256	12,622	16,832	18,124	18,739
United States	121,601	133,700	127,721	132,909	135,047
World Total	*320,390*	*435,050*	*547,147*	*617,914*	*635,284*
US percent of World	*38.0%*	*30.7%*	*23.3%*	*21.5%*	*21.3%*

Source: Oak Ridge National Laboratory, *Transportation Energy Data Book, 27th ed*, table 3.1.

Notes: Data for 1980 and 1990 includes West Germany only.
Data from different years may not be comparable due to differences in survey methodology.

Units: Car registrations in thousands.

Table 4.02:   Motor Vehicle Registrations by State, 2006

	Cars	Trucks	Buses	All Motor Vehicles	Motorcycles
United States	*135,399,945*	*107,943,782*	*821,959*	*244,165,686*	*6,678,958*
Alabama	1,795,596	2,825,636	9,082	4,630,314	104,075
Alaska	242,487	429,901	2,706	675,094	24,122
Arizona	2,189,979	1,987,392	4,961	4,182,332	114,443
Arkansas	958,640	1,027,414	8,201	1,994,255	58,694
California	19,835,554	13,289,690	56,814	33,182,058	726,095
Colorado	858,967	943,027	5,829	1,807,823	117,159
Connecticut	1,999,809	1,041,651	10,492	3,051,952	64,959
Delaware	432,509	378,512	2,167	813,188	22,788
District of Columbia	168,916	47,300	2,889	219,105	1,367
Florida	7,425,148	8,899,488	48,929	16,373,565	588,962
Georgia	4,141,179	4,123,932	21,343	8,286,454	142,276
Hawaii	538,581	464,288	5,671	1,008,540	31,317
Idaho	541,487	729,861	3,767	1,275,115	50,514
Illinois	5,947,468	3,910,742	18,036	9,876,246	293,078
Indiana	2,694,901	2,228,559	31,974	4,955,434	147,544
Iowa	1,744,519	1,593,003	8,429	3,345,951	161,133
Kansas	872,878	1,512,396	3,918	2,389,192	72,078
Kentucky	1,969,142	1,574,731	14,249	3,558,122	58,959
Louisiana	1,950,372	1,900,270	22,102	3,872,744	61,128
Maine	581,797	486,680	3,399	1,071,876	45,488
Maryland	2,656,597	1,819,645	12,155	4,488,397	72,625
Massachusetts	3,310,725	2,063,283	11,207	5,385,215	143,853
Michigan	4,765,547	3,362,440	26,248	8,154,235	248,002
Minnesota	2,512,491	2,174,813	17,610	4,704,914	215,664
Mississippi	1,118,200	869,860	9,521	1,997,581	27,553
Missouri	2,715,297	2,230,390	11,485	4,957,172	85,466
Montana	447,446	616,613	2,503	1,066,562	85,874
Nebraska	832,511	893,627	6,995	1,733,133	36,966
Nevada	679,828	684,806	1,923	1,366,557	56,973

(continued on next page)

Table 4.02: Motor Vehicle Registrations by State, 2006

	Cars	Trucks	Buses	All Motor Vehicles	Motorcycles
United States	*135,399,945*	*107,943,782*	*821,959*	*244,165,686*	*6,678,958*
New Hampshire	585,455	472,635	1,873	1,059,963	70,778
New Jersey	3,692,966	2,241,195	23,827	5,957,988	163,636
New Mexico	699,312	877,956	3,552	1,580,820	43,495
New York	8,528,457	2,685,424	70,015	11,283,896	203,145
North Carolina	3,659,926	2,607,790	33,720	6,301,436	110,637
North Dakota	345,502	364,080	2,587	712,169	25,353
Ohio	6,438,988	4,345,371	44,484	10,828,843	332,355
Oklahoma	1,606,517	1,576,680	18,634	3,201,831	94,289
Oregon	1,427,597	1,538,960	14,822	2,981,379	84,224
Pennsylvania	5,842,819	4,013,315	38,029	9,894,163	330,947
Rhode Island	508,389	295,433	1,726	805,548	31,131
South Carolina	1,964,994	1,470,771	18,078	3,453,843	87,774
South Dakota	375,760	465,580	2,644	843,984	53,481
Tennessee	2,878,136	2,193,213	19,979	5,091,328	134,134
Texas	8,805,316	8,642,899	90,173	17,538,388	355,878
Utah	1,079,455	1,155,325	1,308	2,236,088	50,896
Vermont	309,972	275,951	1,745	587,668	24,543
Virginia	4,031,355	2,586,357	18,264	6,635,976	81,172
Washington	3,087,818	2,590,014	11,665	5,689,497	194,263
West Virginia	734,599	703,706	2,794	1,441,099	40,730
Wisconsin	2,639,984	2,317,130	14,347	4,971,461	271,151
Wyoming	228,057	414,047	3,088	645,192	35,791

Source: US Department of Transportation, Federal Highway Administration, *Highway Statistics 2006*, table MV-1.

Notes: Motorcycles are not included under total for motor vehicles.

Units: Number of motor vehicle registrations.

Table 4.03: Motor Vehicle Tax Receipts by State, 2006

	Registration Fees	Drivers License Fees	Certificate/ Title Fees	Total Receipts
United States	*$16,116,647*	*$1,226,274*	*$1,492,737*	*$29,935,173*
Alabama	141,868	18,443	23,916	232,540
Alaska	41,425	3,376	2,868	51,709
Arizona	67,250	11,081	8,762	337,443
Arkansas	105,796	10,692	3,733	145,614
California	4,521,252	234,078	0	4,986,751
Colorado	197,590	15,532	16,715	724,939
Connecticut	75,163	31,366	17,193	315,096
Delaware	21,717	1,797	4,136	107,754
District of Columbia	11,293	3,527	1,677	75,618
Florida	604,832	53,822	114,405	1,150,203
Georgia	308,865	37,473	52,160	430,152
Hawaii	159,062	3,887	0	175,178
Idaho	58,254	6,312	4,955	153,712
Illinois	1,121,125	18,211	196,256	1,601,033
Indiana	226,130	6,181	19,189	326,985
Iowa	372,260	7,297	9,144	423,533
Kansas	144,894	9,092	6,964	182,499
Kentucky	80,516	13,943	4,226	624,626
Louisiana	76,399	16,651	20,889	200,905
Maine	58,849	6,677	10,337	90,186
Maryland	328,280	30,852	23,218	1,242,019
Massachusetts	182,094	36,235	64,128	338,886
Michigan	853,233	38,433	31,135	1,029,692
Minnesota	515,767	20,381	10,873	581,804
Mississippi	65,277	9,922	5,443	154,657
Missouri	254,344	14,361	19,299	326,159
Montana	111,872	4,487	3,103	153,317
Nebraska	62,728	7,888	6,280	96,373
Nevada	103,991	9,690	14,869	223,018

(continued on next page)

Table 4.03: Motor Vehicle Tax Receipts by State, 2006

	Registration Fees	Drivers License Fees	Certificate/ Title Fees	Total Receipts
United States	*$16,116,647*	*$1,226,274*	*$1,492,737*	*$29,935,173*
New Hampshire	66,737	4,888	9,502	122,887
New Jersey	214,530	62,293	1,113	784,208
New Mexico	90,723	4,205	121,572	362,803
New York	416,350	56,483	133,686	1,089,065
North Carolina	335,478	30,255	66,357	630,496
North Dakota	68,738	677	1,196	84,397
Ohio	625,668	50,052	13,899	948,326
Oklahoma	207,345	16,671	15,805	337,719
Oregon	131,149	19,054	65,358	506,250
Pennsylvania	636,261	54,558	80,302	959,148
Rhode Island	42,466	12,555	4,561	64,913
South Carolina	80,145	17,349	21,851	227,256
South Dakota	65,199	1,766	1,526	73,088
Tennessee	244,424	15,119	11,005	391,879
Texas	1,066,517	96,098	181,611	4,412,352
Utah	55,586	7,055	4,792	120,459
Vermont	38,745	4,612	2,993	123,058
Virginia	67,144	28,756	23,874	869,471
Washington	300,533	32,908	5,462	509,054
West Virginia	59,795	3,000	4,916	272,045
Wisconsin	388,238	22,335	25,413	506,913
Wyoming	42,750	3,898	70	56,985

Source: US Department of Transportation, Federal Highway Administration, *Highway Statistics 2006*, table MV-2.

Notes: Subgroups do not add to total due to groups omitted.

Units: Fees and tax receipts in thousands of dollars.

Table 4.04: Sales, Market Share, and Fuel Economy for Cars and Trucks, 1975, 1990, and 2007

	Sales	Market Share	Fuel Economy
1975			
Cars			
Small	4,088	49.6%	18.3
Midsize	1,631	19.8	13.6
Large	1,555	18.9	13.1
SUVs			
Small	53	2.7%	16.1
Midsize	123	6.2	12.1
Large	11	0.6	12.2
Pickup Trucks			
Small	160	8.1%	22.5
Midsize	56	2.8	21.1
Large	1,126	56.7	13.1
Vans			
Small	2	0.1%	20.6
Midsize	302	15.2	13.3
Large	153	7.7	12.6
Total	*10,224*	*100%*	*NA*
1990			
Cars			
Small	4,999	56.7%	29.8
Midsize	2,342	26.6	26.2
Large	1,092	12.4	23.7
SUVs			
Small	189	5.0%	23.4
Midsize	447	11.7	19.1
Large	72	1.9	16.7
Pickup Trucks			
Small	289	7.6%	24.8
Midsize	600	15.8	24.7
Large	945	24.8	18.0
Vans			
Small	30	0.8%	23.9
Midsize	1,124	29.5	21.8
Large	107	2.8	16.5
Total	*12,615*	*100%*	*NA*

(continued on next page)

Table 4.04: Sales, Market Share, and Fuel Economy for Cars and Trucks, 1975, 1990, and 2007

	Sales	Market Share	Fuel Economy
2007			
Cars			
Small	2,562	33.8%	30.3
Midsize	2,748	36.3	30.8
Large	1,390	18.3	25.3
SUVs			
Small	175	2.4%	22.6
Midsize	2,199	30.2	24.6
Large	1,926	26.4	20.8
Pickup Trucks			
Small	0	0.0%	NA
Midsize	281	3.9	23.7
Large	1,753	24.0	19.7
Vans			
Small	0	0.0%	NA
Midsize	927	12.7	24.7
Large	29	0.4	19.7
Total	*14,870*	*100%*	*NA*

Source: Oak Ridge National Laboratory, *Transportation Energy Data Book, 27th ed*, tables 4.7 and 4.8.

Notes: Market share for cars is out of the total for cars and wagons (not shown); for SUVs, pickup trucks, and vans, it is out of the total for SUVs, pickup trucks, and vans.

Units: Sales in thousands; percent of category total; fuel economy in miles per gallon.

Table 4.05:   Sales of New Cars and Light Trucks, 1970–2006

	Cars			Light Trucks
	Domestic	Import	Total	Total
1970	7,119	1,280	8,399	1,463
1975	7,053	1,571	8,624	2,281
1980	6,580	2,369	8,949	2,440
1981	6,181	2,308	8,489	2,189
1982	5,757	2,200	7,956	2,470
1983	6,795	2,353	9,148	2,984
1984	7,952	2,372	10,324	3,863
1985	8,205	2,775	10,979	4,458
1986	8,215	3,189	11,404	4,594
1987	7,085	3,107	10,192	4,610
1988	7,543	3,004	10,547	4,800
1989	7,098	2,680	9,779	4,610
1990	6,919	2,384	9,303	4,548
1991	6,162	2,028	8,189	4,123
1992	6,286	1,927	8,213	4,629
1993	6,742	1,776	8,518	5,351
1994	7,255	1,735	8,991	6,033
1995	7,129	1,506	8,635	6,053
1996	7,255	1,271	8,526	6,519
1997	6,917	1,355	8,272	6,797
1998	6,762	1,380	8,142	7,299
1999	6,979	1,719	8,698	8,073
2000	6,831	2,016	8,847	8,387
2001	6,325	2,098	8,423	8,700
2002	5,878	2,226	8,103	8,713
2003	5,527	2,083	7,610	8,938
2004	5,357	2,149	7,506	9,361
2005	5,481	2,187	7,667	9,281
2006	5,436	2,345	7,781	8,724

Source: Oak Ridge National Laboratory, *Transportation Energy Data Book, 27th ed*, tables 4.5 and 4.6.

Notes: 'Light Trucks' refers to vehicles weighing less than 10,000 lbs Gross Vehicle Weight Rating (GVWR), and includes SUVs, pickup trucks, and minivans.

Units: Number of cars and light trucks sold in thousands.

Table 4.06: US Motor Vehicle Production and Factory Sales, 1960–2005

Year	Production			Factory Sales		
	Passenger Cars	**Commercial Vehicles**	**Total**	**Passenger Cars**	**Commercial Vehicles**	**Total**
1960	6,703	1,202	7,905	6,675	1,194	7,869
1965	9,335	1,785	11,120	9,306	1,752	11,057
1970	6,550	1,734	8,284	6,547	1,692	8,239
1975	6,717	2,270	8,987	6,713	2,272	8,985
1980	6,376	1,634	8,010	6,400	1,667	8,067
1985	8,186	3,452	11,638	8,002	3,464	11,467
1990	6,078	3,690	9,767	6,050	3,725	9,775
1991	5,440	3,350	8,790	5,407	3,388	8,795
1992	5,667	4,025	9,691	5,685	4,062	9,747
1993	5,982	4,873	10,855	5,962	4,895	10,857
1994	6,601	5,638	12,239	6,549	5,640	12,189
1995	6,340	5,655	11,995	6,310	5,713	12,023
1996	6,083	5,747	11,830	6,140	5,776	11,916
1997	5,934	6,197	12,131	6,070	6,153	12,223
1998	5,554	6,448	12,003	5,677	6,435	12,112
1999	5,638	7,387	13,025	5,428	6,699	12,127
2000	5,542	7,231	12,774	5,504	7,022	12,527
2001	4,879	6,546	11,425	4,884	6,224	11,108
2002	5,019	7,261	12,280	NA	6,964	NA
2003	4,510	7,577	12,087	NA	7,143	NA
2004	4,230	7,731	11,960	NA	7,467	NA
2005	4,321	7,625	11,947	NA	7,767	NA

Source: Bureau of Transportation Statistics, *National Transportation Statistics 2007*, table 1-15.

Notes: 'Factory sales' refers to wholesale sales, and can be greater than the production total due to sales from the previous year's inventory.
Numbers may not add to totals due to rounding.

Units: Production and sales in thousands.

Table 4.07:   World Motor Vehicle Production, 1961–2005

Country	1961	1981	2000	2005
Argentina	136	172	340	320
Australia	231	392	348	389
Austria	13	15	141	253
Belgium	1	257	1,033	927
Brazil	145	780	1,671	2,528
Canada	391	1,323	2,962	2,688
China	NA	NA	2,009	5,708
Czech Republic	76	230	455	605
France	1,205	3,020	3,352	3,499
Germany	2,213	4,116	5,198	5,758
India	54	149	796	1,642
Italy	759	1,433	1,738	1,038
Japan	1,039	11,180	10,145	10,800
South Korea	NA	134	3,115	3,699
Malaysia	NA	NA	295	NA
Mexico	NA	597	1,923	1,684
Netherlands	19	90	267	181
Poland	36	308	556	612
Portugal	NA	NA	247	219
Romania	NA	NA	72	NA
Russia	555	2,198	1,203	1,353
Spain	75	987	3,033	2,753
Sweden	132	313	296	324
Taiwan	NA	NA	365	446
Turkey	NA	47	431	879
United Kingdom	1,447	1,185	1,817	1,803
United States	6,653	7,943	12,771	11,977
Yugoslavia	20	267	NA	NA
World total	*15,200*	*37,136*	*57,528*	*65,750*
US percent of world total	*44%*	*21%*	*22%*	*18%*

Source: Bureau of Transportation Statistics, *National Transportation Statistics 2007*, table 1-22.

Notes: Data includes passenger cars and commercial vehicles.
Prior to 2000, the country of manufacture was considered the producing country. Since then, the country of final assembly is considered the producing country.
Figures may not add to totals due to rounding.

Units: Production in thousands of vehicles.

Table 4.08: Vehicle Miles Traveled (VMT) and VMT per Lane-Mile, by Type of Road, 1980–2006

| | Urban Roads | | | Rural Roads | | |
	Interstate	Other Arterial	Total	Interstate	Other Arterial	Total
Vehicle Miles Traveled						
1980	161,242	484,189	855,265	135,084	262,774	672,030
1985	216,188	578,270	1,044,098	154,357	282,803	730,728
1990	278,901	699,233	1,275,484	200,173	330,866	868,878
1995	341,528	815,170	1,489,534	223,382	368,595	933,289
2000	393,465	900,392	1,663,773	268,180	420,599	1,083,152
2001	399,890	913,726	1,676,379	274,024	426,945	1,105,083
2002	408,618	937,357	1,727,596	279,962	433,805	1,128,160
2003	432,633	973,936	1,805,508	269,945	416,596	1,085,385
2004	454,385	1,020,089	1,892,265	266,996	409,944	1,070,248
2005	469,070	1,048,219	1,951,870	258,790	398,932	1,037,937
2006	477,283	1,060,098	1,977,047	257,913	394,499	1,037,069
VMT per Lane-Mile						
1980	3,327	1,451	613	1,031	518	103
1985	3,773	1,556	677	1,170	555	113
1990	4,483	1,751	764	1,473	640	136
1995	4,784	1,829	810	1,693	695	148
2000	5,323	1,974	869	1,993	778	172
2001	5,370	1,997	852	2,035	787	176
2002	5,440	2,025	861	2,080	797	179
2003	5,436	2,012	856	2,070	780	175
2004	5,479	2,019	860	2,088	771	174
2005	5,455	2,001	862	2,061	753	170
2006	5,427	1,989	856	2,074	744	170

Source: Bureau of Transportation Statistics, *National Transportation Statistics 2008*, table 1-33.

Notes: For urban roads, 'other arterials' refers to other freeways and expressways, and other principal and minor arterials; for rural roads, 'other arterials' refers to principal and minor arterials.
Subgroups may not add to total due to groups omitted.

Units: Vehicle Miles Traveled (VMT) in millions; VMT per Lane-Mile in thousands.

Table 4.09: Vehicle Miles Traveled (VMT) by State, 2006

	Urban	Rural	Total
United States	*1,995,352*	*1,038,401*	*3,033,753*
Alabama	30,922	29,492	60,414
Alaska	2,540	2,427	4,967
Arizona	42,570	19,898	62,468
Arkansas	12,729	20,278	33,007
California	266,768	60,710	327,478
Colorado	33,211	15,430	48,641
Connecticut	27,843	3,900	31,743
Delaware	6,683	2,759	9,442
District of Columbia	3,623	0	3,623
Florida	166,059	37,682	203,741
Georgia	71,860	41,672	113,532
Hawaii	7,719	2,463	10,182
Idaho	6,074	9,124	15,198
Illinois	78,609	28,260	106,869
Indiana	34,579	36,636	71,215
Iowa	12,440	18,915	31,355
Kansas	15,980	14,235	30,215
Kentucky	20,375	27,367	47,742
Louisiana	25,739	19,678	45,417
Maine	4,228	10,816	15,044
Maryland	41,828	14,474	56,302
Massachusetts	50,907	4,229	55,136
Michigan	71,445	32,739	104,184
Minnesota	29,294	27,224	56,518
Mississippi	16,085	25,413	41,498
Missouri	37,828	31,006	68,834
Montana	2,628	8,637	11,265
Nebraska	8,266	11,149	19,415
Nevada	16,500	5,324	21,824

(continued on next page)

Table 4.09:   Vehicle Miles Traveled (VMT) by State, 2006

	Urban	Rural	Total
United States	*1,995,352*	*1,038,401*	*3,033,753*
New Hampshire	7,590	6,024	13,614
New Jersey	68,113	7,258	75,371
New Mexico	11,286	14,501	25,787
New York	107,516	33,832	141,348
North Carolina	63,482	38,033	101,515
North Dakota	2,310	5,580	7,890
Ohio	74,498	36,749	111,247
Oklahoma	25,549	23,140	48,689
Oregon	19,493	15,990	35,483
Pennsylvania	69,191	39,087	108,278
Rhode Island	7,421	879	8,300
South Carolina	25,343	24,856	50,199
South Dakota	2,440	6,728	9,168
Tennessee	41,693	28,903	70,596
Texas	153,855	84,401	238,256
Utah	17,928	8,036	25,964
Vermont	1,910	5,922	7,832
Virginia	49,564	31,531	81,095
Washington	39,986	16,531	56,517
West Virginia	8,569	12,316	20,885
Wisconsin	31,269	28,129	59,398
Wyoming	2,709	6,706	9,415

Source: US Department of Transportation, Federal Highway Administration, *Highway Statistics 2006*, table VM-2.

Notes: US total includes roads in Puerto Rico.
Subgroups may not add to total.

Units: Vehicle Miles Traveled (VMT) in millions.

Table 4.10:   Urban Traffic Congestion Measures, 1982–2005

	Delay per Traveler	Total Delay	Travel Time Index	Fuel Wasted	Cost of Congestion
1982	14	0.8	1.09	0.5	$16.2
1983	15	0.9	1.09	0.5	16.2
1984	16	1.0	1.10	0.6	17.7
1985	18	1.1	1.11	0.7	20.5
1986	21	1.3	1.13	0.8	23.1
1987	22	1.4	1.14	0.9	25.8
1988	25	1.7	1.16	1.1	29.7
1989	27	1.8	1.17	1.2	32.9
1990	27	1.9	1.18	1.3	35.5
1991	28	2.0	1.18	1.3	35.8
1992	29	2.1	1.18	1.4	38.0
1993	30	2.2	1.18	1.5	40.1
1994	30	2.3	1.18	1.5	41.9
1995	31	2.5	1.19	1.7	45.4
1996	33	2.7	1.20	1.8	48.5
1997	34	2.8	1.21	1.9	51.3
1998	34	3.0	1.22	2.0	53.2
1999	35	3.2	1.23	2.1	57.2
2000	34	3.2	1.22	2.2	57.6
2001	35	3.3	1.23	2.3	60.4
2002	35	3.5	1.24	2.4	63.9
2003	36	3.7	1.24	2.5	67.2
2004	37	4.0	1.25	2.7	73.1
2005	38	4.2	1.26	2.9	78.2

Source: Texas Transportation Institute, *The 2007 Urban Mobility Report*, exhibit 3.

Notes: 'Travel Time Index' is the ratio of travel time during the peak period to travel time during free-flow conditions.

Delays refer to the extra time spent traveling at peak congestion periods as opposed to free-flow periods.

'Congestion cost' is the estimated value of fuel consumption (using the state average gas price) and time lost (estimated at $14.60 per hour of person-travel and $77.10 per hour of truck time).

Units: Delay per traveler in hours per year; total delay in bilions of hours; fuel wasted in billions of gallons; total cost in billions of 2005 constant dollars.

Table 4.11: Traffic Congestion in Metropolitan Areas by Population Size, 2005

	Annual Delay per Traveler	Travel Time Index	Wasted Fuel per Traveler	Congestion Cost
Population:				
Over 3 million	54	1.38	38	$3,205
1 million–3 million	37	1.24	25	628
500,000–1 million	28	1.16	18	206
Under 500,000	17	1.09	10	56
All 437 Metropolitan Areas	38	1.26	26	179
Cities over 3 million:				
Los Angeles, CA	72	1.50	57	$9,325
San Francisco, CA	60	1.41	47	7,383
Washington, DC	60	1.37	43	3,968
Atlanta, GA	60	1.34	44	2,747
Dallas, TX	58	1.35	40	2,730
Houston, TX	56	1.36	42	2,581
Detroit, MI	54	1.29	35	2,414
Miami, FL	50	1.38	35	2,331
Phoenix, AZ	48	1.31	34	2,225
Chicago, IL	46	1.47	32	2,174
New York, NY	46	1.39	29	2,076
Boston, MA	46	1.27	31	1,820
Seattle, WA	45	1.30	34	1,687
Philadelphia, PA	38	1.28	24	1,413

Source: Texas Transportation Institute, *The 2007 Urban Mobility Report*, tables 1 and 2.

Notes: 'Travel Time Index' is the ratio of travel time during the peak period to travel time during free-flow conditions.
Delays refer to the extra time spent traveling at peak congestion periods as opposed to free-flow periods.
'Congestion cost' is the estimated value of fuel consumption (using the state average gas price) and time lost (estimated at $14.60 per hour of person-travel and $77.10 per hour of truck time).
Congestion costs for population category ranges are averages for all urgan areas in that range.

Units: Delay per traveler in hours per year; fuel wasted in gallons per traveler per year; total cost in billions of 2005 constant dollars.

Table 4.12:   Bicycle Sales, 1981–2006

	Wheels Under 18 Inches	Wheels 20 Inches and Over	All Wheel Sizes
1981	NA	8.9	NA
1982	NA	6.8	NA
1983	NA	9.0	NA
1984	NA	10.1	NA
1985	NA	11.4	NA
1986	NA	12.3	NA
1987	NA	12.6	NA
1988	NA	9.9	NA
1989	NA	10.7	NA
1990	NA	10.8	NA
1991	NA	11.6	NA
1992	3.7	11.6	15.3
1993	3.8	13.0	16.8
1994	4.2	12.5	16.7
1995	4.1	12.0	16.1
1996	4.5	10.9	15.4
1997	4.2	11.0	15.2
1998	4.7	11.1	15.8
1999	5.9	11.6	17.5
2000	9.0	11.9	20.9
2001	5.4	11.3	16.7
2002	5.9	13.6	19.5
2003	5.6	12.9	18.5
2004	5.3	13.0	18.3
2005	5.8	14.0	19.8
2006	5.5	12.7	18.2

Source: Oak Ridge National Laboratory, *Transportation Energy Data Book*, 27th *ed*, table 8.19.

Notes: Sales data for bicycles with wheel sizes under 20 inches is not available prior to 1992.

Units: Sales in millions.

Table 4.13: Means of Commuting to Work, 1985–2007

	1985	1989	1993	1997	2001	2005	2006	2007
Total Workers	*99,592*	*106,630*	*103,741*	*116,469*	*120,191*	*123,250*	*138,266*	*139,260*
Automobile	86.5%	88.1%	88.0%	87.5%	87.8%	88.4%	86.7%	86.5%
Drives self	72.4	76.3	76.6	77.5	78.2	79.3	76.0	76.1
Carpool	14.1	11.8	11.4	10.0	9.7	9.1	10.7	10.4
2-person	10.4	9.1	8.8	8.0	7.5	7.0	8.3	8.0
3-person	2.0	1.6	1.6	1.3	1.4	1.2	1.4	1.4
4 or more people	1.6	1.1	1.0	0.8	0.8	0.9	1.0	1.0
Mass transit	5.1	4.6	4.6	4.6	4.7	4.4	4.3	4.9
Taxicab	0.1	0.1	0.1	0.1	0.1	0.1	0.1	NA
Bicycle or motorcycle	1.0	0.7	0.7	0.6	0.7	0.6	0.6	1.7
Walked	4.0	3.4	3.1	3.3	2.8	2.3	2.9	2.8
Other	0.3	0.5	0.5	0.7	0.9	0.8	1.4	NA
Work at home	3.0	2.6	3.0	3.1	2.8	3.4	3.9	4.1

Source: Bureau of Transportation Statistics, *National Transportation Statistics 2008*, table 1-38. US Bureau of the Census, *American Community Survey 2007*, 'Commuting Characteristics by Sex,' table S0801.

Notes: Percents may not add to 100.
For 2007 data, 'bicycle' also includes motorcycle and taxicab.

Units: Total workers in thousands; percent of total workers.

Table 4.14:   Commuting Characteristics by Sex, 2007

	Total	Male	Female
Total Workers 16 years and older	*139,259,684*	*75,095,310*	*64,164,374*
Means of Commute:			
Car, truck, or van	86.5%	86.5%	86.5%
Drove alone	76.1	75.6	76.7
Carpooled	10.4	10.9	9.8
2-person carpool	8.0	8.1	7.8
3-person carpool	1.4	1.5	1.3
4-or-more person carpool	1.0	1.2	0.7
Workers per car, truck, or van	*1.24*	*1.24*	*1.23*
Public transit	4.9	4.5	5.3
Walked	2.8	2.9	2.8
Bicycle	0.5	0.7	0.2
Taxicab, motorcycle, or other	1.2	1.6	0.9
Worked at home	4.1	3.9	4.3
Place of Work			
Worked in place of residence	31.0%	29.0%	33.4%
Worked outside place of residence	42.0	43.6	40.1
Worked outside county of residence	23.8	25.9	21.3
Worked outside state of residence	3.8	4.5	3.0

(continued on next page)

Table 4.14: Commuting Characteristics by Sex, 2007

	Total	Male	Female
Workers who did not work from home	*133,583,062*	*72,157,702*	*61,425,360*
Commuting Time:			
Less than 10 minutes	14.2%	13.0%	15.6%
10 to 14 minutes	14.4	13.4	15.6
15 to 19 minutes	15.5	14.7	16.4
20 to 24 minutes	14.5	14.3	14.8
25 to 29 minutes	6.0	5.9	6.0
30 to 34 minutes	13.4	14.1	12.5
35 to 44 minutes	6.3	6.7	5.8
45 to 59 minutes	7.5	8.2	6.8
60 or more minutes	8.2	9.7	6.5
Mean travel time to work (minutes)	*25.3*	*27.0*	*23.4*
Time Leaving for Work			
12:00 a.m. to 4:59 a.m.	4.0%	5.4%	2.5%
5:00 a.m. to 5:29 a.m.	3.7	5.0	2.1
5:30 a.m. to 5:59 a.m.	5.0	6.3	3.4
6:00 a.m. to 6:29 a.m.	9.0	11.0	6.7
6:30 a.m. to 6:59 a.m.	10.4	11.3	9.4
7:00 a.m. to 7:29 a.m.	14.8	14.4	15.3
7:30 a.m. to 7:59 a.m.	13.1	11.0	15.6
8:00 a.m. to 8:29 a.m.	10.9	9.5	12.4
8:30 a.m. to 8:59 a.m.	5.4	4.3	6.8
9:00 a.m. to 11:59 p.m.	23.6	21.7	25.8

Source: US Bureau of the Census, *American Community Survey 2007*, 'Commuting Characteristics by Sex,' table S0801.

Notes: 'Workers' includes members of the armed forces and workers who were at work in the past week.
Means of commute and place of work percentages are calculated out of total workers. Duration of commute and time leaving for work are calculated out of workers who did not work from home.

Units: Total number workers and workers who did not work from home; average persons per vehicle; percent of total; mean commute time in minutes.

Table 4.15: Cost of Owning and Driving an Automobile, 1975–2007

| | Cost per Mile (¢) | | | | Cost per 15,000 Miles ($) | | |
	Gas	Mainte-nance	Tires	Total Cost	Variable Costs	Fixed Costs	Total Cost
1975	4.8¢	1.0¢	0.7¢	14.4¢	$968	$1,186	$2,154
1980	5.9	1.1	0.6	21.2	1,143	2,033	3,176
1985	5.6	1.2	0.7	23.2	1,113	2,371	3,484
1990	5.4	2.1	0.9	33.0	1,260	3,694	4,954
1991	6.6	2.2	0.9	37.3	1,455	4,146	5,601
1992	5.9	2.2	0.9	38.8	1,350	4,474	5,824
1993	5.9	2.4	0.9	38.7	1,380	4,424	5,804
1994	5.6	2.5	1.0	39.4	1,365	4,551	5,916
1995	5.8	2.6	1.2	41.2	1,440	4,745	6,185
1996	5.6	2.8	1.2	42.6	1,440	4,949	6,389
1997	6.6	2.8	1.4	44.8	1,620	5,103	6,723
1998	6.2	3.1	1.4	46.1	1,605	5,303	6,908
1999	5.6	3.3	1.7	47.0	1,590	5,460	7,050
2000	6.9	3.6	1.7	49.1	1,829	5,534	7,363
2001	7.9	3.9	1.8	51.0	2,040	5,614	7,654
2002	5.9	4.1	1.8	50.2	1,770	5,764	7,533
2003	7.2	4.1	1.8	51.7	1,965	5,789	7,754
2004	6.5	5.4	0.7	56.2	1,890	6,541	8,431
2005	9.5	4.9	0.7	52.2	2,265	5,569	7,834
2006	8.9	4.9	0.7	52.2	2,175	5,648	7,823
2007	11.7	4.6	0.7	54.1	2,545	5,576	8,121

Source: Bureau of Transportation Statistics, *National Transportation Statistics 2008*, table 3-14.

Notes: Assumes an average of driving 15,000 miles per year in stop-and-go conditions.
Prior to 2004, oil costs are included under 'gas'; afterwards, they are included under 'maintenance.'
Fixed costs include insurance, license, registration, taxes, depreciation, and finance charges.

Units: Average cost per mile in current cents; average total cost per 15,000 miles in current dollars.

Table 4.16: Cost of Owning and Driving an Automobile by Type of Car, 2006

	Small Sedan	Medium Sedan	Large Sedan	SUV	Minivan
Operating Costs (cents per mile)					
Total Costs	13.0¢	15.5¢	16.8¢	20.1¢	17.0¢
Gasoline & Oil	8.0	9.8	10.7	13.7	11.4
Maintenance	4.5	4.9	5.4	5.6	5.0
Tires	0.5	0.8	0.7	0.8	0.6
Ownership Costs (dollars per year)					
Total Costs	$4,303	$5,642	$6,763	$6,790	$6,328
Insurance	892	902	982	918	843
License, registration, taxes	397	551	658	683	612
Depreciation (15,000 miles annually)	2,503	3,449	4,224	4,254	4,043
Finance charge (10% down; loan @ 6%/5 yrs.)	511	739	899	935	830
Depreciation Adjustments					
Mileage under 15,000 miles annually	-$550	-$950	-$1,150	-$900	-$900
Mileage over 15,000 miles annually	625	1025	1,175	975	975
Total Annual Cost					
10,000 miles per year	$5,053	$6,242	$7,293	$7,900	$7,128
15,000 miles per year	6,253	7,967	9,283	9,805	8,878
20,000 miles per year	7,528	9,767	11,298	11,785	10,703

Source: American Public Transportation Association, *Public Transportation Fact Book, 58th ed*, table 54.

Notes: Data shown is for a popular model of each vehicle type, and assumes ownership of 5 or more years before replacement.
Finance costs assume a 10% down payment, and a 5-year loan at 6% annual interest.

Units: Operating costs in cents per mile; ownership costs, depreciation adjustments, and total annual cost in dollars.

Table 4.17: Fuel Economy Standards for Cars and Light Trucks, 1978–2007

	CAFE Standards		CAFE Estimates		
	Cars	Light trucks	Cars	Light trucks	Combined
1980	20.0	NA	24.3	18.5	23.1
1981	22.0	NA	25.9	20.1	24.6
1982	24.0	17.5	26.6	20.5	25.1
1983	26.0	19.0	26.4	20.7	24.8
1984	27.0	20.0	26.9	20.6	25.0
1985	27.5	19.5	27.6	20.7	25.4
1986	26.0	20.0	28.2	21.5	25.9
1987	26.0	20.5	28.5	21.7	26.2
1988	26.0	20.5	28.8	21.3	26.0
1989	26.5	20.5	28.4	21.0	25.6
1990	27.5	20.0	28.0	20.8	25.4
1991	27.5	20.2	28.4	21.3	25.6
1992	27.5	20.2	27.9	20.8	25.1
1993	27.5	20.4	28.4	21.0	25.2
1994	27.5	20.5	28.3	20.8	24.7
1995	27.5	20.6	28.6	20.5	24.9
1996	27.5	20.7	28.5	20.8	24.9
1997	27.5	20.7	28.7	20.6	24.6
1998	27.5	20.7	28.8	21.0	24.7
1999	27.5	20.7	28.3	20.9	24.5
2000	27.5	20.7	28.5	21.3	24.8
2001	27.5	20.7	28.8	20.9	24.5
2002	27.5	20.7	29.0	21.4	24.7
2003	27.5	20.7	29.5	21.8	25.1
2004	27.5	20.7	29.5	21.5	24.6
2005	27.5	21.0	30.3	22.1	25.4
2006	27.5	21.6	29.8	22.2	25.4
2007	27.5	22.2	31.0	22.9	26.4

Source: Oak Ridge National Laboratory, *Transportation Energy Data Book, 27th ed*, tables 4.17 and 4.18.

Notes: Corporate Average Fuel Economy (CAFE) standards are set by the National Highway Traffic Safety Administration (NHTSA).
Mileage performance estimates are measured by the Environmental Protection Agency (EPA). All mileage calculations are sales-weighted.
'Light trucks' include pickup trucks, SUVs, vans, and minivans.

Units: CAFE standards and estimates in miles per gallon.

Table 4.18: Automobile Fuel Consumption, 1960–2006

	Total Vehicles	Total VMT	Fuel Consumed	Average VMT	Miles per Gallon	Fuel Consumed per Vehicle
1960	61,671	587,000	41,171	9.5	14.3	668
1965	75,258	723,000	49,723	9.6	14.5	661
1970	89,244	917,000	67,819	10.3	13.5	760
1975	106,706	1,034,000	74,140	9.7	13.9	695
1980	121,601	1,112,000	69,982	9.1	15.9	576
1985	127,885	1,247,000	71,518	9.8	17.4	559
1990	133,700	1,408,000	69,568	10.5	20.2	520
1991	128,300	1,358,000	64,317	10.6	21.1	501
1992	126,581	1,372,000	65,436	10.8	21.0	517
1993	127,327	1,375,000	67,048	10.8	20.5	527
1994	127,883	1,406,000	67,874	11.0	20.7	531
1995	128,387	1,438,000	68,072	11.2	21.1	530
1996	129,728	1,469,854	69,221	11.3	21.2	534
1997	129,749	1,502,556	69,892	11.6	21.5	539
1998	131,839	1,549,577	71,695	11.8	21.6	544
1999	132,432	1,569,100	73,283	11.8	21.4	553
2000	133,621	1,600,287	73,065	12.0	21.9	547
2001	137,633	1,628,332	73,559	12.0	22.1	534
2002	135,921	1,658,474	75,471	12.2	22.0	555
2003	135,670	1,672,079	75,455	12.3	22.2	556
2004	136,431	1,699,890	75,402	12.5	23.0	553
2005	136,568	1,708,421	77,418	12.5	22.1	567
2006	135,400	1,682,671	74,983	12.4	22.4	554

Source: Bureau of Transportation Statistics, *National Transportation Statistics 2008*, table 4-11.

Notes: Average VMT, miles per gallon, and fuel consumed per vehicle derived by calculation.

Units: Total vehicles and average VMT in thousands; VMT in millions; miles per gallon; fuel consumed in millions of gallons; fuel consumed per vehicle in gallons.

Table 4.19:   Automobile Fuel Consumption by State, 2006

	Gasoline and Gasohol	Special Fuel	Total Fuel Consumed
United States	*140,320,089*	*40,094,177*	*179,876,883*
Alabama	2,627,049	824,496	3,450,983
Alaska	293,351	237,222	530,573
Arizona	2,870,781	886,254	3,757,035
Arkansas	1,447,192	651,418	2,084,115
California	15,844,687	3,045,851	18,890,538
Colorado	2,164,191	582,166	2,724,715
Connecticut	1,566,875	302,684	1,866,303
Delaware	458,885	70,459	524,764
District of Columbia	131,963	19,641	151,599
Florida	8,692,569	1,794,987	10,487,556
Georgia	4,982,331	1,567,130	6,549,461
Hawaii	483,136	53,710	532,020
Idaho	658,019	264,048	915,487
Illinois	5,189,824	1,535,719	6,717,253
Indiana	3,221,758	1,358,806	4,548,327
Iowa	1,673,188	605,515	2,277,472
Kansas	1,329,522	434,744	1,750,959
Kentucky	2,228,724	888,901	3,117,617
Louisiana	2,621,024	784,876	3,409,534
Maine	704,463	188,426	892,887
Maryland	2,770,954	562,925	3,280,026
Massachusetts	2,826,663	396,090	3,222,753
Michigan	4,879,874	932,524	5,812,398
Minnesota	2,691,672	675,627	3,340,382
Mississippi	1,678,003	643,310	2,304,533
Missouri	3,221,159	1,077,474	4,266,782
Montana	498,343	259,569	757,912
Nebraska	836,683	412,295	1,248,978
Nevada	1,173,077	399,257	1,572,334

(continued on next page)

Table 4.19: Automobile Fuel Consumption by State, 2006

	Gasoline and Gasohol	Special Fuel	Total Fuel Consumed
United States	*140,320,089*	*40,094,177*	*179,876,883*
New Hampshire	717,750	102,060	819,810
New Jersey	4,281,216	968,042	5,249,258
New Mexico	966,209	520,578	1,486,787
New York	5,784,552	1,374,167	7,156,639
North Carolina	4,443,067	1,123,274	5,523,563
North Dakota	352,308	170,425	521,797
Ohio	5,204,068	1,602,008	6,754,016
Oklahoma	1,868,948	780,905	2,597,793
Oregon	1,577,746	546,936	2,124,682
Pennsylvania	5,102,928	1,603,146	6,680,636
Rhode Island	418,396	57,676	465,664
South Carolina	2,556,418	707,354	3,263,772
South Dakota	428,785	191,906	616,403
Tennessee	3,128,807	1,040,979	4,138,498
Texas	11,841,488	4,053,917	15,864,117
Utah	1,061,532	503,317	1,554,147
Vermont	348,236	66,400	414,308
Virginia	4,011,244	1,104,316	5,115,560
Washington	2,730,776	704,820	3,427,529
West Virginia	841,146	295,008	1,136,154
Wisconsin	2,527,993	760,507	3,263,220
Wyoming	360,516	360,312	717,234

Source: US Department of Transportation, Federal Highway Administration, *Highway Statistics 2006*, table MF-21.

Notes: 'Special fuel' refers primarily to diesel fuel mixed with small amounts of liquefied petroleum gas.
Subgroups may not add to total shown.

Units: Motor fuel use in thousands of gallons.

Table 4.20: Gasoline Prices, 1976–2007

	Leaded Regular	Unleaded Regular	Unleaded Premium	All Grades
1976	$1.47	$1.53	NA	NA
1977	1.46	1.53	NA	NA
1978	1.37	1.46	NA	$1.43
1979	1.73	1.82	NA	1.78
1980	2.20	2.30	NA	2.26
1981	2.22	2.33	$2.49	2.29
1982	1.95	2.07	2.26	2.04
1983	1.77	1.90	2.12	1.88
1984	1.67	1.79	2.02	1.77
1985	1.60	1.72	1.92	1.72
1986	1.20	1.30	1.52	1.31
1987	1.23	1.30	1.49	1.31
1988	1.19	1.25	1.46	1.27
1989	1.27	1.30	1.52	1.35
1990	1.41	1.43	1.65	1.49
1991	NA	1.35	1.56	1.42
1992	NA	1.31	1.52	1.38
1993	NA	1.25	1.47	1.33
1994	NA	1.23	1.45	1.30
1995	NA	1.25	1.45	1.31
1996	NA	1.31	1.51	1.37
1997	NA	1.29	1.48	1.35
1998	NA	1.10	1.30	1.16
1999	NA	1.19	1.39	1.25
2000	NA	1.51	1.69	1.56
2001	NA	1.43	1.62	1.50
2002	NA	1.30	1.49	1.38
2003	NA	1.50	1.67	1.54
2004	NA	1.72	1.89	1.76
2005	NA	2.03	2.20	2.07
2006	NA	2.22	2.41	2.26
2007	NA	2.34	2.54	2.38

Source: US Department of Energy, Energy Information Administration, *Annual Energy Review 2007*, table 5.24.

Notes: All prices are in chained 2000 dollars.

Units: Retail price in dollars per gallon.

Table 4.21:   Public Opinion on Gasoline Prices, 2000–2005

1. Question: As a result of the recent rise in gas prices, would you say you have – or have not – done each of the following? (asked June 2004)

	Yes	No	No Opinion
Made more of an effort to find the gas station with the cheapest gas in your area	69%	30%	1%
Seriously considered getting a more fuel-efficient car the next time you buy a vehicle	53	46	1
Cut back significantly on how much you drive	45	54	1
Cut back significantly on your household spending because of the higher gas prices	34	66	0
Altered your summer vacation plans	29	70	1

2. Question: Have recent price increases in gasoline caused any financial hardship for you or your household?

	Yes	No	No Opinion
August 28–30, 2005	69%	31%	0%
April 1–2, 2005	42	58	0
May 21–23, 2004	47	52	1
February 17–19, 2003	35	65	0
May 7–9, 2001	47	53	0
May 23–24, 2000	36	64	0

3. Question: Just your opinion, why would you say the price of gasoline has been increasing so much in recent months? (open-ended, asked May 2004)

Price Factor	Percent
Big Business/oil companies/price gouging/higher profit	22%
War in Iraq	19
OPEC/Saudi Arabia maintaining supply	9
Supply and demand	8
Government/politics	7
President Bush	5
Lack of US refining capability/lack of supply/drilling	4
Gas shortage/lack of production	4
Unrest in the Middle East	4
Economy/inflation	2
Summer vacation time/prices always go up around this time	2
Foreign policy	1
Other	6
No opinion	15

Source: National Renewable Energy Laboratory, *Consumer Views on Transportation and Energy, 3rd ed*, tables 2.2.1, 2.2.2, and 2.2.6.

Notes: Surveys done by Gallup, based on a sample of 400–500 adults.

Units: Percent of survey respondents giving the stated response to each question.

Chapter 5

Public Transportation

Chapter 5 Highlights

Chapter 5 contains data on public transportation, an important intersection of transportation and energy. Public transit riders and trips have increased in the last 10 years, but at a much slower rate than the increase in vehicle-miles traveled on highways (table 5.03, also see 4.08). Public transportation is also, not surprisingly, concentrated in large metropolitan areas. In 2006, around two thirds of the nation's passenger-miles and unlinked passenger-trips were accounted for by the 25 largest transit agencies, and over 80% of the passenger-miles and trips took place in metropolitan areas with populations over 1 million (table 5.01). Tables 5.05 and 5.06 also show further details on the 25 largest public transit agencies and 50 largest metropolitan areas, respectively.

Almost all public transit vehicles use diesel as the primary fuel, except heavy and light rail systems, which primarily use electricity; overall, a growing percentage of transit vehicles are using alternative power sources (tables 5.07–5.10). The cost of riding public transit has been estimated for several permutations, but it is worth noting that they are all much lower than the estimates for the cost of owning a car from chapter 4 (table 5.11, also see tables 4.15 and 4.16). Tables 5.12 and 5.13 contain average fares broken down by mode and fare type, respectively.

Most public transit employees are involved in running the system (that is, operations), and most of those employees work with buses (tables 5.18 and 5.19). About half of the operating expenses are directly generated, coming from fares, advertising revenue, transit agency taxes, etc., while the rest come from grants from various levels of government, especially federal (tables 5.21 and 5.22). Most operating expenses go to employee salaries and other wages, and to vehicle operations (table 5.24).

Table 5.01: Public Transit Summary, 2005

Agencies	6,429	**Operating Expenses**	
Fares collected	$10,269,058,000	*Total*	*$30,294,909,000*
Average fare per unlinked trip	$1.05	Salaries and wages	12,176,601,000
Unlinked Passenger-Trips		Fringe benefits	8,093,269,000
Total	*9,814,683,000*	Fuel and lubricants	1,315,219,000
For 20 largest transit agencies	6,452,819,000	Utilities	974,829,000
percent of total	65.7%	Vehicle operations	13,792,982,000
For cities over 1 million		Vehicle maintenance	5,293,611,000
population	8,259,846,300	Non-vehicle maintenance	2,965,038,000
percent of total	84.2%	**Vehicle Characteristics**	
Passenger-Miles		Total vehicle-miles	4,601,387,000
Total	*49,678,482,000*	Revenue vehicle-miles	4,075,435,000
For 20 largest transit agencies	33,214,702,400	Total vehicle-hours	304,895,000
percent of total	66.9%	Revenue vehicle-hours	275,430,000
For cities over 1 million		Average vehicle speed	14.8
population	43,234,108,500	Vehicles available	150,827
percent of total	87.0%	Average age	9.6
Fuel Consumption		Air-conditioned	93.4%
Diesel fuel	729,918,000	with Wheelchair lifts	48.8%
Other fuel	181,173,000	with Wheelchair ramps	26.0%
Electricity	5,953,991,000	Accessible only via stations	15.3%
Capital Expenses		Diesel of gasoline-powered	66.3%
Total	*$12,383,429,000*	Alternative-powered	30.5%
Rolling stock	3,405,867,000	**Employees**	
Guideway facilities	7,544,543,000	Operating employees	354,458
Other materials and supplies	1,433,019,000	Vehicle operations	224,485
Average trip length (miles)	5.1	Vehicle maintenance	62,898
		Non-vehicle maintenance	30,509
		Capital employees	12,344

Source: American Public Transportation Association, *Public Transportation Fact Book*, 58th ed, tables 3 through 5 and 10.

Notes: Groups may not add to total.
See later tables, glossary, or original data source for definitions.

Units: Number of agencies, trips, miles, vehicles, and employees; fares collected and expenses in dollars; vehicle characteristics as percent of total; diesel and other fuel consumed in gallons; electricity consumed in kilowatt-hours.

Table 5.02:   Public Transit Summary, 2006

Transit Agencies

Total Number	*6,435*
Fares collected	$11,194.90
Average fare per unlinked trip	$1.12

Operating Expenses

Total Expenses	*$32,037.2*
Salaries and wages	12,764.1
Fringe benefits	8,423.5
Services	1,900.4
Materials and supplies	3,604.6
Utilities	1,037.6
Casualty and liability	783.9
Vehicle operations	14,742.8
Vehicle maintenance	5,681.5
Non-vehicle maintenace	3,008.0
General administration	4,301.3

Capital Expenses

Total Expenses	*$13,340.4*
Rolling stock	3,389.8
Guideway facilities	8,357.5
Other materials and supplies	1,593.1

Employees

Operating Employees	*357,484*
Vehicle operations	225,992
Vehicle maintenance	63,806
Non-vehicle maintenance	30,567
General administration	37,118
Capital employees	12,010

Unlinked Passenger Trips

Total Trips	*10,017*
For 25 largest transit agencies	6,929
percent of total	69.2%
For cities over 1 million populaton	8,446
percent of total	84.3%
Average trip length (miles)	5.2

Passenger-Miles

Total Pasenger-miles	*52,154*
For 25 largest transit agencies	36,254
percent of total	69.5%
For cities over 1 million populaton	45,309
percent of total	86.9%

Vehicle Charactristics

Total vehicle-miles	4,648.2
Revenue vehicle-miles	4,151.0
Total vehicle-hours	312.0
Revenue vehicle-hours	281.8
Average vehicle speed	14.7
Revenue vehicles available for meximum service	155,195
Vehicles operated at maximum service	124,822

Fuel Consumption

Diesel fuel consumed	735.1
Other fuel consumed	221.4
Electricity consumed	5,952.0

Source: American Public Transportation Association, *Public Transportation Fact Book*, 59th ed, tables 2 through 4 and 9.

Notes: Groups may not add to total.
See later tables, glossary, or original data source for definitions.

Units: Number of agencies, vehicles, and employees; fares collected and expenses in millions of dollars; passenger-trips, passenger-miles, vehicle-miles, and vehicle-hours in millions; average trip length in miles; diesel and other fuel consumed in million gallons; electricity comsumed in million kilowatt-hours; percent of total.

Table 5.03: Unlinked Passenger Trips and Passenger-Miles by Mode of Travel, 1995–2006

	Bus	Commuter Rail	Paratransit	Heavy Rail	Light Rail	Total
Unlinked Passenger Trips						
1995	4,848	344	88	2,033	251	7,763
1996	4,887	352	93	2,157	261	7,948
1997	5,013	357	99	2,430	262	8,374
1998	5,399	381	95	2,393	276	8,750
1999	5,648	396	100	2,521	292	9,168
2000	5,678	413	105	2,632	320	9,363
2001	5,849	419	105	2,728	336	9,653
2002	5,868	414	103	2,688	337	9,623
2003	5,692	410	111	2,667	338	9,434
2004	5,731	414	114	2,748	350	9,575
2005	5,855	423	125	2,808	381	9,815
2006	5,894	441	126	2,927	407	10,017
Trips per weekday, 2006	*20,203*	*1,512*	*434*	*10,032*	*1,393*	*34,333*
Percent of total	58.8%	4.4%	1.3%	29.2%	4.1%	100%
Passenger miles						
1995	18,818	8,244	607	10,559	860	39,808
1996	19,096	8,351	656	11,530	957	41,378
1997	19,604	8,038	754	12,056	1,035	42,339
1998	20,360	8,704	735	12,284	1,128	44,128
1999	21,205	8,766	813	12,902	1,206	45,857
2000	21,241	9,402	839	13,844	1,356	47,666
2001	22,022	9,548	855	14,178	1,437	49,070
2002	21,841	9,504	853	13,663	1,432	48,324
2003	21,262	9,559	930	13,606	1,476	47,903
2004	21,377	9,719	962	14,354	1,576	49,073
2005	21,825	9,473	1,058	14,418	1,700	49,678
2006	22,821	10,361	1,078	14,721	1,866	52,154
Average trip length, 2006	*3.9*	*23.5*	*8.5*	*5.0*	*4.6*	*5.2*

Source: American Public Transportation Association, *Public Transportation Fact Book, 59th ed*, tables 5 through 8.

Notes: 'Unlinked passenger trips' refers to the number of passengers who board public transportation vehicles. Passengers are counted each time they board vehicles no matter how many vehicles they use to travel from their origin to their destination.
'Passenger-miles' is the cumulative sum of the distances ridden by each passenger.
Data refers to fiscal year indicated. Data for 2006 is preliminary.

Units: Number of unlinked trips and passenger-miles in millions; average weekday trips in thousands; average trip length in miles.

Table 5.04: Trips, Passengers & Expenses for Largest Agencies, 2005

Agency	Primary City	Operating Expenses	Vehicle Revenue Miles	Unlinked Trips	Passenger Miles	Avg Trip Length
MTA New York City Transit Authority	New York, NY	$4,615.5	456.9	2,758.3	10,375.2	3.8
Chicago Transit Authority	Chicago, IL	1,214.6	150.2	492.3	1,936.1	3.9
Los Angeles County Metropolitan Trip Auth	Los Angeles, CA	975.3	106.0	451.5	1,850.2	4.1
Washington Metropolitan Area Transit Authority	Washington, DC	1,035.4	112.8	414.1	1,868.1	4.5
Massachusetts Bay Transportation Authority	Boston, MA	893.1	89.0	394.9	1,738.7	4.4
Southeastern Pennsylvania Trip Authority	Philadelphia, PA	856.2	83.7	334.5	1,475.9	4.4
New Jersey Transit Corp	New York, NY	1,399.5	148.3	244.1	3,065.3	12.6
San Francisco Muni R'way	San Francisco, CA	453.9	25.8	216.9	429.5	2.0
Metropolitan Atlanta Rapid Transit Authority	Atlanta, GA	309.0	48.5	142.4	716.5	5.0
Tri-County Metro Transport Dist of Oregon	Portland, OR	293.5	36.8	104.5	432.6	4.1
Maryland Transit Admin	Baltimore, MD	401.4	40.0	103.4	652.6	6.3
Miami-Dade Transit	Miami, FL	353.5	44.5	103.2	468.5	4.5
San Francisco Bay Area Rapid Transit District	San Francisco, CA	411.9	60.0	99.3	1,255.5	12.6
King County DOT	Seattle, WA	401.3	52.5	98.6	514.9	5.2
MTA Long Island Railroad	New York, NY	944.5	58.7	95.5	1,925.7	20.2
Metropolitan Transit Auth of Harris County, Texas	Houston, TX	308.0	60.1	94.6	552.0	5.8
Denver Regional Transportation District	Denver, CO	295.1	53.4	86.3	443.2	5.1
Metro-North Commuter Railroad Company	New York, NY	715.1	52.0	74.7	1,551.9	20.8
Dallas Area Rapid Transit	Dallas, TX	292.7	37.7	72.6	413.9	5.7
Port Authority Trans-Hudson Corp	New York, NY	196.7	12.9	71.3	307.1	4.3

Source: Federal Transit Administration, National Transit Database, *Report Year 2005 National Transit Summaries and Trends*, pages 109 and 110.

Notes: 'Unlinked passenger trips' refers to number of passengers who board public transportation vehicles. Passengers are counted each time they board vehicles no matter how many vehicles they use to travel from their origin to their destination.

'Passenger-miles' is the cumulative sum of the distances ridden by each passenger. Data is given for the top 20 agencies by passenger trips and passenger-miles.

Units: Operating expenses in millions of dollars; unlinked trips, revenue-miles, and passenger-miles in millions; average trip length in miles.

Table 5.05: Largest Transit Agencies, Passenger Trips and Miles, 2006

Agency	Primary City	Unlinked Passenger Trips	Passenger-Miles
MTA New York City Transit Authority	New York, NY	2,803,463.9	10,234,418.5
Chicago Transit Authority	Chicago, IL	494,729.1	1,897,672.7
Los Angeles County Metropolitan Trip Authority	Los Angeles, CA	482,815.9	1,979,256.3
Washington Metropolitan Area Transit Authority	Washington, DC	408,988.3	2,014,974.3
Massachusetts Bay Transportation Authority	Boston, MA	380,260.7	1,767,605.8
Southeastern Pennsylvania Transport Authority	Philadelphia, PA	323,050.5	1,434,210.2
New Jersey Transit Corporation	New York, NY	255,294.3	3,201,667.1
San Francisco Municipal Railway	San Francisco, CA	210,848.3	419,290.8
Metropolitan Atlanta Rapid Transit Authority	Atlanta, GA	138,403.3	749,676.6
Miami-Dade Transit	Miami, FL	107,094.1	487,682.6
Maryland Transit Administration	Baltimore, MD	107,024.1	689,097.6
King County DOT	Seattle, WA	106,273.6	538,831.7
San Francisco Bay Area Rapid Transit District	San Francisco, CA	103,654.1	1,307,104.7
Metropolitan Transit Authority of Harris County, Texas	Houston, TX	102,477.6	605,236.7
Tri-County Metropolitan Trp District of Oregon	Portland, OR	101,575.2	436,730.2
MTA Long Island Railroad	New York, NY	99,520.0	2,207,016.6
MTA Bus Company	New York, NY	99,169.4	587,082.8
Denver Regional Transportation District	Denver, CO	86,571.4	472,644.2
Part Authority Trans-Hudson Corporation	New York, NY	78,283.0	338,486.5
Metro-North Commuter Railroad Company	New York, NY	77,070.7	1,785,643.1
Dallas Area Rapid Transit	Dallas, TX	77,010.1	421,096.5
Metro Transit	Minneapolis, MN	73,356.6	314,330.2
Northeast IL Regional Commuter Corp	Chicago, IL	72,064.3	1,636,188.8
City and County of Honolulu Department of Transport Services	Honolulu, HI	71,168.3	328,124.8
Greater Cleveland Regional Transit Authority	Cleveland, OH	69,199.2	NA
Southern California Regional Rail Authority	Los Angeles, CA	NA	400,170.6

Source: American Public Transportation Association, *Public Transportation Fact Book, 59th ed*, tables 3 and 4.

Notes: 'Unlinked passenger trips' refers to number of passengers who board public transportation vehicles. Passengers are counted each time they board vehicles no matter how many vehicles they use to travel from their origin to their destination.
'Passenger-miles' is the cumulative sum of the distances ridden by each passenger.
Data is given for the top 25 agencies by passenger trips and passenger-miles.

Units: Number of unlinked passenger trips and passenger-miles in thousands.

Table 5.06: Public Transit Passengers and Expenses for 50 Largest Metropolitan Areas, 2006

	Directional Route-miles	Vehicle Revenue-Miles	Passenger-Miles	Unlinked Passenger-Trips	Operating Expenses	Recovery Ratio
New York, NY	17,270	869.6	19,831.6	3,556.9	$9,269.7	54.6%
Los Angeles, CA	12,234	228.4	3,160.8	700.4	1,815.0	24.9
Chicago, IL	7,322	233.8	3,943.2	610.7	2,059.6	36.3
Philadelphia, PA	4,708	101.7	1,591.0	342.0	979.0	37.3
Miami, FL	5,254	105.1	845.0	162.7	649.8	20.1
Dallas, TX	1,943	54.5	501.7	86.0	390.1	12.0
Boston, MA	4,325	94.9	1,796.2	386.7	975.5	35.6
Washington, DC	6,660	146.9	2,371.6	461.0	1,384.6	40.3
Detroit, MI	2,934	32.4	298.7	51.3	293.9	12.3
Houston, TX	3,846	61.0	605.2	102.5	317.0	17.8
Atlanta, GA	3,193	60.4	889.4	148.5	347.8	30.8
San Francisco, CA	4,913	143.6	2,377.1	420.2	1,440.7	36.1
Phoenix, AZ	2,740	40.4	282.6	64.3	198.0	21.4
Seattle, WA	4,647	94.5	1,106.9	168.6	874.8	18.8
San Diego, CA	5,096	54.4	568.3	96.1	264.2	35.6
Minneapolis, MN	4,126	45.2	402.6	85.2	306.4	28.3
St. Louis, MO	2,914	32.6	280.4	52.3	193.0	20.9
Baltimore, MD	2,962	45.6	694.4	108.5	432.5	27.4
Tampa, FL	2,154	21.5	127.3	24.9	100.8	16.9
Denver, CO	5,049	54.0	472.6	86.6	320.1	21.2
Cleveland, OH	2,213	29.5	297.4	70.2	230.5	18.3
Pittsburgh, PA	3,545	44.0	319.3	71.7	344.0	24.1
Portland, OR	1,972	41.4	469.8	107.5	330.8	22.8
San Jose, CA	1,683	25.1	172.7	40.9	282.5	13.2
Riverside, CA	2,461	22.2	122.8	22.7	110.4	14.1
Cincinnati, OH	1,686	17.6	152.4	29.3	100.4	28.5
Virginia Beach, VA	1,771	14.7	109.1	24.0	62.1	24.6
Sacramento, CA	3,017	19.6	164.5	34.7	163.3	18.3
Kansas City, MO	1,378	13.1	64.4	15.2	76.2	13.3
San Antonio, TX	1,876	26.7	175.9	42.7	118.7	14.7

(continued on next page)

Table 5.06: Public Transit Passengers and Expenses for 50 Largest Metropolitan Areas, 2006

	Directional Route-miles	Vehicle Revenue- Miles	Passenger- Miles	Unlinked Passenger- Trips	Operating Expenses	Recovery Ratio
Las Vegas, NV	1,455	23.7	229.4	67.7	$189.5	36.8%
Milwaukee, WI	1,949	25.6	155.1	50.7	158.5	31.4
Indianapolis, IN	737	8.9	51.1	10.0	43.1	19.3
Providence, RI	2,164	15.1	108.3	21.2	95.1	27.9
Orlando, FL	1,344	20.8	162.8	25.3	86.8	22.1
Columbus, OH	889	9.3	61.2	15.0	67.4	19.6
New Orleans, LA	184	5.1	39.4	10.7	92.8	3.7
Buffalo, NY	1,352	10.6	80.2	23.8	100.5	24.4
Memphis, TN	1,872	8.7	61.3	11.7	45.9	19.8
Austin, TX	1,727	17.6	131.5	35.4	128.1	4.3
Bridgeport, CT	839	5.7	29.0	10.1	34.6	30.5
Salt Lake City, UT	1,713	30.2	299.3	38.6	136.8	17.5
Jacksonville, FL	757	16.3	68.3	11.7	81.7	25.8
Louisville, KY	1,752	11.8	56.7	15.0	58.5	12.3
Hartford, CT	1,522	17.3	111.1	16.3	70.2	28.9
Richmond, VA	598	8.2	50.3	14.3	37.0	23.3
Charlotte, NC	1,782	15.1	106.8	21.2	78.1	16.1
Nashville, TN	808	6.1	38.2	7.9	34.7	24.4
Oklahoma City, OK	807	3.7	15.0	2.9	17.1	14.3
Tucson, AZ	582	9.9	65.7	17.8	52.8	16.4

Source: Federal Transit Administration, *National Transit Database, Report Year 2006 National Transit Summaries and Trends*, pages 45 through 47.

Notes: Metropolitan areas are ranked by population according to the 2000 Census.
Recovery ratio is calculated as the ratio of fare revenues to operating expenditures.
Data for some agencies may be understated because not all agencies report data to the federal government, or it may be overstated, because some agencies also serve other metropolitan areas, but only agency-total data is given.

Units: Route-miles, revenue-miles, and passenger miles in millions; operating expenses in millions of dollars; recovery ratio as percent.

Table 5.07: Diesel Consumption by Mode, and Non-Diesel Consumption by Fuel Type, 1995–2006

	1995	1998	2001	2004	2006
Diesel	678.3	739.6	744.6	730.7	735.1
Bus	563.8	606.6	587.2	550.5	536.7
Commuter Rail	63.1	69.2	72.2	72.0	78.6
Paratransit	29.0	38.3	54.9	73.0	86.8
Ferryboat	22.3	25.3	30.3	35.1	33.5
Non-diesel	71.5	89.9	112.1	164.7	221.4
Compressed natural gas	10.7	37.3	66.2	111.8	146.6
Gasoline	42.8	35.6	26.6	24.3	26.3
Liquefied natural gas	2.2	5.3	13.8	17.3	20.2
Propane	3.7	6.6	4.7	5.7	5.3

Source: American Public Transportation Association, *Public Transportation Fact Book*, 59th ed, tables 28 and 29.

Notes: Data for 2006 is preliminary.
Groups may not add to total.
Ferryboat data excludes international, rural, rural interstate, island, and urban park ferries.

Units: Fuel consumed in millions of gallons.

Table 5.08: Electric Power Consumption by Mode, 1995–2006

	Commuter Rail	Heavy Rail	Light Rail	Trolley	Total
1995	1,253	3,401	288	100	5,068
1996	1,255	3,332	321	69	5,007
1997	1,270	3,253	361	78	4,988
1998	1,299	3,280	381	74	5,073
1999	1,322	3,385	416	75	5,237
2000	1,370	3,549	463	77	5,510
2001	1,354	3,646	487	74	5,610
2002	1,334	3,683	510	73	5,649
2003	1,383	3,632	507	69	5,643
2004	1,449	3,684	553	68	5,825
2005	1,484	3,769	571	67	5,954
2006	1,478	3,709	634	62	5,952

Source: American Public Transportation Association, *Public Transportation Fact Book*, 59*th* ed, table 27.

Notes: Groups may not add to total.

Units: Electricity consumed in million kilowatt-hours.

Table 5.09:   Public Transit Power Sources by Mode, 2006

	Bus	Commuter Rail Car	Heavy Rail	Light Rail	Paratransit	Total
Total Vehicles	*57,616*	*6,070*	*11,154*	*2,070*	*11,970*	*94,831*
Percent using alternative power	19.1%	49.6%	100%	98.8%	6.3%	33.8%
Vehicles by Mode						
CNG	7,488	0	0	0	311	7,829
CNG blends	169	0	0	0	2	171
Clean diesel	618	0	0	0	207	825
Diesel	46,266	18	0	24	7,714	54,947
Electric & diesel	750	0	0	0	0	804
Electric 3rd rail or caternary	0	3,008	11,151	2,046	0	17,114
Gasoline	336	0	0	0	3,498	7,803
Liquefied natural gas	1,092	0	0	0	38	1,130
Propane	310	0	0	0	161	471
Unpowered	0	3,044	3	0	0	3,096

Source: American Public Transportation Association, *Public Transportation Fact Book*, 58th ed, tables 18 and 20.

Notes: Here, 'alternative' refers to any power source other than straight diesel or gasoline. Not all subgoups are included; figures may not add to total.
CNG = Compressed Natural Gas

Units: Number of vehicles; percent of total.

Table 5.10:   Altenative-Power Vehicles by Mode, 1995–2006

	Bus	Self-Propelled Commuter Rail	Commuter Rail Locomotive	Paratransit	Heavy Rail	Light Rail	Ferryboat
1995	6.3%	NA	NA	11.2%	NA	NA	NA
1996	6.4	NA	NA	14.0	99.9%	100.0%	2.0%
1997	5.6	NA	NA	13.8	100.0	100.0	2.0
1998	6.5	NA	NA	13.2	100.0	100.0	31.9
1999	7.5	99.5%	42.1%	11.4	100.0	100.0	32.6
2000	7.9	98.7	43.1	8.5	100.0	100.0	32.7
2001	9.8	99.5	23.6	5.8	100.0	100.0	37.3
2002	11.8	99.5	28.6	5.1	100.0	100.0	36.5
2003	13.0	99.5	27.6	5.1	100.0	100.0	40.3
2004	13.3	99.5	28.6	5.1	100.0	98.9	40.3
2005	16.0	99.4	29.3	4.9	100.0	100.0	41.5
2006	20.8	99.3	10.5	6.4	100.0	98.0	58.2
2007	22.4	99.4	10.2	5.3	100.0	98.4	58.8

Source: American Public Transportation Association, *Public Transportation Fact Book, 59th ed*, table 16.

Notes: An alternative-power vehicle is defined as any vehicle that is powered by something other than straight diesel or gasoline.

Units: Percent of total vehicles by mode.

Table 5.11: Estimated Cost of Riding Public Transit

Base Fare	$0.50	$1.00	$1.50	$2.00	$2.50	$3.00
Base Annual Cost (472 Trips)	$236.00	$472.00	$708.00	$944.00	$1,180.00	$1,416.00
Using monthly pass with 20% discount	188.80	377.60	566.40	755.20	944.00	1,132.80

Additional Surcharges

$0.25 transfer	$94.40
$2.00 zone/distance	755.20
$0.50 peak-hour	188.80
$0.25 express service	94.40
$2.00 daily parking	755.20

Total Annual Cost with Surcharges

	$0.50	$1.00	$1.50	$2.00	$2.50	$3.00
Base cost with discount	$188.80	$377.60	$566.40	$755.20	$944.00	$1,132.80
Transfer only	283.20	472.00	660.80	849.60	1,038.40	1,227.20
Distance only	944.00	1,132.80	1,321.60	1,510.40	1,699.20	1,888.00
Distance and peak-hour	1,132.80	1,321.60	1,510.40	1,699.20	1,888.00	2,076.80
Distance and express	1,038.40	1,227.20	1,416.00	1,604.80	1,793.60	1,982.40
Distance and parking	1,699.20	1,888.00	2,076.80	2,265.60	2,454.40	2,643.20

Source: American Public Transportation Association, *Public Transportation Fact Book*, 58th ed, table 53.

Notes: Figures are based on 472 trips per year (2 trips per day for 365 days, minus weekends, 7 holidays, 10 vacation days, and 8 sick days).
Annual costs with surcharges are calculated using the 20% monthly pass discount.

Units: Estimated cost in dollars per year.

Table 5.12: Passenger Fares Summary, 1995–2006

	Unlinked Trip	Adult Base Cash Fare		Percent of Systems With:		
	Fares Received	Highest	Average	Peak Period Surcharges	Transfer Surcharges	Zone or Distance Surcharges
1995	0.876	$7.00	$0.992	6.5%	23.8%	36.9%
1996	0.933	7.00	1.047	7.0	22.9	32.6
1997	0.888	7.00	1.058	7.0	22.9	32.6
1998	0.871	7.00	1.065	6.1	21.9	32.9
1999	0.903	4.00	1.087	6.5	26.8	35.0
2000	0.934	5.00	1.128	7.5	21.6	33.2
2001	0.921	7.00	1.194	7.0	20.1	32.4
2002	0.899	9.00	1.238	4.5	21.3	28.5
2003	0.970	10.00	1.327	5.4	20.4	29.1
2004	1.021	10.00	1.367	7.6	19.7	29.9
2005	1.016	12.50	1.384	6.1	19.2	24.6
2006	1.118	12.50	1.438	7.1	18.9	24.6

Source: American Public Transportation Association, *Public Transportation Fact Book, 59th ed*, table 50.

Notes: Average adult fare is an unweighted average of all transit agencies' adult fares, excluding surcharges.
Average adult fare and system percentages are based on a sample from the APTA's fare database.
'Unlinked trip' refers to the number of passengers who board public transportation vehicles. Fractions of fares for unlinked trips occur because passengers are counted each time they board vehicles no matter how many vehicles they use to travel from their origin to their destination.
Data for 2006 is preliminary.

Units: Fares paid per unlinked trip; fees in dollars; percent of total systems.

Table 5.13: Passenger Fares by Mode, 1995–2006

	Bus	Commuter Rail	Paratransit	Heavy Rail	Light Rail	Total
Total Fares						
1995	$3,287.2	$1,077.5	$146.3	$2,018.2	$126.5	$6,800.9
1996	3,515.0	1,145.6	156.9	2,321.5	144.2	7,416.3
1997	3,557.8	1,177.6	170.4	2,350.9	138.6	7,545.7
1998	3,991.2	1,255.2	141.5	2,297.4	149.7	7,969.6
1999	4,175.0	1,308.7	158.6	2,323.3	163.5	8,282.4
2000	4,375.5	1,374.6	171.6	2,482.7	181.2	8,745.8
2001	4,356.7	1,438.7	181.5	2,532.6	203.8	8,891.1
2002	4,106.2	1,447.4	193.5	2,492.5	226.1	8,648.9
2003	4,269.6	1,552.2	244.0	2,654.3	229.1	9,149.3
2004	4,546.5	1,614.7	253.5	2,902.8	232.8	9,774.6
2005	4,764.0	1,727.9	286.3	3,006.9	248.7	10,269.1
2006	5,329.2	1,860.9	309.2	3,217.8	293.2	11,194.9
Average Fare per Unlinked Trip						
1995	$0.68	$3.13	$1.66	$0.99	$0.50	$0.88
1996	0.72	3.25	1.69	1.08	0.55	0.93
1997	0.71	3.30	1.72	0.97	0.53	0.90
1998	0.74	3.29	1.49	0.96	0.54	0.91
1999	0.74	3.30	1.59	0.92	0.56	0.90
2000	0.77	3.33	1.63	0.94	0.57	0.93
2001	0.74	3.43	1.73	0.93	0.61	0.92
2002	0.70	3.50	1.88	0.93	0.67	0.90
2003	0.75	3.79	2.20	1.00	0.68	0.97
2004	0.79	3.90	2.22	1.06	0.67	1.02
2005	0.81	4.08	2.29	1.07	0.65	1.05
2006	0.89	4.22	2.45	1.10	0.72	1.12

Source: American Public Transportation Association, *Public Transportation Fact Book, 59th ed*, tables 48 and 49.

Notes: Data for 2006 is preliminary.
Groups may not add to total.

Units: Fares in millions of dollars; average fare in dollars.

Table 5.14: Estimated Fuel Savings by Commuting to Work Using Public Transportation

Length of Trip	2 Miles	5 Miles	10 Miles	20 Miles	40 Miles	60 Miles
Miles traveled per year	944	2,360	4,720	9,440	18,880	28,320

Fuel Savings, based on Fuel Efficiency of:

	2 Miles	5 Miles	10 Miles	20 Miles	40 Miles	60 Miles
15 MPG	62.9	157.3	314.7	629.3	1,258.7	1,888.0
20 MPG	47.2	118.0	236.0	472.0	944.0	1,416.0
25 MPG	37.8	94.4	188.8	377.6	755.2	1,132.8
30 MPG	31.5	78.7	157.3	314.7	629.3	944.0
35 MPG	27.0	67.4	134.9	269.7	539.4	809.1
40 MPG	23.6	59.0	118.0	236.0	472.0	708.0

Source: American Public Transportation Association, *Public Transportation Fact Book*, 58th ed, table 29.

Notes: Miles traveled per year is based on 472 trips per year: 2 trips per day for 365 days, minus weekends, 7 holidays, 10 vacation days, and 8 sick days.

Units: Miles traveled per year; estimated fuel savings per person in gallons per year.

Table 5.15: Vehicle-Miles Operated and Vehicle-Hours by Mode, 1995–2006

	Bus	Commuter Rail	Paratransit	Heavy Rail	Light Rail	Total
Vehicles-Miles Operated						
1995	2,183.7	237.7	506.5	537.2	34.6	3,550.2
1996	2,220.5	241.9	548.3	543.1	37.6	3,650.3
1997	2,244.6	250.7	585.3	557.7	41.2	3,745.8
1998	2,174.6	259.5	670.9	565.7	43.8	3,793.6
1999	2,275.9	265.9	718.4	577.7	48.7	3,972.2
2000	2,314.8	270.9	758.9	595.2	52.8	4,080.8
2001	2,376.5	277.3	789.3	608.1	54.3	4,196.2
2002	2,411.1	283.7	802.6	620.9	61.0	4,276.7
2003	2,420.8	286.0	864.0	629.9	64.3	4,363.4
2004	2,471.0	294.7	889.5	642.4	67.4	4,470.8
2005	2,484.8	303.4	978.3	646.2	69.2	4,601.4
2006	2,494.9	314.8	1,013.0	652.1	74.3	4,684.2
Vehicle-Hours Operated						
1995	162.9	7.2	34.9	27.6	2.5	238.5
1996	165.5	7.3	37.0	28.0	2.7	244.2
1997	167.0	7.5	39.5	28.8	2.8	249.5
1998	164.0	7.9	44.1	29.3	2.9	252.3
1999	170.1	8.5	48.2	29.9	3.2	264.3
2000	174.3	9.4	50.9	30.9	3.5	274.0
2001	179.4	8.8	53.8	31.6	3.6	281.7
2002	182.7	8.8	54.4	32.0	4.1	286.8
2003	184.2	9.0	58.8	31.8	4.2	293.1
2004	189.7	9.3	61.5	32.8	4.4	302.8
2005	186.2	9.5	65.8	33.3	4.7	304.9
2006	189.3	10.0	68.3	33.7	5.1	312.0

Source: American Public Transportation Association, *Public Transportation Fact Book*, 59th ed, tables 10 and 11.

Notes: 'Vehicle-hours' refers to the total time a vehicle is in operation (from the time it pulls out from its garage to go into revenue service to the time it pulls in from revenue service). 'Vehicle-miles' refers to the distance a vehicle travels from the time it pulls out from its garage to go into revenue service to the time it pulls in from revenue service.
Groups may not add to total.
Data for 2006 is preliminary.

Units: Number of vehicle-miles operated and vehicle-hours in millions.

Table 5.16: Vehicles with Specified Amenities by Mode, 2007

	Bus	Light Rail	Heavy Rail	Commuter Rail
Two-way radio	93.2%	96.5%	83.7%	55.2%
Public address system	81.3	87.6	98.3	90.9
Automated stop announcement	39.6	56.0	34.9	19.8
Automatic passenger counter	17.0	NA	NA	NA
Passenger-operator intercom	NA	24.2	51.3	NA
Security or CCTV-type camera	38.2	35.9	2.7	0.9
Exterior bicycle rack	62.7	NA	NA	NA
Automatic vehicle locator or GPS	54.3	47.9	2.9	16.1
Traffic light preemption	3.2	28.4	NA	NA

Source: American Public Transportation Association, *Public Transportation Fact Book*, 59th *ed*, tables 19 through 22.

Notes: CCTV = Closed-Circuit Television.
GPS = Global Positioning System.
Data is based on a sample from the annual American Public Transit Association database, and is not expanded to national totals.

Units: Percent of total vehicles by mode.

Table 5.17: Wheelchair-Accessible Vehicles by Mode, 1995–2007

	Bus	Commuter Rail	Paratransit	Heavy Rail	Light Rail	Trolleybus
1995	59.8%	43.3%	89.1%	93.3%	49.2%	51.0%
1996	64.1	67.0	90.7	93.7	54.4	51.2
1997	67.6	70.5	92.8	93.7	56.2	48.9
1998	72.5	71.8	93.0	94.2	73.1	49.8
1999	76.6	62.5	92.4	98.3	77.4	51.0
2000	81.0	64.0	93.1	98.5	76.7	51.2
2001	86.2	66.0	90.9	98.6	77.1	51.2
2002	90.7	66.7	94.4	98.7	78.5	65.1
2003	93.0	68.4	94.1	98.7	82.2	69.5
2004	94.8	70.5	94.3	98.7	84.2	73.3
2005	96.7	75.6	93.1	98.7	87.3	88.7
2006	95.5	85.4	91.4	98.6	79.9	95.4
2007	97.9	81.7	89.7	99.0	86.8	92.6

Source: American Public Transportation Association, *Public Transportation Fact Book*, 59*th* ed, table 17.

Notes: 'Accessible vehicles' includes accessibiliy via lift, ramp, and station.

Units: Percent of total vehicles.

Table 5.18: Public Transit Employees by Function, 1995–2006

| | Operating Employees | | | | | Capital Employees | Total Employees |
	Vehicle Operations	Vehicle Maintenance	Non-vehicle Maintenance	General Administration	Total	Total	Total
1995	190,675	51,905	27,329	30,582	300,491	10,695	311,186
1996	199,615	54,645	27,239	33,445	314,944	11,682	326,626
1997	207,510	53,322	27,232	32,695	320,759	13,081	333,840
1998	209,047	57,128	28,335	33,242	327,752	10,963	338,715
1999	215,185	59,018	28,914	34,768	337,885	11,938	349,823
2000	221,885	61,155	29,527	35,274	347,841	11,753	359,594
2001	228,091	62,404	29,963	36,808	357,266	13,490	370,756
2002	227,470	62,679	30,520	40,053	360,722	13,048	373,770
2003	209,392	59,007	29,139	40,444	337,982	12,984	350,987
2004	216,824	60,160	30,653	38,233	345,871	12,774	358,645
2005	224,485	62,898	30,509	36,566	354,458	12,344	366,802
2006	225,992	63,806	30,567	37,118	357,484	12,010	369,494

Source: American Public Transportation Association, *Public Transportation Fact Book, 59th ed*, table 24.

Notes: Operating employees are involved directly in the operation of a transit system.
Capital employees are those whose labor costs are reimbursed under a capital grant or are otherwise capitalized.
Excludes approximately 10,000–20,000 individuals not employed by transit agencies, but whose compensation is classified as 'services' (e.g., boiler repair or marketing consultant).
Data for 2006 is preliminary.
Groups may not add to total.

Units: Number of employees.

Table 5.19:   Operating Employees by Mode, 1995–2006

	Bus	Commuter Rail	Paratransit	Heavy Rail	Light Rail	Total
1995	181,973	22,320	39,882	45,644	4,935	300,491
1996	190,152	22,604	44,667	45,793	5,728	314,944
1997	196,861	21,651	44,029	45,935	5,940	320,759
1998	198,644	22,488	48,406	45,163	6,024	327,752
1999	204,179	22,896	51,186	46,311	6,058	337,885
2000	211,095	23,518	52,021	47,087	6,572	347,841
2001	214,674	23,851	55,846	47,865	7,021	357,266
2002	214,825	24,391	56,746	48,464	7,598	360,722
2003	205,478	24,813	42,935	48,327	7,619	337,982
2004	212,122	25,296	43,642	47,211	8,184	345,871
2005	217,332	25,321	46,624	47,806	8,181	354,458
2006	221,302	25,314	46,178	48,323	8,448	357,484

Source: American Public Transportation Association, *Public Transportation Fact Book, 59ᵗʰ ed*, table 23.

Notes: Operating employees are involved directly in the operation of a transit system.
Excludes capital employees (those whose labor costs are reimbursed under a capital grant or are otherwise capitalized) and approximately 10,000–20,000 individuals not employed by transit agencies, but whose compensation is classified as a service (e.g., boiler repair or marketing consultant).
Data for 2006 is preliminary.
Groups may not add to total.

Units: Number of employees.

Table 5.20: Employee Compensation, 1995–2006

	Employees	Salaries and Wages	Fringe Benefits	Compensation	Compensation per Employee
1995	311,186	$8,213.1	$4,484.0	$12,697.1	$40,802
1996	326,626	8,437.6	4,401.4	12,839.0	39,308
1997	333,840	8,771.7	4,503.7	13,275.4	39,766
1998	338,715	9,211.2	4,843.6	14,054.8	41,494
1999	349,823	9,495.1	5,052.3	14,547.4	41,585
2000	359,594	10,400.2	5,412.9	15,813.1	43,975
2001	370,756	10,626.9	5,705.6	16,332.5	44,052
2002	373,770	11,197.4	6,246.9	17,444.3	46,671
2003	350,987	11,634.0	6,913.4	18,547.4	52,844
2004	358,645	12,487.4	8,172.0	20,659.4	57,604
2005	366,802	12,176.6	8,093.3	20,269.9	55,261
2006	369,494	12,764.1	8,423.5	21,187.6	57,342

Source: American Public Transportation Association, *Public Transportation Fact Book, 59th ed*, table 25.

Notes: 'Employees' excludes approximately 10,000–20,000 individuals not employed by transit agencies, but whose compensation is classified as a service (e.g., boiler repair, marketing consultant).

'Compensation' is the sum of 'Salaries and Wages' and 'Fringe Benefits' (payments or accruals to others (insurance companies, governments, etc.) on behalf of an employee, and payments and accruals direct to an employee arising from something other than work.

Data for 2006 is preliminary.

Units: Number of employees; salaries, benefits, and total compensation in millions of dollars; compensation per employee in dollars.

Table 5.21: Capital Funding by Source, 1995–2006

	Federal	State	Local	Directly Generated	Total
1995	$3,422.2	$1,020.3	$888.2	$1,899.6	$7,230.3
1996	3,592.8	915.9	926.0	1,649.1	7,083.8
1997	4,275.6	1,037.0	898.8	1,638.1	7,849.5
1998	3,919.0	932.2	1,032.2	2,009.4	7,892.8
1999	3,960.4	911.5	1,128.2	2,974.6	8,974.7
2000	4,525.6	1,030.5	1,469.2	2,561.7	9,587.0
2001	5,768.5	1,066.6	1,304.4	3,279.2	11,418.7
2002	5,215.6	1,496.5	2,582.9	3,552.5	12,847.5
2003	5,277.5	1,681.9	2,397.8	3,883.5	13,240.6
2004	5,171.0	1,841.9	2,407.7	3,825.4	13,246.0
2005	4,824.8	1,563.2	2,716.3	3,279.2	12,383.4
2006	5,808.3	1,776.6	2,071.9	3,683.6	13,340.4

Source: American Public Transportation Association, *Public Transportation Fact Book*, 59th *ed*, table 40.

Notes: 'Capital funds' are used to pay expenses related to the purchase of equipment. 'Directly generated funds' include passenger fares, advertising revenue, donations, bond proceeds, and taxes imposed by the transit agency.

Units: Funding in millions of dollars.

Table 5.22: Operating Funding by Source, 1995–2006

	Agency Funds			Government Funds					All Funds
	Passenger Fares	Other	Total	Direct	Local	State	Federal	Total	Total
1995	$6,800.9	$1,268.0	$8,068.9	$1,544.2	$3,980.9	$3,829.6	$817.0	$10,171.7	$18,240.6
1996	7,416.3	1,232.8	8,649.1	1,695.4	4,128.5	4,081.8	596.4	10,502.1	19,151.2
1997	7,545.7	1,444.8	8,990.5	1,863.6	4,095.1	3,918.7	647.0	10,524.4	19,514.9
1998	7,969.6	1,731.3	9,700.9	1,953.4	4,376.9	4,279.4	751.2	11,360.9	21,061.8
1999	8,282.4	1,363.1	9,645.5	2,284.5	4,539.8	4,878.6	871.8	12,574.7	22,220.2
2000	8,745.8	2,257.8	11,003.6	1,958.9	5,318.8	4,967.1	994.2	13,239.0	24,242.6
2001	8,891.1	1,634.8	10,525.9	1,944.7	5,986.6	5,700.9	1,129.9	14,762.1	25,288.0
2002	8,648.9	2,390.3	11,039.2	2,211.3	5,343.9	6,718.6	1,319.4	15,593.2	26,632.4
2003	9,149.3	2,520.5	11,669.8	2,544.7	5,557.6	6,632.8	1,616.2	16,351.3	28,021.2
2004	9,774.6	2,372.7	12,147.3	2,587.5	6,184.3	6,713.2	2,085.9	17,570.9	29,718.1
2005	10,269.1	2,289.5	12,558.6	2,693.6	6,657.8	7,494.5	2,303.4	19,149.3	31,707.8
2006	11,194.9	2,349.9	13,544.8	2,796.6	7,105.2	7,674.3	2,591.9	20,168.0	33,712.8

Source: American Public Transportation Association, *Public Transportation Fact Book, 59ᵗʰ ed*, table 47.

Notes: Operating funds are used to pay expenses related to running a transit agency.
Agency funds are generated by the transit agency through sources other than taxation.
'Other' agency funds include freight tariffs, auxiliary transportation revenues, non-transportation revenue, and subsidies from other sectors.
Directly generated funds are from taxation generated by the transit agency.

Units: Funding in millions of dollars.

Table 5.23: Capital Expenses by Mode and Type, 2005 and 2006

2005

	Bus	Commuter Rail	Paratransit	Heavy Rail	Light Rail	Total
Total Expenses	*$3,252.4*	*$2,488.3*	*$248.6*	*$3,455.1*	*$2,488.6*	*$12,383.4*
Facilities	586.5	152.2	30.0	380.9	217.2	1,375.9
Guideway	347.7	897.7	0.0	1,124.0	1,584.9	3,979.0
Stations	327.9	346.6	4.4	846.7	225.7	1,964.7
Administrative buildings	177.4	3.8	15.2	21.5	6.0	225.0
Rolling stock	1,326.3	945.8	168.7	479.2	311.8	3,405.9
Other vehicles	24.9	5.5	1.0	15.4	2.1	49.3
Fare revenue collection	73.3	3.7	1.3	51.8	14.9	153.9
Systems	182.7	56.0	19.1	383.7	51.7	696.1
Other	205.7	77.0	8.9	151.8	74.3	533.7

2006

	Bus	Commuter Rail	Paratransit	Heavy Rail	Light Rail	Total
Total Expenses	*$3,687.7*	*$2,487.5*	*$208.8*	*$3,692.4*	*$2,999.6*	*$13,340.4*
Facilities	521.3	188.6	23.3	373.1	243.8	1,367.4
Guideway	370.3	1,049.2	0.0	1,095.1	2,026.1	4,551.7
Stations	436.6	343.6	2.0	1,083.5	308.5	2,257.0
Administrative buildings	123.1	4.3	10.2	15.0	28.6	181.5
Rolling stock	1,728.1	713.3	143.9	419.3	250.7	3,389.8
Other vehicles	26.0	7.7	1.1	37.7	2.6	75.7
Fare revenue collection	83.0	5.1	1.3	109.5	20.3	219.8
Systems	230.7	64.3	18.6	444.4	71.3	833.4
Other	168.7	111.4	8.2	114.8	47.6	464.2

Source: American Public Transportation Association, *Public Transportation Fact Book*, 58th ed, table 39; 59th ed, table 39.

Notes: Capital expenses are those related to the purchase of equipment. All data is preliminary.

Units: Expenses in millions of dollars.

Table 5.24: Operating Expenses, by Function and Object Class, 1995–2006

	1995	1998	2000	2003	2006
Total Operating Expenses	*$17,848.7*	*$19,738.5*	*$22,645.5*	*$26,851.6*	*$32,037.2*
By Function Class					
Vehicle operations	$8,281.9	$9,176.7	$10,110.9	$11,935.5	$14,742.8
Vehicle maintenance	3,218.2	3,579.2	4,267.1	4,822.1	5,681.5
Non-vehicle maintenance	1,829.0	1,783.9	2,177.7	2,545.7	3,008.0
General administration	2,589.5	3,065.8	3,328.8	3,962.4	4,301.3
By Object Class					
Salaries and wages	$8,213.1	$9,211.2	$10,400.2	$11,634.0	$12,764.1
Fringe benefits	4,484.0	4,843.6	5,412.9	6,913.4	8,423.5
Services	849.3	1,170.7	1,289.6	1,614.6	1,900.4
Materials and supplies	1,613.4	1,851.5	2,259.6	2,428.2	3,604.6
Utilities	628.9	660.8	719.8	809.9	1,037.6
Casualty and liability	512.8	473.9	506.5	693.7	783.9
Purchased transportation	1,930.1	2,132.9	2,761.0	3,585.8	4,303.6

Source: American Public Transportation Association, *Public Transportation Fact Book, 59th ed*, tables 44 and 45.

Notes: 'Operating expenses' are those involved in running a transit agency.
Object-classed expenses are grouped on the basis of goods and services purchased.

Units: Expenses in millions of dollars.

Chapter 6

Transportation Safety

Chapter 6 Highlights

Chapter 6 contains information on transportation safety. Of the nearly 45,000 transportation fatalities in 2006, almost all (close to 95%) were highway/motor vehicle accidents (table 6.01). The number and rate of motor vehicle fatalities and injuries has decreased steadily since 1988, however (table 6.02). Males aged 16–24 are the most likely to die in an accident (table 6.03). Automobile crashes involving rollover are much more likely to result in a fatality, and sport utility vehicles are much more likely to roll over in all types of accidents (table 6.05). On a positive note, alcohol-related deaths have dropped steadily since 1982, and the percentage of fatalities involving alcohol has dropped from 60% to 41% in 2006 (table 6.06). In 2007, only 31.7% of fatalities involved a significant level of alcohol impairment (table 6.08). Seat-belt use has increased as well (table 6.10). Motorcycles remain the most dangerous type of motor vehicle, comprising over 11% of the total automotive fatalities despite making up less than 3% of motor vehicles (table 6.11, also see table 4.02).

Fatalities involving aircraft remain rare, and very few of those came on planes with 10 or more seats; rather, most deaths came from small, private planes (tables 6.12 and 6.13). Fatalities involving boating or railroad crossings have declined as well (tables 6.17 and 6.19). Most public transportation fatalities in 2004 involved rail transit, while most injuries and collisions were on buses (table 6.20). Reported crimes varied by mode of transportation according to the type of crime involved (table 6.21).

In addition, chapter 6 contains state-by-state breakdowns of motor vehicle fatalities (table 6.04), alcohol-related and alcohol-impaired motor vehicle fatalities (tables 6.07 and 6.08), speeding-related fatalities (table 6.09), seat-belt use (table 6.10), motorcycle fatalities (table 6.11), and alcohol-related boating accidents and fatalities (table 6.18).

Table 6.01: Fatalities, Injuries, and Accidents by Mode of Transportation, 2000 and 2006

	2000			2006		
	Fatalities	**Injuries**	**Accidents**	**Fatalities**	**Injuries**	**Accidents**
Total	*44,384*	*3,259,673*	*NA*	*44,912*	*2,604,648*	*NA*
Air	764	357	1,985	766	287	1,603
US air carriers	92	29	56	50	9	31
Commuter carriers	5	7	12	2	1	3
On-demand air taxi	71	12	80	16	16	54
General aviation	596	309	1,837	698	261	1,515
Highway	41,945	3,188,750	6,394,000	42,642	2,575,000	5,973,000
Passenger car occupants	20,699	2,051,609	4,926,243	17,800	1,475,000	4,341,688
Motorcyclists	2,897	57,723	68,783	4,810	88,000	101,474
Light truck occupants	11,526	886,566	3,207,738	12,721	857,000	3,355,291
Large truck occupants	754	30,832	437,861	805	23,000	367,920
Bus occupants	22	17,769	55,594	27	10,000	51,554
Pedestrians	4,763	77,625	NA	4,784	61,000	NA
Pedacyclists	693	51,160	NA	773	44,000	NA
Other	591	15,466	NA	922	18,000	NA
Railroad	937	11,643	6,485	911	8,189	5,823
Highway-rail grade crossing	425	1,219	3,502	368	1,021	2,920
Railroad	512	10,424	2,983	543	7,168	2,903
Transit	295	56,697	24,261	213	18,327	8,851
Highway-rail grade crossing	20	123	148	21	172	141
Transit	275	56,574	24,113	192	18,155	8,710
Waterborne	888	5,112	13,143	797	5,245	10,367
Vessel-related	53	150	5,403	48	177	5,400
Not related to vessel	134	607	NA	39	594	NA
Recreational boating	701	4,355	7,740	710	4,474	4,967
Pipeline	38	81	380	19	32	386
Hazardous liquid pipeline	1	4	146	0	2	110
Gas pipeline	37	77	234	19	30	276

Source: Bureau of Transportation Statistics, *National Transportation Statistics 2008*, tables 2-1 to 2-3.

Notes: Figures may not add to total due to rounding and subgroups left out. See source document for further notes.

Units: Number of transportation-related fatalities, injuries, and accidents by mode.

Table 6.02: Motor Vehicle Injuries and Fatalities, 1988–2007

		Fatalities			Injuries	
	Number	Per 100,000 Population	Per 100 Million VMT	Number	Per 100,000 Population	Per 100 Million VMT
1988	47,087	19.26	2.32	3,416,000	1,397	169
1989	45,582	18.47	2.17	3,284,000	1,330	157
1990	44,599	17.88	2.08	3,231,000	1,295	151
1991	41,508	16.46	1.91	3,097,000	1,228	143
1992	39,250	15.39	1.75	3,070,000	1,204	137
1993	40,150	15.58	1.75	3,149,000	1,222	137
1994	40,716	15.64	1.73	3,266,000	1,255	139
1995	41,817	15.91	1.73	3,465,000	1,319	143
1996	42,065	15.86	1.69	3,483,000	1,313	140
1997	42,013	15.69	1.64	3,348,000	1,250	131
1998	41,501	15.36	1.58	3,192,000	1,181	121
1999	41,717	15.30	1.55	3,236,000	1,187	120
2000	41,945	14.86	1.53	3,189,000	1,130	116
2001	42,196	14.79	1.51	3,033,000	1,063	108
2002	43,005	14.93	1.51	2,926,000	1,015	102
2003	42,884	14.75	1.48	2,889,000	993	100
2004	42,836	14.59	1.44	2,788,000	950	94
2005	43,510	14.67	1.46	2,699,000	910	90
2006	42,642	14.24	1.41	2,575,000	860	85
2007	41,059	NA	1.37	2,491,000	NA	83

Source: National Highway Traffic Safety Administration, *Traffic Safety Facts 2006*, table 2; National Highway Traffic Safety Administration, *Traffic Safety Facts 2007 Preview*, tables 1 and 2.

Notes: Results for 2007 are based on preliminary data.

Units: Number of fatalities and injuries; rate per 100,000 population and 100 million vehicle-miles traveled.

Table 6.03: Persons Killed or Injured in Car Accidents by Sex and Age, 2006

	Male		Female		Total	
	Number	Rate per 100,000	Number	Rate per 100,000	Number	Rate per 100,000
Fatalities						
Total	29,722	20.15	12,747	8.39	42,642	14.24
4 and under	293	2.81	284	2.85	578	2.83
5–9	291	2.89	225	2.34	516	2.62
10–15	622	4.87	455	3.74	1,079	4.32
16–19	3,883	35.70	1,755	17.02	5,658	26.70
21–24	3,624	41.41	1,059	12.97	4,701	27.79
25–24	5,460	26.55	1,687	8.50	7,169	17.74
35–44	4,536	20.76	1,808	8.29	6,361	14.57
45–54	4,533	21.29	1,673	7.61	6,232	14.40
55–64	2,856	18.76	1,305	7.98	4,178	13.23
65–74	1,626	18.75	976	9.53	2,611	13.80
75 and over	1,892	27.08	1,496	13.17	3,406	18.57
Injuries						
Total	1,221,000	828	1,354,000	891	2,575,000	860
4 and under	30,000	289	26,000	258	56,000	274
5–9	31,000	308	32,000	333	63,000	320
10–15	55,000	433	65,000	536	121,000	484
16–19	197,000	1,810	213,000	2,067	410,000	1,935
21–24	132,000	1,503	141,000	1,729	273,000	1,612
25–24	234,000	1,137	236,000	1,188	470,000	1,162
35–44	196,000	897	218,000	999	414,000	948
45–54	156,000	734	188,000	855	344,000	795
55–64	102,000	670	120,000	735	222,000	704
65–74	50,000	576	61,000	591	111,000	585
75 and over	38,000	540	54,000	474	92,000	499

Source: National Highway Traffic Safety Administration, *Traffic Safety Facts 2006*, table 56.

Notes: Subgroups may not add to total.
Rates per 100,000 population are based on counts from the US Bureau of the Census.
Fatality total includes 173 fatalities of unknown gender.

Units: Number of deaths and injuries; rate per 100,000 population.

Table 6.04:   Motor Vehicle Fatalities by State, 2005–2007

	2005	2006	2007	% Change, 2005–2007
United States	*43,510*	*42,708*	*41,059*	*-5.6%*
Alabama	1,148	1,207	1,110	-3.3
Alaska	73	74	84	15.1
Arizona	1,179	1,293	1,066	-9.6
Arkansas	654	665	650	-0.6
California	4,333	4,240	3,974	-8.3
Colorado	606	535	554	-8.6
Connecticut	278	311	277	-0.4
Delaware	133	148	117	-12.0
District of Columbia	48	37	44	-8.3
Florida	3,518	3,357	3,214	-8.6
Georgia	1,729	1,693	1,641	-5.1
Hawaii	140	161	138	-1.4
Idaho	275	267	252	-8.4
Illinois	1,363	1,254	1,249	-8.4
Indiana	938	902	898	-4.3
Iowa	450	439	445	-1.1
Kansas	428	468	416	-2.8
Kentucky	985	913	864	-12.3
Louisiana	963	987	985	2.3
Maine	169	188	183	8.3
Maryland	614	652	614	0.0
Massachusetts	441	429	417	-5.4
Michigan	1,129	1,086	1,088	-3.6
Minnesota	559	494	504	-9.8
Mississippi	931	911	884	-5.0
Missouri	1,257	1,096	992	-21.1
Montana	251	264	277	10.4
Nebraska	276	269	256	-7.2

(continued on next page)

Table 6.04: Motor Vehicle Fatalities by State, 2005–2007

	2005	2006	2007	% Change, 2005–2007
United States	*43,510*	*42,708*	*41,059*	*-5.6%*
Nevada	427	431	373	-12.6
New Hampshire	166	127	129	-22.3
New Jersey	747	771	724	-3.1
New Mexico	488	484	413	-15.4
New York	1,434	1,454	1,333	-7.0
North Carolina	1,547	1,554	1,675	8.3
North Dakota	123	111	111	-9.8
Ohio	1,321	1,238	1,257	-4.8
Oklahoma	803	765	754	-6.1
Oregon	487	478	455	-6.6
Pennsylvania	1,616	1,525	1,491	-7.7
Rhode Island	87	81	69	-20.7
South Carolina	1,094	1,045	1,066	-2.6
South Dakota	186	191	146	-21.5
Tennessee	1,270	1,284	1,210	-4.7
Texas	3,536	3,531	3,363	-4.9
Utah	282	287	299	6.0
Vermont	73	87	66	-9.6
Virginia	947	962	1,027	8.4
Washington	649	633	568	-12.5
West Virginia	374	410	431	15.2
Wisconsin	815	724	756	-7.2
Wyoming	170	195	150	-11.8

Source: National Highway Traffic Safety Administration, *Traffic Safety Facts 2006*, table 5; *2007*, table 5.

Notes: Total for US does not include Puerto Rico (457 deaths in 2005, 509 deaths in 2006, and 452 deaths in 2007).

Units: Number of fatalities resulting from automobile accidents within 30 days; percent change from 2005 to 2007.

Table 6.05:   Rollover Accidents by Vehicle Type, 2006

	Fatal Crashes		Injury Crashes	
	Number	% Rollover	Number	% Rollover
Total	*53,008*	*21.6%*	*3,097,000*	*5.3%*
Cars	24,087	17.0	1,794,000	3.4
Light trucks				
Pickup	10,547	27.8	446,000	6.8
SUV	8,261	35.1	499,000	9.8
Van	3,395	16.9	229,000	4.3
Other light truck	87	16.1	28,000	5.5
Large Truck	4,732	14.7	80,000	8.6
Bus	299	3.0	11,000	0.5
Other	1,600	15.6	11,000	33.6

	Property-Damage Only Crashes		All Crashes	
	Number	% Rollover	Number	% Rollover
Total	*7,330,000*	*1.4%*	*10,481,000*	*2.6%*
Cars	4,046,000	0.9	5,864,000	1.7
Light trucks				
Pickup	1,131,000	2.0	1,588,000	3.6
SUV	1,188,000	2.4	1,696,000	4.7
Van	532,000	0.6	764,000	1.8
Other light truck	81,000	1.0	109,000	2.2
Large Truck	300,000	2.6	385,000	4.0
Bus	41,000	NA	52,000	0.1
Other	11,000	4.8	24,000	19.3

Source: National Highway Traffic Safety Administration, *Traffic Safety Facts 2006*, table 37.

Notes: Rollover is defined as any vehicle rotation of 90 degrees or more about any true longitudinal or lateral axis. Includes rollovers occurring as a first harmful event or subsequent event.

Units: Number of crashes by type; percent involving a vehicle rollover.

Table 6.06: Alcohol-Related Automobile Deaths by Highest Blood-Alcohol Level, 1982–2006

	Total Fatalities	No Alcohol Involved	BAC = .01 to .07	BAC > .08
1982	43,945	40%	7%	53%
1983	42,589	42	6	52
1984	44,257	44	7	49
1985	43,825	47	7	46
1986	46,087	46	8	47
1987	46,390	48	7	45
1988	47,087	49	7	44
1989	45,582	51	6	43
1990	44,599	49	7	44
1991	41,508	51	6	42
1992	39,250	53	6	40
1993	40,150	55	6	39
1994	40,716	57	6	37
1995	41,817	58	6	36
1996	42,065	58	6	36
1997	42,013	60	5	34
1998	41,501	60	6	34
1999	41,717	60	6	34
2000	41,945	59	6	35
2001	42,196	59	6	35
2002	43,005	59	6	35
2003	42,884	60	6	34
2004	42,836	61	5	34
2005	43,443	61	5	33
2006	42,642	59	6	35

Source: National Highway Traffic Safety Administration, *Traffic Safety Facts 2005*, table 13; National Highway Traffic Safety Administration, *Traffic Safety Facts 2006*, 'Alcohol-Related Fatalities,' table 1.

Notes: Alcohol-related deaths include any fatality involving at least one participant with a blood-alcohol level (BAC) of .01 g/dL or above. A BAC of .08 g/dL is typically considered the legal threshold for impairment.

Units: Number of automobile fatalities involving alcohol; percent involving the specified level of alcohol.

Table 6.07:   Alcohol-Related Automobile Deaths by State, 2006

	Number of Fatalities	% Involving Alcohol	% With Blood Alcohol Above .08
United States	*42,642*	*41%*	*32%*
Alabama	1,208	39	32
Alaska	74	31	27
Arizona	1,288	45	32
Arkansas	665	38	30
California	4,236	42	30
Colorado	535	42	33
Connecticut	301	43	36
Delaware	148	39	29
District of Columbia	37	48	32
Florida	3,374	41	28
Georgia	1,693	36	27
Hawaii	161	52	39
Idaho	267	40	31
Illinois	1,254	47	35
Indiana	899	36	27
Iowa	439	34	28
Kansas	468	36	29
Kentucky	913	30	24
Louisiana	982	48	37
Maine	188	39	27
Maryland	651	41	30
Massachusetts	430	40	32
Michigan	1,085	41	31
Minnesota	494	37	31
Mississippi	911	41	35
Missouri	1,096	46	35
Montana	263	48	39
Nebraska	269	33	26
Nevada	432	43	33

(continued on next page)

Table 6.07: Alcohol-Related Automobile Deaths by State, 2006

	Number of Fatalities	% Involving Alcohol	% With Blood Alcohol Above .08
United States	*42,642*	*41%*	*32%*
New Hampshire	127	41	37
New Jersey	772	44	29
New Mexico	484	38	28
New York	1,456	38	27
North Carolina	1,559	36	27
North Dakota	111	45	37
Ohio	1,238	39	30
Oklahoma	765	34	26
Oregon	477	41	31
Pennsylvania	1,525	39	32
Rhode Island	81	51	36
South Carolina	1,037	50	41
South Dakota	191	42	36
Tennessee	1,287	40	32
Texas	3,475	48	39
Utah	287	24	19
Vermont	87	33	30
Virginia	963	39	31
Washington	630	47	36
West Virginia	410	39	31
Wisconsin	724	50	42
Wyoming	195	41	34

Source: National Highway Traffic Safety Administration, *Traffic Safety Facts,* '2006 Traffic Safety Assessment–Alcohol-Related Fatalities,' table 11.

Notes: Alcohol-related deaths include any fatality involving at least one participant with a blood-alcohol level (BAC) of .01 g/dL or above. A BAC of .08 g/dL is typically considered the standard threshold for impairment.
Fatality totals for the US exclude Puerto Rico.

Units: Number of automobile fatalities; percent involving the specified level of alcohol.

Table 6.08: Alcohol-Impaired Automobile Fatalities by State, 2006 and 2007

	2006		2007		Overall
	Number of Fatalities	% Impaired	Number of Fatalities	% Impaired	% Change, 2006–2007
United States	*42,708*	*31.6%*	*41,059*	*31.7%*	*-3.7%*
Alabama	1207	31.2	1110	35.0	3.2
Alaska	74	25.7	84	35.7	57.9
Arizona	1,293	30.9	1,066	31.5	-15.8
Arkansas	665	30.1	650	28.0	-9.0
California	4,240	30.0	3,974	29.1	-9.2
Colorado	535	33.5	554	30.7	-5.0
Connecticut	311	36.3	277	36.5	-10.6
Delaware	148	29.1	117	42.7	16.3
District of Columbia	37	35.1	44	34.1	15.4
Florida	3,357	27.6	3,214	27.7	-3.9
Georgia	1,693	26.8	1,641	26.9	-2.9
Hawaii	161	37.3	138	32.6	-25.0
Idaho	267	32.2	252	27.8	-18.6
Illinois	1,254	35.6	1,249	34.7	-2.7
Indiana	902	27.2	898	25.6	-6.1
Iowa	439	27.1	445	23.8	-10.9
Kansas	468	26.7	416	27.4	-8.8
Kentucky	913	23.7	864	24.3	-2.8
Louisiana	987	37.6	985	37.4	-0.8
Maine	188	27.7	183	36.1	26.9
Maryland	652	29.0	614	29.2	-5.3
Massachusetts	429	33.6	417	35.0	1.4
Michigan	1,086	30.8	1,088	28.0	-9.0
Minnesota	494	30.2	504	31.3	6.0
Mississippi	911	36.8	884	34.2	-9.9
Missouri	1,096	35.2	992	34.1	-12.4
Montana	264	39.4	277	38.3	1.9
Nebraska	269	26.4	256	30.1	8.5
Nevada	431	33.4	373	31.6	-18.1

(continued on next page)

Table 6.08: Alcohol-Impaired Automobile Fatalities by State, 2006 and 2007

	2006		2007		Overall
	Number of Fatalities	% Impaired	Number of Fatalities	% Impaired	% Change, 2006–2007
United States	*42,708*	*31.6%*	*41,059*	*31.7%*	*-3.7%*
New Hampshire	127	36.2	129	26.4	-26.1
New Jersey	771	28.3	724	27.5	-8.7
New Mexico	484	28.1	413	32.2	-2.2
New York	1,454	29.8	1,333	28.8	-11.3
North Carolina	1,554	27.1	1,675	29.1	15.7
North Dakota	111	37.8	111	47.7	26.2
Ohio	1,238	31.2	1,257	31.1	1.3
Oklahoma	765	26.0	754	29.0	10.1
Oregon	478	31.0	455	33.0	1.4
Pennsylvania	1,525	32.3	1,491	33.5	1.6
Rhode Island	81	37.0	69	36.2	-16.7
South Carolina	1,045	40.1	1,066	43.4	10.5
South Dakota	191	35.1	146	30.8	-32.8
Tennessee	1,284	32.2	1,210	32.2	-5.8
Texas	3,531	39.6	3,363	38.4	-7.7
Utah	287	18.5	299	17.1	-3.8
Vermont	87	29.9	66	33.3	-15.4
Virginia	962	31.0	1,027	32.3	11.4
Washington	633	34.9	568	34.3	-11.8
West Virginia	410	25.6	431	32.9	35.2
Wisconsin	724	42.4	756	41.4	2.0
Wyoming	195	32.3	150	32.7	-22.2

Source: National Highway Traffic Safety Administration, *2007 Traffic Safety Annual Assessment–Alcohol-Impaired Driving Fatalities*, table 13.

Notes: A driver is considered 'impaired' if he or she has a blood-alcohol level (BAC) of .08 g/dL or above. Alcohol-impaired deaths include any fatality involving at least one impaired participant.
Fatality totals for the US exclude Puerto Rico.

Units: Number of alcohol-impaired fatalities; percent of total fatalities, percent change.

Table 6.09: Speeding-Related Traffic Fatalities by State, 2006

	Total Fatalities	Speeding-Related	% Speeding-Related	Interstate	Non-Interstate
US Summary	*42,642*	*13,543*	*31.8%*	*1,744*	*9,762*
Alabama	1,208	567	46.9	73	464
Alaska	74	30	40.5	4	22
Arizona	1,288	578	44.9	118	340
Arkansas	665	96	14.4	11	79
California	4,236	1,403	33.1	261	945
Colorado	535	182	34.0	25	133
Connecticut	301	92	30.6	11	76
Delaware	148	34	23.0	5	29
District of Columbia	37	3	8.1	0	3
Florida	3,374	714	21.2	85	523
Georgia	1,693	407	24.0	43	306
Hawaii	161	77	47.8	8	67
Idaho	267	83	31.1	9	48
Illinois	1,254	555	44.3	77	469
Indiana	899	194	21.6	25	161
Iowa	439	31	7.1	0	30
Kansas	468	128	27.4	14	96
Kentucky	913	160	17.5	12	144
Louisiana	982	257	26.2	33	210
Maine	188	72	38.3	7	59
Maryland	651	237	36.4	25	201
Massachusetts	430	148	34.4	34	106
Michigan	1,085	219	20.2	34	173
Minnesota	494	128	25.9	14	109
Mississippi	911	365	40.1	45	292
Missouri	1,096	470	42.9	55	334
Montana	263	112	42.6	9	34
Nebraska	269	64	23.8	13	37

(continued on next page)

Table 6.09: Speeding-Related Traffic Fatalities by State, 2006

	Total Fatalities	Speeding-Related	% Speeding-Related	Interstate	Non-Interstate
US Summary	*42,642*	*13,543*	*31.8%*	*1,744*	*9,762*
Nevada	432	159	36.8	30	90
New Hampshire	127	42	33.1	3	38
New Jersey	772	56	7.3	6	43
New Mexico	484	173	35.7	29	88
New York	1,456	448	30.8	32	293
North Carolina	1,559	539	34.6	32	493
North Dakota	111	40	36.0	2	23
Ohio	1,238	253	20.4	25	218
Oklahoma	765	269	35.2	37	139
Oregon	477	145	30.4	9	112
Pennsylvania	1,525	675	44.3	50	597
Rhode Island	81	42	51.9	4	38
South Carolina	1,037	412	39.7	58	286
South Dakota	191	48	25.1	8	32
Tennessee	1,287	296	23.0	17	208
Texas	3,475	1,474	42.4	215	747
Utah	287	61	21.3	15	37
Vermont	87	33	37.9	7	26
Virginia	963	296	30.7	47	234
Washington	630	253	40.2	27	212
West Virginia	410	75	18.3	9	54
Wisconsin	724	283	39.1	9	249
Wyoming	195	65	33.3	23	15

Source: National Highway Traffic Safety Administration, *Traffic Safety Facts 2006*, table 118.

Notes: Fatalities on roads with unknown speed limits are not included in the totals for interstate and non-interstate, but are included in speeding death total.

Units: Number of fatalities; percent of total.

Table 6.10: Seat Belt Use by State, 2000–2007

	2000	2002	2004	2006	2007
United States	*71.0%*	*75.0%*	*80.0%*	*81.0%*	*82.0%*
Alabama	70.6	78.7	80.0	82.9	82.3
Alaska	61.0	65.8	76.7	83.2	82.4
Arizona	75.2	73.7	95.3	78.9	80.9
Arkansas	52.4	63.7	64.2	69.3	69.9
California	88.9	91.1	90.4	93.4	94.6
Colorado	65.1	73.2	79.3	80.3	81.1
Connecticut	76.3	78.0	82.9	83.5	85.8
Delaware	66.1	71.2	82.3	86.1	86.6
District of Columbia	82.6	84.6	87.1	85.4	87.1
Florida	64.8	75.1	76.3	80.7	79.1
Georgia	73.6	77.0	86.7	90.0	89.0
Hawaii	80.4	90.4	95.1	92.5	97.6
Idaho	58.6	62.9	74.0	79.8	78.5
Illinois	70.2	73.8	83.0	87.8	90.1
Indiana	62.1	72.2	83.4	84.3	87.9
Iowa	78.0	82.4	86.4	89.6	91.3
Kansas	61.6	61.3	68.3	73.5	75.0
Kentucky	60.0	62.0	66.0	67.2	71.8
Louisiana	68.2	68.6	75.0	74.8	75.2
Maine	NA	NA	72.3	77.2	79.8
Maryland	85.0	85.8	89.0	91.1	93.1
Massachusetts	50.0	51.0	63.3	66.9	68.7
Michigan	83.5	82.9	90.5	94.3	93.7
Minnesota	73.4	80.1	82.1	83.3	87.8
Mississippi	50.4	62.0	63.2	73.6	71.8
Missouri	67.7	69.4	75.9	75.2	77.2
Montana	75.6	78.4	80.9	79.0	79.6
Nebraska	70.5	69.7	79.2	76.0	78.7

(continued on next page)

Table 6.10: Seat Belt Use by State, 2000–2007

	2000	2002	2004	2006	2007
United States	*71.0%*	*75.0%*	*80.0%*	*81.0%*	*82.0%*
Nevada	78.5	74.9	86.6	91.2	92.2
New Hampshire	NA	NA	NA	63.5	63.8
New Jersey	74.2	80.5	82.0	90.0	91.4
New Mexico	86.6	87.6	89.7	89.6	91.5
New York	77.3	82.8	85.0	83.0	83.5
North Carolina	80.5	84.1	86.1	88.5	88.8
North Dakota	47.7	63.4	67.4	79.0	82.2
Ohio	65.3	70.3	74.1	81.7	81.6
Oklahoma	67.5	70.1	80.3	83.7	83.1
Oregon	83.6	88.2	92.6	94.1	95.3
Pennsylvania	70.7	75.7	81.8	86.3	86.7
Rhode Island	64.4	70.8	76.2	74.0	79.1
South Carolina	73.9	66.3	65.7	72.5	74.5
South Dakota	53.4	64.0	69.4	71.3	73.0
Tennessee	59.0	66.7	72.0	78.6	80.2
Texas	76.6	81.1	83.2	90.4	91.8
Utah	75.7	80.1	85.7	88.6	86.8
Vermont	61.6	84.9	79.9	82.4	87.1
Virginia	69.9	70.4	79.9	78.7	79.9
Washington	81.6	92.6	94.2	96.3	96.4
West Virginia	49.8	71.6	75.8	88.5	89.6
Wisconsin	65.4	66.1	72.4	75.4	75.3
Wyoming	66.8	66.6	70.1	63.5	72.2

Source: National Highway Traffic Safety Administration, Traffic Safety Facts, *Seat Belt Use in 2006*, table 1; *2007*, table 1.

Notes: Not all states reported data for all years.

Units: Percent of drivers and passengers observed to use seat belts.

Table 6.11:   Motorcycle Fatalities by State, 2006

	Number of Fatalities	% Change from 2005	% of Total Motor Vehicle Fatalities
United States	*4,810*	*5.1%*	*11.3%*
Alabama	105	69.4	8.7
Alaska	9	125.0	12.2
Arizona	142	2.9	11.0
Arkansas	76	20.6	11.4
California	506	7.9	11.9
Colorado	74	-14.9	13.8
Connecticut	53	23.3	17.6
Delaware	12	-42.9	8.1
District of Columbia	1	-83.3	2.7
Florida	562	20.1	16.7
Georgia	154	6.9	9.1
Hawaii	27	-10.0	16.8
Idaho	38	46.2	14.2
Illinois	132	-16.5	10.5
Indiana	110	0.0	12.2
Iowa	57	26.7	13.0
Kansas	64	82.9	13.7
Kentucky	98	10.1	10.7
Louisiana	95	26.7	9.7
Maine	23	53.3	12.2
Maryland	84	-1.2	12.9
Massachusetts	50	-10.7	11.6
Michigan	114	-8.1	10.5
Minnesota	67	13.6	13.6
Mississippi	55	41.0	6.0
Missouri	93	2.2	8.5
Montana	26	-7.1	9.9
Nebraska	18	5.9	6.7
Nevada	50	-10.7	11.6

(continued on next page)

Table 6.11: Motorcycle Fatalities by State, 2006

	Number of Fatalities	% Change from 2005	% of Total Motor Vehicle Fatalities
United States	*4,810*	*5.1%*	*11.3%*
New Hampshire	21	-52.3	16.5
New Jersey	87	42.6	11.3
New Mexico	43	13.2	8.9
New York	192	18.5	13.2
North Carolina	150	-1.3	9.6
North Dakota	4	-33.3	3.6
Ohio	158	-11.2	12.8
Oklahoma	64	-16.9	8.4
Oregon	44	-8.3	9.2
Pennsylvania	188	-8.3	12.3
Rhode Island	16	14.3	19.8
South Carolina	109	2.8	10.5
South Dakota	22	0.0	11.5
Tennessee	140	8.5	10.9
Texas	346	-4.9	10.0
Utah	24	4.3	8.4
Vermont	10	-28.6	11.5
Virginia	69	0.0	7.2
Washington	80	8.1	12.7
West Virginia	38	11.8	9.3
Wisconsin	93	0.0	12.8
Wyoming	17	-15.0	8.7

Source: National Highway Traffic Safety Administration, *Traffic Safety Facts 2006: Comparison of Motorcycle Rider Fatalities in Traffic Crashes, 2005-2006*, table 2.

Notes: Fatality totals for the US exclude Puerto Rico.

Units: Number of fatalities among mototcycle riders; percent change from previous year; percent of total motor vehicle fatalities.

Table 6.12: Air Carrier Accidents and Fatalities, 1987–2007

	Accidents		Fatalities		Accidents per 100,000 Flight Hours	
	Total	Fatal	Total	Aboard	Total	Fatal
1987	2,494	446	837	822	9.18	1.63
1988	2,388	460	797	792	8.65	1.66
1989	2,242	432	769	766	7.97	1.52
1990	2,242	444	770	765	7.85	1.55
1991	2,197	439	800	786	7.91	1.57
1992	2,111	451	867	865	8.51	1.82
1993	2,064	401	744	740	9.03	1.74
1994	2,021	404	730	723	9.08	1.81
1995	2,056	413	735	728	8.21	1.63
1996	1,908	361	636	619	7.65	1.45
1997	1,844	350	631	625	7.19	1.36
1998	1,905	365	625	619	7.44	1.41
1999	1,905	340	619	615	6.50	1.16
2000	1,837	345	596	585	6.57	1.21
2001	1,727	325	562	558	6.78	1.27
2002	1,715	345	581	575	6.69	1.33
2003	1,740	352	633	630	6.68	1.34
2004	1,617	314	559	559	6.49	1.26
2005	1,670	321	563	558	7.20	1.38
2006	1,518	306	703	543	6.33	1.27
2007	1,631	284	491	486	6.84	1.19

Source: National Transportation Safety Board, *Aviation Accident Statistics 2006*, table 10; *2007*, table 10.

Notes: Data for 2007 is preliminary.
Flight hours are estimated by the Federal Aviation Administration.

Units: Number of accidents and fatalities; rate per 100,000 flight hours.

Table 6.13: Accidents for US Aircraft with 10 or More Seats, 1987–2007

	Accidents				Accidents per Million Hours Flown			
	Major	Serious	Injury	Damage	Major	Serious	Injury	Damage
1987	5	1	12	16	0.470	0.094	1.127	1.503
1988	4	2	13	11	0.359	0.180	1.167	0.987
1989	8	4	6	10	0.710	0.355	0.532	0.887
1990	4	3	10	7	0.329	0.247	0.823	0.576
1991	5	2	10	9	0.424	0.170	0.849	0.764
1992	3	3	10	2	0.243	0.243	0.809	0.162
1993	1	2	12	8	0.079	0.157	0.944	0.630
1994	4	0	12	7	0.305	0.000	0.914	0.533
1995	3	2	14	17	0.222	0.148	1.037	1.259
1996	6	0	18	13	0.436	0.000	1.309	0.946
1997	2	4	24	19	0.126	0.253	1.515	1.200
1998	0	3	21	26	0.000	0.178	1.249	1.546
1999	2	2	20	27	0.114	0.114	1.139	1.538
2000	3	3	20	30	0.109	0.109	1.093	1.475
2001	5	1	19	21	0.281	0.056	1.067	1.179
2002	1	1	14	25	0.058	0.058	0.810	1.446
2003	2	3	24	25	0.114	0.172	1.374	1.431
2004	4	0	15	11	0.212	0.000	0.794	0.583
2005	2	3	11	24	0.103	0.155	0.567	1.238
2006	2	2	7	22	0.104	0.104	0.363	1.142
2007	0	2	14	10	0.000	0.104	0.725	0.518

Source: National Transportation Safety Board, *Aviation Accident Statistics 2006*, table 2; *2007*, table 2.

Notes: All data refers to aircraft operating under 14 CFR 121 (see Glossary).
'Major' refers to an accident in which either an aircraft was destroyed, there were multiple fatalities, or there was one fatality and an aircraft was substantially damaged.
'Serious' refers to an accident in which either there was one fatality without serious damage to an aircraft, or there was at least one serious injury and an aircraft was seriously damaged.
'Injury' refers to an accident in which there was at least one serious injury (but no fatalities) and no substantial damage to an aircraft.
'Damage' refers to an accident in which no one was killed or seriously injured, but an aircraft was substantially damaged.

Units: Number of accidents; rate per million aircraft-hours.

Table 6.14: Fatal Aircraft Accidents by First Phase of Operation, 1990–2006

	Air Carriers	Commuter Air Carriers	Total Accidents
1990–1996			
Total Fatal Accidents	*27*	*28*	*55*
Approach/descent/landing	6	12	18
Takeoff/climb	10	3	13
Cruise (in-flight)	2	7	9
Standing (static)	4	2	6
Maneuvering	1	3	4
Other/not reported	4	1	5
1997–2006			
Total Fatal Accidents	*25*	*15*	*40*
Approach/descent/landing	3	4	7
Takeoff/climb	7	5	12
Cruise (in-flight)	6	3	9
Standing (static)	4	0	4
Maneuvering	0	2	2
Other/not reported	5	1	6

Source: Bureau of Transportation Statistics, *National Transportation Statistics 2007*, tables 2-11 and 2-12.

Notes: 'Air carriers' refers to aircraft operating under designation 14 CFR 121, which prior to 1997 included aircraft with more than 30 seats or a payload capacity of more than 7,500 lbs. Since 1997, it also includes aircraft with 10 or more seats that were formerly included under 14 CFR 135.

'Commuter air carriers' refers to aircraft operating under 14 CFR 35, which prior to 1997 included aircraft with 30 or fewer seats. Since 1997, it includes only aircraft with fewer than 10 seats. Because of this change in definition, it is difficult to compare pre-1997 data with more recent data.

'First phase of operation' refers to the phase of flight in which the problem leading to the accident first occurred.

The data is divided due to changes in the definitions of 14 CFR 121 and 14 CFR 135 starting in 1997, which caused many aircraft to be reclassified.

Units: Number of aircraft involved in fatal accidents.

Table 6.15: Aircraft Damaged or Destroyed Through Sabotage, Suicide, or Terrorism, 1986–2007

Date	Location	Operator	Fatalities Total	Aboard Flight
April 2, 1986	Near Athens, Greece	Trans World	4	4
December 7, 1987	San Luis Obispo, CA	Pacific Southwest	43	43
December 21, 1988	Lockerbie, Scotland	Pan American	270	259
April 17, 1992	Lexington, KY	Mesaba Airlines	0	0
April 7, 1994	Memphis, TN	Federal Express	0	0
September 11, 2001	New York, NY	American Airlines	*	92
September 11, 2001	New York, NY	United Airlines	*	65
September 11, 2001	Arlington, VA	American Airlines	*	64
September 11, 2001	Shanksville, PA	United Airlines	*	44

Source: National Transportation Safety Board, *Aviation Accident Statistics 2007*, table 12.

Notes: Fatalities resulting from the September 11, 2001 terrorist attacks are excluded, other than those of the passengers on board the aircraft.

Units: Number of fatalities among passengers and overall.

Table 6.16: Waterborne Transportation Accidents and Property Damage, 1970–2005

	Fatalities	Injuries	Accidents	Vessels Involved	Property Damage
1970	178	105	2,582	4,063	NA
1975	243	97	3,310	5,685	NA
1980	206	180	4,624	7,694	NA
1985	131	172	3,439	5,694	NA
1990	85	175	3,613	5,494	NA
1991	30	110	2,222	3,514	NA
1992	97	170	5,583	7,190	$201.7
1993	105	171	6,126	7,913	181.5
1994	77	182	6,743	9,030	264.4
1995	53	154	5,349	7,802	159.0
1996	55	254	5,260	7,695	200.8
1997	48	120	5,504	7,802	158.2
1998	69	130	5,767	7,824	234.9
1999	58	152	5,526	7,265	177.1
2000	53	150	5,403	7,103	180.5
2001	53	210	4,958	6,439	100.9
2002	65	183	5,719	6,915	502.3
2003	62	251	5,018	5,773	196.5
2004	50	216	4,907	5,975	215.4
2005	61	155	4,901	6,193	811.0

Source: Bureau of Transportation Statistics, *National Transportation Statistics 2007*, table 2-41.

Notes: 'Fatalities' include people who died or were declared missing following an accident. Since accidents can involve more than one vessel, the number of vessels involved is given separately, and exceeds the number of accidents.

Units: Number of incidents and vessels; property damage in millions of current dollars.

Table 6.17: Recreational Boating Safety, 1995–2007

	Number			Per 100,000 Registered Boats		
	Fatalities	**Injuries**	**Accidents**	**Fatalities**	**Injuries**	**Accidents**
1995	829	4,141	8,019	7.1	35.3	68.3
1996	709	4,442	8,026	6.0	37.4	67.6
1997	821	4,555	8,047	6.7	37.0	65.4
1998	815	4,612	8,061	6.5	36.7	64.1
1999	734	4,315	7,931	5.8	33.9	62.3
2000	701	4,355	7,740	5.5	34.1	60.6
2001	681	4,274	6,419	5.3	33.2	49.9
2002	750	4,062	5,705	5.8	31.6	44.4
2003	703	3,888	5,438	5.5	30.4	42.5
2004	676	3,363	4,904	5.3	26.3	38.4
2005	697	3,451	4,969	5.4	26.7	38.4
2006	710	3,474	4,967	5.6	27.3	39.0
2007	685	3,673	5,191	5.3	28.5	40.3

Source: US Coast Guard, *Boating Statistics 2005*, pages 4 and 5; *2007*, tables 29 and 31.

Notes: Boat registration is handled by the individual states, whose methods may differ. Since fatalities occur on both registered and unregistered boats, fatality rates contain some uncertainty.
The federal threshold of property damage for reporting accidents was $500 prior to July 2001, and $2,000 thereafter.

Units: Number of incidents; rate per 100,000 registered boats.

Table 6.18: Alcohol Use in Boating Accidents, Fatalities, and Injuries, by State, 2007

	Accidents		Fatalities		Non-fatal Injuries	
	Total	% With Alcohol Contributing	Total	% With Alcohol Contributing	Total	% With Alcohol Contributing
United States	*5,191*	*8.1%*	*685*	*22.9%*	*3,673*	*10.2%*
Alabama	96	19.8	11	27.3	50	28.0
Alaska	48	16.7	17	41.2	24	16.7
Arizona	167	7.8	8	37.5	118	17.8
Arkansas	81	19.8	18	33.3	55	50.9
California	601	5.7	55	20.0	482	7.9
Colorado	54	7.4	7	14.3	41	4.9
Connecticut	61	8.2	8	37.5	38	10.5
Delaware	15	6.7	2	0.0	2	0.0
District of Columbia	4	0.0	0	NA	0	NA
Florida	663	5.7	75	26.7	387	4.9
Georgia	139	5.8	18	16.7	101	5.0
Hawaii	10	0.0	2	0.0	6	0.0
Idaho	63	4.8	8	0.0	23	0.0
Illinois	107	13.1	13	15.4	60	18.3
Indiana	32	9.4	7	57.1	18	11.1
Iowa	47	25.5	9	55.6	31	12.9
Kansas	24	12.5	6	16.7	14	21.4
Kentucky	59	16.9	13	46.2	45	20.0
Louisiana	119	15.1	30	20.0	99	17.2
Maine	90	7.8	15	33.3	56	5.4
Maryland	170	4.7	10	20.0	120	4.2
Massachusetts	36	16.7	9	33.3	32	3.1
Michigan	185	2.7	34	11.8	111	1.8
Minnesota	123	13.8	15	13.3	105	14.3
Mississippi	31	12.9	7	14.3	32	18.8
Missouri	168	7.7	7	57.1	148	7.4
Montana	24	12.5	4	0.0	16	25.0
Nebraska	31	12.9	7	42.9	46	4.3

(continued on next page)

Table 6.18: Alcohol Use in Boating Accidents, Fatalities, and Injuries, by State, 2007

	Accidents		Fatalities		Non-fatal Injuries	
	Total	% With Alcohol Contributing	Total	% With Alcohol Contributing	Total	% With Alcohol Contributing
United States	*5,191*	*8.1%*	*685*	*22.9%*	*3,673*	*10.2%*
Nevada	76	2.6	5	0.0	53	3.8
New Hampshire	54	5.6	6	16.7	27	0.0
New Jersey	136	0.7	8	0.0	52	3.8
New Mexico	38	5.3	1	100.0	23	17.4
New York	180	7.8	21	38.1	133	6.0
North Carolina	158	12.0	19	21.1	129	18.6
North Dakota	10	0.0	0	NA	9	0.0
Ohio	121	14.0	14	35.7	79	16.5
Oklahoma	56	12.5	12	25.0	71	19.7
Oregon	60	3.3	9	11.1	33	6.1
Pennsylvania	64	6.3	11	18.2	59	6.8
Rhode Island	44	9.1	4	0.0	22	22.7
South Carolina	104	4.8	16	0.0	72	13.9
South Dakota	12	8.3	2	0.0	10	10.0
Tennessee	146	8.2	17	17.6	100	8.0
Texas	197	8.6	46	15.2	164	6.7
Utah	71	1.4	5	0.0	80	0.0
Vermont	3	0.0	1	0.0	0	NA
Virginia	145	4.1	12	8.3	108	3.7
Washington	97	13.4	26	38.5	74	9.5
West Virginia	26	11.5	7	14.3	23	13.0
Wisconsin	119	8.4	18	22.2	77	23.4
Wyoming	8	25.0	4	25.0	5	60.0

Source: US Coast Guard, *Boating Statistics 2007*, tables 8 and 30.

Notes: Alcohol is said to be a contributing factor if it acted as a direct or indirect cause of the accident.
The total for the United States includes areas outside the 50 states (Puerto Rico, Guam, Virgin Islands, Americna Samoa, North Marianas, and 3 or more miles offshore).

Units: Number of incidents; percent with alcohol as a contributing factor.

Table 6.19:   Railroad-Crossing Fatalities, 1980–2007

	Passengers	Employees	Trespassers	Total
1980	4	108	566	1,417
1985	3	52	474	1,036
1990	3	43	700	1,297
1991	8	39	663	1,194
1992	3	46	646	1,170
1993	58	57	675	1,279
1994	5	34	682	1,226
1995	0	43	660	1,146
1996	12	42	620	1,039
1997	6	48	646	1,063
1998	4	34	644	1,008
1999	14	43	570	932
2000	4	28	570	937
2001	3	26	673	971
2002	7	31	646	951
2003	3	25	635	868
2004	3	29	621	895
2005	16	30	593	888
2006	2	23	648	910
2007	4	22	630	856

Source: Bureau of Transportation Statistics, *National Transportation Statistics 2008*, table 2-35.

Notes: Includes fatalities occuring between trains and other vehicles or pedestrians at railroad-crossings.
Groups shown do not add to total. Some data has been revised from earlier editions.

Units: Number of railroad fatalities.

Table 6.20: Public Transportation Fatalities, Injuries, and Accidents, by Mode, 2004

	Fatalities	Injuries	Collisions	Property Damage
Total	*248*	*18,982*	*7,703*	*$43,373*
Automated guideway	1	15	0	0
Commuter rail	86	1,364	50	15,373
Paratransit	0	296	214	964
Heavy rail	59	4,738	150	3,678
Light rail	22	633	459	2,757
Bus	77	11,898	6,802	20,461
Vanpool	3	38	28	140

Source: American Public Transportation Association, *Public Transportation Fact Book, 58th ed*, tables 32, 33, 35, and 36.

Notes: Data for paratransit, buses, and vanpools may understate incidents because many of these systems do not report data to the Federal Transit Administration.
Only injuries requiring immediate medical treatment are considered.
Only collisions and property damage resulting in at least $7,500 in property damage are considered.

Units: Number of fatalities, injuries, and collisions; property damage in thousands of dollars.

Table 6.21: Crimes Reported on Transit Vehicles by Transit Mode, 2005 and 2006

	Motor Bus	Commuter Rail	Demand-responsive	Heavy Rail	Light Rail	Total
2005						
Violent Crime						
Homicide	1	0	0	0	0	1
Rape	11	2	0	4	6	23
Robbery	535	107	2	630	377	1,656
Aggravated assault	760	115	6	249	177	1,332
Property Crime						
Theft	1,593	1,224	2	2,204	856	6,007
Vehicle theft	382	54	0	490	434	1,361
Burglary	142	112	1	25	105	393
Arson	11	2	0	2	12	27
Arrests						
Other assaults	703	181	3	462	164	1,530
Vandalism	568	276	5	209	233	1,298
Trespassing	1,138	730	12	634	677	3,220
Fare evasion	21,787	194	2	15,901	91,701	129,590
2006						
Violent Crime						
Homicide	0	2	0	0	0	2
Rape	1	0	0	3	1	5
Robbery	730	126	14	861	463	2,222
Aggravated assault	1,007	172	19	334	217	1,768
Property Crime						
Theft	1,520	1,449	13	2,527	847	6,409
Vehicle theft	229	126	8	388	298	1,051
Burglary	100	154	1	54	367	681
Arson	13	1	0	5	6	26
Arrests						
Other assaults	1,023	196	29	630	214	2,141
Vandalism	589	507	5	213	408	1,748
Trespassing	1,392	1,033	36	853	1,151	4,503
Fare evasion	4,372	11,768	448	12,611	96,868	126,092

Source: Bureau of Transportation Statistics, *National Transportation Statistics 2007*, table 2-34; *2008*, table 2-34.

Notes: 'Demand responsive' refers to vehicles on a nonfixed route and schedule, that operate in response to calls from passengers or their agents to the transit operator or dispatcher. Data is from transit agencies in urbanized areas with populations over 200,000.

Units: Number of crimes reported or arrests made.

Chapter 7

Travel and Shipping

Chapter 7 Highlights

Chapter 7 contains information on travel and shipping. Since 1980, passenger-miles traveled have increased greatly for air and highway modes of transit, but only slightly for public transit systems, including railways and Amtrak (table 7.01). The vast majority (nearly 90%) of personal trips over 50 miles are taken by car, although total trip-miles are about even between cars and airplanes, because planes are used for longer trips. Most long-distance trips are taken for pleasure, either vacation or visiting relatives (table 7.02). Over 80% of passenger boardings took place at the 50 busiest airports, which showed nearly a 29% increase in passengers from 1996 to 2007 (table 7.04). For foreign trips, the most common distinations and origins were Japan, the United Kingdom, and Mexico (table 7.05 – Canada is usually the most frequent destination or place of origin but that data was not available). Just under three quarters of flights were reported as being on-time in 2007, down slightly from previous years (table 7.06).

Over 70% of domestic US freight (by value and weight) went by truck (table 7.09). The top goods for shipment by value were electronic goods, motor vehicle products, textiles and leather, and pharmaceuticals, while the top goods by weight were coal, gasoline, and minerals (table 7.10). From 1970 to 2003, the amount of crude oil shipped by pipeline decreased while the amount shipped by water increased; the opposite pattern held for refined petroleum products (table 7.12). Table 7.13 lists the top 50 gateways for foreign trade and the type of transit involved; nearly half of the total value came from water ports, which comprised 21 of the top 50 gateways. Waterborne freight has increased in recent years, especially for foreign imports (table 7.14).

Table 7.01:   Passenger-Miles Traveled by Mode, 1980–2005

	Air	Highway	Transit	Intercity Rail/ Amtrak
1980	219,068	2,653,510	39,854	4,503
1985	290,136	3,012,953	39,581	4,825
1990	358,873	3,561,209	41,143	6,057
1991	350,185	3,600,322	40,703	6,273
1992	365,564	3,697,719	40,241	6,091
1993	372,130	3,768,066	39,384	6,199
1994	398,199	3,837,512	39,585	5,921
1995	414,688	3,868,070	39,808	5,545
1996	446,652	3,968,386	41,378	5,050
1997	463,112	4,089,366	42,339	5,166
1998	476,362	4,200,635	44,128	5,304
1999	502,457	4,304,270	45,857	5,330
2000	531,329	4,390,076	47,666	5,498
2001	502,406	4,643,794	49,070	5,559
2002	482,310	4,667,038	48,324	5,468
2003	505,158	4,721,869	47,903	5,680
2004	557,893	4,844,452	49,073	5,511
2005	583,689	4,884,557	NA	5,381

Source: Bureau of Transportation Statistics, *National Transportation Statistics 2007*, table 1-37.

Notes: 'Transit' includes buses, light rail, heavy rail, trolley buses, commuter rail, demand-responsive transportation, and ferry boats, except for 1980 data, which excludes demand-responsive and most rural and smaller systems.

Transit rail modes measure distance traveled in car-miles, which measure the distance traveled by each car on a train (e.g., a 10-car train traveling 1 mile would travel 10 car-miles).

Units: Number of passenger-miles traveled in millions.

Table 7.02:   Long-Distance Travel in the US, 2001

	Person-trips	Person-miles	Personal-use Vehicle Trips	Personal-use Vehicle-miles
Total	*2,617,126*	*1,360,813*	*2,336,094*	*760,325*
By Principal Means of Transportation				
Personal-use vehicle	89.3%	55.9%	NA	NA
Airplane	7.4	41.0	NA	NA
Commercial airplane	7.1	40.5	NA	NA
Bus	2.1	2.0	NA	NA
Intercity	0.9	0.7	NA	NA
Charter or tour	1.2	1.3	NA	NA
Train	0.8	0.8	NA	NA
Ship, boat, or ferry	0.1	0.3	NA	NA
By Roundtrip Distance				
Under 200 miles	47.7%	12.9%	51.8%	22.4%
200–299 miles	17.4	8.2	18.8	14.0
300–499 miles	14.4	10.7	15.2	17.9
500–999 miles	10.3	13.6	9.9	20.7
1,000–1,999 miles	5.1	13.9	3.1	12.8
2,000 miles or more	5.1	40.8	1.3	12.1
Mean	520	NA	325	NA
Median	209	NA	194	NA
By Main Purpose of Trip				
Commute	12.6%	5.0%	13.6%	7.6%
Business	15.3	20.5	13.5	13.2
Pleasure	56.0	60.8	56.6	62.7
Visit relatives	25.3	26.2	26.1	29.0
Leisure	30.1	33.5	30.0	33.0
By Nights Away From Home				
None	56.2%	23.6%	60.0%	36.7%
1–3 nights	31.4	31.7	31.2	37.5
4–7 nights	8.8	24.0	6.6	16.4
8 more more nights	3.6	20.7	2.2	9.4
Mean, excluding none	3.5	NA	3.0	NA

Source: Bureau of Transportation Statistics, *Transportation Statistics Annual Report, December 2006*, table F-1.

Notes: For round trips to destinations at least 50 miles away.
Groups may not add to total; not all groups are shown.

Units: Number of trips in thousands; number of person-miles and vehicle-miles in millions; percent of total; mean and median distance in miles; mean time away from home in nights.

Table 7.03:   Air Traffic Activity, 2005–2007

	2005	2006	2007
Aircraft Handled by FAA Air Route Traffic Control Centers			
Total	*47,812*	*46,300*	*46,748*
Air carrier	24,871	24,486	24,891
Air taxi	10,007	9,437	9,826
General aviation	8,313	8,255	8,246
Military	3,991	4,122	3,785
Airport Operations Logged by FAA Towers			
Total	*46,202*	*44,663*	*44,067*
Air carrier	13,253	13,132	13,445
Air taxi	10,770	10,138	9,897
General aviation	20,490	19,714	19,170
Military	1,689	1,679	1,555
Instrument Operations Logged by FAA Towers			
Total	*46,884*	*45,793*	*45,073*
Air carrier	14,153	14,108	14,480
Air taxi	12,654	11,948	11,645
General aviation	17,313	17,095	16,487
Military	2,764	2,642	2,461
Flight Services Logged By:			
Total	*23,414*	*20,596*	*8,511*
Flight service stations	895	852	796
Automated flight service stations	22,519	19,744	7,715

Source: Federal Aviation Administration, *Administrator's Fact Book, April 2007*, page 8; *January 2008*, page 8; *July 2008*, page 8.

Notes: All data for 2007 is preliminary as of April 10, 2008.

Units: Number of aircraft handled in thousands.

Table 7.04: Passengers Boarded at 50 Busiest US Airports, 1996 and 2007

	Enplaned Passengers, 1996	Enplaned Passengers, 2007	Percent Change, 1996–2007
William B. Hartsfield-Atlanta Intl	30,407,111	42,703,736	40.4%
Chicago O'Hare Intl	30,526,401	34,213,188	12.1
Dallas/Ft Worth Intl	26,639,351	28,183,932	5.8
Los Angeles Intl	22,799,083	23,795,532	4.4
Denver Intl	15,246,315	23,731,234	55.7
McCarran Intl	14,116,485	21,490,165	52.2
Phoenix Sky Harbor Intl	14,807,863	20,563,541	38.9
George Bush Intercontinental	11,621,912	20,091,915	72.9
Detroit Metro Wayne County	14,117,157	17,278,955	22.4
Minneapolis-St Paul Intl	12,616,095	16,895,319	33.9
John F. Kennedy Intl	9,703,787	16,753,232	72.6
Newark Intl	12,952,399	16,613,599	28.3
Orlando Intl	10,846,685	16,590,473	53.0
Charlotte-Douglas Intl	10,007,911	16,506,138	64.9
Philadelphia Intl	8,571,888	15,314,696	78.7
Seattle-Tacoma Intl	11,486,892	14,912,345	29.8
San Francisco Intl	16,308,203	14,848,751	-8.9
Miami Intl	11,907,895	13,475,854	13.2
Gen. Edward Lawrence Logan Intl	10,653,824	12,484,054	17.2
La Guardia	9,593,965	12,107,802	26.2
Salt Lake City Intl	9,462,849	10,560,206	11.6
Fort Lauderdale - Hollywood Intl	4,848,058	10,499,884	116.6
Washington Dulles Intl	4,758,242	10,392,761	118.4
Baltimore-Washington Intl	5,907,427	10,293,142	74.2
Chicago Midway	4,436,034	9,127,806	105.8
Tampa Intl	5,720,761	9,126,130	59.5
Honolulu Intl	9,035,709	9,090,304	0.6
San Diego Intl / Lindbergh Field	6,549,170	9,046,624	38.1
Ronald Reagan Washington National	6,771,891	8,934,441	31.9
Cincinnati-Northern Kentucky Intl	7,301,767	7,727,434	5.8

(continued on next page)

Table 7.04: Passengers Boarded at 50 Busiest US Airports, 1996 and 2007

	Enplaned Passengers, 1996	Enplaned Passengers, 2007	Percent Change, 1996–2007
Portland Intl	6,125,579	7,129,216	16.4
Lambert-St Louis Intl	13,546,822	7,085,075	-47.7
Metropolitan Oakland Intl	4,684,494	7,065,844	50.8
Kansas City Intl	4,820,290	5,816,384	20.7
Cleveland-Hopkins Intl	5,286,823	5,554,715	5.1
Memphis Intl	3,944,376	5,545,386	40.6
Sacramento Intl	3,321,408	5,315,066	60.0
San Jose Intl	4,825,943	5,183,512	7.4
Luis Munoz Marin Intl	4,549,722	5,051,698	11.0
John Wayne-Orange County	3,532,746	4,945,927	40.0
Raleigh-Durham Intl	2,879,935	4,940,400	71.5
Nashville Intl	3,254,956	4,866,879	49.5
Pittsburgh Intl	9,348,286	4,856,561	-48.0
William P. Hobby	4,026,140	4,236,251	5.2
Austin-Bergstrom Intl	2,829,581	4,173,476	47.5
Indianapolis Intl	3,328,005	4,078,718	22.6
Love Field	3,540,539	3,982,921	12.5
Southwest Florida Intl	1,945,044	3,886,365	99.8
San Antonio Intl	3,319,535	3,821,289	15.1
Columbus Intl	NA	3,768,621	NA
Total top 50	*461,383,023*	*594,657,497*	*28.9*
All airports	*558,559,160*	*726,354,887*	*30.0*

Source: Bureau of Transportation Statistics, *National Transportation Statistics 2007*, table 1-41. US Department of Transportation, Bureau of Transportation Statistics, *Air Carrier Summary Data*, table T3: US Air Carrier Airport Activity Statistics, accessed online September 8, 2008.

Notes: Order is based on 2007 rankings.
Measures enplaned passengers on large certified air carriers in the 50 states, DC, and other US territories.

Units: Number of passenger-miles traveled in millions.

Table 7.05:   Travel to and From Foreign Countries, by Country, 2006

	Departures	Arrivals
Total Passengers (excludes Canada)	59,477	62,951
United States airports	35,686	32,735
Foreign airports	23,791	30,217
Selected Countries of Departure/Arrival:		
Australia	879	808
Bahama Islands	1,252	1,509
Belgium	351	364
Bermuda	289	358
Brazil	1,147	1,154
China/Taiwan	1,048	1,141
Colombia	790	787
Denmark	359	350
Dominican Republic	1,695	1,961
France	3,008	2,941
Germany	4,134	4,252
Greece	101	163
Haiti	285	302
Hong Kong	978	1,002
Ireland	993	1,319
Israel	475	576
Italy	1,310	1,301
Jamaica	1,335	1,499
Japan	5,708	5,769
Mexico	7,615	8,471
Netherlands	1,877	1,944
Netherland Antilles	414	441
Panama Republic	463	468
Philippines	341	496
South Korea	1,386	1,545
Spain	862	855
Switzerland	699	712
United Kingdom	8,156	8,432
Venezuela	552	535

Source: Bureau of Transportation Statistics, *National Transportation Statistics 2008*, tables 1-42 and 1-43.

Notes: Figures for travel to and from Canada come from a separate source, which is unavailable at this time, and are not included in the US or foreign totals.

Units: Number of passengers in thousands.

Table 7.06: Flight Delays and Cancellations, 1995–2007

	Total Flights	% On-time	Departed Late	Arrived Late	Cancelled	Diverted
1995	5,327	78.6%	828	1,039	92	10
1996	5,352	74.5	974	1,220	129	14
1997	5,412	78.0	847	1,084	98	12
1998	5,385	77.2	870	1,070	145	13
1999	5,528	76.1	937	1,153	154	14
2000	5,683	72.6	1,132	1,356	187	14
2001	5,968	77.4	954	1,104	231	13
2002	5,271	82.1	717	868	65	8
2003	6,489	82.0	834	1,058	101	11
2004	7,129	78.1	1,188	1,421	128	14
2005	7,141	77.4	1,279	1,466	134	14
2006	7,142	75.5	1,425	1,616	122	16
2007	7,453	73.4	1,572	1,803	161	17

Source: US Dept of Transportation, Research and Innovative Technology Administration, *Transportation Statistics Annual Report 2007*, table C-3.

Notes: Departures and arivals are considered late if they are more than 15 minutes later than the scheduled time.

Cancellations must be listed within a carrier's reservation system within 7 days of the scheduled departure and then not take off.

Diverted flights must take off from the scheduled airport, but land at a different airport than the scheduled arrival.

Units: Number of flights in thousands; percent of total flights.

Table 7.07: Passengers Boarded and Denied Boarding by US Air Carriers, 1990–2007

| | Boarded | Denied Boarding | | |
	Total	Voluntary	Involuntary	Total
1990	420,696	561	67	628
1991	429,190	599	47	646
1992	445,271	718	46	764
1993	449,184	632	51	683
1994	457,286	771	53	824
1995	460,277	794	49	842
1996	480,555	899	58	957
1997	502,960	1,018	54	1,071
1998	514,170	1,091	45	1,136
1999	523,081	1,024	46	1,070
2000	543,344	1,062	57	1,120
2001	477,970	861	39	900
2002	467,205	803	34	837
2003	485,797	727	42	769
2004	522,308	702	45	747
2005	516,553	552	45	597
2006	552,445	619	55	674
2007	571,661	622	64	686

Source: Bureau of Transportation Statistics, *National Transportation Statistics 2008*, table 1-58.

Notes: Passengers who are denied boarding are those who hold confirmed reservations and are 'bumped' due to overbooking. Does not include those affected by canceled, delayed, or diverted flights.
Some figures have been adjusted from previous reports.

Units: Number of passengers in thousands.

Table 7.08: Aviation Forecasts, 2005, 2007, and 2009

	Estimated FY 2005	Estimated FY 2007	Estimated FY 2009
FAA Facility Workload			
Type of Aircraft Handled			
Total	*47.5*	*46.8*	*51.0*
Air carrier	25.0	25.0	27.5
Air taxi/commuter	10.1	9.7	10.6
General aviation	8.4	8.3	9.1
Military	4.1	3.8	3.8
Operations Logged			
Airport	63.1	61.1	65.0
Instrument	49.0	45.4	47.9
Civil aviation			
Certified Route Air Carrier			
Revenue passenger enplanements	587.3	605.6	677.1
Revenue passenger miles	709.1	749.4	876.9
Air carrier aircraft	4,974	4,980	5,511
General Aviation			
Hours flown*	28.3	27.9	31.3
Active aircraft*	214.6	225.0	238.1
Estimated Fuel Consumed by US Domestic Civil Aviation			
Jet Fuel			
Air carrier	19,356	19,583	22,778
General aviation	1,009	1,650	2,387
Aviation Gas			
Air carrier	2	2	2
General aviation	290	348	365
*Active pilots**	*609,603*	*590,349*	*591,830*

Source: Federal Aviation Administration, *Administrator's Fact Book, April 2007*, page 22; *July 2008*, page 22.

Notes: *Calendar years 2005, 2007 and 2009 (projected), respectively.
As of March 30, 2008.

Units: Aircraft handled, operations logged, revenue passenger enplanements, and hours flown in millions; revenue passenger miles in billions; jet fuel consumed in millions of gallons; number of pilots in thousands.

Table 7.09: Freight Activity in the US, Value and Weight of Shipments by Mode, 1993, 1997, and 2002

	Value			Weight		
	1993	1997	2002	1993	1997	2002
Total for All Modes	$5,846.3	$6,944.0	$8,397.2	9,688.5	11,089.7	11,667.9
Single modes	4,941.5	5,719.6	7,049.4	8,922.3	10,436.5	11,086.7
Truck	4,403.5	4,981.5	6,235.0	6,385.9	7,700.7	7,842.8
For-hire truck	2,625.1	2,901.3	3,757.1	2,808.3	3,402.6	3,657.3
Private truck	1,755.8	2,036.5	2,445.3	3,543.5	4,137.3	4,149.7
Rail	247.4	319.6	310.9	1,544.1	1,549.8	1,873.9
Water	61.6	75.8	89.3	505.4	563.4	681.2
Shallow draft	40.7	53.9	57.5	362.5	414.8	458.6
Great Lakes	NA	1.5	0.8	33.0	38.4	38.0
Deep draft	19.7	20.4	31.0	109.9	110.2	184.6
Air	139.1	229.1	265.0	3.1	4.5	3.8
Pipeline	89.8	113.5	149.2	483.6	618.2	685.0
Multiple modes	662.6	945.9	1,079.2	225.7	216.7	216.7
Parcel, US Postal Service, or courier	563.3	855.9	987.7	18.9	23.7	25.5
Truck and rail	83.1	75.7	69.9	40.6	54.2	43.0
Truck and water	9.4	8.2	14.4	68.0	33.2	23.3
Rail and water	3.6	1.8	3.3	79.2	79.3	105.0
Other multiple modes	3.2	4.3	3.8	18.9	26.2	19.8
Other/unknown modes	242.3	278.6	268.6	540.5	436.5	364.6

Source: Bureau of Transportation Statistics, *National Transportation Statistics 2007*, table 1-52.

Notes: Single-mode truck shipments include only those that went by private truck, for-hire truck, or a combination of both.
'Pipeline' excludes most shipments of crude oil.
Numbers may not add to total.
Data for 2002 changed from the 1987 Standard Industrial Classification system (SIC) to the 1997 North American Industry Classification System (NAICS); caution is advised when directly comparing the results for 2002 with those of previous years.

Units: Value in billions of dollars; weight in millions of tons.

Table 7.10: Domestic Freight Shipments for Selected Products, 2002

	Value	Tons	Ton-miles	Value per Ton	Miles per Shipment
All Commodities	*$8,397.2*	*11,667.9*	*3,137.9*	*$719.7*	*546*
Live animals and fish	7.4	6.1	1.6	1,211.2	530
Cereal grains	53.8	561.1	264.2	95.9	138
Animal feed and products of animal origin	52.1	228.0	51.2	228.7	167
Meat, fish, seafood, and their preparations	201.3	84.5	41.4	2,382.1	162
Milled grain and bakery products	113.4	109.3	49.0	1,037.2	189
Alcoholic beverages	109.0	89.4	25.7	1,218.7	55
Tobacco products	69.9	4.4	1.0	15,988.1	334
Metallic ores and concentrates	14.0	98.3	63.0	142.7	474
Coal	22.9	1,239.9	686.3	18.4	120
Gasoline and aviation turbine fuel	279.4	1,063.6	117.2	262.7	52
Fuel oils	116.1	549.0	55.5	211.5	32
Other coal and petroleum products	82.1	448.0	93.0	183.3	102
Basic chemicals	153.7	347.7	116.0	442.0	417
Pharmaceutical products	479.1	24.3	11.3	19,741.1	693
Fertilizers	34.0	264.3	87.6	128.8	157
Plastics and rubber	325.7	140.0	80.8	2,326.7	424
Wood products	158.6	345.9	120.2	458.4	242
Pulp, newsprint, paper, and paperboard	102.5	137.1	78.2	747.8	206
Paper or paperboard articles	103.7	69.2	23.4	1,498.5	282
Printed products	134.5	34.0	17.0	3,952.7	816
Textiles and leather	466.4	51.2	31.8	9,104.3	940
Nonmetallic mineral products	150.0	968.0	135.9	154.9	357
Base metal (primary or semifinished forms, or finished basic shapes)	259.8	328.1	121.3	792.0	270
Machinery	484.2	63.4	34.5	7,637.7	377
Electronic and other electrical equipment, components, and office equipment	890.8	49.6	30.3	17,962.6	713
Motorized and other vehicles and parts	748.6	133.1	59.0	5,624.5	395
Precision instruments and apparatus	225.1	18.4	3.9	12,264.1	922
Furniture, mattresses, lamps, and lighting	139.7	32.5	13.7	4,293.2	515
Waste and scrap	37.9	217.2	48.0	174.4	166
Mixed freight	840.3	299.9	52.8	2,801.8	329

Source: US Bureau of the Census, 2002 Economic Census, *Commodity Flow Survey*, table 5a.
Notes: Estimates exclude shipments of crude oil.
Figures may not add to total.
Units: Value in billions of dollars; weight in million tons; distance in billion ton-miles; value per ton in dollars; average distance in miles.

Table 7.11: Average Length of Haul for Domestic Freight by Mode, 1960–2004

	Air	Truck	Rail	Coastwise Water	Lakewise Water	Crude Oil Pipeline	Petroleum Product Pipeline
1960	953	272	461	1,496	522	325	269
1965	943	259	503	1,501	494	320	335
1970	1,014	263	515	1,509	506	300	357
1975	1,082	286	541	1,362	530	633	516
1980	1,052	363	616	1,915	536	871	414
1985	1,157	366	665	1,972	524	777	391
1990	1,389	391	726	1,604	553	812	387
1991	1,346	398	751	1,705	535	822	379
1992	1,391	410	763	1,762	519	830	379
1993	1,347	407	794	1,650	514	790	406
1994	1,221	392	817	1,652	508	778	414
1995	1,160	416	843	1,652	514	797	402
1996	1,181	426	842	1,526	508	779	413
1997	1,077	435	851	1,330	507	781	413
1998	1,078	442	835	1,261	505	767	420
1999	1,001	458	835	1,279	501	766	418
2000	982	473	843	1,251	506	NA	NA
2001	973	485	859	1,228	509	NA	NA
2002	NA	NA	853	1,219	529	NA	NA
2003	NA	NA	862	1,248	530	NA	NA
2004	NA	NA	902	1,269	538	NA	NA

Source: Bureau of Transportation Statistics, *National Transportation Statistics 2007*, table 1-35.

Notes: Average length of haul is calculated by dividing ton-miles by total weight of haul.

Units: Average haul length in miles.

Table 7.12:   Crude Oil and Pretroleum Transportation by Mode, 1975–2003

	Total	Pipelines	Water Carriers	Motor Carriers	Railroads
Crude Oil					
1975	331.5	86.9%	12.2%	0.4%	0.5%
1980	753.0	48.2	51.4	0.3	0.1
1985	786.2	42.5	57.1	0.2	0.1
1990	628.2	53.3	46.4	0.2	0.1
1995	586.0	57.3	42.3	0.3	0.1
1996	543.2	62.3	37.3	0.3	0.1
1997	486.9	69.3	30.3	0.3	0.1
1998	454.1	73.6	26.0	0.4	0.1
1999	423.0	75.9	23.6	0.3	0.1
2000	376.0	75.4	24.2	0.3	0.1
2001	376.6	73.6	26.0	0.3	0.1
2002	384.0	74.6	24.9	0.3	0.1
2003	380.4	74.8	24.7	0.3	0.1
Refined Petroleum Products					
1975	515.2	42.5%	50.0%	5.1%	2.4%
1980	492.3	45.8	46.8	5.0	2.4
1985	409.3	56.2	34.5	6.6	2.7
1990	448.6	55.6	35.2	6.3	2.9
1995	458.9	57.8	33.4	5.4	3.5
1996	479.0	58.6	32.2	5.8	3.3
1997	469.6	59.4	31.6	5.5	3.4
1998	475.7	60.1	30.9	5.6	3.4
1999	489.9	60.5	30.1	5.6	3.7
2000	497.3	59.1	30.8	6.1	4.0
2001	493.2	60.6	29.6	6.0	3.8
2002	480.6	62.3	27.4	6.1	4.1
2003	502.9	60.8	29.0	6.3	3.8

Source: Bureau of Transportation Statistics, *National Transportation Statistics 2007*, table 1-55.

Notes: The large increase in crude oil transport by water between 1975 and 1980 reflects the opening of the Alaska pipeline, moving crude oil to US-based refineries.

Units: Total transportation in ton-miles; percent of total by mode of transport.

Table 7.13: Top 50 Foreign Trade Gateways in US, 2006

Gateway	Type	Total Shipment Value	Imports	Exports
Port of Los Angeles, CA	Water	$170.0	$143.7	$26.3
Port of New York, NY and NJ	Water	149.3	116.1	33.2
JFK International Airport, NY	Air	147.8	79.4	68.4
Port of Detroit, MI	Land	137.2	64.5	72.8
Port of Long Beach, CA	Water	134.7	113.3	21.4
Port of Laredo, TX	Land	104.0	58.2	45.8
Port of Houston, TX	Water	102.9	60.9	41.9
Los Angeles International Airport, CA	Air	79.1	38.0	41.0
Chicago, IL	Air	78.1	46.7	31.3
Port of Buffalo-Niagara Falls, NY	Land	75.5	40.0	35.5
Port of Huron, MI	Land	70.3	44.9	25.5
San Francisco International Airport, CA	Air	63.8	34.3	29.5
Port of Charleston, SC	Water	55.1	39.1	16.1
Port of El Paso, TX	Land	46.7	25.7	21.0
Anchorage, AK	Air	44.6	33.2	11.5
Port of Norfolk Harbor, VA	Water	44.5	27.1	17.4
Dallas-Fort Worth, TX	Air	41.6	24.1	17.5
Port of Savannah, GA	Water	39.7	26.1	13.6
Port of Baltimore, MD	Water	36.6	27.0	9.6
Port of Seattle, WA	Water	34.6	26.0	8.6
New Orleans, LA	Air	34.1	20.0	14.2
Port of Oakland, CA	Water	33.3	23.6	9.8
Atlanta, GA	Air	33.2	20.9	12.4
Port of Tacoma, WA	Water	32.6	27.7	4.9
Miami International Airport, FL	Air	30.3	9.6	20.7
Port of Otay Mesa Station, CA	Land	28.6	18.7	9.9
Port of New Orleans, LA	Water	26.0	14.5	11.5
Cleveland, OH	Air	25.8	9.7	16.1

(continued on next page)

Table 7.13:   Top 50 Foreign Trade Gateways in US, 2006

Gateway	Type	Total Shipment Value	Imports	Exports
Port of Morgan City, LA	Water	$25.6	$25.4	$0.1
Port of Beaumont, TX	Water	22.0	20.2	1.9
Port of Jacksonville, FL	Water	21.2	12.5	8.7
Port of Philadelphia, PA	Water	20.7	19.0	1.7
Port of Miami, FL	Water	20.3	11.4	8.9
Port of Hidalgo, TX	Land	20.0	11.8	8.3
Port of Champlain-Rouses Pt., NY	Land	19.9	12.8	7.2
Port of Corpus Christi, TX	Water	19.0	15.7	3.3
Port of Nogales, AZ	Land	18.9	12.5	6.3
Port of Port Everglades, FL	Water	18.6	10.5	8.0
Port of Blaine, WA	Land	17.1	8.4	8.8
Port of Pembina, ND	Land	15.4	6.9	8.5
Newark, NJ	Air	15.2	12.1	3.1
Washington, DC	Air	15.1	10.0	5.1
Port of Portland, OR	Water	14.1	11.5	2.6
Port of Texas City, TX	Water	13.7	12.0	1.6
Boston Logan Airport, MA	Air	13.6	5.3	8.3
San Juan International Airport, PR	Air	12.6	5.0	7.6
Port of Brownsville. TX	Land	12.4	5.6	6.8
Port of Sweetgrass, MT	Land	12.2	6.0	6.3
Port of Alexandria Bay, NY	Land	12.2	7.5	4.7
Port of Portal, ND	Land	11.9	5.1	6.8
Total for top 50	*NA*	*2,271.9*	*1,460.0*	*811.9*

Source: Bureau of Transportation Statistics, *National Transportation Statistics 2008*, table 1-47.

Notes: Gateways are ranked by total value of shipments.
Totals exclude imports valued under $1,250 and exports valued under $2,500.

Units: Value of shipments in billions of current (2006) dollars.

Table 7.14: Waterborne Freight, 1967–2006

	Overall	Foreign			Domestic			
	Total	Total	Imports	Exports	Total	Inland	Coastal	Great Lakes
1967	1,336.6	466.0	276.0	190.0	870.6	398.6	214.6	153.6
1970	1,531.7	581.0	339.3	241.6	950.7	472.1	238.4	157.1
1975	1,695.0	748.7	476.6	272.1	946.3	503.9	231.9	129.3
1980	1,998.9	921.4	517.5	403.9	1,077.5	535.0	329.6	115.1
1985	1,788.4	774.3	412.7	361.6	1,014.1	534.7	309.8	92.0
1990	2,163.9	1,041.6	600.0	441.6	1,122.3	622.6	298.6	110.2
1991	2,092.1	1,013.6	555.4	458.2	1,078.6	600.4	294.5	103.4
1992	2,132.1	1,037.5	586.7	450.8	1,094.6	621.0	285.1	107.4
1993	2,128.2	1,060.0	648.8	411.3	1,068.2	607.3	271.7	109.9
1994	2,214.8	1,115.7	719.5	396.2	1,099.0	618.4	277.0	114.8
1995	2,240.4	1,147.4	672.7	474.7	1,093.0	620.3	266.6	116.1
1996	2,284.1	1,183.4	732.6	450.8	1,100.7	622.1	267.4	114.9
1997	2,333.1	1,220.6	788.3	432.3	1,112.5	630.6	263.1	122.7
1998	2,339.5	1,245.4	840.7	404.7	1,094.1	625.0	249.6	122.2
1999	2,322.6	1,260.8	860.8	400.0	1,061.8	624.6	228.8	113.9
2000	2,424.6	1,354.8	939.7	415.0	1,069.8	628.4	226.9	114.4
2001	2,393.3	1,350.8	951.8	399.0	1,042.5	619.8	223.6	100.0
2002	2,340.3	1,319.3	934.9	384.3	1,021.0	608.0	216.4	101.5
2003	2,394.3	1,378.1	1,004.8	373.3	1,016.1	609.6	223.5	89.8
2004	2,551.9	1,504.9	1,089.1	415.8	1,047.1	626.2	220.6	103.5
2005	2,527.6	1,498.7	1,096.9	401.8	1,028.9	624.0	213.7	96.2
2006	2,588.4	1,564.9	1,130.9	434.0	1,023.5	627.6	201.8	96.9

Source: US Army Corps of Engineers, Institute for Water Resources, *Waterborne Commerce of the United States: Calendar Year 2006*, tables 1-1 to 1-3.

Notes: Starting in 1996, domestic totals exclude shipments of fish.
Groups may not add to total.
Inland, coastal, and Great Lakes shipments are also known as internal, coastwise, and lakewise, respectively.

Units: Freight in millions of short tons.

Chapter 8

Roads & Infrastructure

Chapter 8 Highlights

Chapter 8 contains data on roads and the travel infrastructure. In the last few decades, highway system miles, transit rail systems, and gas pipelines have increased, while large Class I railway systems and oil pipelines have gone down (table 8.01). While roadway miles have increased overall, the increase is due to roads in urban areas. Rural roadway miles have actually decreased, which may be due either to the amount of road or the reclassification of areas as urban or rural (table 8.02). Table 8.03 rates the condition of the pavement on US roadways for 2000 and 2006. In addition, table 8.04 gives a state-by-state breakdown of urban and rural interstates, and total roads. Highway bridges in the US were also rated, and a lower percentage of US highway bridges were rated functionally deficient or obsolete in 2007 than in 1990 (table 8.05).

The number of highway vehicles and public transit vehicles have increased since 1990, while rail cars have decreased and waterborne transport has remained about the same (table 8.07). There were more aircraft and airports in 2006 than in 1995 and 2000, but fewer pilots (table 8.08). Over three quarters of the airport runways in the US were considered to be in good condition in 2006 (table 8.09).

Since 1990, there have been 401 commercial space launches, most from the United States, Russia, or elsewhere in Europe (table 8.10). Public transit buses have become almost completely compliant with ADA access regulations (table 8.11, also see table 5.17). Pipelines for oil have declined since 1980, but gas pipelines have increased significantly in the same period (table 8.12), while there are fewer ships in the US fleet, comprising a smaller share of the world's total (table 8.13).

Table 8.01: Total System Mileage by Mode, 1960–2006

	Highway	Class I Railway	Commuter Rail	Heavy Rail	Light Rail	Oil Pipeline	Gas Pipeline
1960	3,545.7	207.3	NA	NA	NA	190.9	631.0
1965	3,689.7	199.8	NA	NA	NA	210.9	767.5
1970	3,730.1	196.5	NA	NA	NA	218.7	913.3
1975	3,838.1	191.5	NA	NA	NA	225.9	979.3
1980	3,859.8	164.8	NA	NA	NA	218.4	1,051.8
1985	3,863.9	145.8	3.57	1.29	0.38	213.6	1,118.9
1990	3,866.9	119.8	4.13	1.35	0.48	208.8	1,189.2
1991	3,883.9	116.6	4.04	1.37	0.55	203.8	1,208.2
1992	3,901.1	113.1	4.01	1.40	0.56	196.5	1,216.1
1993	3,905.2	110.4	4.09	1.45	0.54	194.0	1,277.2
1994	3,906.6	109.3	4.09	1.46	0.56	190.4	1,288.4
1995	3,912.2	108.3	4.16	1.46	0.57	181.9	1,277.6
1996	3,919.7	105.8	3.68	1.48	0.64	177.5	1,323.6
1997	3,945.9	102.1	4.42	1.53	0.66	179.9	1,331.8
1998	3,906.3	100.6	5.17	1.53	0.68	178.6	1,351.2
1999	3,917.2	99.4	5.19	1.54	0.80	177.5	1,340.3
2000	3,936.2	99.3	5.21	1.56	0.83	177.0	1,369.3
2001	3,948.3	97.8	5.21	1.57	0.90	158.2	1,373.5
2002	3,966.5	100.1	6.83	1.57	0.96	161.0	1,411.4
2003	3,974.1	99.1	6.81	1.60	1.00	159.9	1,424.2
2004	3,981.5	97.7	6.88	1.60	1.19	161.7	1,462.3
2005	3,995.6	95.8	7.12	1.62	1.19	159.5	1,437.5
2006	4,016.7	94.9	8.08	1.60	1.19	169.3	NA

Source: Bureau of Transportation Statistics, *National Transportation Statistics 2008*, table 1-1.

Notes: System mileage for transit systems (commuter rail, heavy rail, and light rail) is calculated in directional route-miles, the distance in each direction over which vehicles travel while in revenue service, without regard to the number of lanes or existing rail tracks.

Units: System miles in thousands.

Table 8.02: Roadway Lane-Miles by Functional System, 1980–2006

	1980	1985	1990	1995	2000	2005	2006
Total Lane-miles	*7,922.2*	*8,018.0*	*8,051.1*	*8,158.3*	*8,224.2*	*8,371.7*	*8,420.6*
Urban							
Total	1,395.2	1,542.3	1,670.5	1,840.1	1,915.5	2,263.4	2,308.6
Interstates	48.5	57.3	62.2	71.4	73.9	86.0	87.9
Other arterials	333.7	371.6	399.4	445.8	456.2	523.8	532.9
Collectors	145.1	162.4	167.8	185.0	188.6	225.5	231.9
Local	868.0	951.0	1,041.1	1,137.9	1,196.8	1,428.0	1,455.9
Rural							
Total	6,526.9	6,475.7	6,380.6	6,318.1	6,308.7	6,108.4	6,112.0
Interstates	131.0	131.9	135.9	131.9	134.6	125.6	124.4
Other arterials	507.1	510.0	517.3	530.7	540.5	529.6	525.7
Collectors	1,431.3	1,466.8	1,467.6	1,417.4	1,414.7	1,373.3	1,372.9
Local	4,457.6	4,367.0	4,259.8	4,238.1	4,219.0	4,079.9	4,089.0

Source: Bureau of Transportation Statistics, *National Transportation Statistics 2008*, table 1-6.

Notes: For urban roads, 'other arterials' refers to other freeways and expressways, and other principal and minor arterials; for rural roads, 'other arterials' refers to principal and minor arterials. Subgroups do not add to total due to groups omitted.
The figures given assume that rural minor collectors and urban and rural local roads are two lanes wide.

Units: Number of lane-miles in thousands.

Table 8.03:   Condition of US Roadways, 2000 and 2006

	Miles Reported	Poor	Mediocre	Fair	Good	Very good
2000						
Urban						
Interstate	13,139	6.5%	21.7%	21.4%	37.1%	13.3%
Other freeways and expressways	8,796	2.8	8.1	50.7	31.6	6.8
Other principal arterials	47,890	13.2	16.8	45.1	19.4	5.4
Minor arterials	88,338	10.0	16.0	39.8	16.9	17.3
Collectors	86,030	14.7	17.4	35.7	14.2	18.0
Rural						
Interstate	32,888	2.1%	12.2%	16.9%	44.8%	23.9%
Other principal arterials	97,297	0.8	3.2	38.7	42.9	14.4
Minor arterials	136,096	1.7	5.3	46.2	35.6	11.2
Collectors	388,488	8.5	12.7	43.7	22.0	13.2
2006						
Urban						
Interstate	15,899	2.4%	19.0%	18.4%	41.4%	18.7%
Other freeways and expressways	10,659	2.9	23.9	22.7	40.1	10.3
Other principal arterials	61,064	17.5	35.6	17.3	21.4	8.2
Minor arterials	101,637	12.2	14.6	40.1	16.2	16.9
Collectors	106,843	18.8	16.1	35.1	12.9	17.1
Rural						
Interstate	30,512	1.0%	9.0%	12.8%	46.5%	30.7%
Other principal arterials	94,500	1.7	14.4	18.5	46.5	18.9
Minor arterials	134,914	3.3	21.1	22.2	41.5	11.8
Collectors	378,753	6.2	11.7	47.0	23.4	11.7

Source: Bureau of Transportation Statistics, *National Transportation Statistics 2008*, table 1-26.

Notes: Condition ratings are according to the International Roughness Rating (IRI).

Units: Number of lane-miles reported; percent of total.

Table 8.04: Roadway Lane-Miles by State, 2006

	All Roads	Urban		Rural	
	Total	Total	Interstate	Total	Interstate
United States	*8,420.6*	*2,308.6*	*87.9*	*6,112.0*	*124.4*
Alabama	200.1	47.6	1.7	152.5	2.2
Alaska	30.0	5.1	0.3	24.8	2.1
Arizona	130.9	52.1	1.0	78.8	3.9
Arkansas	202.2	24.3	0.9	177.9	1.9
California	380.3	206.4	8.9	173.9	5.9
Colorado	182.9	42.7	1.3	140.2	2.8
Connecticut	45.3	32.8	1.6	12.5	0.2
Delaware	13.4	6.6	0.3	6.8	0.0
District of Columbia	3.5	3.5	0.1	0.0	0.0
Florida	267.8	182.8	4.1	85.0	3.4
Georgia	249.5	82.9	3.4	166.6	3.2
Hawaii	9.4	5.3	0.3	4.1	0.0
Idaho	96.7	10.3	0.4	86.4	2.1
Illinois	291.3	90.8	4.1	200.5	5.5
Indiana	199.2	46.5	1.5	152.7	3.5
Iowa	235.0	25.5	0.7	209.6	2.5
Kansas	286.0	28.5	1.0	257.5	2.6
Kentucky	162.7	27.2	1.2	135.5	2.4
Louisiana	128.1	36.1	1.7	92.0	2.2
Maine	46.6	6.3	0.3	40.3	1.2
Maryland	68.3	39.1	1.9	29.2	0.9
Massachusetts	75.8	59.5	2.8	16.2	0.4
Michigan	256.0	81.1	3.4	174.9	2.6
Minnesota	271.7	37.4	1.2	234.4	2.7
Mississippi	154.8	23.5	0.8	131.3	2.0
Missouri	262.6	42.6	2.2	220.0	3.2
Montana	149.2	6.3	0.2	142.9	4.5
Nebraska	189.9	13.6	0.3	176.2	1.7
Nevada	70.9	16.6	0.6	54.3	1.8

(continued on next page)

Table 8.04:   Roadway Lane-Miles by State, 2006

| | All Roads | Urban | | Rural | |
	Total	Total	Interstate	Total	Interstate
United States	*8,420.6*	*2,308.6*	*87.9*	*6,112.0*	*124.4*
New Hampshire	32.3	10.0	0.4	22.3	0.6
New Jersey	83.9	68.8	2.5	15.1	0.4
New Mexico	133.7	18.3	0.7	115.4	3.4
New York	240.8	106.2	4.4	134.5	3.4
North Carolina	217.9	71.2	2.8	146.7	2.2
North Dakota	175.8	4.1	0.2	171.7	2.1
Ohio	265.8	100.6	4.6	165.1	3.3
Oklahoma	234.2	35.0	1.2	199.2	2.7
Oregon	132.6	27.3	0.9	105.3	2.3
Pennsylvania	252.7	96.2	3.1	156.5	4.3
Rhode Island	13.8	11.2	0.3	2.6	0.1
South Carolina	139.4	36.9	1.4	102.6	2.4
South Dakota	170.9	6.1	0.3	164.8	2.4
Tennessee	192.9	49.6	2.3	143.3	2.8
Texas	651.5	192.6	6.1	458.9	8.9
Utah	91.4	23.2	1.3	68.2	2.9
Vermont	29.6	3.0	0.2	26.6	1.1
Virginia	156.9	50.4	2.6	106.5	2.7
Washington	174.0	50.7	1.9	123.3	2.1
West Virginia	76.3	9.9	0.8	66.4	1.5
Wisconsin	236.2	48.4	1.2	187.8	2.0
Wyoming	57.8	5.7	0.4	52.1	3.3

Source: US Department of Transportation, Federal Highway Administration, *Highway Statistics 2006*, table HM-60.

Notes: The figures given assume that rural minor collectors and urban and rural local roads are two lanes wide.

Units: Number of lane-miles in thousands.

Table 8.05:   Condition of US Highway Bridges, 1990–2007

	1990	1995	2000	2005	2007
Total Bridges	572,205	581,135	589,674	595,363	599,893
% Structurally deficient	24.1%	18.0%	14.7%	12.8%	12.0%
% Functionally obsolete	17.5	13.9	13.8	13.5	13.5
Urban	108,770	122,537	133,384	142,408	151,102
% Structurally deficient	15.5%	12.4%	NA	8.8%	8.5%
% Functionally obsolete	27.8	22.4	22.0	22.0	21.9
Rural	463,435	458,598	456,290	452,955	448,791
% Structurally deficient	26.1%	19.4%	NA	14.0%	13.2%
% Functionally obsolete	15.1	11.7	11.4	10.8	10.7

Source:	Bureau of Transportation Statistics, *National Transportation Statistics 2007*, table 1-27.
Notes:	Bridges are considered structurally deficient if significant load-carrying elements are found to be in poor or worse condition due to deterioration and/or damage, or the adequacy of the waterway opening provided by the bridge is determined to be extremely insufficient to the point of causing intolerable traffic interruptions.
	Functional obsolescence occurs as a result of differences in design requirements and traffic demands from the time a bridge was built to the present day.
	Includes bridges in the 50 states, DC, and Puerto Rico.
	Percentages were calculated by Information Publications from totals given in the source table.
Units:	Number of bridges; percent of total.

Table 8.06: Number of US Air Carriers, Railroads, and Pipeline Operators, 1995–2005

	1995	2000	2005
Air Carriers	96	91	82
Major carriers	11	15	17
Other	85	76	65
Railroads	541	560	560
Class I railroads	11	8	7
Other	530	552	553
Pipeline Operators	2,387	2,172	2,166
Hazardous liquid	209	243	235
Natural gas transmission	975	844	929
Natural gas distribution	1,444	1,363	1,291
Interstate motor carriers*	346,000	560,593	679,744
Marine vessel operators	1,381	1,114	733

Source: Bureau of Transportation Statistics, *National Transportation Statistics 2007*, table 1-2.

Notes: 'Major carriers' are those with at least $1 billion in annual operating revenue. Figures for other air carriers may be underreported.

Due to overlap between types, the total number of pipeline operators may be lower than the sum of the subgroups.

Class I railroads are the largest designation of railroad, with an annual operating revenue over approximately $320 million.

* Fiscal year, October through September.

Units: Number of carriers.

Table 8.07: Number of Aircraft, Vehicles, Vessels, and Other Conveyance, 1990–2005

	1990	1995	2000	2005
Air				
Air carrier	6,083	7,411	8,055	8,225
General aviation	198,000	188,089	217,533	224,352
Highway				
Total registered vehicles	193,057,376	205,427,212	225,821,241	247,421,120
Passenger car	133,700,496	128,386,775	133,621,420	136,568,083
Motorcycle	4,259,462	3,897,191	4,346,068	6,227,146
Other 2-axle, 4-tire vehicle	48,274,555	65,738,322	79,084,979	95,336,839
Single-unit truck	4,486,981	5,023,670	5,926,030	6,395,240
Bus	626,987	685,503	746,125	807,053
Transit				
Motor bus	58,714	67,107	75,013	82,027
Light rail cars	910	1,048	1,327	1,645
Heavy rail cars	10,567	10,166	10,311	11,110
Trolley	610	695	652	615
Commuter rail	4,982	5,164	5,498	6,392
Rail				
Class I freight cars	658,902	583,486	560,154	474,839
Class I locomotive	18,835	18,812	20,028	22,779
Amtrak passenger car	1,863	1,722	1,894	1,186
Amtrak locomotive	318	313	378	258
Water				
Non-self-propelled vessels	31,209	31,360	33,152	32,052
Self-propelled vessels	8,236	8,281	8,202	8,976
Oceangoing steam and motor ships	635	512	461	357
Recreational boats	10,996,253	11,734,710	12,782,143	12,942,414

Source: Bureau of Transportation Statistics, *National Transportation Statistics 2007*, table 1-11.

Notes: 'Other 2-axle 4-tire vehicle' includes pickup trucks and SUVs.
Class I railroads are the largest designation, and have annual operating revenues over an inflation-adjusted threshold – for 2005, approximately $320 million.

Units: Number of vehicles.

Table 8.08: Number of Airports, Planes, and Pilots, 1995–2006

	1995	2000	2005	2006
Airports				
Total Airports	*18,224*	*19,281*	*19,854*	*19,990*
Public use	5,415	5,317	5,270	5,233
% with lighted runways	74.3%	75.9%	76.8%	77.2%
% with paved runways	73.3%	74.3%	74.8%	75.3%
Private use	12,809	13,964	14,584	14,757
% with lighted runways	6.4%	7.2%	9.2%	9.5%
% with paved runways	33.0%	32.0%	33.2%	33.3%
Aircraft (general aviation fleet)				
Total Aircraft	*188,089*	*217,533*	*224,352*	*221,943*
Fixed wing	162,342	183,276	185,373	182,186
Piston	152,788	170,513	167,608	163,743
Turbojet	4,559	7,001	9,823	10,379
Turboprop	4,995	5,762	7,942	8,063
Rotorcraft	5,830	7,150	8,728	9,159
Pilots				
Total Pilots	*NA*	*625,581*	*609,737*	*597,109*
Student	NA	93,064	87,213	84,866
Private	NA	251,561	228,619	219,233
Commercial	NA	121,858	120,614	117,610
Airline transport	NA	141,596	141,992	141,935
Female pilots	NA	36,757	36,584	36,101
Flight instructors	NA	80,931	90,555	91,343

Source: Bureau of Transportation Statistics, *National Transportation Statistics 2008*, table 1-3.
Federal Aviation Administration, *Administrator's Fact Book, 2000*, page 21; *April 2007*, pages 16 and 25; *July 2008*, page 25.
Federal Aviation Administration, *General Aviation and Air Taxi Activity and Avionics Surveys CY 2005*, table 1.1; *CY 2006*, table 1.2.

Notes: 'Airports' includes civil and joint-use military airports, heliports, STOLports (short takeoff and landing), and seaplane bases in the US and its territories.
Airport data for 2006 has been revised from previous estimates.

Units: Number of airports, aircraft, and pilots; percent of total airports.

Table 8.09:   Condition of US Airport Runways, 1986–2006

	1986	1993	2000	2002	2004	2006
National Plan of Integrated Airport Systems (NPIAS) Airports						
Total	*3,243*	*3,294*	*3,361*	*3,358*	*3,356*	*3,365*
Good condition	61%	68%	73%	71%	75%	77%
Fair condition	28	25	22	24	21	19
Poor condition	11	7	5	5	4	4
Commercial Service Airports						
Total	*550*	*554*	*546*	*536*	*513*	*517*
Good condition	78%	79%	79%	79%	82%	79%
Fair condition	15	18	19	19	16	18
Poor condition	7	3	2	2	2	3

Source: Bureau of Transportation Statistics, *National Transportation Statistics 2008*, table 1-24.

Notes: National Plan of Integrated Airport Systems (NPIAS) are designated by the FAA, and include all commercial service airports, reliever airports, and some general aviation airports, but exclude several smaller types of landing areas. NPIAS airports account for most passenger travel. 'Commercial service airports' refers to public airports receiving scheduled commercial service, with at least 2,500 passengers per year.

Units: Number of airports; percent with specified runway quality.

Table 8.10: Commercial Space Launches by Country, 1990–2007

	Total Launches	United States	Europe	Russia	Ukraine	China	Sea Launch
Total	*401*	*140*	*127*	*90*	*1*	*18*	*24*
1990	15	9	5	0	0	1	0
1991	12	6	6	0	0	0	0
1992	14	6	6	0	0	2	0
1993	11	5	6	0	0	0	0
1994	15	5	8	0	0	2	0
1995	23	12	8	0	0	3	0
1996	24	11	9	2	0	2	0
1997	38	17	11	7	0	3	0
1998	41	22	9	5	1	4	0
1999	39	15	8	13	0	1	2
2000	35	7	12	13	0	0	3
2001	16	3	8	3	0	0	2
2002	24	5	10	8	0	0	1
2003	17	5	4	5	0	0	3
2004	15	6	1	5	0	0	3
2005	18	1	5	8	0	0	4
2006	21	2	5	9	0	0	5
2007	23	3	6	12	0	0	1

Source: Bureau of Transportation Statistics, *National Transportation Statistics 2008*, table 1-36.

Notes: 'Sea launch' is an international venture involving organizations in 4 countries that uses its own launch facility outside national borders, and is overseen by the FAA.
Data includes orbital launches only.

Units: Number of space launches by country.

Table 8.11: ADA-Accessible Buses, 1995, 2000, and 2006

	1995		2000		2006	
	Number ADA-Equipped	% of Total	Number ADA-Equipped	% of Total	Number ADA-Equipped	% of Total
Size of Bus						
Small	4,539	84.5%	8,366	94.5%	11,315	98.1%
Medium	2,561	66.0	6,926	92.9	10,891	99.1
Large	27,420	59.2	37,581	79.9	44,385	97.8
Articulated	861	50.2	1,712	85.5	2,289	99.8
Total	*35,381*	*61.7*	*54,585*	*83.6*	*68,880*	*98.1*

Source: Bureau of Transportation Statistics, *National Transportation Statistics 2008*, table 1-8.

Notes: Small buses have fewer than 25 seats.
Medium buses have between 25 and 35 seats.
Large buses have over 35 seats.
'Articulated' refers to extra-long buses measuring between 54 and 60 feet.

Units: Number of ADA-equipped buses; percent of total.

Table 8.12:   Oil and Gas Pipelines in US, 1960–2006

	Crude Oil Pipelines			Gas Pipelines		
	Total Oil	**Crude Lines**	**Product Lines**	**Total Gas**	**Distribution Mains**	**Transmission Pipelines**	**Gathering Lines**
1960	190.9	141.1	49.9	630.9	391.4	183.7	55.8
1965	210.9	149.4	61.4	767.5	494.5	211.3	61.7
1970	218.7	146.3	72.4	913.3	594.8	252.2	66.3
1975	225.9	145.7	80.2	979.3	648.2	262.6	68.5
1980	218.4	129.8	88.6	1,051.8	701.8	266.5	83.5
1985	213.6	117.8	95.8	1,118.9	753.4	271.2	94.3
1990	208.8	118.8	89.9	1,189.2	864.6	292.2	32.4
1991	203.8	115.9	88.0	1,218.2	891.4	294.1	32.7
1992	196.5	110.7	85.9	1,216.1	892.0	291.5	32.6
1993	194.0	107.2	86.7	1,277.2	951.8	293.3	32.1
1994	190.4	103.3	87.1	1,288.4	955.6	301.5	31.3
1995	181.9	97.0	84.9	1,277.6	949.8	296.9	30.9
1996	177.5	92.6	84.9	1,323.6	1,001.8	292.2	29.6
1997	179.9	91.5	88.4	1,331.8	1,003.1	294.0	34.7
1998	178.6	87.7	91.0	1,351.2	1,022.1	300.1	29.0
1999	177.5	86.4	91.1	1,340.3	1,007.5	301.0	31.8
2000	177.0	85.5	91.5	1,369.3	1,045.6	296.6	27.1
2001	158.2	NA	NA	1,373.5	1,066.3	287.1	20.1
2002	160.9	NA	NA	1,411.4	1,079.6	309.5	22.3
2003	159.6	NA	NA	1,424.2	1,097.9	304.0	22.3
2004	161.7	NA	NA	1,462.3	1,139.8	298.9	23.7
2005	159.5	NA	NA	1,437.5	1,117.8	296.4	23.3
2006	169.3	NA	NA	1,534.3	1,214.0	300.4	19.9

Source: Bureau of Transportation Statistics, *National Transportation Statistics 2008*, table 1-10.

Notes: 'Crude lines' includes trunk and gathering lnes.
'Gas pipelines' excludes service pipes.
'Transmission pipelines' includes about 5,000–6,000 miles of underground storage pipe for data after 1975.
'Gathering lines' figures before 1990 include field line mileage.

Units: Miles of pipeline in thousands.

Table 8.13: US Merchant Fleet: Number, Size, and Share of World Fleet, 1980–2006

	1980	1990	2000	2002	2005	2006
Total World Fleet	*24,867*	*23,596*	*28,318*	*28,761*	*28,956*	*31,477*
Total US Fleet	*864*	*636*	*454*	*426*	*391*	*347*
% of World fleet	3%	3%	2%	1%	1%	1%
Freighters	471	367	286	276	123	96
Total carrying capacity	*6,885*	*7,265*	*6,680*	*6,404*	*1,674*	*1,379*
General cargo ships	259	166	136	126	123	96
Container ships	121	92	90	90	90	76
Tankers	308	233	142	120	100	89
Total carrying capacity	*16,152*	*15,641*	*8,447*	*6,552*	*5,228*	*4,974*
Passenger/cargo combinations	65	10	11	12	15	19
Total carrying capacity	*446*	*91*	*99*	*100*	*82*	*107*
Bulk carriers	20	26	15	18	21	18
Total carrying capacity	*607*	*1,270*	*604*	*797*	*670*	*543*

Source: Bureau of Transportation Statistics, *National Transportation Statistics 2008*, table 1-23.

Notes: Includes oceangoing ships of 1,000 metric tons and over.
'General cargo' includes barges.

Units: Number of ships; carrying capacity in deadweight (metric) tons (2,240 lbs).

Part III: Environment

(ip)

**Essential
Topics
Series**

Chapter 9

Natural Resources

Chapter 9 Highlights

Chapter 9 contains data on natural resources in the US. The period from 1998–2004 showed a net increase in wetland and deepwater habitat areas for the first time since measurements began (table 9.01). The nation's wadeable streams have been assessed on a variety of dimensions: generally, streams in the western United States are the least disturbed (table 9.03). Most people (280 million out of 300 million) use community water systems (CWSs) for their drinking water; of those served by CWSs, surface water systems serve 70% of the population, despite comprising only 23% of the systems (table 9.05). Table 9.06 lists drinking water violations reported to state agencies or the EPA, for a variety of violation types. For people served by CWSs, the highest percentage affected by violations live in the District of Columbia, New York, Oklahoma, and South Carolina (table 9.07). Most violations reported were related to bacterial contamination (table 9.08).

Since 1982, the amount of land used for crop land or grazing has decreased. Soil erosion is also down, and the amount of land considered at highest risk for erosion has also decreased (table 9.12). Table 9.09 lists the number of endangered plants and animals for each state, with the highest numbers residing in Hawaii and California.

The chapter also features state-by-state breakdowns of land and water area, land use, and soil erosion (tables 9.02, 9.10, and 9.11, respectively).

Table 9.01: Wetlands and Deepwater Habitats in the US, 1998 and 2004

	1998 Area	2004 Area	% Change, 1998–2004
Wetlands and Deepwater Habitat Total	*148,618.8*	*149,058.5*	*0.3%*
Wetlands			
Total Wetlands	*107,562.3*	*107,754.0*	*0.2%*
Intertidal Wetlands	5,328.7	5,300.3	-0.5
Marine	130.4	128.6	-1.4
Estuarine intertidal non-vegetated	594.1	600.0	1.0
Estuarine intertidal vegetated	4,604.2	4,571.7	-0.7
Freshwater Wetlands	102,233.6	102,453.8	0.2
Freshwater non-vegetated	5,918.7	6,633.9	12.1
Freshwater ponds	5,534.3	6,229.6	12.6
Freshwater vegetated	96,414.9	95,819.8	-0.5
Freshwater emergent	26,289.6	26,147.0	-0.5
Freshwater forested	51,483.1	52,031.4	1.1
Freshwater shrub	18,542.2	17,641.4	-4.9
Deepwater Habitats			
Total Deepwater	*41,046.6*	*41,304.5*	*0.6%*
Lacustrine	16,610.5	16,773.4	1.0
Riverine	6,765.5	6,813.3	0.7
Estuarine subtidal	17,680.5	17,717.8	0.2

Source: US Fish & Wildlife Service, *Status and Trends of Wetlands in the Coterminous United States, 1998 to 2004*, table 2.

Notes: Generally, 'wetlands' are defined as lands where saturation with water is the dominant factor determining the nature of soil development and the types of plant and animal communities living in the soil and on its surface.

Marine systems are exposed to the open ocean, while estuarine systems are usually partially enclosed by land, but have some access to the ocean, diluted by contact with freshwater sources.

Deepwater habitats are permanently flooded, and not classified as wetlands.

For further definitions, readers are referred to the glossary or to the Fish & Wildlife Service.

Units: Area in thousands of acres; percent change.

Table 9.02: Land and Water Area in the US by State

	Total Area	Land			Water		
	Total	Total	Total	Inland	Coastal	Great Lakes	Territorial
United States	*3,794,083*	*3,537,438*	*256,645*	*78,797*	*42,225*	*60,251*	*75,372*
Alabama	52,419	50,744	1,675	956	519	0	200
Alaska	663,267	571,951	91,316	17,243	27,049	0	47,024
Arizona	113,998	113,635	364	364	0	0	0
Arkansas	53,179	52,068	1,110	1,110	0	0	0
California	163,696	155,959	7,736	2,674	222	0	4,841
Colorado	104,094	103,718	376	376	0	0	0
Connecticut	5,543	4,845	699	161	538	0	0
Delaware	2,489	1,954	536	72	371	0	93
District of Columbia	68	61	7	7	0	0	0
Florida	65,755	53,927	11,828	4,672	1,311	0	5,845
Georgia	59,425	57,906	1,519	1,016	48	0	455
Hawaii	10,931	6,423	4,508	38	0	0	4,470
Idaho	83,570	82,747	823	823	0	0	0
Illinois	57,914	55,584	2,331	756	0	1,575	0
Indiana	36,418	35,867	551	316	0	235	0
Iowa	56,272	55,869	402	402	0	0	0
Kansas	82,277	81,815	462	462	0	0	0
Kentucky	40,409	39,728	681	681	0	0	0
Louisiana	51,840	43,562	8,278	4,154	1,935	0	2,189
Maine	35,385	30,862	4,523	2,264	613	0	1,647
Maryland	12,407	9,774	2,633	680	1,843	0	110
Massachusetts	10,555	7,840	2,715	423	977	0	1,314
Michigan	96,716	56,804	39,912	1,611	0	38,301	0
Minnesota	86,939	79,610	7,329	4,783	0	2,546	0
Mississippi	48,430	46,907	1,523	785	590	0	148
Missouri	69,704	68,886	818	818	0	0	0
Montana	147,042	145,552	1,490	1,490	0	0	0
Nebraska	77,354	76,872	481	481	0	0	0
Nevada	110,561	109,826	735	735	0	0	0

(continued on next page)

Table 9.02: Land and Water Area in the US by State

| | Total Area | Land | | | Water | | |
	Total	Total	Total	Inland	Coastal	Great Lakes	Territorial
United States	*3,794,083*	*3,537,438*	*256,645*	*78,797*	*42,225*	*60,251*	*75,372*
New Hampshire	9,350	8,968	382	314	0	0	68
New Jersey	8,721	7,417	1,304	396	401	0	507
New Mexico	121,590	121,356	234	234	0	0	0
New York	54,556	47,214	7,342	1,895	981	3,988	479
North Carolina	53,819	48,711	5,108	3,960	0	0	1,148
North Dakota	70,700	68,976	1,724	1,724	0	0	0
Ohio	44,825	40,948	3,877	378	0	3,499	0
Oklahoma	69,898	68,667	1,231	1,231	0	0	0
Oregon	98,381	95,997	2,384	1,050	80	0	1,254
Pennsylvania	46,055	44,817	1,239	490	0	749	0
Rhode Island	1,545	1,045	500	178	9	0	314
South Carolina	32,020	30,110	1,911	1,008	72	0	831
South Dakota	77,117	75,885	1,232	1,232	0	0	0
Tennessee	42,143	41,217	926	926	0	0	0
Texas	268,581	261,797	6,784	5,056	404	0	1,324
Utah	84,899	82,144	2,755	2,755	0	0	0
Vermont	9,614	9,250	365	365	0	0	0
Virginia	42,774	39,594	3,180	1,006	1,728	0	446
Washington	71,300	66,544	4,756	1,553	2,537	0	666
West Virginia	24,230	24,078	152	152	0	0	0
Wisconsin	65,498	54,310	11,188	1,830	0	9,358	0
Wyoming	97,814	97,100	713	713	0	0	0

Source: US Bureau of the Census, *Statistical Abstract of the United States 2007*, table 345.

Notes: Area is calculated from measurements collected during the 2000 Decennial Census.

Units: Area in square miles.

Table 9.03: Condition of Wadeable Streams by Region, 2004–2005

	National Total	Eastern Highlands	Plains and Lowlands	West
Total Stream Length	*671,051*	*276,362*	*242,264*	*152,425*
Biological Condition				
Good	28.2%	18.2%	29.0%	45.1%
Fair	24.9	20.5	29.0	25.8
Poor	41.9	51.8	40.0	27.4
Phosphorous Concentration				
Good	48.8%	32.8%	61.5%	58.5%
Fair	16.1	15.1	13.3	22.8
Poor	30.9	42.6	24.9	18.5
Nitrogen Concentration				
Good	43.3%	31.6%	51.9%	51.4%
Fair	20.7	16.4	20.4	27.9
Poor	31.8	42.4	27.1	20.5
Salinity				
Good	82.5%	78.8%	81.9%	90.1%
Fair	10.4	10.4	12.6	7.1
Poor	2.9	1.3	5.0	2.6
Acidification				
Good	93.2%	87.1%	96.4%	99.3%
Fair	0.5	0.0	1.4	0.0
Poor	2.1	3.4	1.9	0.5
Streambed Sediments				
Good	50.1%	36.2%	59.1%	60.3%
Fair	19.7	25.4	12.5	20.8
Poor	24.9	28.0	26.4	17.4

(continued on next page)

Table 9.03: Condition of Wadeable Streams by Region, 2004–2005

	National Total	Eastern Highlands	Plains and Lowlands	West
Total Stream Length	*671,051*	*276,362*	*242,264*	*152,425*
In-Stream Fish Habitat				
Good	51.5%	55.8%	37.7%	66.4%
Fair	24.9	26.4	25.0	21.1
Poor	19.5	8.3	37.0	12.3
Riparian Vegetative Cover				
Good	47.6%	42.2%	47.5%	57.1%
Fair	28.3	30.7	24.5	30.5
Poor	19.3	17.6	26.0	12.2
Riparian Disturbance				
Good	23.6%	21.3%	18.8%	34.6%
Fair	46.8	40.4	55.1	45.8
Poor	25.5	28.8	25.8	19.4

Source: Envioronmental Protection Agency, Office of Water, *Wadeable Streams Assessment, December 2006*, figures 13 and 15 through 22.

Notes: 'National' includes the continental 48 states.
'Biological condition' is based on the Macroinvertebrate Index, which combines several measures of overall biological health for a stream.
Concentrations for phosphorous, nitrogen, and salt (salinity) are based on the least-disturbed reference sites in the region.
Ratings for acidification are based on a stream's ability to neutralize acidity introduced by acid rain.
Ratings for streambed sediments, fish habitats, and riparian vegetative cover and disturbance are based on the least-disturbed referenced sites in the region.
Percentages for streams that were not assessed are not included.

Units: Total length of streams in miles; percent of total.

Table 9.04: US Water Quality Conditions by Type of Water Body, 2000

	Rivers and Streams	Lakes, Reservoirs, and Ponds	Coastal Resources	Great Lakes Shoreline	Ocean Shoreline
Total Size	*3,692,830*	*40,603,893*	*87,369*	*5,521*	*58,618*
Assessed	699,946	17,339,080	31,072	5,066	3,221
% of total assessed	19%	43%	36%	92%	6%
Percent Assessed as:					
Good	53%	47%	45%	0%	79%
Good but threatened	8	8	4	22	7
Polluted	39	45	51	78	14
Amount Impaired, by Source of Pollution:					
Agriculture	128,859	3,158,393	2,811	75	NA
Atmospheric deposition	NA	983,936	3,692	71	NA
Construction	NA	NA	NA	NA	29
Contaminated sediments	NA	NA	NA	519	NA
Forestry	28,156	NA	NA	NA	NA
Habitat modification	37,654	NA	NA	62	NA
Hydrologic modification	53,850	1,413,624	2,171	NA	NA
Industrial discharges/ point sources	NA	NA	4,116	NA	76
Land disposal of wastes	NA	856,586	NA	61	123
Municipal point sources	27,988	943,715	5,779	NA	89
Nonpoint sources	NA	1,045,036	NA	NA	142
Resource extraction	27,695	NA	1,913	NA	NA
Septic tanks	NA	NA	NA	61	103
Urban runoff & storm sewers	34,871	13,699,327	5,045	152	241

Source: US Bureau of the Census, *Statistical Abstract of the United States 2007*, table 356.

Notes: 'Coastal resources' includes tidal estuaries, shoreline waters, and coral reefs.

Units: Length of rivers and streams, Great Lakes shoreline, and ocean shoreline in miles; size of lakes, reservoirs, and ponds in acres; area of coastal resources in square miles; percent of total.

Table 9.05:   Public Water Systems by Source and Type, 2005 and 2006

	Number of Systems	% of Systems	Population Served	% of Population
2005				
Community water systems	51.8	100%	280,669.3	100%
Ground water	40.0	77	89,539.2	32
Surface water	11.7	23	191,130.1	68
Non-transient non-community water system	19.0	100%	6,021.4	100%
Ground water	18.4	97	5,410.4	90
Surface water	0.6	3	611.0	10
Transient non-community water system	85.8	100%	12,107.0	100%
Ground water	83.9	98	11,305.6	93
Surface water	1.9	2	801.4	7
2006				
Community water systems	52.3	100%	281,700.1	100%
Ground water	40.3	77	85,034.9	30
Surface water	12.0	23	196,665.2	70
Non-transient non-community water system	19.0	100%	6,008.3	100%
Ground water	18.4	97	5,406.7	90
Surface water	0.6	3	601.6	10
Transient non-community water system	85.3	100%	13,980.7	100%
Ground water	83.3	98	11,281.4	81
Surface water	1.9	2	2,699.3	19

Source: Environmental Protection Agency, *Factoids: Drinking Water and Ground Water Statistics for 2005*, page 4; *2006*, page 4.

Notes: Community water systems (CWS) are public water systems that supply water to the same population year-round.
Non-transient non-community water systems (NTNCWS) regularly supply water to at least 25 of the same people at least 6 months of the year, but not year-round (such as schools, factories, and office buildings).
Transient non-community water systems (TNCWS) provide water to places such as gas stations or campgrounds where people do not remain for long periods of time.

Units: Number of systems and population served in thousands; percent of total by system type.

Table 9.06: Drinking Water Violations Reported by System and Violation Type, 2001–2006

	2001	2002	2003	2004	2005	2006
Community Water Supply						
Maximum contaminant level						
Violations	5,231	4,693	4,884	5,562	9,739	9,242
Systems	3,241	3,193	3,069	3,455	4,472	4,438
Population affected	11,165,733	8,800,095	16,082,938	15,060,424	19,228,465	16,918,011
Treatment technique						
Violations	2,493	2,408	2,299	2,168	3,036	2,790
Systems	1,572	1,482	1,458	1,409	1,625	1,538
Population affected	15,474,893	9,245,467	16,969,087	16,588,301	16,879,450	16,612,762
Monitoring/reporting						
Violations	63,476	80,635	68,840	96,225	124,605	67,301
Systems	13,639	12,430	12,880	13,693	14,403	13,106
Population affected	52,618,908	32,503,639	49,812,213	51,043,156	62,511,599	52,415,065
Other violations						
Violations	11,455	11,759	12,671	14,459	18,414	19,245
Systems	8,631	8,386	8,109	8,947	10,258	9,600
Population affected	25,780,359	17,809,478	12,726,332	17,833,120	23,442,800	23,372,794
Total						
Violations	82,655	99,495	88,695	118,420	155,798	98,585
Systems	20,996	20,232	20,343	21,200	22,902	22,902
Population affected	77,845,089	56,644,512	81,672,086	79,058,089	91,626,483	83,638,885
Non-Transient Non-Community Water Supply						
Maximum contaminant level						
Violations	1,258	1,336	1,391	1,381	1,980	1,903
Systems	921	1,005	1,029	1,033	1,207	1,227
Population affected	359,556	302,322	266,522	288,280	352,038	409,163
Treatment technique						
Violations	696	720	680	681	853	827
Systems	515	529	495	474	550	539
Population affected	222,120	165,522	140,053	130,242	164,644	170,672
Monitoring/reporting						
Violations	NA	38,805	32,578	37,514	54,561	33,512
Systems	NA	5,322	4,758	4,963	5,591	5,150
Population affected	NA	1,566,034	1,434,673	1,402,090	1,668,159	1,674,286
Other violations						
Violations	305	227	503	538	717	2,063
Systems	213	155	317	356	491	1,059
Population affected	82,910	57,016	85,026	88,003	122,177	277,538

(continued on next page)

Table 9.06: Drinking Water Violations Reported by System and Violation Type, 2001–2006

	2001	2002	2003	2004	2005	2006
Transient Non-Community Water Supply						
Maximum contaminant level						
Violations	4,596	4,837	5,082	5,032	5,043	5,287
Systems	3,687	3,858	4,071	3,974	3,977	4,082
Population affected	558,780	504,967	541,950	549,673	542,026	1,297,464
Treatment technique						
Violations	677	626	573	415	502	474
Systems	256	249	245	195	215	211
Population affected	46,987	60,692	40,518	51,915	86,648	50,372
Monitoring/reporting						
Violations	NA	39,451	35,005	38,705	37,505	32,767
Systems	NA	19,191	17,439	17,334	17,556	15,575
Population affected	NA	2,154,654	2,160,890	2,207,974	2,264,085	2,166,907
Other violations						
Violations	1,467	2,339	8,640	3,028	4,800	19,010
Systems	826	1,142	3,685	1,697	2,284	6,417
Population affected	118,847	137,795	340,950	234,291	344,411	642,080

Source: Environmental Protection Agency, *Factoids: Drinking Water and Ground Water Statistics for 2005*, pages 11 through 12; *2006*, pages 11 through 12.

Notes: Community water systems (CWS) are public water systems that supply water to the same population year-round.

Non-transient non-community water systems (NTNCWS) regularly supply water to at least 25 of the same people at least 6 months of the year, but not year-round (such as schools, factories, and office buildings).

Transient non-community water systems (TNCWS) provide water to places such as gas stations or campgrounds where people do not remain for long periods of time.

For explanations of the violation detection types (maximum contaminant level, treatment technique, and monitoring/reporting), readers are referred to the glossary or the EPA.

Units: Number of violations reported, systems involved, and number of people affected.

Table 9.07: Public Water Systems and Health Violations by State, 2006

	Systems	% with Violations	Population Served	% with Violations
United States	*154,723*	*3%*	*294,713,545*	*9%*
Alabama	636	3	5,371,331	2
Alaska	1,546	21	624,387	12
Arizona	1,602	9	5,644,140	4
Arkansas	1,090	15	2,590,244	10
California	7,320	8	38,345,096	1
Colorado	1,952	7	5,398,768	2
Connecticut	2,736	14	2,846,787	4
Delaware	516	9	948,875	19
District of Columbia	5	33	609,570	98
Florida	6,028	10	18,404,071	5
Georgia	2,458	6	7,566,335	5
Hawaii	130	9	1,334,704	7
Idaho	2,001	16	1,173,608	12
Illinois	5,868	11	12,225,068	8
Indiana	4,406	10	5,270,497	3
Iowa	1,990	6	2,775,377	8
Kansas	1,052	13	2,588,408	13
Kentucky	510	12	4,778,826	9
Louisiana	1,518	15	5,056,671	15
Maine	1,955	24	879,027	15
Maryland	3,639	7	5,224,568	1
Massachusetts	1,731	9	9,212,301	7
Michigan	11,724	11	8,895,949	2
Minnesota	7,392	4	4,750,264	5
Mississippi	1,339	3	3,180,199	4
Missouri	2,740	13	5,251,194	6
Montana	2,076	11	921,974	7
Nebraska	1,348	20	1,530,665	10
Nevada	588	16	2,481,071	5

(continued on next page)

Table 9.07: Public Water Systems and Health Violations by State, 2006

	Systems	% with Violations	Population Served	% with Violations
United States	*154,723*	*3%*	*294,713,545*	*9%*
New Hampshire	2,381	17	1,240,262	15
New Jersey	3,902	5	9,255,927	5
New Mexico	1,283	14	1,751,869	12
New York	9,762	7	21,071,391	47
North Carolina	6,740	15	7,272,551	7
North Dakota	512	7	573,409	9
Ohio	5,384	8	10,804,812	13
Oklahoma	1,603	18	3,578,511	26
Oregon	2,641	12	3,313,737	4
Pennsylvania	9,629	7	11,915,054	4
Rhode Island	484	20	1,060,886	16
South Carolina	1,412	9	3,534,809	23
South Dakota	672	11	699,027	7
Tennessee	1,122	9	5,722,715	14
Texas	6,471	9	23,934,619	10
Utah	942	12	2,499,440	6
Vermont	1,371	16	594,481	15
Virginia	3,054	13	6,867,710	5
Washington	4,117	11	6,268,971	4
West Virginia	1,176	10	1,516,417	9
Wisconsin	11,410	9	4,806,250	15
Wyoming	759	10	550,722	4

Source: Environmental Protection Agency, *Factoids: Drinking Water and Ground Water Statistics for 2006*, pages 5 and 6.

Notes: Systems with reported health violations include only Community Water Systems (CWSs), public water systems that supply water to the same population year-round.

Units: Number of systems and population served; percent of CWSs with reported health-based violations; percent of CWS-served people.

Table 9.08: Public Water Supply Violations Reported by Type of Violation, 2005 and 2006

	Systems	Violations	Population Served
2005			
Microbial			
Total coliform rule/turbidity	7,101	9,113	9,142,908
Stage 1 disinfectants-by-products	1,627	4,926	6,028,863
Surface water treatment rule	772	1,463	2,046,650
Interim enhanced and long-term 1 surface water treatment rule	249	672	664,287
Organic			
Volatile organic contaminants	34	50	109,752
Synthetic organic compounds	25	35	32,133
Inorganic			
Arsenic	57	96	175,860
Nitrates	540	1,124	1,756,890
Lead and copper	1,181	1,653	5,257,317
Other inorganic contaminants	200	517	608,472
Radionuclides	395	943	2,352,058

(continued on next page)

Table 9.08: Public Water Supply Violations Reported by Type of Violation, 2005 and 2006

	Systems	Violations	Population Served
2006			
Microbial			
Total coliform rule/turbidity	7,184	9,349	11,311,784
Stage 1 disinfectants-by-products	1,534	4,321	4,436,438
Surface water treatment rule	679	1,386	9,097,527
Interim enhanced and long-term 1 surface water treatment rule	229	516	4,842,748
Organic			
Volatile organic contaminants	31	69	125,113
Synthetic organic compounds	20	32	16,725
Inorganic			
Arsenic	330	448	409,096
Nitrates	535	912	1,266,952
Lead and copper	1,150	1,564	2,084,912
Other inorganic contaminants	148	397	304,635
Radionuclides	363	1,277	1,542,734

Source: Environmental Protection Agency, *Factoids: Drinking Water and Ground Water Statistics for 2005*, page 13; *2006*, page 13.

Notes: Entries in the 'microbial' category refer to testing methods. Readers are referred to the glossary or the EPA for more information.
'Other inorganic coumpounds' refers to regulated inorganic contaminants (such as arsenic) other than copper, lead, nitrate, and nitrite.

Units: Number of violations reported and systems; population served by those systems.

Table 9.09:   Endangered or Threatened Species by State, 2008

	Animals			Plants			All Species		
	Endan-gered	Threat-ened	Total	Endan-gered	Threat-ened	Total	Endan-gered	Threat-ened	Total
United States	*973*	*189*	*1,162*	*599*	*148*	*747*	*1,572*	*337*	*1,909*
Alabama	57	22	79	10	7	17	67	29	96
Alaska	7	6	13	1	0	1	8	6	14
Arizona	24	13	37	11	7	18	35	20	55
Arkansas	17	5	22	3	3	6	20	8	28
California	85	36	121	136	45	181	221	81	302
Colorado	10	6	16	6	7	13	16	13	29
Connecticut	10	6	16	1	1	2	11	7	18
Delaware	9	4	13	1	4	5	10	8	18
District of Columbia	2	0	2	0	0	0	2	0	2
Florida	36	20	56	43	11	54	79	31	110
Georgia	26	13	39	16	7	23	42	20	62
Hawaii	71	5	76	264	9	273	335	14	349
Idaho	8	7	15	0	4	4	8	11	19
Illinois	18	0	18	1	8	9	19	8	27
Indiana	21	2	23	2	3	5	23	5	28
Iowa	7	1	8	0	5	5	7	6	13
Kansas	7	3	10	0	2	2	7	5	12
Kentucky	29	2	31	4	4	8	33	6	39
Louisiana	12	9	21	2	1	3	14	10	24
Maine	8	2	10	1	2	3	9	4	13
Maryland	12	6	18	4	3	7	16	9	25
Massachusetts	14	5	19	2	1	3	16	6	22
Michigan	12	3	15	1	7	8	13	10	23
Minnesota	6	3	9	1	3	4	7	6	13
Mississippi	22	11	33	3	1	4	25	12	37
Missouri	14	4	18	2	6	8	16	10	26
Montana	7	4	11	0	3	3	7	7	14
Nebraska	7	1	8	1	3	4	8	4	12
Nevada	21	7	28	2	6	8	23	13	36
New Hampshire	5	3	8	2	1	3	7	4	11
New Jersey	11	4	15	1	5	6	12	9	21

(continued on next page)

Table 9.09: Endangered or Threatened Species by State, 2008

	Animals			Plants			All Species		
	Endangered	Threatened	Total	Endangered	Threatened	Total	Endangered	Threatened	Total
United States	*973*	*189*	*1,162*	*599*	*148*	*747*	*1,572*	*337*	*1,909*
New Mexico	20	10	30	7	6	13	27	16	43
New York	13	6	19	1	5	6	14	11	25
North Carolina	25	7	32	18	9	27	43	16	59
North Dakota	4	1	5	0	1	1	4	2	6
Ohio	14	3	17	1	5	6	15	8	23
Oklahoma	12	5	17	0	2	2	12	7	19
Oregon	13	19	32	10	7	17	23	26	49
Pennsylvania	11	1	12	1	2	3	12	3	15
Rhode Island	10	3	13	1	1	2	11	4	15
South Carolina	15	6	21	13	6	19	28	12	40
South Dakota	8	1	9	0	0	0	8	1	9
Tennessee	52	9	61	12	7	19	64	16	80
Texas	52	9	61	23	6	29	75	15	90
Utah	12	5	17	11	13	24	23	18	41
Vermont	3	2	5	2	0	2	5	2	7
Virginia	38	8	46	7	8	15	45	16	61
Washington	11	14	25	3	6	9	14	20	34
West Virginia	10	3	13	4	2	6	14	5	19
Wisconsin	7	2	9	0	6	6	7	8	15
Wyoming	4	2	6	1	3	4	5	5	10

Source: US Fish & Wildlife Service, Threatened and Endangered Species System (TESS), http://ecos.fws.gov/tess_public/StartTESS.do (accessed October 14, 2008).

Notes: As of October 14, 2008. Counts are based on the number of species occurring in each state, which may differ from the number listed for the state (some species may be listed for the state but not occur there, and some may occur there but not be listed).

Each plant or animal listed was either designated 'endangered' or 'threatened' by the US Fish & Wildlife Service's Endangered Species Program.

US total includes species found in American Samoa, Guam, Puerto Rico, and the Virgin Islands.

States may not add to total due to some species' being listed in multiple states.

Units: Number of species.

Table 9.10:   Land Use by State, 2003

	Cropland	Pasture Land	Forest Land	Developed Land	Water Areas	Federal Land	Total Area
United States	*367,900*	*131,100*	*402,400*	*72,900*	*48,600*	*399,100*	*NA*
Alabama	2,509.0	3,400.8	21,530.0	2,723.9	1,281.4	997.9	33,423.8
Arizona	933.9	82.0	4,141.4	1,910.5	187.1	30,426.2	72,964.4
Arkansas	7,522.0	5,322.1	15,007.8	1,603.3	900.9	3,104.2	34,036.9
California	9,468.2	1,188.6	13,903.2	5,925.1	1,870.1	46,639.0	101,510.2
Colorado	8,348.0	1,001.8	3,289.0	1,870.7	328.2	23,796.9	66,624.5
Connecticut	172.2	128.7	1,706.0	941.5	127.7	14.5	3,194.7
Delaware	457.5	22.9	340.6	264.6	289.2	31.0	1,533.5
Florida	2,873.2	3,619.4	12,732.7	5,852.7	3,089.4	3,784.2	37,533.7
Georgia	4,151.9	2,798.1	21,893.2	4,572.0	1,053.5	2,124.0	37,740.5
Idaho	5,452.6	1,316.6	4,006.9	811.5	554.0	33,563.3	53,487.5
Illinois	23,980.5	2,254.0	3,949.3	3,347.3	725.8	491.1	36,058.7
Indiana	13,315.6	1,897.7	3,816.5	2,421.0	364.4	472.4	23,158.4
Iowa	25,511.1	3,460.5	2,301.3	1,779.3	478.1	172.4	36,016.5
Kansas	26,466.3	2,397.8	1,549.3	2,025.3	539.9	504.0	52,660.8
Kentucky	5,478.5	5,147.9	10,510.1	2,000.2	626.8	1,295.4	25,863.4
Louisiana	5,435.0	2,249.3	13,337.7	1,801.7	3,819.0	1,310.0	31,376.8
Maine	384.5	137.4	17,620.3	810.1	1,253.0	207.2	20,966.2
Maryland	1,516.6	456.7	2,369.5	1,346.4	1,660.3	168.9	7,869.9
Massachusetts	251.7	135.9	2,664.9	1,572.6	366.9	97.1	5,339.0
Michigan	8,097.2	2,158.2	16,708.2	3,915.2	1,116.4	3,273.6	37,349.2
Minnesota	21,099.6	3,590.6	16,356.5	2,321.8	3,141.3	3,336.1	54,009.9
Mississippi	4,975.5	3,223.9	16,754.6	1,676.3	884.3	1,794.8	30,527.3
Missouri	13,677.9	10,673.6	12,549.9	2,710.5	845.9	1,919.4	44,613.9
Montana	14,526.6	3,594.4	5,402.0	1,069.1	1,036.3	27,092.0	94,110.0
Nebraska	19,552.3	1,849.9	812.1	1,233.9	473.5	647.6	49,509.6
Nevada	636.1	269.5	314.0	474.7	431.2	59,868.9	70,763.1

(continued on next page)

Table 9.10: Land Use by State, 2003

	Cropland	Pasture Land	Forest Land	Developed Land	Water Areas	Federal Land	Total Area
United States	*367,900*	*131,100*	*402,400*	*72,900*	*48,600*	*399,100*	*NA*
New Hampshire	124.6	89.3	3,898.7	635.2	236.9	763.2	5,941.0
New Jersey	527.9	101.6	1,604.5	1,923.9	526.2	148.3	5,215.6
New Mexico	1,548.7	232.1	5,477.6	1,364.8	153.6	26,448.5	77,823.3
New York	5,358.9	2,584.1	17,598.5	3,465.4	1,282.1	205.3	31,360.8
North Carolina	5,512.8	1,832.3	15,456.1	4,667.2	2,772.6	2,507.5	33,709.3
North Dakota	24,266.5	951.2	466.5	1,007.3	1,084.2	1,784.8	45,250.7
Ohio	11,243.3	2,271.3	7,225.1	3,856.4	400.7	373.3	26,444.8
Oklahoma	8,971.3	8,458.1	7,367.9	2,130.7	1,079.0	1,148.3	44,738.1
Oregon	3,701.0	1,761.3	12,733.6	1,313.1	825.2	31,260.4	62,161.0
Pennsylvania	5,124.3	2,000.0	15,630.7	4,265.5	476.9	724.3	28,995.2
Rhode Island	20.3	26.5	373.7	219.5	151.4	3.5	813.3
South Carolina	2,367.9	1,093.4	11,161.2	2,468.8	799.5	1,036.2	19,939.3
South Dakota	17,086.6	1,985.4	503.1	981.2	880.1	3,112.2	49,358.0
Tennessee	4,750.0	4,756.6	11,959.3	2,616.4	784.2	1,302.6	26,973.6
Texas	25,562.3	15,836.3	10,613.1	9,656.4	4,085.1	2,909.9	171,051.9
Utah	1,682.1	722.4	1,875.6	736.9	1,800.6	34,278.8	54,338.9
Vermont	586.5	314.4	4,129.4	346.5	260.8	422.6	6,153.6
Virginia	2,862.4	2,904.5	13,181.5	2,936.6	1,936.1	2,646.4	27,087.1
Washington	6,493.8	1,080.1	12,707.1	2,279.4	1,542.7	11,923.5	44,035.3
West Virginia	820.6	1,472.4	10,556.2	1,011.8	178.8	1,211.9	15,508.2
Wisconsin	10,303.6	3,081.2	14,528.2	2,595.3	1,287.7	1,845.3	35,920.0
Wyoming	2,161.1	1,081.0	948.6	656.7	440.4	28,748.0	62,602.8

Source: National Resources Conservation Service, *National Resources Inventory 2003–Land Use*, pages 9 through 12.

Notes: Only the continental 48 states are shown.
'Cropland' includes cultivated and non-cultivated land.

Units: Land area in thousand acres.

Table 9.11: Soil Erosion for Cropland by State, 2003

	Water Erosion	Wind Erosion	Highly Erodable Cropland	Non-HEL Cropland
United States	*970,600*	*776,400*	*100,200*	*267,700*
Alabama	12,932.5	0.0	660.9	1,848.1
Arizona	547.2	8,319.7	835.7	98.2
Arkansas	23,672.1	0.0	280.6	7,241.4
California	3,178.0	*	557.5	8,910.7
Colorado	13,031.6	86,731.0	6,422.7	1,925.3
Connecticut	438.0	0.0	49.3	122.9
Delaware	906.2	0.0	17.6	439.9
Florida	3,859.1	0.0	54.5	2,818.7
Georgia	19,467.2	0.0	450.3	3,701.6
Idaho	12,218.5	15,546.5	2,177.6	3,275.0
Illinois	95,783.7	0.0	3,626.4	20,354.1
Indiana	42,056.5	3,885.3	1,912.4	11,403.2
Iowa	128,581.1	10,886.4	7,186.9	18,324.2
Kansas	55,210.5	35,449.3	8,100.7	18,365.6
Kentucky	13,285.4	0.0	2,983.9	2,494.6
Louisiana	16,734.9	0.0	242.8	5,192.2
Maine	527.7	0.0	98.8	285.7
Maryland	5,520.7	0.0	516.6	1,000.0
Massachusetts	235.7	0.0	58.7	193.0
Michigan	11,845.6	13,898.3	523.0	7,574.2
Minnesota	36,867.2	92,339.2	1,510.1	19,589.5
Mississippi	22,901.2	0.0	723.2	4,252.3
Missouri	56,533.3	0.0	5,439.5	8,238.4
Montana	16,670.8	42,739.1	8,753.1	5,773.5
Nebraska	51,248.9	32,034.8	6,576.0	12,976.3
Nevada	32.6	2,203.3	271.8	364.3

(continued on next page)

Table 9.11: Soil Erosion for Cropland by State, 2003

	Water Erosion	Wind Erosion	Highly Erodable Cropland	Non-HEL Cropland
United States	*970,600*	*776,400*	*100,200*	*267,700*
New Hampshire	93.0	0.0	29.5	95.1
New Jersey	1,860.6	0.0	125.3	402.6
New Mexico	1,238.0	20,047.7	1,379.9	168.8
New York	11,420.1	0.0	1,676.3	3,682.6
North Carolina	16,881.5	0.0	1,309.4	4,203.4
North Dakota	32,779.3	117,325.8	4,583.0	19,683.5
Ohio	22,938.3	1,592.4	2,095.4	9,147.9
Oklahoma	22,874.8	13,221.2	2,207.1	6,764.2
Oregon	5,831.2	5,588.6	732.4	2,968.6
Pennsylvania	18,476.6	0.0	3,097.4	2,026.9
Rhode Island	42.6	0.0	*	19.9
South Carolina	6,556.3	0.0	213.5	2,154.4
South Dakota	31,427.0	34,203.6	2,320.8	14,765.8
Tennessee	16,950.3	0.0	2,085.7	2,664.3
Texas	64,834.7	190,493.4	8,995.1	16,567.2
Utah	1,230.5	5,010.8	557.0	1,125.1
Vermont	792.6	0.0	177.9	408.6
Virginia	9,763.8	0.0	1,313.3	1,549.1
Washington	26,341.0	31,429.6	2,775.2	3,718.6
West Virginia	990.6	0.0	468.2	352.4
Wisconsin	31,754.3	1,759.0	2,993.7	7,309.9
Wyoming	1,184.9	6,974.2	1,039.3	1,121.8

Source: National Resources Conservation Service, *National Resources Inventory 2003–Soil Erosion*, pages 14 through 21.

Notes: Only the continental 48 states are shown.
'Highly Erodable Land' (HEL) is land with an erodibility index (a numerical expression of soil's potential for loss due to erosion) of at least 8.
* Not shown because the margin of error is larger than the estimate.

Units: Erosion in thousand tons of soil lost; cropland area in thousand acres.

Table 9.12: Land Use and Soil Erosion, by Category, 1982–2003

	1982	1992	1997	2001	2003
Land Use					
Crop land	419.9	381.3	376.4	369.5	367.9
Cultivated	375.8	334.3	326.4	314.0	309.9
Non-cultiivated	44.1	47.0	50.0	55.5	58.0
CRP land	0.0	34.0	32.7	31.8	31.5
Grazing land	610.9	592.9	582.4	579.3	576.4
Grazed forest land	64.3	61.0	58.0	55.2	54.3
Pasture land	131.1	125.2	119.5	119.2	117.0
Range land	415.5	406.8	404.9	404.9	405.1
Forest land	402.4	403.6	404.7	404.8	405.6
Other rural	48.2	49.4	50.4	50.1	50.2
Developed land	72.9	86.5	97.6	105.2	108.1
Water areas	48.6	49.4	49.9	50.3	50.4
Federal land	399.1	401.5	401.7	401.9	401.9
Soil Erosion					
Water Erosion	1,671.8	1,168.8	1,039.1	992.4	970.6
Wind Erosion	1,389.6	985.3	837.9	780.1	776.4
Highly Erodable Land (HEL)	**123.6**	**104.1**	**102.8**	**NA**	**100.2**
Eroding at or below soil tolerance rates	40.8	40.5	45.3	NA	46.1
Eroding above soil loss tolerance rates	82.8	63.6	57.5	NA	54.1
Non-HEL land	**296.3**	**277.2**	**273.6**	**NA**	**267.7**
Eroding at or below soil tolerance rates	210.0	216.3	222.4	NA	219.8
Eroding above soil loss tolerance rates	86.3	60.9	51.2	NA	47.9

Source: National Resources Conservation Service, *National Resources Inventory 2003–Land Use*, pages 5 and 8.
National Resources Conservation Service, *National Resources Inventory 2003–Soil Erosion*, pages 5 and 6.

Notes: 'CRP' refers to the Conservation Reserve Program, a federal program established under the Food Security Act of 1985 to assist private landowners to convert highly erodible cropland to vegetative cover for 10 years.
'Highly Erodable Land' (HEL) is land with an erodibility index (a numerical expression of soil's potential for loss due to erosion) of at least 8.
The soil loss tolerance rate is the maximum rate of annual soil loss that will permit crop productivity to be sustained economically and indefinitely on a given soil.

Units: Land area in million acres; erosion in million tons of soil lost.

Chapter 10

Greenhouse Gases & Climate Change

Chapter 10 contains information on greenhouse gases and climate change. At the moment, climate change (also known as global warming) may be the highest-profile environmental issue in the world. Most of the debate focuses on the role of "greenhouse gases" (carbon dioxide, methane, nitrous oxide, and others), and the degree to which humans are responsible for rising temperatures. The EPA's Greenhouse Gas inventory is the agency's annual report on greenhouse gas emissions.

The vast majority (over 80%) of greenhouse gas emissions come from carbon dioxide (table 10.01). Almost 95% of CO_2 emissions are from fossil fuel combustion, while most nitrous oxide comes from agriculture, and most methane comes from landfills, fermentation, and natural gas systems (table 10.02). The transportation and industrial economic sectors are responsible for the most greenhouse emissions, followed by the residential and commercial sectors (table 10.03). Almost all energy-related emissions are in the form of CO_2 from fossil fuel combustion (table 10.04). Of all CO_2 released, the highest amount is generated by the electricity-generating sector, followed by transportation and industry (table 10.05). Most transportation releases are from motor fuel: gasoline in cars and light trucks (including pickup trucks and SUVs), and diesel in large trucks (table 10.06). The two countries with the highest CO_2 emissions from fossil fuels are the United States and China, followed by Russia, India, and Japan (table 10.11).

Industrial emissions are not dominated by CO_2; about an equal amount of emissions (by CO_2 equivalents) come from HFCs (hydrofluorocarbons), PFCs (perfluorocarbons), and SF_6 (sulfur hexafluoride). These gases all have high CO_2 equivalents, which may account for the high figures, even with low masses of emissions (table 10.07). Most methane and nitrous oxide releases come from agriculture and waste (table 10.09). The greenhouse gas inventory also tracks the so-called "indirect" greenhouse gases: carbon monoxide, nitrogen oxides, non-methane volatile organic compounds (NMVOCs), and sulfur dioxide, all of which are released primarily by fossil fuel burning (table 10.10). While emissions have increased, there has also been a small increase in the amount of carbon sequestration (the removal of carbon from the atmosphere), usually by plants (table 10.13).

The Intergovernmental Panel on Climate Change (IPCC) is a UN-affiliated group of scientists studying the causes, extent, and effects of global climate change. Table 10.14 contains an excerpt from the IPCC's Fourth Assessment Report from 2007 summarizing several projected scenarios for climate change. Table 10.12 contains projections of US emissions through 2030.

Finally, this chapter contains a list of Global Warming Potential (GWP) values, which are used to convert emissions into CO_2 equivalents, the equivalent weight of carbon dioxide that would have the same effect as the quantity of each gas released (table 10.15).

Table 10.01: Greenhouse Gas Emissions, 1985–2006

	Based on Weight			Based on Global Warming Potential				
	Carbon Dioxide	Methane	Nitrous Oxide	Carbon Dioxide	Methane	Nitrous Oxide	HFC, PFC, and SF$_6$	Total
1985	4,638.3	30.0	1.1	4,638.3	689.7	330.7	70.5	5,729.3
1986	4,642.5	29.4	1.1	4,642.5	676.5	323.8	75.0	5,717.8
1987	4,800.2	29.9	1.1	4,800.2	688.3	323.4	77.8	5,889.8
1988	5,012.6	30.1	1.1	5,012.6	692.0	316.9	91.3	6,112.8
1989	5,105.8	30.2	1.1	5,105.8	693.8	332.8	94.5	6,226.9
1990	5,017.5	30.8	1.1	5,017.5	708.4	333.7	87.1	6,146.7
1991	4,969.4	30.8	1.2	4,969.4	707.7	342.9	79.0	6,098.9
1992	5,078.7	30.9	1.2	5,078.7	709.7	350.0	83.7	6,222.1
1993	5,203.0	29.8	1.2	5,203.0	684.8	349.5	82.9	6,320.2
1994	5,288.3	29.8	1.3	5,288.3	685.6	374.9	85.3	6,434.0
1995	5,343.4	29.4	1.2	5,343.4	675.9	357.1	94.9	6,471.2
1996	5,531.0	28.5	1.2	5,531.0	656.0	357.6	110.6	6,655.2
1997	5,606.7	28.5	1.2	5,606.7	654.6	350.5	118.0	6,729.8
1998	5,632.5	27.4	1.2	5,632.5	631.3	347.9	134.4	6,746.1
1999	5,703.1	26.8	1.2	5,703.1	615.8	346.3	133.9	6,799.1
2000	5,890.5	26.4	1.2	5,890.5	608.0	341.9	138.0	6,978.4
2001	5,806.3	25.8	1.1	5,806.3	593.9	336.6	128.6	6,865.4
2002	5,875.9	26.0	1.1	5,875.9	598.6	332.5	137.8	6,944.9
2003	5,940.4	26.2	1.1	5,940.4	603.7	331.7	136.6	7,012.4
2004	6,019.9	26.3	1.2	6,019.9	605.9	358.3	149.4	7,133.5
2005	6,045.0	26.4	1.2	6,045.0	607.3	368.0	161.2	7,181.4
2006	5,934.4	26.3	1.3	5,934.4	605.1	378.6	157.6	7,075.6

Source: Energy Information Administration, *Annual Energy Review 2007*, table 12.1.

Notes: Estimations of global warming potential are given with reference to carbon dioxide (that is, CO_2 has a value of 1).
HFCs are hydrofluourocarbons.
PFCs are perfluorocarbons.
SF_6 is sulfur hexafluoride.
Emissions shown are the result of human activity only.
Much data has been revised since its original publication.
Data for 2006 is preliminary.

Units: Gases by weight in millions of metric tons; gases by global warming potential in millions of metric tons carbon dioxide.

Table 10.02: Greenhouse Gas Emissions by Gas and Activity, 1990–2006

	1990	2000	2005	2006
Carbon Dioxide (CO_2)				
Total Carbon Dioxide	*5,068.5*	*5,939.7*	*6,074.3*	*5,983.1*
Fossil fuel combustion	4,724.1	5,577.1	5,731.0	5,637.9
Non-energy use of fuels	117.2	141.4	139.1	138.0
Cement manufacture	33.3	41.2	45.9	45.7
Iron and steel production	86.2	66.6	46.6	49.1
Natural gas systems	33.7	29.4	29.5	28.5
Municipal solid waste combustion	10.9	17.5	20.7	20.9
Ammonia manufacture and urea consumption	16.9	16.4	12.8	12.4
Lime manufacture	12.0	14.9	15.1	15.8
Limestone and dolomite use	5.5	6.0	7.4	8.6
Soda ash manufacture and consumption	4.1	4.2	4.2	4.2
Aluminum production	6.8	6.1	4.2	3.9
Titanium dioxide production	1.2	1.8	1.8	1.9
Phosphoric acid production	1.5	1.4	1.4	1.2
CO_2 consumption	1.4	1.4	1.3	1.6
Zinc production	0.9	1.1	0.5	0.5
Lead production	0.3	0.3	0.3	0.3
Silicon carbide production and consumption	0.4	0.2	0.2	0.2
Land-use change and forestry sink	-737.7	-673.6	-878.6	-883.7
International bunker fuels	113.7	101.1	122.6	127.1
Wood biomass and ethanol consumption	4.2	9.2	22.6	30.3
Methane (CH_4)				
Total Methane	*606.1*	*574.3*	*539.7*	*555.3*
Landfills	149.6	120.8	123.7	125.7
Enteric fermentation	126.9	124.6	124.5	126.2
Natural gas systems	124.7	126.5	102.5	102.4
Coal mining	84.1	60.4	57.1	58.5
Manure management	31.0	38.8	41.8	41.4
Petroleum systems	33.9	30.3	28.3	28.4
Wastewater treatment	23.0	24.6	23.8	23.9
Forest land remaining forest land	4.5	19.0	12.3	24.6
Stationary combustion rice cultivation	7.4	6.6	6.5	6.2
Abandoned coal mines	6.0	7.4	5.6	5.4
Mobile combustion	4.7	3.4	2.5	2.4
Iron and steel production	1.3	1.2	1.0	0.9
Field burning of agricultural residues	0.7	0.8	0.9	0.8

(continued on next page)

Table 10.02: Greenhouse Gas Emissions by Gas and Activity, 1990–2006

	1990	2000	2005	2006
Nitrous Oxide (N$_2$O)				
Total Nitrous Oxide	*383.4*	*385.9*	*370.1*	*367.9*
Agricultural soil management	269.4	262.1	265.2	265.0
Mobile combustion	43.5	52.5	36.3	33.1
Nitric acid production	17.0	18.6	15.8	15.6
Stationary combustion	12.8	14.6	14.8	14.5
Manure management	12.1	13.7	13.9	14.3
Wastewater treatment	6.3	7.6	8.0	8.1
Adipic adic production	15.3	6.2	5.9	5.9
Settlements remaining settlements	1.0	1.2	1.5	1.5
N$_2$O product usage	4.4	4.9	4.4	4.4
Forest land remaining forest land	0.5	2.2	1.6	2.8
Field burning of agricultural residues	0.4	0.5	0.5	0.5
Municipal solid waste combustion	0.5	0.4	0.4	0.4
International bunker fuels	1.0	0.9	1.1	1.1
HFCs, PFCs, and SF$_6$				
Total HFCs, PFCs, and SF$_6$	*36.9*	*100.1*	*121.4*	*124.5*
Substitution of ozone-depleting substances	0.3	71.2	105.4	110.4
HCFC-22 production	36.4	28.6	15.8	13.8
Electrical transmission and distribution	26.7	15.1	14.0	13.2
Semiconductor manufacture	0.2	0.3	0.2	0.3
Aluminum production	18.5	8.6	3.0	2.5
Magnesium production and processing	5.4	3.0	3.3	3.2
Total Emissions	*6,148.3*	*7,032.6*	*7,129.9*	*7,054.2*
Net emissions (sources and sinks)	5,410.6	6,359.0	6,251.3	6,170.5

Source: Environmental Protection Agency, *2008 Inventory of US Greenhouse Gas Emissions and Sinks: 1990-2006*, table ES-2.

Notes: Negative values indicate greenhouse gas sinks (processes that absorb emitted gases). Sinks are only included in the net emissions total.
Estimates for international bunker fuels and biomass consumption are not included in totals.
Groups may not add to total.

Units: Emissions and sinks in million metric tons of CO$_2$ equivalents.

Table 10.03: Emissions by Economic Sector, 1990–2006

	1990	2000	2005	2006
Grand Total	*6,148.3*	*7,032.6*	*7,129.9*	*7,054.2*
Industrial				
Total Industrial	*2,100.4*	*2,174.3*	*2,038.3*	*2,029.2*
Direct emissions	1,460.3	1,432.9	1,354.3	1,371.5
CO_2	1,070.1	1,091.3	1,065.8	1,084.6
CH_4	286.5	258.3	226.7	227.1
N_2O	40.4	33.7	30.0	29.9
HFC, PFC, SF_6	63.3	49.6	31.7	30.0
Electricity-related	640.1	741.4	683.9	657.7
CO_2	627.7	733.1	676.8	650.9
N_2O	2.9	3.3	3.0	2.9
SF_6	9.2	4.8	3.9	3.6
Transportation				
Total Transportation	*1,547.2*	*1,921.0*	*1,992.0*	*1,974.5*
Direct emissions	1,544.1	1,917.5	1,987.2	1,969.5
CO_2	1,496.9	1,810.2	1,880.0	1,865.9
CH_4	4.5	3.2	2.3	2.1
N_2O	42.7	51.5	35.2	32.0
HFCs	NA	52.6	69.7	69.5
Electricity-related	3.1	3.5	4.8	5.0
CO_2	3.1	3.4	4.7	5.0
Commercial				
Total Commercial	*946.3*	*1,141.9*	*1,212.5*	*1,204.4*
Direct emissions	396.9	390.3	400.4	394.6
CO_2	216.1	228.0	221.9	210.1
CH_4	173.8	147.6	149.9	152.0
N_2O	7.0	9.3	10.1	10.2
HFCs	NA	5.5	18.5	22.4
Electricity-related	549.3	751.6	812.0	809.8
CO_2	538.7	743.2	803.5	801.5
N_2O	2.5	3.3	3.6	3.6
SF_6	7.9	4.9	4.7	4.5

(continued on next page)

Table 10.03: Emissions by Economic Sector, 1990–2006

	1990	2000	2005	2006
Grand Total	*6,148.3*	*7,032.6*	*7,129.9*	*7,054.2*
Residential				
Total Residential	*952.4*	*1,160.7*	*1,241.7*	*1,187.8*
Direct emissions	346.9	387.7	376.0	344.8
CO_2	340.1	372.1	358.5	326.5
CH_4	4.4	3.4	3.3	3.1
N_2O	2.1	2.1	2.4	2.3
HFCs	0.3	10.1	11.9	12.9
Electricity-related	605.5	773.0	865.6	843.0
CO_2	593.8	764.4	856.6	834.4
N_2O	2.8	3.4	3.8	3.7
SF_6	8.7	5.0	5.0	4.7
Agriculture				
Total Agriculture	*567.9*	*587.4*	*584.9*	*595.8*
Direct emissions	506.8	528.0	521.3	533.6
CO_2	53.8	58.4	53.4	51.6
CH_4	170.3	190.8	186.4	199.1
N_2O	282.6	278.8	281.5	282.9
Electricity-related	61.2	59.4	63.6	62.3
CO_2	60.0	58.7	63.0	61.6

Source: Environmental Protection Agency, *2008 Inventory of US Greenhouse Gas Emissions and Sinks: 1990-2006*, table 2-16.

Notes: Emissions related to electrical generation are included with other end-use sectors, in proportion to the amount of electricity they use.

Units: Emissions in million metric tons of CO_2 equivalents.

Table 10.04: Energy-Related Emissions by Gas and Source, 1990–2006

	1990	2000	2005	2006
Total Energy-related	*5,203.9*	*6,067.8*	*6,174.4*	*6,076.9*
Carbon Dioxide				
Total Carbon Dioxide	*4,886.4*	*5,765.7*	*5,920.5*	*5,825.6*
Fossil fuel combustion	4,724.1	5,577.1	5,731.0	5,637.9
Electricity generation	1,809.6	2,283.1	2,314.9	2,380.2
Transportation	1,473.5	1,801.5	1,849.3	1,862.6
Industrial	849.9	858.8	861.0	850.9
Residential	344.4	385.0	370.8	360.9
Commercial	218.5	237.6	231.9	223.2
Non-energy use of fuels	117.2	141.4	139.1	138.0
Natural gas systems	33.7	29.4	29.5	28.5
Municipal solid waste combustion	10.9	17.5	20.7	20.9
Petroleum systems	0.4	0.3	0.3	0.3
Wood biomass and ethanol consumption	219.4	227.3	227.4	234.7
Wood	215.2	218.1	204.8	204.4
Ethanol	4.2	9.2	22.6	30.3
International bunker fuels*	113.7	101.1	122.6	127.1
Methane				
Total Methane	*260.7*	*234.5*	*202.3*	*203.3*
Coal mining	84.1	60.4	57.1	58.5
Abandoned underground coal mines	6.0	7.4	5.6	5.4
Mobile combustion	4.7	3.4	2.5	2.4
Natural gas systems	124.7	126.5	102.5	102.4
Petroleum systems	33.9	30.3	28.3	28.4
Stationary combustion	7.4	6.6	6.5	6.2
International bunker fuels*	0.2	0.1	0.2	0.2
Nitrous Oxide				
Total Nitrous Oxide	*56.8*	*67.5*	*51.5*	*48.0*
Mobile combustion	43.5	52.5	36.3	33.1
Municipal solid waste combustion	0.5	0.4	0.4	0.4
Stationary combustion	12.8	14.6	14.8	14.5
International bunker fuels*	1.0	0.9	1.1	1.1

Source: Environmental Protection Agency, *2008 Inventory of US Greenhouse Gas Emissions and Sinks: 1990-2006*, table 2-4.

Notes: * Excluded from totals, but presented for informational purposes.

Units: Emissions in million metric tons of CO_2 equivalents.

Table 10.05: CO_2 Emissions from Fossil Fuel Burning by Sector, 1990–2006

	1990	2000	2005	2006
Total, All Sectors	*4,724.1*	*5,577.1*	*5,731.0*	*5,637.9*
Transportation				
Transportation Total	*1,488.1*	*1,801.6*	*1,874.5*	*1,861.0*
Combustion	1,485.1	1,798.2	1,869.8	1,856.0
Electricity	3.0	3.4	4.7	4.9
Industrial				
Industrial Total	*1,527.5*	*1,645.1*	*1,579.6*	*1,567.1*
Combustion	844.9	860.3	847.3	862.2
Electricity	682.5	784.7	732.3	704.9
Residential				
Residential Total	*929.5*	*1,129.7*	*1,206.4*	*1,151.9*
Combustion	340.1	372.1	358.5	326.5
Electricity	589.4	757.6	847.9	825.4
Commercial				
Commercial Total	*750.8*	*964.6*	*1,017.3*	*1,003.0*
Combustion	216.1	228.0	221.9	210.1
Electricity	534.7	736.6	795.4	792.9
Electricity Generation				
Total	*1,809.6*	*2,282.3*	*2,380.2*	*2,328.2*

Source: Environmental Protection Agency, *2008 Inventory of US Greenhouse Gas Emissions and Sinks: 1990-2006*, table 2-5.

Notes: Emissions from electricity generation are not included in total; rather, they are distributed among the transportation, industrial, residential, and commercial sectors by the proportion of the total electricity used by the sectors.
Groups may not add to total.

Units: Emissions in million metric tons of CO_2 equivalents.

Table 10.06: CO_2 Emissions From Transportation Fossil Fuel Combustion, by Fuel and Vehicle Type, 1990–2006

	1990	2000	2005	2006
Total with Bunkers	*1,601.8*	*1,902.7*	*1,997.1*	*1,988.1*
Total, Excluding Bunkers	*1,488.1*	*1,801.6*	*1,874.5*	*1,861.0*
Gasoline				
Total Gasoline	*982.8*	*1,135.7*	*1,181.2*	*1,170.0*
Cars	621.0	639.9	654.2	630.4
Light trucks	308.9	446.0	476.0	488.0
Other trucks	38.7	36.0	34.7	35.2
Buses	0.3	0.4	0.4	0.4
Motorcycles	1.7	1.8	1.6	1.9
Recreational boats	12.1	11.6	14.3	14.1
Diesel				
Total Diesel	*272.7*	*401.0*	*462.2*	*472.1*
Automobiles	7.8	3.6	4.2	4.1
Light trucks	11.3	19.8	25.5	26.4
Other trucks	188.3	305.1	356.5	365.4
Buses	7.9	10.1	10.6	10.9
Locomotives	35.1	41.7	45.1	46.0
Recreational boats	1.9	2.7	3.1	3.2
Ships & other boats	8.8	11.7	7.9	7.4
Ship bunkers	11.6	6.3	9.3	8.7
Jet Fuel				
Total Jet Fuel	*222.6*	*253.8*	*246.3*	*239.5*
Commercial aircraft	136.7	164.2	150.4	142.1
Military aircraft	33.9	20.5	16.9	14.8
General aviation	6.3	9.2	11.4	11.4
Aircraft bunkers	45.7	59.9	67.5	71.1
Aviation Gasoline				
Total Aviation Gasoline	*3.1*	*2.5*	*2.4*	*2.3*

(continued on next page)

Table 10.06: CO_2 Emissions From Transportation Fossil Fuel Combustion, by Fuel and Vehicle Type, 1990–2006

	1990	2000	2005	2006
Residual Fuel Oil				
Total Residual Fuel Oil	*80.1*	*69.9*	*66.0*	*64.9*
Ships & boats	23.7	34.9	20.2	17.7
Ship bunkers	56.4	35.0	45.8	47.2
Natural Gas				
Total Natural Gas	*36.1*	*35.7*	*33.2*	*33.2*
Pipeline	36.1	35.2	32.3	32.4
Propane				
Total Propane	*1.4*	*0.7*	*1.1*	*1.1*
Light trucks	0.5	0.3	0.4	0.4
Other trucks	0.8	0.4	0.6	0.6
Electricity				
Total Electricity	*3.0*	*3.4*	*4.7*	*4.9*
Rail	3.0	3.4	4.7	4.9

Source: Environmental Protection Agency, *2008 Inventory of US Greenhouse Gas Emissions and Sinks: 1990-2006*, table 3-7.

Notes: 'Light trucks' weigh less than 8,500 pounds.
'Other trucks' include both medium and heavy-duty trucks, which weigh over 8,500 pounds.
'Propane' refers to the use of Liquefied Propane Gas.
Estimates of emissions from bunker fuels are excluded from official estimates, but are included here for informational purposes.

Units: Emissions in million metric tons of CO_2 equivalents.

Table 10.07: Emissions from Industrial Processes, 1990–2006

	1990	2000	2005	2006
Total Industrial Emissions	*299.9*	*326.5*	*315.5*	*320.9*
Carbon Dioxide (CO_2)				
Total CO_2	*175.0*	*166.5*	*145.9*	*149.5*
Cement manufacture	33.3	41.2	45.9	45.7
Iron and steel production	86.2	66.6	46.6	49.1
Ammonia production	16.9	16.4	12.8	12.4
Lime manufacture	12.0	14.9	15.1	15.8
Limestone and dolemite use	5.5	6.0	7.4	8.6
Aluminum production	6.8	6.1	4.2	3.9
Soda ash manufacture and consumption	4.1	4.2	4.2	4.2
Petrochemical production	2.2	3.0	2.8	2.6
Methane (CH_4)				
Total CH_4	*2.2*	*2.5*	*2.0*	*2.0*
Petrochemical production	0.9	1.2	1.1	1.0
Iron and steel production	1.3	1.2	1.0	0.9
Nitrous Oxide (N_2O)				
Total N_2O	*32.3*	*24.8*	*21.7*	*21.6*
Nitric acid production	17.0	18.6	15.8	15.6
Adipic acid production	15.3	6.2	5.9	5.9
HFCs, PFCs, and SF_6				
Total	*90.4*	*132.7*	*145.8*	*147.8*
Substitution of ozone-depleting substances	0.3	71.2	105.4	110.4
HCFC-22 production	36.4	28.6	15.8	13.8
Electrical transmission and distribution	26.7	15.1	14.0	13.2

Source: Environmental Protection Agency, *2008 Inventory of US Greenhouse Gas Emissions and Sinks: 1990-2006*, table 2-6.

Notes: HFCs are hydrofluourocarbons.
PFCs are perfluorocarbons.
SF_6 is sulfur hexafluoride.
Not all subgroups are shown, and may not add to total.

Units: Emissions in million metric tons of CO_2 equivalents.

Table 10.08: Carbon Intensity of Fossil Fuel Combustion by Sector, 1990–2006

	1990	2000	2004	2005	2006
All Sectors	*72.7*	*72.7*	*72.9*	*73.1*	*73.0*
Residential	57.3	56.7	56.9	56.6	56.7
Commercial	59.2	57.1	57.6	57.6	57.5
Industrial	63.7	62.6	63.6	64.0	64.2
Transportation	71.0	71.0	71.0	71.1	71.1
Electricity generation, all sources	86.7	85.6	85.4	85.0	84.6
Electricity, excluding nuclear and renewable sources	59.0	59.9	59.6	59.9	58.8

Source: Environmental Protection Agency, *2007 Inventory of US Greenhouse Gas Emissions and Sinks: 1990-2005*, tables 3-8 and 3-9; *2008*, tables 3-8 and 3-9.

Notes: Total does not include nuclear or renewable power consumption.

Units: Carbon intensity in million metric tons of CO_2 equivalent per quadrillion Btu.

Table 10.09: Methane and Nitrous Oxide Emissions from Agriculture and Waste, 1990–2006

	1990	2000	2005	2006
Methane				
Agriculture	165.7	171.7	174.0	174.4
Enteric fermentation	126.9	124.6	124.5	126.2
Manure management	31.0	38.8	41.8	41.4
Dairy cattle	12.0	15.8	17.9	17.9
Beef cattle	2.5	2.4	2.3	2.5
Swine	13.1	17.4	17.9	17.5
Sheep	0.1	0.1	0.1	0.1
Poultry	2.8	2.6	2.6	2.7
Horses	0.5	0.5	0.8	0.8
Rice cultivation	7.1	7.5	6.8	5.9
Field burning of agricultural residues	0.7	0.8	0.9	0.8
Waste	172.9	146.7	149.0	151.1
Landfills	149.6	120.8	123.7	125.7
Wastewater treatment	23.0	24.6	23.8	23.9
Nitrous Oxide				
Agriculture	281.8	276.3	279.6	279.8
Soil management	269.4	262.1	265.2	265.0
Manure management	39.0	13.7	13.9	14.3
Dairy cattle	3.5	3.6	3.7	3.8
Beef cattle	5.5	6.7	6.5	6.7
Swine	1.2	1.4	1.5	1.5
Sheep	0.1	0.1	0.1	0.1
Poultry	1.5	1.7	1.7	1.8
Horses	0.2	0.2	0.4	0.4
Field burning of agricultural residues	0.4	0.5	0.5	0.5
Wastewater treatment	6.3	7.6	8.0	8.1
Agriculture total	*447.5*	*447.9*	*453.6*	*454.1*
Waste total	*179.6*	*155.6*	*158.7*	*161.0*

Source: Environmental Protection Agency, *2008 Inventory of US Greenhouse Gas Emissions and Sinks: 1990-2006*, tables 2-10, 2-11, and 6-6.

Notes: Total shown includes only methane (CH_4) and nitrous oxide (NO_2). Groups may not add to total.

Units: Emissions in million metric tons of CO_2 equivalents.

Table 10.10: Emissions of Indirect Greenhouse Gases, 1990–2006

	1990	2000	2005	2006
Nitrogen Oxides				
Total Nitrogen Oxides	*21,645*	*19,203*	*15,569*	*14,869*
Mobile fossil fuel combustion	10,920	10,310	8,739	8,287
Stationary fossil fuel combustion	9,883	8,002	5,853	5,610
Industrial processes	591	626	519	515
Oil and gas activities	139	111	316	315
Municipal solid waste combustion	82	114	97	97
Agricultural burning	28	35	39	38
Carbon Monoxide				
Total Carbon Monoxide	*130,461*	*92,777*	*72,365*	*68,372*
Mobile fossil fuel combustion	119,360	83,559	63,154	59,213
Stationary fossil fuel combustion	5,000	4,340	4,860	4,844
Municipal solid waste combustion	978	1,670	1,437	1,437
Industrial processes	4,125	2,217	1,724	1,724
Agricultural burning	691	792	860	825
Oil and gas activities	302	146	321	322
Non-Methane Volatile Organic Compounds (NMVOCs)				
Total NMVOCs	*20,930*	*15,228*	*14,444*	*14,082*
Mobile fossil fuel combustion	10,932	7,230	6,289	5,991
Solvent use	5,216	4,384	3,846	3,839
Industrial processes	2,422	1,773	1,890	1,849
Stationary fossil fuel combustion	912	1,077	1,545	1,538
Oil and gas activities	554	389	528	523
Municipal solid waste combustion	222	257	235	232
Waste	673	119	111	110
Sulfur Dioxide				
Total Sulfur Dioxide	*20,935*	*14,829*	*13,114*	*12,258*
Stationary fossil fuel combustion	18,407	12,848	11,573	10,784
Industrial processes	1,307	1,031	797	793
Mobile fossil fuel combustion	793	632	508	451
Oil and gas activities	390	286	213	207
Municipal solid waste combustion	38	29	22	22

Source: Environmental Protection Agency, *2008 Inventory of US Greenhouse Gas Emissions and Sinks: 1990-2006*, table ES-10.

Notes: Indirect greenhouse gases include nitrogen oxides (NO_x), carbon monoxide (CO), non-methane volatile organic compounds (NMVOCs), and sulfur diooxide (SO_2).

Units: Emissions in thousand metric tons.

Table 10.11: World Carbon Dioxide Emissions from Fossil Fuels, 2005

	Coal	Petroleum	Natural Gas	Fossil Fuel Total
World Total	*11,357.2*	*10,995.5*	*5,840.1*	*28,192.7*
North America	*2,330.0*	*3,169.4*	*1,488.4*	*6,987.8*
Canada	153.0	289.9	188.3	631.3
Mexico	35.4	264.2	98.7	398.2
United States	2,141.7	2,614.0	1,201.4	5,957.0
Central and South America	*80.5*	*747.7*	*268.0*	*1,096.2*
Argentina	3.2	63.4	80.0	146.6
Brazil	40.8	279.2	40.5	360.6
Chile	15.8	33.5	16.8	66.2
Colombia	10.2	36.2	12.4	58.8
Ecuador	0.0	21.5	2.4	23.9
Peru	3.7	24.5	3.1	31.3
Venezuela	0.1	80.0	71.2	151.3
Europe	*1,355.7*	*2,209.5*	*1,109.5*	*4,674.7*
Austria	16.5	42.7	19.0	78.2
Belgium	18.9	82.5	34.4	135.8
Czech Republic	67.7	27.2	17.9	112.8
France	48.5	265.2	101.6	415.3
Germany	318.0	339.7	186.5	844.2
Greece	35.0	62.6	5.5	103.2
Italy	60.5	241.8	164.3	466.6
Netherlands	47.0	140.2	82.5	269.7
Poland	198.5	57.7	28.4	284.6
Portugal	12.2	44.0	8.7	65.0
Romania	33.0	32.6	33.8	99.3
Spain	88.5	230.9	67.8	387.1
Turkey	94.6	82.4	53.0	230.0
United Kingdom	141.8	243.2	192.1	577.2
Eurasia	*693.7*	*566.4*	*1,317.7*	*2,577.8*
Kazakhstan	105.4	33.2	59.4	198.0
Russia	441.7	379.4	874.9	1,696.0
Ukraine	126.3	46.0	170.2	342.6
Uzbekistan	4.1	22.5	91.4	118.0

(continued on next page)

Table 10.11: World Carbon Dioxide Emissions from Fossil Fuels, 2005

	Coal	Petroleum	Natural Gas	Fossil Fuel Total
World Total	*11,357.2*	*10,995.5*	*5,840.1*	*28,192.7*
Middle East	*35.4*	*823.5*	*591.8*	*1,450.8*
Iran	4.2	221.3	225.2	450.7
Iraq	0.0	79.0	19.2	98.1
Israel	30.8	32.8	1.4	65.0
Saudi Arabia	0.0	272.9	139.4	412.4
United Arab Emirates	0.0	55.7	82.1	137.8
Africa	*385.5*	*413.5*	*243.9*	*1,042.9*
Algeria	2.2	31.3	54.6	88.1
Egypt	3.1	90.5	68.2	161.8
Nigeria	0.0	43.3	61.9	105.2
South Africa	347.8	71.5	4.6	423.8
Asia and Oceania	*6,476.3*	*3,065.4*	*820.7*	*10,362.5*
Australia	231.5	122.1	53.0	406.6
China	4,341.0	880.2	101.5	5,322.7
India	791.1	303.5	71.2	1,165.7
Indonesia	96.3	179.0	84.2	359.5
Japan	416.9	643.2	170.3	1,230.4
North Korea	69.6	3.9	0.0	73.5
South Korea	196.3	240.4	63.0	499.6
Malaysia	22.3	68.1	65.2	155.5
Pakistan	15.4	52.5	53.6	121.5
Singapore	0.0	121.0	12.9	133.9
Taiwan	149.4	113.5	21.4	284.4
Thailand	45.5	129.3	59.3	234.2

Source: Energy Information Administration, *International Energy Annual 2005*, tables H.1co2, H.2co2, H.3co2, and H.4co2.

Notes: Total for fossil fuels includes CO_2 emitted burning petroleum products, coal, and natural gas. Total for Europe excludes countries in the former USSR.

Units: Emissions in million metric tons CO_2.

Table 10.12: Projected Carbon Dioxide Emissions by Sector and Source, 2006–2030

	2006	2010	2015	2020	2025	2030
All Sectors						
Grand Total	5,890	6,011	6,226	6,384	6,571	6,851
Petroleum	2,581	2,555	2,636	2,650	2,676	2,767
Natural gas	1,163	1,256	1,279	1,262	1,245	1,231
Coal	2,134	2,188	2,299	2,459	2,638	2,841
Other	12	12	12	12	12	12
Per capita CO_2 emissions	19.6	19.3	19.2	18.9	18.7	18.7
Residential						
Residential Total	1,204	1,259	1,280	1,324	1,379	1,451
Petroleum	100	91	92	92	90	88
Natural gas	237	263	274	281	284	282
Coal	1	1	1	1	1	1
Electricity	866	904	913	949	1,004	1,079
Commercial						
Commercial Total	1,046	1,079	1,176	1,265	1,367	1,474
Petroleum	53	46	48	49	49	49
Natural gas	155	162	175	184	193	201
Coal	6	8	8	8	8	8
Electricity	832	864	945	1,024	1,117	1,216
Industrial						
Industrial Total	1,652	1,693	1,718	1,718	1,716	1,733
Petroleum	421	435	442	432	428	436
Natural gas	399	430	435	434	437	433
Coal	189	186	185	204	206	217
Electricity	642	640	656	649	645	647

(continued on next page)

Table 10.12: Projected Carbon Dioxide Emissions by Sector and Source, 2006–2030

	2006	2010	2015	2020	2025	2030
Transportation						
Transportation Total	*1,989*	*1,980*	*2,052*	*2,077*	*2,110*	*2,193*
Petroleum	1,952	1,940	2,010	2,032	2,062	2,145
Natural gas	33	36	38	40	43	43
Electricity	4	4	5	5	5	5
Electric Power						
Electric Power Total	*2,344*	*2,413*	*2,519*	*2,627*	*2,771*	*2,948*
Petroleum	55	43	44	45	47	48
Natural gas	340	365	358	323	289	272
Coal	1,938	1,993	2,105	2,247	2,423	2,615
Other	12	12	12	12	12	12

Source: Energy Information Administration, *Annual Energy Outlook 2008 with Projections to 2030*, table A18.

Notes: Emissions for electricity are distributed by end-use sector.
'Electric power' sector totals are not included in the grand total.
'Other' includes emissions from geothermal power and and non-biogenic emissions from municipal solid waste.
Data for 2006 is from the projection model, and may differ slightly from the official 2006 estimates.
Groups may not add to total.

Units: Emissions in million metric tons CO_2; per capita emission in tons of CO_2 per person per year.

Table 10.13: Storage of Carbon Dioxide from Land and Land-Use Changes, 1990–2006

	1990	2000	2005	2006
Total Net Storage	*737.7*	*673.6*	*878.6*	*883.7*
Forest land remaining forest land	621.7	550.7	743.6	745.1
Cropland remaining cropland	30.1	38.4	41.0	41.8
Land converted to cropland	-14.7	-9.4	-9.4	-9.4
Grassland remaining grassland	1.9	16.4	16.3	16.2
Land converted to grassland	14.3	16.3	16.3	16.3
Settlements remaining settlements	60.6	82.4	93.3	95.5
Other (landfilled yard trimmings and food scraps)	23.9	11.5	10.0	10.5

Source: Environmental Protection Agency, *2008 Inventory of US Greenhouse Gas Emissions and Sinks: 1990-2006*, table 7-1.

Notes: Positive values represent the removal of CO_2 gas from the atmosphere (called 'sequestration'). Negative values indicate emission of CO_2 gas.

Units: Sequestration (storage) in million metric tons of CO_2.

Table 10.14: Projected Global Temperature Increase and Sea Level Rise, End of 21st Century

| | Temperature Change | | Sea Level Rise |
	Best Estimate	Likely Range	Likely Range
Baseline scenario	0.6°	0.3°-0.9°	NA
B1 scenario (600 ppm)	1.8°	1.1°-2.9°	0.18-0.38
A1T scenario (700 ppm)	2.4°	1.4°-3.8°	0.20-0.45
B2 scenario (800 ppm)	2.4°	1.4°-3.8°	0.20-0.43
A1B scenario (850 ppm)	2.8°	1.7°-4.4°	0.21-0.48
A2 scenario (1,250 ppm)	3.4°	2.0°-5.4°	0.23-0.51
A1FI scenario (1,550 ppm)	4.0°	2.4°-6.4°	0.26-0.59

Source: Intergovernmental Panel on Climate Change, *Climate Change 2007: The Physical Science Basis. Contribution of Working Group I to the Fourth Assessment Report of the Intergovernmental Panel on Climate Change: Summary for Policymakers*, table SPM.3.

Notes: Temperature change and sea level rise is measured in terms of the average global temperature from 2090–2099 compared to the global average from 1980–1999. Global temperature scenarios are based on the 2000 IPCC report *Special Report on Emission Scenarios*, based on the following projected CO_2 equivalent concentrations at the end of the 21st century:

    B1:   600 ppm.
    A1T: 700 ppm.
    B2:   800 ppm.
    A1B: 850 ppm.
    A2:   1,250 ppm.
    A1FI: 1,550 ppm.

The baseline case assumes a constant level of CO_2 equivalent concentrations from the year 2000.

The science behind climate change predictions is quite complex; see the IPCC's Fourth Assessment Report (AR4) for further explanations of the scenarios and the underlying data and methodology.

Units: Projected temperature change in degrees Celsius; projected sea level rise in meters.

Table 10.15: Global Warming Potentials of Greenhouse Gases

Gas	GWP
CO_2	1
CH_4	21
N_2O	310
HFC-23	11,700
HFC-32	650
HFC-125	2,800
HFC-134a	1,300
HFC-143a	3,800
HFC-152a	140
HFC-227ea	2,900
HFC-236fa	6,300
HFC-4310mee	1,300
CF_4	6,500
C_2F_6	9,200
C_4F_{10}	7,000
C_6F_{14}	7,400
SF_6	23,900

Source: Environmental Protection Agency, *2008 Inventory of US Greenhouse Gas Emissions and Sinks: 1990-2006*, table ES-1.

Notes: Global Warming Potentials (GWPs) are used to generate CO_2 equivalents, the typical unit in estimating greenhouse gas emisisons, based on a gas' greenhouse potential relative to CO_2. For example, methane (CH_4) has 21 times the potential of CO_2 (for equal quantities by weight) to alter climate and temperature, so 1 ton of methane released has an equal atmospheric effect as 21 tons of CO_2. Values shown here were provided by the Interogvernmental Panel on Climate Change (IPCC).

The GWP value for CH_4 includes its direct greenhouse effects, as well as its indirect effects in producing ozone and wator vapor in the atmosphere, but does not its indirect effects in the formation of CO_2.

See source material for details on chemicals.

Units: Global Warming Potential (GWP) relative to carbon dioxide.

Chapter 11

Pollution &
Chemical Exposure

Chapter 11 collects information on pollution and human exposure to chemicals. Much of the data on chemical releases comes from the EPA's Toxic Release Inventory (TRI) program. The TRI report shows a decrease in chemical releases from 1998 to 2006, especially for on-site disposal (table 11.01). Three of the top 20 counties for disposal are in Nevada (table 11.03), and the top sources of toxic materials are mining, electrical utilities, chemicals, and metals (table 11.04). Table 11.04 also lists the amount of carcinogens, lead, mercury, and dioxin released. Toluene and copper were the most recycled chemicals, propylene and methanol were the most used for energy recovery, and methanol and hydrochloric acid were the most treated chemicals (table 11.06). The report also gives a state-by-state breakdown of toxic chemical releases by method of disposal and specific compounds (tables 11.02 and 11.05).

The EPA's Air Quality division keeps track of emissions of pollutants like carbon monoxide, ammonia, nitrogen oxides, particulate matter, sulfur dioxide, volatile organic compounds, and lead. Emissions decreased across the board from 1980 to 2007 (table 11.08, also see details in tables 11.09–11.13). Also shown is data on emissions from vehicles by type of vehicle and pollutant emitted (table 11.14) and automobile emissions by type of fuel and automobile (table 11.15). The highest emissions were for carbon monoxide, most of which (over 68% in 2007) came from highway and off-highway vehicles (tables 11.09 and 11.15). Lead emissions have dropped drastically, from 220,000 tons in 1970 to 4,000 in 2000, likely due in large part to the introduction of unleaded gasoline (table 11.16).

The CDC measures levels of human exposure to various chemicals. Tables in this chapter show the 95th percentile level for several chemicals in blood, urine, or fatty tissue (table 11.18). Secondhand smoke exposure for non-smokers is higher among males, younger people, and Black Americans (table 11.19). A CDC program measuring blood lead levels found the highest levels of exposure in Alabama, Kansas, and Missouri (table 11.20). The CDC also provides two rankings of the chemicals that pose the greatest threat to health through exposure: the Completed Exposure Pathway (CEP) and Comprehensive Environmental Response, Compensation, and Recovery Act (CERCLA) lists (tables 11.21 and 11.22, respectively).

People's opinion of whether we should relax environmental standards to promote more oil and gas production is sharply divided by political affiliation, with Republicans more likely to support such measures, and Democrats most likely to oppose them. In general, people are less optimistic about state of the environment in the United States and the world in general than they are for their own communities. People are also generally supportive of environmental proposals setting higher pollution or greenhouse gas emission standards for industry, but are less open to proposals opening the Alaskan wildlife refuge to oil drilling (table 11.24).

Table 11.01: Toxic Chemical Disposal and Other Releases, 2001–2006

	2001	2002	2003	2004	2005	2006
Facilities	25,758	25,051	24,445	24,197	23,797	22,880
Chemical forms	96,725	94,070	92,086	91,183	90,244	87,870
Total Disposal	*5,584.8*	*4,750.5*	*4,442.2*	*4,238.7*	*4,353.9*	*4,248.9*
On-site Disposal:						
Total On-site Disposal	*5,088.4*	*4,260.0*	*3,958.7*	*3,726.5*	*3,820.6*	*3,725.5*
Air emissions	1,630.2	1,613.6	1,584.0	1,540.4	1,512.6	1,408.3
Fugitive air	211.9	199.9	198.5	196.2	192.3	184.4
Stack air	1,418.3	1,413.7	1,385.5	1,344.2	1,320.3	1,223.9
Surface water discharges	243.2	242.5	229.7	245.1	250.4	243.0
Underground injection	215.6	227.0	229.2	238.1	231.7	219.8
On-site land	2,999.4	2,176.8	1,915.7	1,702.9	1,825.9	1,854.5
Off-site Disposal:						
Total Off-site Disposal	*496.4*	*490.5*	*483.5*	*512.2*	*533.4*	*523.3*
Storage only	5.9	9.1	5.9	7.9	5.5	6.2
Solidification/stabilization (metals only)	64.5	103.3	78.5	78.0	72.7	98.0
Wastewater treatment (metals only)	3.8	3.6	2.3	2.1	6.3	2.2
Transfers to POTW (metals)	2.2	2.0	1.9	1.7	1.8	2.8
Underground injection	15.4	8.6	7.9	12.2	13.2	16.6
Landfill/surface impoundments	336.3	277.5	310.1	324.2	338.4	320.7
Land treatment	7.3	10.0	9.5	8.9	10.6	6.7
Other land disposal	28.7	42.3	32.4	40.1	46.7	33.9
Other off-site management	16.2	15.2	14.6	14.2	16.5	15.8
Waste broker	12.1	12.9	15.6	17.4	16.1	14.1
Unknown	3.8	5.9	4.9	5.6	5.7	6.4

Source: Environmental Protection Agency, *2006 TRI Public Data Release*, table B-3.

Notes: This information does not indicate whether (or to what degree) the public has been exposed to chemicals. See www.epa.gov/tri/tridata for a discussion of using Toxic Release Inventory (TRI) data to estimate exposures and risks.
Groups may not add to total.

Units: Number of facilities and chemical forms; amount of waste disposed in millions of pounds.

Table 11.02: Toxic Material Disposal by State and Disposal Site, 2006

	On-site Disposal	Off-site Disposal	Total
United States	*3,725,545.6*	*523,319.6*	*4,248,865.2*
Alabama	95,800.3	25,270.0	121,070.3
Alaska	667,332.8	289.4	667,622.2
Arizona	96,262.9	2,336.5	98,599.4
Arkansas	39,681.9	10,820.6	50,502.5
California	36,110.6	6,868.1	42,978.7
Colorado	18,503.3	6,197.4	24,700.7
Connecticut	3,466.5	1,461.1	4,927.6
Delaware	11,085.8	4,740.5	15,826.3
District of Columbia	19.8	1.0	20.9
Florida	116,285.8	3,114.5	119,400.3
Georgia	126,375.6	3,387.0	129,762.6
Hawaii	2,788.6	230.7	3,019.3
Idaho	66,344.5	887.0	67,231.4
Illinois	87,669.1	24,889.4	112,558.5
Indiana	136,298.1	100,571.6	236,869.7
Iowa	34,023.6	12,794.1	46,817.7
Kansas	23,462.8	4,049.2	27,512.1
Kentucky	89,648.3	7,476.5	97,124.8
Louisiana	123,629.7	7,950.8	131,580.4
Maine	9,215.5	1,336.6	10,552.1
Maryland	36,692.4	3,073.8	39,766.2
Massachusetts	4,871.0	2,098.9	6,969.9
Michigan	66,510.4	20,664.1	87,174.5
Minnesota	23,538.2	2,565.7	26,103.9
Mississippi	58,691.5	2,069.3	60,760.8
Missouri	105,437.2	4,424.0	109,861.1
Montana	42,172.3	1,151.4	43,323.8
Nebraska	30,197.4	4,622.3	34,819.8
Nevada	215,929.3	1,169.7	217,099.1

(continued on next page)

Table 11.02: Toxic Material Disposal by State and Disposal Site, 2006

	On-site Disposal	Off-site Disposal	Total
United States	*3,725,545.6*	*523,319.6*	*4,248,865.2*
New Hampshire	4,069.3	104.1	4,173.4
New Jersey	18,176.8	3,586.8	21,763.6
New Mexico	23,466.1	247.3	23,713.4
New York	29,136.7	6,380.1	35,516.8
North Carolina	117,379.8	16,715.0	134,094.8
North Dakota	13,607.2	8,705.6	22,312.8
Ohio	230,077.4	61,266.5	291,343.9
Oklahoma	25,422.8	4,230.1	29,652.9
Oregon	22,791.4	1,065.3	23,856.7
Pennsylvania	101,065.4	53,011.9	154,077.3
Rhode Island	321.6	177.1	498.7
South Carolina	62,701.9	12,627.0	75,328.9
South Dakota	6,638.6	564.2	7,202.7
Tennessee	116,861.9	14,555.7	131,417.5
Texas	209,160.8	29,297.8	238,458.6
Utah	145,860.0	2,334.6	148,194.6
Vermont	171.0	433.3	604.3
Virginia	65,974.1	4,807.9	70,782.0
Washington	27,388.7	2,109.0	29,497.7
West Virginia	85,046.8	16,528.4	101,575.2
Wisconsin	30,435.0	15,563.9	45,998.9
Wyoming	14,225.5	1,213.8	15,439.3

Source: Environmental Protection Agency, *2006 TRI Public Data Release*, table B-11.

Notes: This information does not indicate whether (or to what degree) the public has been exposed to chemicals. See www.epa.gov/tri/tridata for a discussion of using Toxic Release Inventory (TRI) data to estimate exposures and risks.
Groups may not add to total.

Units: Amount of toxic materials disposed in thousands of pounds.

Table 11.03: Top 20 Counties for Toxic Material Disposal, 2006

	Facilities	Chemical Forms	On-Site Disposal	Off-Site Disposal	Total
Northwest Arctic County, AK	2	16	615,323,007	24	615,323,031
Salt Lake County, UT	68	249	120,298,576	717,082	121,015,658
Humboldt County, NV	6	58	84,605,790	4,701	84,610,491
Gila County, AZ	5	39	73,185,027	1,295,421	74,480,448
Lucas County, OH	56	317	56,221,926	788,559	57,010,485
Elko County, NV	5	55	52,485,680	1,492	52,487,172
Lake County, IN	54	397	15,348,298	36,164,176	51,512,474
Juneau County, AK	1	10	44,450,428	0	44,450,428
Jefferson County, OH	8	71	22,505,778	18,364,752	40,870,531
Harris County, TX	319	2,215	31,344,516	8,980,283	40,324,800
Escambia County, FL	17	114	37,576,422	244,724	37,821,146
Brazoria County, TX	35	400	36,599,288	329,885	36,929,173
Spencer County, IN	4	31	35,779,863	1,027,714	36,807,577
Reynolds County, MO	5	14	36,581,663	0	36,581,663
Montgomery County, IN	10	43	125,506	33,634,072	33,759,578
Humphreys County, TN	8	69	28,811,138	3,466,490	32,277,629
Owyhee County, ID	3	32	31,330,041	5,084	31,335,125
Peoria County, IL	17	97	23,246,679	8,028,222	31,274,902
Iron County, MO	3	13	26,955,766	1,873,106	28,828,872
Eureka County, NV	4	34	28,798,283	16,596	28,814,879

Source: Environmental Protection Agency, *2006 TRI Public Data Release*, tables B-12a to B-12c.

Notes: This information does not indicate whether (or to what degree) the public has been exposed to chemicals. See www.epa.gov/tri/tridata for a discussion of using Toxic Release Inventory (TRI) data to estimate exposures and risks.
Groups may not add to total.
Rankings are based on total TRI disposed.

Units: Amount of toxic materials disposed in pounds.

Table 11.04: Toxic Material Disposal by Type of Compound, 2006

	Carcinogens	Lead	Mercury	Dioxin	Total
All Releases	*819,511.6*	*446,246.4*	*5,138.0*	*130,277.28*	*4,248,865.2*
Coal mining	1,938.0	713.6	4.1	6.70	16,863.8
Metal mining	494,364.0	378,928.4	4,523.6	8.39	1,216,444.1
Electric utilities	42,228.3	7,476.8	148.7	725.70	1,022,110.4
Food, beverages, and tobacco	3,539.0	134.4	3.1	29.86	163,836.6
Textiles	417.1	34.5	0.0	0.67	3,749.6
Apparel	55.8	2.5	NA	NA	116.2
Leather	639.9	0.0	NA	NA	1,447.9
Wood products	5,551.6	70.7	0.1	485.38	21,655.6
Paper	12,082.6	540.9	13.7	668.42	211,586.7
Printing and publishing	76.8	7.0	NA	NA	12,934.3
Petroleum	6,419.2	191.2	4.9	452.32	76,145.4
Chemicals	72,476.7	2,549.0	60.6	121,167.77	514,343.1
Plastics and rubber	27,435.0	82.1	0.0	0.36	63,999.8
Stone, clay, and glass	5,976.5	608.6	1.6	10.48	34,107.5
Cement	1,344.3	578.7	12.0	151.70	10,937.8
Primary metals	51,027.0	28,026.3	26.2	6,432.80	468,564.0
Fabricated metals	8,165.5	1,045.8	0.0	0.04	62,781.9
Machinery	1,752.2	124.1	1.1	NA	9,626.1
Computers and electronics	876.0	426.0	0.1	NA	9,222.8
Electrical equipment	2,678.5	1,388.2	9.5	0.27	9,387.0
Transportation equipment	20,546.3	131.5	0.0	0.53	60,594.3
Furniture	876.9	8.0	NA	1.83	9,812.7
Miscellaneous manufacturing	1,552.8	41.0	0.5	NA	7,934.5
Chemical wholesalers	160.4	0.6	0.2	NA	1,286.0
Petroleum bulk terminals	417.2	24.4	0.0	NA	3,282.2
Hazardous waste	51,004.7	17,839.7	327.2	132.26	204,350.6
Other	5,909.2	5,272.6	0.7	1.80	31,744.4

Source: Environmental Protection Agency, *2006 TRI Public Data Release*, tables B-8, B-21, B-24, B-27, and B-30.

Notes: 'Lead' includes lead and lead compounds.
'Mercury' includes mercury and mercury compounds.
'Dioxin' includes dioxin and dioxin-like compounds.
This information does not indicate whether (or to what degree) the public has been exposed to chemicals. See www.epa.gov/tri/tridata for a discussion of using Toxic Release Inventory (TRI) data to estimate exposures and risks.
Groups may not add to total.

Units: Amount of carcinogens, lead compounds, mercury compounds, and total disposal in thousands of pounds; amount of dioxin in grams.

Table 11.05: Toxic Material Disposal by Type
of Compound and State, 2006

	Carcinogens	Lead	Mercury	Dioxin	Total
United States	*819,511.6*	*446,246.4*	*5,138.0*	*130,277.28*	*4,248,865.2*
Alabama	14,570.2	4,208.5	204.5	336.46	121,070.3
Alaska	245,693.3	239,867.4	59.4	1.00	667,622.2
Arizona	22,093.4	15,525.2	130.0	14.09	98,599.4
Arkansas	4,381.1	1,093.3	2.6	79.26	50,502.5
California	10,910.5	4,401.5	43.7	219.91	42,978.7
Colorado	6,499.1	6,192.2	4.3	6.16	24,700.7
Connecticut	1,341.5	494.2	22.0	4.86	4,927.6
Delaware	722.5	94.4	4.6	28,470.09	15,826.3
District of Columbia	1.0	0.9	NA	NA	20.9
Florida	12,753.1	828.2	8.1	96.12	119,400.3
Georgia	8,844.2	799.1	6.7	548.18	129,762.6
Hawaii	202.6	110.7	0.1	5.09	3,019.3
Idaho	9,726.4	6,268.4	5.5	3.01	67,231.4
Illinois	9,693.6	2,142.5	9.8	40.53	112,558.5
Indiana	24,779.9	6,513.1	9.9	399.00	236,869.7
Iowa	3,608.3	1,026.8	4.2	150.21	46,817.7
Kansas	2,932.8	234.8	3.5	139.03	27,512.1
Kentucky	6,873.3	1,284.6	6.9	1,702.89	97,124.8
Louisiana	23,237.9	1,311.7	18.5	1,700.62	131,580.4
Maine	773.4	16.4	0.1	27.51	10,552.1
Maryland	1,425.9	205.6	5.7	104.57	39,766.2
Massachusetts	950.3	163.2	0.4	8.60	6,969.9
Michigan	7,103.3	716.1	6.1	25,813.85	87,174.5
Minnesota	2,906.3	406.1	2.0	165.24	26,103.9
Mississippi	4,882.3	507.5	12.2	28,175.42	60,760.8
Missouri	40,905.4	38,271.1	7.8	33.80	109,861.1
Montana	10,900.3	7,411.0	6.2	5.50	43,323.8
Nebraska	1,936.0	984.6	2.4	4.94	34,819.8
Nevada	157,461.5	54,996.5	4,325.1	6.38	217,099.1

(continued on next page)

Table 11.05: Toxic Material Disposal by Type of Compound and State, 2006

	Carcinogens	Lead	Mercury	Dioxin	Total
United States	*819,511.6*	*446,246.4*	*5,138.0*	*130,277.28*	*4,248,865.2*
New Hampshire	104.5	12.7	0.3	1.21	4,173.4
New Jersey	1,380.3	517.5	1.4	41.16	21,763.6
New Mexico	12,919.3	12,333.7	20.9	2.95	23,713.4
New York	3,219.5	536.2	15.3	53.92	35,516.8
North Carolina	7,557.3	1,120.6	6.7	348.47	134,094.8
North Dakota	1,419.6	142.9	3.1	7.27	22,312.8
Ohio	25,432.9	6,305.8	20.2	280.94	291,343.9
Oklahoma	3,506.6	614.5	5.5	29.96	29,652.9
Oregon	8,066.8	331.8	4.4	10.95	23,856.7
Pennsylvania	14,976.4	4,155.4	21.1	308.29	154,077.3
Rhode Island	121.2	10.4	0.0	NA	498.7
South Carolina	8,595.7	631.6	2.8	55.21	75,328.9
South Dakota	802.0	591.8	1.8	2.75	7,202.7
Tennessee	17,458.2	6,708.7	15.4	11,378.11	131,417.5
Texas	38,916.0	2,300.4	26.2	24,510.80	238,458.6
Utah	14,521.3	6,713.7	44.7	4,533.21	148,194.6
Vermont	261.2	2.5	4.9	0.11	604.3
Virginia	3,426.1	738.4	3.6	30.27	70,782.0
Washington	7,509.5	4,956.7	0.8	120.90	29,497.7
West Virginia	5,313.7	800.9	11.1	36.05	101,575.2
Wisconsin	4,102.1	522.1	11.6	235.71	45,998.9
Wyoming	607.5	110.1	2.8	9.11	15,439.3

Source: Environmental Protection Agency, *2006 TRI Public Data Release*, tables B-11, B-22, B-25, B-28, and B-31.

Notes: 'Lead' includes lead and lead compounds.
'Mercury' includes mercury and mercury compounds.
'Dioxin' includes dioxin and dioxin-like compounds.
This information does not indicate whether (or to what degree) the public has been exposed to chemicals. See www.epa.gov/tri/tridata for a discussion of using Toxic Release Inventory (TRI) data to estimate exposures and risks.
Groups may not add to total.

Units: Amount of carcinogens, lead compounds, mercury compounds, and total disposal in thousands of pounds; amount of dioxin in grams.

Table 11.06: Top Chemicals for Recycling,
Energy Recovery, and Treatment, 2006

	Recycling	Energy Recovery	Total treated
Toluene	968.2	225.9	374.7
Copper	813.8	NA	NA
Methanol	628.1	462.3	1,218.6
Lead compounds	529.7	NA	NA
Cumene	461.0	NA	NA
Zinc compounds	412.4	NA	NA
n-Hexane	353.4	66.8	89.8
Ethylene glycol	336.3	88.6	83.7
Copper compounds	296.1	NA	NA
Freon 113	291.3	NA	NA
Chlorine	274.7	NA	203.8
1,2-Dichloroethane	254.8	44.7	62.9
Acrylonitrile	198.3	NA	NA
Xylene (mixed isomers)	177.3	163.3	81.7
Ammonia	156.5	146.1	425.4
Manganese	141.8	NA	NA
Lead	140.0	NA	NA
Trichloroethylene	139.9	NA	NA
Dichloromethane	128.8	NA	NA
Vinyl chloride	120.0	NA	NA
Propylene	NA	536.3	384.2
Ethylene	NA	413.2	576.4
Sulfuric acid	NA	104.0	522.1
Styrene	NA	60.3	NA
Benzene	NA	50.2	63.1
Ethylbenzene	NA	41.9	NA

(continued on next page)

Table 11.06: Top Chemicals for Recycling, Energy Recovery, and Treatment, 2006

	Recycling	Energy Recovery	Total treated
n-Butyl alcohol	NA	40.2	NA
Propylene oxide	NA	38.6	NA
tert-Butyl alcohol	NA	36.9	NA
Chloroethane	NA	35.9	NA
Acetophenone	NA	35.6	NA
Glycol ethers	NA	29.6	NA
Cyclohexane	NA	29.4	NA
Hydrochloric acid	NA	NA	1,118.5
Nitrate compounds	NA	NA	320.3
Nitric acid	NA	NA	280.3
Formic acid	NA	NA	249.7
Hydrogen fluoride	NA	NA	241.5
Carbonyl sulfide	NA	NA	140.5
Formaldehyde	NA	NA	87.2
Carbon disulfide	NA	NA	63.9
Top 20 Subtotal	*6,822.5*	*2,649.8*	*6,588.2*
All Compounds	*8,838.4*	*3,151.6*	*7,973.7*

Source: Environmental Protection Agency, *2006 TRI Public Data Release*, tables E-2, E-14, and E-26.

Notes: Only the top 20 chemicals for each method are given.
This information does not indicate whether (or to what degree) the public has been exposed to chemicals. See www.epa.gov/tri/tridata for a discussion of using Toxic Release Inventory (TRI) data to estimate exposures and risks.
Groups may not add to total.

Units: Amount of chemicals in millions of pounds.

Table 11.07: Toxic Chemicals in Waste by Type of Process, 2005 and 2006

	Amount	Percent of Total
2005		
Total Chemicals	*25,081.4*	*100%*
Recycled	8,973.0	35.8
On-site	6,955.6	27.7
Off-site	2,017.4	8.0
Used for Energy Recovery	3,018.8	12.0
On-site	2,410.9	9.6
Off-site	607.9	2.4
Treated	8,637.3	34.4
On-site	8,061.7	32.1
Off-site	575.7	2.3
Waste managed (disposed of or otherwise released)	4,452.2	17.8
On-site	3,788.1	15.1
Off-site	664.1	2.7
Non-production-related waste managed	23.7	NA
2006		
Total Chemicals	*24,368.2*	*100%*
Recycled	8,838.4	36.3
On-site	6,656.5	27.3
Off-site	2,182.0	9.0
Used for Energy Recovery	3,151.6	12.9
On-site	2,604.5	10.7
Off-site	547.0	2.2
Treated	7,973.7	32.7
On-site	7,425.6	30.5
Off-site	548.2	2.2
Waste managed (disposed of or otherwise released)	4,404.5	18.1
On-site	3,720.7	15.3
Off-site	683.8	2.8
Non-production-related waste managed	18.2	NA

Source: Environmental Protection Agency, *2005 TRI Public Data Release*, table E-1; *2006*, table E-1.

Notes: 'Non-production-related waste managed' is excluded from percentages.
This information does not indicate whether (or to what degree) the public has been exposed to chemicals. See www.epa.gov/tri/tridata for a discussion of using Toxic Release Inventory (TRI) data to estimate exposures and risks. Groups may not add to total.

Units: Waste in millions of pounds; percent of total.

Table 11.08: Pollutant Emissions, by Chemical, 1980–2007

	1980	1985	1990	1995	2000	2005	2007
Carbon monoxide	185,408	176,845	154,188	126,778	114,465	96,619	88,254
Ammonia	NA	NA	4,320	4,659	4,907	4,143	4,131
Nitrogen oxides	27,080	25,757	25,527	24,955	22,599	18,711	17,025
Particulate matter <10 μm							
With condensibles	7,013	41,323	27,753	25,820	23,748	21,285	17,374
Without condensibles	7,013	41,323	27,753	25,820	22,962	18,416	14,455
Particulate matter <2.5 μm							
With condensibles	NA	NA	7,560	6,929	7,287	5,536	5,450
Without condensibles	NA	NA	7,560	6,929	6,503	3,082	2,958
Sulfur dioxide	25,926	23,307	23,077	18,619	16,348	14,714	12,925
Volatile organic compounds	31,107	27,403	24,108	22,042	17,511	19,976	18,423

Source: Environmental Protection Agency, National Emissions Inventory, *Current Emissions Trends 1970-2007*, accessed online at www.epa.gov/ttn/chief/trends/index.html.

Notes: 'Particulate matter' is a mixture of extremely small particles and liquid droplets. Particles smaller than 10 micrometers (μm) can pass through the nose and throat into the lungs. Particles between 2.5 and 10 μm in diameter are known as 'inhalable coarse particles.' Particles under 2.5 μm are known as 'fine particles.'

'Condensibles' are gases that may condense to form liquid or solid particulate matter. They are sometimes included in particulate matter data and sometimes not. Separate figures for particulate matter with and without condensibles have only been tracked since 1999.

'Volatile organic compounds' (VOCs) are a precursor to ozone, a pollutant tracked by the EPA.

'Nitrogen oxides' includes several forms comprising different mixtures of nitrogen and oxygen, but the majority of the chemicals released (by weight) are nitrogen dioxide (NO_2).

Data for 2007 is preliminary and may be subject to revision.

Units: Amount of chemicals released in thousands of tons.

Table 11.09: Carbon Monoxide Emissions by Source, 1980–2007

	1980	1985	1990	1995	2000	2005	2007
Total Emissions	*185,408*	*176,845*	*154,188*	*126,778*	*114,465*	*96,619*	*88,254*
Fuel combustion							
Electrical utilities	322	291	363	372	484	655	689
Industrial	750	670	879	1,056	1,219	1,268	1,253
Other	6,230	7,525	4,269	4,506	3,081	3,345	3,362
Chemical and product manufacturing	2,151	1,845	1,183	1,223	361	284	284
Metals processing	2,246	2,223	2,640	2,380	1,295	987	986
Petroleum and related industry	1,723	462	333	348	161	357	356
Other industrial	830	694	537	624	592	490	489
Solvent utilization	NA	2	5	6	51	2	2
Storage and transport	NA	49	76	25	169	118	118
Waste disposal and recycling	2,300	1,941	1,079	1,185	1,849	1,594	1,593
Highway vehicles	143,827	134,187	110,255	83,881	68,061	48,222	41,610
Off-highway	16,685	19,029	21,447	23,874	24,178	20,804	18,762
Miscellaneous	8,344	7,927	11,122	7,298	12,964	18,493	18,750

Source: Environmental Protection Agency, *National Emissions Inventory, Current Emissions Trends 1970-2007*, accessed online at www.epa.gov/ttn/chief/trends/index.html.

Notes: Data for 2007 is preliminary and may be subject to revision.

Units: Amount of carbon monoxide (CO) released in thousands of tons.

Table 11.10: Ammonia Emissions by Source, 1990–2007

	1990	1995	2000	2005	2007
Total Emissions	*4,320*	*4,659*	*4,907*	*4,143*	*4,131*
Fuel combustion					
Electrical utilities	0	0	11	27	32
Industrial	17	18	31	17	16
Other	8	8	8	17	17
Chemical and product manufacturing	183	183	26	23	23
Metals processing	6	6	2	3	3
Petroleum and related industry	43	43	10	3	3
Other industrial	38	40	50	177	159
Storage and transport	0	0	5	1	1
Waste disposal and recycling	82	93	83	26	26
Highway vehicles	155	222	275	307	307
Off-highway	31	37	3	3	3
Miscellaneous	3,757	4,009	4,403	3,539	3,541

Source: Environmental Protection Agency, *National Emissions Inventory, Current Emissions Trends 1970-2007*, accessed online at www.epa.gov/ttn/chief/trends/index.html.

Notes: Data for 2007 is preliminary and may be subject to revision.

Units: Amount of ammonia (NH_3) released in thousands of tons.

Table 11.11: Sulfur Dioxide Emissions by Source, 1980–2007

	1980	1985	1990	1995	2000	2005	2007
Total Emissions	*25,926*	*23,307*	*23,077*	*18,619*	*16,348*	*14,714*	*12,925*
Fuel combustion							
Electrical utilities	17,469	16,272	15,909	12,080	11,396	10,469	8,973
Industrial	2,951	3,169	3,550	3,357	2,139	1,784	1,705
Other	971	579	831	793	628	578	577
Chemical and product manufacturing	280	456	297	286	338	259	258
Metals processing	1,842	1,042	726	530	313	213	213
Petroleum and related industry	734	505	430	369	316	257	232
Other industrial	918	425	399	403	410	327	323
Solvent utilization	NA	1	0	1	1	0	0
Storage and transport	NA	4	7	2	6	5	5
Waste disposal and recycling	33	34	42	47	34	26	26
Highway vehicles	394	455	503	335	260	145	91
Off-highway	323	354	371	406	437	516	396
Miscellaneous	11	11	12	10	70	135	126

Source: Environmental Protection Agency, *National Emissions Inventory, Current Emissions Trends 1970-2007*, accessed online at www.epa.gov/ttn/chief/trends/index.html.

Notes: Data for 2007 is preliminary and may be subject to revision.

Units: Amount of sulfur dioxide (SO_2) released in thousands of tons.

Table 11.12: Nitrogen Oxide Emissions by Source, 1980–2007

	1980	1985	1990	1995	2000	2005	2007
Total Emissions	*27,080*	*25,757*	*25,527*	*24,955*	*22,599*	*18,711*	*17,025*
Fuel combustion							
Electrical utilities	7,024	6,127	6,663	6,384	5,330	3,856	3,331
Industrial	3,555	3,209	3,035	3,144	2,723	2,042	1,941
Other	741	712	1,196	1,298	766	733	728
Chemical and product manufacturing	213	262	168	158	105	70	70
Metals processing	65	87	97	98	89	69	69
Petroleum and related industry	72	124	153	110	122	354	346
Other industrial	205	327	378	399	479	429	413
Solvent utilization	0	2	1	3	4	7	7
Storage and transport	0	2	3	6	15	19	19
Waste disposal and recycling	111	87	91	99	129	111	110
Highway vehicles	11,493	10,932	9,592	8,876	8,394	6,407	5,563
Off-highway	3,353	3,576	3,781	4,113	4,167	4,403	4,164
Miscellaneous	248	310	369	267	276	211	264

Source: Environmental Protection Agency, *National Emissions Inventory, Current Emissions Trends 1970-2007*, accessed online at www.epa.gov/ttn/chief/trends/index.html.

Notes: Nitrogen oxides (often abbreviated as NO_x) referred to here include nitric oxide (NO) and nitrogen dioxide (NO_2).
Data for 2007 is preliminary and may be subject to revision.

Units: Amount of nitrogen oxides (NO_x) released in thousands of tons.

Table 11.13: Particulate Matter Emissions by Source, 1980–2007

	1980	1985	1990	1995	2000	2005	2007
PM-10							
Total Emissions	7,013	41,323	27,753	25,820	23,748	21,285	17,374
Fuel combustion							
Electrical utilities	879	280	295	268	687	625	565
Industrial	679	247	270	302	320	339	329
Other	887	1,009	631	610	465	463	465
Chemical and product manufacturing	148	58	77	67	55	40	40
Metals processing	622	220	214	212	140	81	79
Petroleum and related industry	138	63	55	40	38	25	23
Other industrial	1,846	611	583	511	378	976	963
Waste disposal and recycling	273	278	271	287	362	289	288
Highway vehicles	432	408	387	304	230	183	172
Off-highway	257	304	328	339	322	313	297
Miscellaneous	852	37,736	24,536	22,765	20,650	17,883	14,087
PM-2.5							
Total Emissions	NA	NA	7,560	6,929	7,287	5,536	5,450
Fuel combustion							
Electrical utilities	NA	NA	121	107	587	508	442
Industrial	NA	NA	177	203	260	178	172
Other	NA	NA	611	589	447	421	420
Chemical and product manufacturing	NA	NA	47	42	46	30	30
Metals processing	NA	NA	157	134	118	54	52
Petroleum and related industry	NA	NA	27	22	27	18	17
Other industrial	NA	NA	284	256	254	354	349
Waste disposal and recycling	NA	NA	234	247	333	268	268
Highway vehicles	NA	NA	323	245	173	127	114
Off-highway	NA	NA	300	311	295	292	276
Miscellaneous	NA	NA	5,233	4,726	4,688	3,256	3,281

Source: Environmental Protection Agency, *National Emissions Inventory, Current Emissions Trends 1970-2007*, accessed online at www.epa.gov/ttn/chief/trends/index.html.

Notes: All groups include condensible material. Data for 2007 is preliminary and may be subject to revision.

Units: Amount of particulate matter smaller than 10 micrometers (PM-10) and 2.5 micrometers (PM-2.5) released in thousands of tons.

Table 11.14: Pollutants Emitted by Vehicles, 2002

	Carbon Monoxide	Nitrogen Oxides	Volatile Organic Compounds	Sulfur Dioxide	PM-10	PM-2.5
All Emissions	*112.05*	*21.10*	*16.54*	*15.35*	*22.15*	*6.80*
Transportation Emissions						
Total	*66.60*	*9.44*	*5.93*	*0.49*	*10.99*	*1.85*
On-road	62.16	7.37	4.54	0.28	0.20	0.15
Off-road	4.44	2.07	1.38	0.22	0.12	NA
Aircraft	0.26	0.08	0.02	<0.01	<0.01	<0.01
Railroads	0.09	0.89	0.04	0.05	0.02	0.02
Marine vessels	0.13	1.01	0.03	0.16	0.04	0.04
Other off-road	3.97	0.09	1.30	NA	0.05	0.04

Source: Bureau of Transportation Statistics, *National Transportation Statistics 2007*, tables 4-40 through 4-45.

Notes: 'PM-10' is particulate matter less than 10 micrometers in diameter.
'PM-2.5' is particulate matter less than 2.5 micrometers in diameter.

Units: Emissions in millions of tons.

Table 11.15: Estimated Average Vehicle Emissions Rates by Fuel Type, 1990–2007

	1990	1995	2000	2005	2007
Gasoline (Unreformulated)					
Light-Duty Vehicles					
Hydrocarbons	4.00	2.62	1.88	1.25	1.04
Carbon monoxide	42.89	26.60	18.53	12.57	10.28
Nitrogen oxides	2.70	1.78	1.29	0.92	0.73
Light-Duty Trucks					
Hydrocarbons	5.05	3.32	2.43	1.54	1.31
Carbon monoxide	56.23	37.51	26.81	16.23	13.52
Nitrogen oxides	2.62	1.84	1.54	1.21	1.02
Heavy-Duty Vehicles					
Hydrocarbons	6.40	4.24	2.84	1.88	1.54
Carbon monoxide	85.61	54.16	31.08	16.73	13.55
Nitrogen oxides	7.19	6.11	5.26	4.28	3.33
Motorcycles					
Hydrocarbons	2.74	2.40	2.31	2.30	2.29
Carbon monoxide	15.15	14.67	14.59	14.58	14.59
Nitrogen oxides	1.26	1.26	1.25	1.25	1.25
Diesel					
Light-Duty Vehicles					
Hydrocarbons	0.68	0.77	0.80	0.58	0.36
Carbon monoxide	1.49	1.69	1.78	1.57	1.21
Nitrogen oxides	1.83	1.89	1.81	1.32	0.85
Light-Duty Trucks					
Hydrocarbons	1.59	1.67	1.02	0.80	0.63
Carbon monoxide	2.67	2.85	1.77	1.37	1.06
Nitrogen oxides	2.71	2.46	1.76	1.37	1.09
Heavy-Duty Vehicles					
Hydrocarbons	2.21	1.23	0.79	0.54	0.48
Carbon monoxide	10.06	6.32	4.10	3.05	2.66
Nitrogen oxides	23.34	20.49	18.05	11.45	9.60

(continued on next page)

Table 11.15: Estimated Average Vehicle Emissions Rates by Fuel Type, 1990–2007

	1990	1995	2000	2005	2007
Reformulated Gasoline					
Light-Duty Vehicles					
Hydrocarbons	NA	2.34	1.48	1.02	0.85
Carbon monoxide	NA	22.78	15.36	11.44	9.29
Nitrogen oxides	NA	1.78	1.24	0.90	0.72
Light-Duty Trucks					
Hydrocarbons	NA	3.02	1.96	1.28	1.09
Carbon monoxide	NA	31.86	22.25	14.47	12.03
Nitrogen oxides	NA	1.84	1.47	1.20	1.01
Heavy-Duty Vehicles					
Hydrocarbons	NA	3.86	2.28	1.51	1.23
Carbon monoxide	NA	46.02	25.87	13.89	11.25
Nitrogen oxides	NA	6.13	5.18	4.36	3.39
Motorcycles					
Hydrocarbons	NA	2.24	2.04	2.04	2.03
Carbon monoxide	NA	12.64	12.56	12.56	12.56
Nitrogen oxides	NA	1.26	1.25	1.25	1.25

Source: Bureau of Transportation Statistics, *National Transportation Statistics 2008*, tables 4-38 and 4-39.

Notes: Light-duty vehicles are defined as passenger cars with a GVWR (Gross Vehicle Weight Rating) less than 6,000 pounds.

Light-duty trucks include pickups and minivans with a GVWR under 8,500 pounds.

Heavy-duty vehicles have a GVWR over 8,500 pounds. Emissions estimates assume conditions of an ambient temperature of 75 °F, a daily temperature range of 60–84 °F, and an average traffic speed of 27.6 miles per hour.

For more information about the estimation process, please see the source document.

Hydrocarbon estimates for gasoline vehicles include both exhaust and nonexhaust emissions; all other estimates are for exhaust emissions only.

The Unreformulated Gasoline category assumes that no reformulated gasoline is used. The Reformulated category assumes that all gasoline used is reformulated.

Units: Emissions in grams per vehicle per mile for hyrdocarbons, carbon monoxide (CO), and nitrogen oxides (NO_x).

Table 11.16: Lead Emissions, 1970–2000

	1970	1980	1990	1995	2000
Total Emissions	*220.88*	*74.16*	*4.98*	*3.93*	*4.23*
Transportation					
Total	173.36	61.39	1.04	0.56	0.56
Highway vehicles	171.96	60.50	0.42	0.02	0.02
Aircraft	1.40	0.89	0.62	0.54	0.55
Non-transportation					
Total	47.52	12.77	3.94	3.37	3.66
Fuel combustion	10.62	4.30	0.50	0.49	0.50
Industrial processes	26.36	3.94	2.48	2.27	2.35
Waste disposal and recycling	2.20	1.21	0.80	0.60	0.81
Miscelleneous	8.34	3.32	0.16	<0.01	<0.01

Source: Bureau of Transportation Statistics, *National Transportation Statistics 2007*, table 4-46.

Notes: The sale and use of lead-containing gasoline, which acounted for most airborne lead emissions, has been severely restricted since in 1973.

Units: Lead emissions in thousands of tons.

Table 11.17: Air Quality Index for Metropolitan Areas, 1990–2007

City	Days with Air Quality Index (AQI) over 100					# Trend Sites
	1990	1995	2000	2005	2007	
Akron, OH	26	21	14	30	22	7
Albany-Schenectady-Troy, NY	7	12	3	8	13	5
Albuquerque, NM	7	3	7	9	1	17
Allentown-Bethlehem-Easton, PA	22	18	18	16	12	5
Atlanta, GA	60	53	62	28	34	19
Austin-San Marcos, TX	10	28	14	9	4	1
Bakersfield, CA	144	133	164	122	131	17
Baltimore, MD	50	57	39	36	45	17
Baton Rouge, LA	46	31	47	29	17	15
Bergen-Passaic, NJ	0	0	1	4	1	6
Birmingham, AL	50	50	68	35	41	21
Boston, MA-NH	0	0	0	4	3	12
Buffalo-Niagara Falls, NY	13	12	7	23	18	10
Charleston-North Charleston, SC	4	1	9	8	5	10
Charlotte-Gastonia-Rock Hill, NC-SC	60	32	40	26	33	9
Chicago, IL	13	29	17	29	23	40
Cincinnati, OH-KY-IN	32	33	22	33	39	18
Cleveland-Lorain-Elyria, OH	17	30	29	36	22	27
Columbus, OH	14	27	16	20	13	7
Dallas, TX	0	36	44	33	11	7
Dayton-Springfield, OH	28	28	14	22	11	7
Denver, CO	18	11	15	11	21	22
Detroit, MI	17	20	17	38	21	32
El Paso, TX	17	6	15	8	6	12
Fort Lauderdale, FL	3	3	5	1	7	12
Fort Worth-Arlington, TX	30	52	38	43	12	6
Fresno, CA	101	91	164	95	93	20
Gary, IN	14	30	18	19	11	16
Grand Rapids-Muskegon-Holland, MI	20	32	15	31	22	13
Greensboro-Winston Salem-High Point, NC	31	25	29	14	21	9
Greenville-Spartanburg-Anderson, SC	16	30	47	22	14	9
Harrisburg-Lebanon-Carlisle, PA	19	28	17	19	19	8
Hartford, CT	17	26	14	19	16	6
Honolulu, HI	0	0	2	2	0	11
Houston, TX	66	82	57	49	25	23

(continued on next page)

Table 11.17: Air Quality Index for Metropolitan Areas, 1990–2007

City	Days with Air Quality Index (AQI) over 100					# Trend Sites
	1990	1995	2000	2005	2007	
Indianapolis, IN	28	39	17	34	24	27
Jacksonville, FL	5	1	3	6	8	14
Jersey City, NJ	21	21	9	13	12	8
Kansas City, MO-KS	6	34	23	26	10	15
Knoxville, TN	47	60	65	39	51	19
Las Vegas, NV-AZ	6	6	6	9	7	8
Little Rock-North Little Rock, AR	22	24	29	19	11	6
Los Angeles-Long Beach, CA	181	124	83	60	59	44
Louisville, KY-IN	27	41	29	39	30	17
Memphis, TN-AR-MS	50	56	52	37	35	14
Miami, FL	2	8	8	0	3	11
Middlesex-Somerset-Hunterdon, NJ	32	31	19	22	21	4
Milwaukee-Waukesha, WI	19	23	9	24	11	16
Minneapolis-St. Paul, MN-WI	4	9	8	7	5	20
Monmouth-Ocean, NJ	29	34	19	27	21	4
Nashville, TN	46	46	49	26	35	19
Nassau-Suffolk, NY	24	20	12	19	14	5
New Haven-Meriden, CT	0	0	2	3	0	2
New Orleans, LA	25	37	33	16	17	13
New York, NY	23	25	26	23	20	18
Newark, NJ	37	33	17	18	21	16
Norfolk-Virginia Beach-Newport News, VA-NC	24	22	23	12	9	7
Oakland, CA	4	13	12	6	5	19
Oklahoma City, OK	14	29	16	12	4	9
Omaha, NE-IA	3	4	3	1	1	13
Orange County, CA	65	20	11	0	9	8
Orlando, FL	13	9	14	8	8	13
Philadelphia, PA-NJ	57	54	37	35	40	42
Phoenix-Mesa, AZ	20	41	35	23	11	26
Pittsburgh, PA	27	36	40	54	44	39
Portland-Vancouver, OR-WA	15	4	5	4	5	12
Providence-Fall River-Warwick, RI-MA	18	17	13	13	11	8
Raleigh-Durham-Chapel Hill, NC	37	10	16	12	17	6
Richmond-Petersburg, VA	23	28	17	23	19	9
Riverside-San Bernardino, CA	185	154	171	141	135	44

(continued on next page)

Table 11.17: Air Quality Index for Metropolitan Areas, 1990–2007

City	Days with Air Quality Index (AQI) over 100					# Trend Sites
	1990	1995	2000	2005	2007	
Rochester, NY	14	10	2	0	7	1
Sacramento, CA	86	61	65	58	32	21
St. Louis, MO-IL	30	46	30	47	34	35
Salt Lake City-Ogden, UT	2	8	23	32	28	13
San Antonio, TX	8	32	5	10	3	2
San Diego, CA	143	94	58	26	33	26
San Francisco, CA	0	3	4	2	2	12
San Jose, CA	9	16	0	3	0	4
San Juan-Bayamon, PR	0	0	0	0	1	10
Scranton-Wilkes Barre-Hazleton, PA	16	25	8	12	7	12
Seattle-Bellevue-Everett, WA	5	0	8	2	4	10
Springfield, MA	28	17	7	16	21	10
Syracuse, NY	1	10	2	8	8	5
Tacoma, WA	7	3	15	4	7	4
Tampa-St. Petersburg-Clearwater, FL	20	14	29	15	12	24
Toledo, OH	15	15	9	25	5	6
Tucson, AZ	7	14	5	8	1	20
Tulsa, OK	27	39	21	19	2	8
Ventura, CA	106	100	57	36	22	14
Washington, DC-MD-VA-WV	38	54	35	36	38	39
West Palm Beach-Boca Raton, FL	0	0	1	0	2	4
Wilmington-Newark, DE-MD	0	47	24	22	25	9
Youngstown-Warren, OH	0	14	11	17	14	8

Source: Environmental Protection Agency, Air Quality Index Information, 'Number of Days with Air Quality Index Values Greater than 100 at Trend Sites, 1990-2007, and All Sites in 2007.'

Notes: The Air Quality Index (AQI) is based on levels of major pollutants (particulate matter, sulfur dioxide, carbon monoxide, ozone, and nitrogen dioxide), and provides a single number that represents the worst daily air quality experienced in an urban area. An AQI over 100 for a given day indicates that at least one pollutant exceeded air quality standards; therefore, air quality would be in the unhealthful range on that day.
Data shown is for trend sites only, not all monitoring sites.
Monitoring sites are labeled 'trend sites' if they have complete data for at least 8 of the 10 last years.
Particulate matter data prior to 1999 includes only particles under 10 micrometers in diameter; data after 1999 also includes particles under 2.5 micrometers.
Data may differ from previous versions of the report.

Units: Number of trend sites and days with AQI over 100.

Table 11.18: Human Exposure to Chemicals, 2005

	Cadmium	Lead	Mercury*	Antimony	Uranium	p,p'-DDT
Total Population	*1.20*	*2.6*	*NA*	*0.34*	*0.046*	*26.5*
By Gender						
Male	1.22	3.2	NA	0.39	0.046	21.6
Female	1.17	2.2	3.99	0.31	0.040	36.3
By Race/Hispanic Origin						
Mexican American	0.766	3.2	4.13	0.36	0.054	236
Black (non-Hispanic)	1.51	3.7	5.18	0.45	0.030	40.9
White (non-Hispanic)	1.17	2.4	3.62	0.34	0.036	17.7
By Age						
6–11	0.282	2.6	NA	0.33	0.037	NA
12–19	0.442	1.9	NA	0.46	0.041	NA
20–59	1.28	NA	NA	NA	NA	NA
20 and older	NA	2.8	NA	0.33	0.046	28.1

Source: US Department of Health & Human Services, Centers for Disease Control, *Third National Report on Human Exposure to Environmental Chemicals, Execuive Summary*, pages 3, 4, and 10.

Notes: Figures given are the 95th percentile for urine levels of the specified chemicals. The 95th percentile is used as the standard for what constitutes unusually high levels for the population.
A high level of a chemical does not necessarily lead to health problems, but depends on several other factors as well; for more information, see the original report or the Centers for Disease Control.
* Data for mercury is given only for females between the ages of 16 and 49.

Units: Chemical levels in micograms per liter of urine (µg/L), except for DDT, which is in nanograms per gram of lipid (ng/g).

Table 11.19: Secondhand Smoke Exposure
for Nonsmokers, 1999–2002

Exposure Measured by Contine Levels in the Blood

	1999–2000	2001–2002
Total Population Age 3 and Over	*1.96*	*2.19*
By Age		
3–11 years	3.37	3.21
12–19 years	2.56	3.12
20 years and older	1.48	1.38
By Gender		
Male	2.39	2.44
Female	1.85	1.76
By Race/Hispanic Origin		
Mexican-American	1.21	2.11
Black (non-Hispanic)	2.34	3.12
White (non-Hispanic)	1.92	1.88

Source: US Department of Health & Human Services, *Centers for Disease Control, Third National Report on Human Exposure to Environmental Chemicals*, table 32.

Notes: This study tracked the concentration of contine, a metabolite of nicotine which is considered the best way of measuring exposure to tobacco smoke. Since only nonsmokers were included, the level of contine is considered an indication of the level of exposure to secondhand smoke.

Figures given are the 95th percentile for contine levels. The 95th percentile is used as the standard for what constitutes unusually high levels for the population.

The given data was sampled by the National Health and Nutrition Examination Survey (NHANES) for 1999–2002.

Units: Serum (blood) concentrations of contine in nanograms per mililiter (ng/mL).

Table 11.20: Blood Lead Levels in Adults by State, 2005

	Over 25 µg/dL	Over 40 µg/dL
United States	*8.31*	*1.35*
Alabama	29.56	9.43
Alaska	6.91	1.57
Arizona	0.66	0.07
California	2.40	0.36
Connecticut	3.52	0.81
Florida	2.71	0.93
Georgia	8.55	1.25
Hawaii	0.49	0.16
Illinois	5.12	0.61
Indiana	19.74	3.80
Iowa	16.58	1.02
Kansas	34.05	1.44
Kentucky	8.41	0.85
Maine	3.88	1.05
Maryland	1.60	0.32
Massachusetts	5.79	1.25
Michigan	2.77	0.70
Minnesota	4.65	0.36
Missouri	29.08	3.41
Montana	0.86	0.22
Nebraska	4.47	0.64
New Hampshire	7.54	0.71
New Jersey	8.62	1.03
New Mexico	0.58	0.12
New York	5.61	1.10

(continued on next page)

Table 11.20: Blood Lead Levels in Adults by State, 2005

	Over 25 µg/dL	Over 40 µg/dL
United States	*8.31*	*1.35*
North Carolina	3.14	1.00
Ohio	13.05	2.61
Oklahoma	2.95	0.68
Oregon	3.31	0.57
Pennsylvania	20.85	2.83
Rhode Island	7.60	1.30
South Carolina	12.01	3.35
Texas	2.26	0.28
Utah	4.04	1.32
Washington	1.59	0.42
Wisconsin	6.96	0.66
Wyoming	15.69	1.87

Source: Centers for Disease Control, *Adult Blood Lead Epidemiology and Surveillance (ABLES), Blood Level Lead Data, 2002-2005*, accessed online at www.cdc.gov/niosh/topics/ABLES/ables.html.

Notes: The Adult Blood Lead Epidemiology and Surveillance (ABLES) is a state-based program that measures blood levels of lead in adults in participating states.

The threshold for high lead levels in blood is 25 µg per deciliter (micrograms per every tenth of a liter). Data for adults over 40 µg/dL (considered a very high level) is also included.

Figures given are an estimate of the prevalence in the overall population, and are based on new cases as well as previously reported cases.

Only residents of the specified states are included.

Units: Rate per 100,000 resident adults with specified blood lead level.

Table 11.21: Chemical Exposures at Hazardous Waste Sites, Completed Exposure Pathway Ranking, 2007

Ranking	Chemical	Priority Sites	All Sites
1	Lead	284	476
2	Arsenic	231	405
3	Trichloroethylene	301	391
4	Tetrachloroethylene	219	309
5	Benzene	147	242
6	Cadmium	151	236
7	Chromium	138	216
8	Mercury	100	189
9	Volatile Organic Compounds NOS	124	185
10	Polychlorinated Biphenyls	117	184
11	Manganese	101	180
12	Zinc	102	170
13	Copper	96	165
14	Benzo(A)Pyrene	68	139
15	1,1,1-Trichloroethane	108	134
16	Chloroform	93	126
17	Antimony	80	124
17	Nickel	75	124
19	1,1-Dichloroethene	98	122
19	Vinyl Chloride	95	122
21	Polycyclic Aromatic Hydrocarbons	78	118
22	Methylene Chloride	73	116
23	Toluene	68	114
24	Barium	60	110
25	Benzo(A)Anthracene	50	102
26	1,2-Dichloroethane	78	99
26	Iron	62	99
26	Vanadium	53	99
29	Di(2-Ethylhexyl)Phthalate	64	96
30	Benzo(B)Fluoranthene	39	94
31	Chrysene	45	93
32	1,1-Dichloroethane	75	92
33	Carbon Tetrachloride	59	90
34	Metals NOS	55	88
35	Beryllium	44	86

(continued on next page)

Table 11.21: Chemical Exposures at Hazardous Waste Sites, Completed Exposure Pathway Ranking, 2007

Ranking	Chemical	Priority Sites	All Sites
36	Benzo(K)Fluoranthene	37	83
36	Phenanthrene	35	83
38	Indeno(1,2,3-Cd)Pyrene	36	82
39	Naphthalene	41	81
40	Dibenzo(A,H)Anthracene	32	75
41	Dieldrin	37	74
42	Ethylbenzene	43	73
43	Xylenes	39	72
44	Thallium	36	71
45	Aluminum	43	70
46	Pentachlorophenol	43	68
47	*p,p'*-DDT	41	66
47	Cobalt	30	66
49	Benzo(Ghi)Perylene	25	63
50	Sodium	34	61

Source: Centers for Disease Control, *Agency for Toxic Substances & Disease Registry, 2007 Completed Exposure Pathway (CEP) Site Count Report*, accessed online at www.adtdr.cdc.gov/cep/index.html.

Notes: The Agency for Toxic Substances & Disease Registry (ASTDR) publishes the 'Completed Exposure Pathway' (CEP) for cases in which a contaminant found in the population is linked to a specific source. The CEP ranks chemicals based on the number of exposure sites.

A similar source from the ASTDR, the CERCLA list of priority substances, ranks chemicals according to an algorithm based on toxicity, frequency of occurrence, and possibility for human exposure. Since the CEP list does not look at toxicity, the two lists differ in their rankings. In addition, the CERCLA list only accounts for waste sites designated on the National Priority List (NPL), while the CEP list receives reports from all sites.

Only the top 50 chemicals are shown from the larger CEP list.

NOS = Not Otherwise Specified.

Units: Number of sites reporting exposure.

Table 11.22: Chemical Exposures at Hazardous Waste Sites, CERCLA Ranking, 2007

Rank in 2007	Chemical	Points	Rank in 2005
1	Arsenic	1,672.58	1
2	Lead	1,534.07	2
3	Mercury	1,504.69	3
4	Vinyl Chloride	1,387.75	4
5	Polychlorinated Biphenyls	1,365.78	5
6	Benzene	1,355.96	6
7	Cadmium	1,324.22	8
8	Polycyclic Aromatic Hydrocarbons	1,316.98	7
9	Benzo(A)Pyrene	1,312.45	9
10	Benzo(B)Fluoranthene	1,266.55	10
11	Chloroform	1,223.03	11
12	p,p'-DDT	1,193.36	12
13	Aroclor 1254	1,182.63	13
14	Aroclor 1260	1,177.77	14
15	Dibenzo(A,H)Anthracene	1,165.88	15
16	Trichloroethylene	1,154.73	16
17	Dieldrin	1,150.91	17
18	Hexavalent Chromium	1,149.98	18
19	White Phosphorus	1,144.77	19
20	Chlordane	1,133.21	21
21	p,p'-DDE	1,132.49	20
22	Hexachlorobutadiene	1,129.63	22
23	Coal Tar Creosote	1,124.32	23
24	Aldrin	1,117.22	25
25	p,p'-DDD	1,114.83	24
26	Benzidine	1,114.24	26
27	Aroclor 1248	1,112.20	27
28	Cyanide	1,099.48	28
29	Aroclor 1242	1,093.14	29
30	Aroclor	1,091.52	62
31	Toxaphene	1,086.65	30
32	Gamma-hexachlorocyclohexane	1,081.63	32
33	Tetrachloroethylene	1,080.43	31
34	Heptachlor	1,072.67	33
35	1,2-Dibromoethane	1,064.06	34

(continued on next page)

Table 11.22: Chemical Exposures at Hazardous Waste Sites, CERCLA Ranking, 2007

Rank in 2007	Chemical	Points	Rank in 2005
36	Beta-hexachlorocyclohexane	1,060.22	37
37	Acrolein	1,059.07	36
38	Disulfoton	1,058.85	35
39	Benzo(A)Anthracene	1,057.96	38
40	3,3'-Dichlorobenzidine	1,051.61	39
41	Endrin	1,048.57	41
42	Beryllium	1,046.12	40
43	Delta-hexachlorocyclohexane	1,038.27	42
44	1,2-Dibromo-3-Chloropropane	1,035.55	43
45	Pentachlorophenol	1,028.01	45
46	Heptachlor Epoxide	1,027.12	44
47	Carbon Tetrachloride	1,023.32	46
48	Aroclor 1221	1,018.41	47
49	Cobalt	1,015.57	50
50	*o,p'*-DDT	1,014.71	49

Source: Centers for Disease Control, Agency for Taxic Substances & Disease Registry, *2007 CERCLA Priority List of Hazardous Substances*, accessed online at www.adtdr.cdc.gov/cercla.

Notes: The Agency for Toxic Substances & Disease Registry (ASTDR) publishes the Comprehensive Environmental Response, Compensation, and Liability Act (CERCLA) to determine which chemicals represent the greatest potential threat to human health. The CERCLA list uses an algorithm based on toxicity, frequency of occurrence, and possibility for human exposure, and looks only at those sites designated on the National Priority List (NPL), the EPA's list of the most serious uncontrolled or abandoned hazardous waste sites in the United States.

A similar list is the 'Completed Exposure Pathway' (CEP) for cases in which a contaminant found in the population is linked to a specific source; however, the CEP ranks chemicals solely based on the number of exposure sites, and receives reports from all sites, not just NPL sites. As a result, the two lists will differ.

Only the top 50 chemicals are shown from the larger CERCLA list.

Units: Most hazardous chemicals, ranked by computer algorithm score.

Table 11.23: Oil Spills by Size, 1973–2004

	Under 1,000 Gallons	1,000–10,000 Gallons	10,000–100,000 Gal	100,000–1 Million Gal	Over 1 Million Gal	Total Spill Volume
	242,716	*7,227*	*1,408*	*268*	*30*	*235,299.7*
1973	8,473	425	89	24	3	15,253.6
1974	9,157	664	149	27	2	15,698.7
1975	8,647	526	97	19	3	21,520.1
1976	8,812	514	78	16	2	18,517.9
1977	8,912	443	91	13	0	8,189.1
1978	10,061	486	84	11	2	10,864.1
1979	9,277	451	89	16	1	20,893.6
1980	7,931	357	73	20	2	12,597.0
1981	7,421	324	60	5	1	8,921.0
1982	7,032	366	71	13	2	10,344.8
1983	7,503	339	62	10	2	8,379.8
1984	7,841	331	68	14	4	18,005.9
1985	5,824	286	47	9	3	8,436.2
1986	4,853	107	22	11	0	4,282.0
1987	4,698	112	23	8	0	3,608.9
1988	4,850	115	24	8	1	6,586.0
1989	6,462	114	30	6	1	13,478.7
1990	7,988	136	45	7	1	7,915.0
1991	8,419	121	27	2	0	1,876.0
1992	9,340	121	28	2	0	1,875.7
1993	8,840	113	16	3	0	2,067.4
1994	8,811	124	21	4	0	2,489.3
1995	8,938	80	17	3	0	2,638.2
1996	9,226	89	15	5	0	3,117.8
1997	8,542	69	12	1	0	942.6
1998	8,221	84	8	2	0	885.3
1999	8,452	70	16	1	0	1,172.4
2000	8,277	65	10	2	0	1,431.4
2001	7,472	72	14	1	0	854.5
2002	4,445	41	10	1	0	638.9
2003	4,144	42	6	0	0	401.1
2004	3,847	40	6	4	0	1,416.7

Source: US Coast Guard, Office of Investigations and Analysis, 'Pollution Incidents In and Around US Waters: A Spill/Release Compendium 1969–2004,' accessed online from the Coast Guard's website. Unfortunately, due to a site redesign, the original data is no longer available online.

Notes: Covers oil spills taking place in US territorial waters and investigated by the Coast Guard.

Units: Number of oil spills; total volume in thousands of gallons.

Table 11.24: Public Opinion on Environmental Issues, 2003–2005

1. Question: Do you favor or oppose relaxing some environmental standards to increase oil and gas production in the United States? (asked April 2004)

Political affiliation	Favor	Oppose	Unsure
All	46%	43%	11%
Democrats	34	54	12
Republicans	63	26	11
Independents	40	49	11

2. Question: Right now, do you think the quality of the environment is getting better, staying about the same, or getting worse? (asked May 2005; aided question)

Level	Getting better	About the same	Getting worse	Don't know
In your community	17%	54%	28%	1%
In the United States	16	33	50	1
Worldwide	10	22	63	5

3. Question: I am going to read rome specific environmental proposals. For each one, please say whether you generally favor or oppose it. (asked March 2003)

Proposal	Favor	Oppose	No opinion
Setting higher standards and pollution standards for business and industry	80%	19%	1%
Imposing mandatory controls on carbon dioxide emissions and other greenhouse gases	75	22	3
More strongly enforcing federal environmental regulations	75	21	4
Setting higher auto emissions standards for automobiles	73	24	NA
Expanding the use of nuclear energy	43	51	6
Opening up the Arctic National Wildlife Refuge in Alaska for oil exploration	41	55	4

Source: National Renewable Energy Laboratory, *Consumer Views on Transportation and Energy*, 3rd ed, tables Q2.3.4, Q2.3.6, and Q2.3.7.

Notes: Surveys done by Fox News/Opinion Dynamics (question 1: 900 adults), Yale Environment Survey (question 2: 1,002 adults), and Gallup (question 3: 526 adults).

Units: Percent of survey respondents giving the stated response to each question.

Chapter 12

Waste & Recycling

Chapter 12 Highlights

Chapter 12 contains information on waste and recycling in the United States. Fatalities, injuries, and property damage in the transportation of hazardous materials all experienced a sharp spike in 2005, but it is not entirely clear whether this is due to an increase in hazardous materials transportation overall or a higher rate of accidents. Injuries and fatalities came back down for 2006. (table 12.01). Flammable liquids were the most commonly transported class of material, trucks were the most common means of transport (followed by pipelines), and gasoline and other flammable liquids were the most common chemicals (table 12.02). Texas and California were the most common sources and destinations for interstate shipments of hazardous materials (table 12.04). Table 12.03 also gives a state-by-state breakdown of the amount of hazardous waste generated, managed, shipped, and received. The most common waste management method was deepwell (underground) injection (table 12.05). The industries that generated the greatest amount of hazardous waste in 2005 were manufacturers of chemicals, coal and petroleum products, and synthetic fibers and resins (table 12.06). Table 12.07 gives the number of National Priority List hazardous waste sites in each state for 2007 and 2008.

The amount of municipal solid waste (also known as "garbage" or "trash") has increased greatly in recent decades; at the same time, the portion of waste that is recovered, either through recycling or composting, is up from 6% in 1960 to over 32% in 2006, with another 12% of waste generated in 2006 going to combustion for energy recovery (tables 12.08 through 12.10). The most generated material in 2006 was paper (and paperboard materials), followed by plastics; paper and nonferrous metals were the most-heavily recycled materials (table 12.09). Containers and packaging (especially corrugated boxes) comprised the bulk of products generated and recycled (table 12.12, with a more detailed breakdown in 12.11). Yard clippings were also very likely to be recovered (table 12.10).

Table 12.01: Hazardous Material Transportation Fatalities, Injuries, Incidents, and Property Damage, 1990–2006

	1990	1995	2000	2005	2006
Fatalities	8	7	16	34	6
Air	0	0	0	0	0
Highway	8	7	16	24	6
Rail	0	0	0	10	0
Water	0	0	0	0	0
Liquid pipeline	3	3	1	2	0
Gas pipeline	6	18	37	14	19
Injuries	423	400	251	945	233
Air	39	33	5	78	2
Highway	311	296	164	175	192
Rail	73	71	82	692	24
Water	0	0	0	0	15
Liquid pipeline	7	11	4	2	2
Gas pipeline	69	53	77	45	29
Incidents	8,879	14,853	17,557	15,925	20,310
Air	297	817	1,419	1,654	2,410
Highway	7,296	12,869	15,063	13,457	17,128
Rail	1,279	1,155	1,058	745	704
Water	7	12	17	69	68
Liquid pipeline	180	188	146	137	107
Gas pipeline	198	161	234	352	272
Property Damages	$32,353	$30,900	$78,132	$55,806	$70,374
Air	142	100	272	198	671
Highway	20,190	22,141	51,030	40,039	58,904
Rail	11,952	8,485	26,547	15,455	10,740
Water	70	174	283	114	59
Liquid pipeline	15,700	32,500	180,200	94,800	48,000
Gas pipeline	18,900	20,900	41,300	767,000	71,000

Source: Bureau of Transportation Statistics, *National Transportation Statistics 2008*, tables 2-6 and 2-46.

Notes: Incidents include accidents, as well as any unintentional release of hazardous material while in transit or storage.

'Water' includes only nonbulk marine transport. Bulk marine shipments are handled by the Coast Guard and are not reported here.

Property damage under $30,000 is rounded to the nearest $100; over $30,000, it is rounded to the nearest $1,000. Some data has been revised from previous editions.

Units: Number of fatalities, injuries, and incidents; property damage in thousands of current dollars.

Table 12.02: Hazardous Materials Transported, by Hazard Class, Mode of Transport, and Chemical, 2002

	Value	Weight	Distance	Miles per Shipment
Total	$660.2	2,191.5	326.7	136
By Hazard Class				
Explosives	1.2%	0.2%	0.5%	651
Gases	11.2	9.7	11.4	95
Flammable liquids	74.3	81.6	66.9	106
Flammable solids	1.0	0.5	1.3	158
Oxidizers and organic peroxides	0.8	0.6	1.3	407
Toxic materials	1.3	0.4	1.3	626
Radioactive materials	0.9	0.0	0.0	NA
Corrsoive materials	5.8	4.1	11.1	301
Miscellaneous	3.6	2.8	6.2	368
By Mode				
Single-mode	97.6%	98.5%	95.5%	105
Truck	63.6	52.9	33.7	86
For hire	28.8	20.5	19.9	285
Private	34.3	32.0	13.5	38
Rail	4.7	5.0	22.1	695
Water	7.1	10.4	21.6	NA
Airplane	0.2	0.0	0.0	2,080
Pipeline	22.0	30.2	NA	NA
Multiple-mode	1.5	0.9	3.8	849
Parcel, US post, or courier	0.6	0.0	0.0	837
Other	0.8	0.8	3.8	1,371
Unknown mode	0.9	0.6	0.7	57

(continued on next page)

Table 12.02: Hazardous Materials Transported, by Hazard Class, Mode of Transport, and Chemical, 2002

	Value	Weight	Distance	Miles per Shipment
Total	*$660.2*	*2,191.5*	*326.7*	*136*
By Chemical				
Anhydrous ammonia	0.3%	0.5%	0.8%	NA
Carbon dioxide	0.2	NA	NA	58
Chlorine	0.3	0.4	0.8	114
Compressed nitrogen	0.3	0.9	NA	84
Compressed oxygen	0.4	NA	NA	NA
Petroleum gas	2.9	2.7	3.7	47
Benzene	0.6	0.5	0.4	438
Gas oil, diesel fuel, light heating oil	4.1	5.9	3.7	41
Gasoline	40.9	46.1	33.4	57
Kerosene	0.4	0.6	0.3	19
Methanol	NA	NA	NA	201
Petroleum distillates NOS	0.8	0.5	0.6	213
Sodium hydroxide	0.8	1.1	3.0	203
Sulfuric acid	0.2	0.7	1.0	218
Aviation fuel	2.5	3.5	3.0	97
Ethylene	0.6	0.5	0.2	NA
Compressed hyrocarbon gas mixture	0.6	1.0	1.1	164
Flammable liquids NOS	14.4	19.6	14.3	52
Liquid tars	0.4	0.9	1.4	162
Elevated temperature liquid NOS	1.0	1.9	3.8	174
Other	27.8	10.3	26.0	283

Source: US Bureau of the Census, 2002 Economic Census, *Commodity Flow Survey: Hazardous Materials 2002*, tables 1a, 2a, and 3.

Notes: 'Pipeline' excludes most crude oil shipments.
NOS = 'Not Otherwise Specified'
Groups may not add to total.

Units: Total value in billions of dollars; total weight in million tons; total distance in million ton-miles; percent of total; miles per shipment.

Table 12.03: Hazardous Waste Generated, Managed, Shipped, and Received, by State, 2005

	Generated	Managed	Shipped	Received	Interstate Shipments	Interstate Receipts
United States	*38,347,011*	*43,923,861*	*7,686,291*	*8,545,857*	*4,262,187*	*4,244,053*
Alabama	874,749	955,711	210,013	120,868	163,471	86,984
Alaska	2,356	33,567	1,196	149	1,048	0
Arizona	24,294	34,121	26,479	35,573	18,293	17,213
Arkansas	443,735	596,549	284,497	273,294	206,222	200,730
California	747,221	2,083,754	710,785	1,770,296	199,749	42,288
Colorado	95,475	105,157	53,941	23,368	38,942	6,154
Connecticut	43,980	17,056	55,413	22,714	47,825	11,704
Delaware	14,441	534	14,122	373	14,034	280
District of Columbia	281	0	293	0	293	0
Florida	237,078	1,481,638	39,038	18,040	35,090	6,661
Georgia	480,269	862,647	321,356	6,944	319,506	4,361
Hawaii	1,458	6	1,444	400	1,098	0
Idaho	25,924	114,245	28,858	136,002	6,198	135,020
Illinois	1,164,127	1,199,813	407,699	437,479	138,865	325,874
Indiana	1,017,416	1,313,125	426,551	642,508	208,480	420,538
Iowa	52,708	786	52,450	546	52,348	114
Kansas	229,151	1,129,142	132,177	193,929	22,088	182,947
Kentucky	1,152,075	1,089,239	206,322	86,914	183,336	61,415
Louisiana	5,460,262	5,471,449	385,071	362,705	131,105	109,123
Maine	4,130	1,080	3,493	2,390	3,443	1,930
Maryland	39,715	111,112	58,373	127,135	56,192	86,577
Massachusetts	372,703	324,393	70,051	28,046	58,950	8,902
Michigan	295,807	422,586	316,230	440,019	154,524	314,537
Minnesota	249,503	306,216	62,141	303,553	52,238	269,936
Mississippi	1,599,450	1,902,007	27,118	56,696	20,077	55,733
Missouri	89,842	339,520	70,091	199,926	50,091	169,960
Montana	7,218	1,256	6,008	0	6,008	0
Nebraska	30,901	35,012	33,649	36,110	33,209	32,169
Nevada	12,947	58,939	16,639	61,996	8,863	50,072

(continued on next page)

Table 12.03: Hazardous Waste Generated, Managed, Shipped, and Received, by State, 2005

	Generated	Managed	Shipped	Received	Interstate Shipments	Interstate Receipts
United States	*38,347,011*	*43,923,861*	*7,686,291*	*8,545,857*	*4,262,187*	*4,244,053*
New Hampshire	6,126	0	6,150	0	6,150	0
New Jersey	993,071	920,655	322,377	166,198	213,296	117,505
New Mexico	944,636	947,872	5,947	8,977	5,751	8,374
New York	1,124,198	1,200,503	195,511	286,495	118,526	64,883
North Carolina	384,112	373,208	106,536	91,110	97,051	31,573
North Dakota	549,686	548,066	1,569	611	1,549	141
Ohio	2,145,356	2,079,408	946,652	853,197	571,767	500,400
Oklahoma	211,939	219,642	38,533	48,203	31,072	42,325
Oregon	40,332	102,215	32,070	93,930	26,703	67,453
Pennsylvania	360,820	510,014	316,788	467,186	169,710	328,389
Rhode Island	6,292	35,118	10,318	38,594	9,576	36,478
South Carolina	177,734	139,438	219,231	177,372	164,723	119,984
South Dakota	992	1	1,153	133	1,153	50
Tennessee	776,095	721,541	67,784	23,699	64,776	20,475
Texas	15,224,158	14,872,774	886,180	600,289	190,226	155,761
Utah	78,101	329,301	77,801	154,354	19,097	77,012
Vermont	3,451	390,607	2,758	253	2,731	78
Virginia	134,416	115,896	82,969	36,790	67,129	20,144
Washington	141,918	46,515	120,672	33,251	89,702	9,854
West Virginia	72,602	36,803	46,417	11,822	46,073	10,084
Wisconsin	108,327	72,586	111,484	53,752	92,805	31,868
Wyoming	3,067	206,910	2,313	0	2,313	0

Source: Environmental Protection Agency, *National Biennial RCRA Hazardous Waste Report 2005*, exhibits 1.1, 2.2, 3.1, 3.5, and 4.1.

Notes: Figures include only solid waste assigned a Federal Hazardous Waste Code and regulated by the EPA's Resource Conservation and Recovery Act (RCRA). Wastes not specifically regulated by the EPA but assigned State Hazardous Waste Codes are not included.

Units: Amount of waste in tons.

Table 12.04: Hazardous Materials Shipped, by State of Origin and Destination, 2002

	Origin			Destination		
	Value	Weight	Distance	Value	Weight	Distance
Total	*$660.2*	*2,191.5*	*326.7*	*$660.2*	*2,191.5*	*326.7*
Alabama	1.3%	1.4%	0.9%	1.5%	1.4%	1.2%
California	10.3	9.1	4.8	11.3	9.3	9.9
Florida	2.7	2.6	1.0	4.2	4.3	9.3
Georgia	2.6	2.1	1.3	2.5	2.2	1.7
Illinois	6.2	5.5	5.3	4.7	4.4	4.5
Indiana	2.4	2.9	1.7	3.0	3.1	1.5
Kentucky	1.8	1.9	1.3	1.8	1.7	2.6
Louisiana	8.1	10.2	19.0	5.8	7.2	4.2
Michigan	3.6	2.8	1.5	3.5	3.1	2.7
Mississippi	1.3	1.7	5.1	1.4	1.6	1.3
Missouri	NA	NA	NA	1.4	1.2	0.9
New Jersey	3.4	4.2	3.4	3.5	3.9	5.0
New York	2.3	2.1	3.4	2.3	2.2	2.7
North Carolina	2.0	1.3	0.9	2.1	1.4	1.5
Ohio	4.2	3.7	2.6	4.3	4.8	5.3
Pensylvania	3.8	2.3	1.7	2.8	2.4	1.6
Tennessee	2.8	2.4	2.2	2.4	2.3	2.4
Texas	19.3	21.3	22.1	18.2	21.0	17.6
Utah	1.5	2.0	3.2	0.9	1.3	0.7
Washington	2.3	2.4	1.9	2.0	2.2	2.5
West Virginia	0.4	NA	NA	NA	NA	NA
Other states	17.7	16.9	15.9	20.3	19.0	20.8

Source: US Bureau of the Census, 2002 Economic Census, *Commodity Flow Survey: Hazardous Materials 2002*, tables 5a and 5b.

Notes: Groups may not add to total.
Detail given only for selected states.

Units: Total value in billions of dollars; total weight in million tons; total distance in million ton-miles; percent of total.

Table 12.05: Top 15 Methods of Hazardous Waste Management, 2005

Method	Tons Managed	Number of Sites
Total	*43,923,861*	*1,550*
Deepwell or underground injection	21,846,692	46
Other treatment	4,221,555	381
Other disposal	3,433,990	118
Aqueous organic treatment	3,356,122	78
Landfill/surface impoundment	2,037,543	68
Energy recovery	1,719,390	99
Aqueous inorganic treatment	1,705,585	190
Incineration	1,437,996	164
Metals recovery	1,420,320	137
Fuel blending	1,174,625	105
Sludge treatment	516,002	61
Stabilization	425,931	149
Other recovery	328,180	74
Solvents recovery	296,681	493
Land treatment/application/farming	3,248	20

Source: Environmental Protection Agency, *National Biennial RCRA Hazardous Waste Report 2005*, exhibit 2.6.

Notes: Figures include only solid waste assigned a Federal Hazardous Waste Code and regulated by the EPA's Resource Conservation and Recovery Act (RCRA). Wastes not specifically regulated by the EPA but assigned State Hazardous Waste Codes are not included. Columns may not add to total.

Units: Number of sites; amount of waste in tons.

Table 12.06: 50 Largest Generators of Hazardous Waste by NAICS Category, 2005

Rank	Description	Tons Generated
1	Basic Chemical Manufacturing	21,082,216
2	Petroleum and Coal Products Manufacturing	5,083,753
3	Resin, Synthetic Rubber, and Artificial Synthetic Fibers and Filaments Manufacturing	1,825,181
4	Waste Treatment and Disposal	1,753,682
5	Iron and Steel Mills and Ferroalloy Manufacturing	1,486,675
6	Semiconductor and Other Electronic Component Manufacturing	992,437
7	Nonferrous Metal (except Aluminum) Production and Processing	939,050
8	Coating, Engraving, Heat Treating, and Allied Activities	531,812
9	Pharmaceutical and Medicine Manufacturing	513,768
10	Remediation and Other Waste Management Services	373,958
11	Alumina and Aluminum Production and Processing	342,883
12	Other Electrical Equipment and Component Manufacturing	333,213
13	Motor Vehicle Parts Manufacturing	301,837
14	Electric Power Generation, Transmission and Distribution	182,897
15	Paint, Coating, and Adhesive Manufacturing	164,464
16	Waste Collection	155,920
17	Other Chemical Product and Preparation Manufacturing	148,594
18	Other Fabricated Metal Product Manufacturing	143,145
19	Warehousing and Storage	139,730
20	National Security and International Affairs	118,372
21	Forging and Stamping	115,439
22	Chemical and Allied Products Merchant Wholesalers	107,081
23	Pesticide, Fertilizer, and Other Agricultural Chemical Manufacturing	95,288
24	Hardware Manufacturing	88,129
25	Aerospace Product and Parts Manufacturing	76,711
26	Steel Product Manufacturing from Purchased Steel	75,224
27	Sawmills and Wood Preservation	66,187
28	Business Support Services	47,899
29	Pulp, Paper, and Paperboard Mills	47,125
30	Plastics Product Manufacturing	46,449

(continued on next page)

Table 12.06: 50 Largest Generators of Hazardous Waste by NAICS Category, 2005

Rank	Description	Tons Generated
31	Printing and Related Support Activities	43,908
32	Motor Vehicle Manufacturing	42,593
33	Cutlery and Handtool Manufacturing	35,884
34	Support Activities for Water Transportation	35,512
35	Other Miscellaneous Manufacturing	31,809
36	Soap, Cleaning Compound, and Toilet Preparation Manufacturing	30,948
37	Miscellaneous Durable Goods Merchant Wholesalers	30,743
38	Foundries	30,270
39	Support Activities for Road Transportation	28,928
40	Nonscheduled Air Transportation	26,172
41	Colleges, Universities, and Professional Schools	26,155
42	Support Activities for Air Transportation	22,791
43	Scientific Research and Development Services	22,166
44	Automotive Parts, Accessories, and Tire Stores	18,478
45	Converted Paper Product Manufacturing	18,117
46	Metal Ore Mining	16,276
47	Deep Sea, Coastal, and Great Lakes Water Transportation	16,161
48	Chemical and Allied Products Wholesalers	15,999
49	Executive, Legislative, and Other General Government Support	15,897
50	Engine, Turbine, and Power Transmission Equipment Manufacturing	15,640
	Top 50 Total	*37,903,569*

Source: Environmental Protection Agency, *National Biennial RCRA Hazardous Waste Report 2005*, exhibit 1.9.

Notes: Figures include only solid waste assigned a Federal Hazardous Waste Code and regulated by the EPA's Resource Conservation and Recovery Act (RCRA). Wastes not specifically regulated by the EPA but assigned State Hazardous Waste Codes are not included. Columns may not add to total.

Units: Amount of waste in tons.

Table 12.07: Hazardous Waste Sites on the National Priority List by State, 2007 and 2008

	2007	2008		2007	2008
United States	*1,370*	*1,258*	*United States*	*1,370*	*1,258*
Alabama	13	13	Montana	14	14
Alaska	5	5	Nebraska	13	13
Arizona	8	9	Nevada	1	1
Arkansas	10	9	New Hampshire	20	20
California	94	94	New Jersey	114	114
Colorado	17	18	New Mexico	13	13
Connecticut	14	14	New York	86	86
Delaware	14	14	North Carolina	31	32
District of Columbia	1	1	North Dakota	0	0
Florida	48	49	Ohio	30	31
Georgia	15	15	Oklahoma	10	8
Hawaii	3	3	Oregon	12	12
Idaho	6	6	Pennsylvania	93	94
Illinois	42	43	Rhode Island	12	12
Indiana	30	31	South Carolina	25	25
Iowa	11	11	South Dakota	2	2
Kansas	10	11	Tennessee	13	13
Kentucky	14	14	Texas	42	46
Louisiana	11	10	Utah	15	15
Maine	12	12	Vermont	11	11
Maryland	17	17	Virginia	29	30
Massachusetts	31	31	Washington	48	48
Michigan	65	65	West Virginia	9	9
Minnesota	25	25	Wisconsin	37	37
Mississippi	4	4	Wyoming	2	2
Missouri	26	29			

Source: Environmental Protection Agency, Superfund National Priorities List, accessed online via www.epa.gov/superfund/sites/query/basic.htm.

Notes: The National Priorities List is a list of national priorities among the known releases or threatened releases of hazardous substances, pollutants, or contaminants throughout the United States and its territories. The NPL is intended primarily to guide the EPA in determining which sites warrant further investigation. Includes sites currently on the final NPL list.

Total for United States excludes 12 sites in Puerto Rico, 2 sites in Guam, and 2 sites in the US Virgin Islands for 2007, and 13 sites in Puerto Rico, 2 sites in Guam, and 2 sites in the US Virgin Islands for 2008.

NPL database was accessed November 1, 2007 and September 12, 2008.

Units: Number of sites.

Table 12.08: Generation and Recovery of
Municipal Solid Waste, 1960–2006

	1960	1970	1980	1990	2000	2005	2006
Total Weight							
Total Generation	88.1	121.1	151.6	205.2	238.3	248.2	251.3
Recovery of materials	5.6	8.0	14.5	33.2	69.3	79.1	81.8
for recycling	5.6	8.0	14.5	29.0	52.8	58.6	61.0
for composting	0.0	0.0	0.0	4.2	16.5	20.6	20.8
Combusion with energy recovery	0.0	0.4	2.7	29.7	33.7	33.4	31.4
Discards to landfill	82.5	112.7	134.4	142.3	135.3	135.6	138.2
Per Capita Daily							
Total Generation	2.68	3.25	3.66	4.50	4.64	4.59	4.60
Recovery of materials	0.17	0.22	0.35	0.73	1.35	1.46	1.50
for recycling	0.17	0.22	0.35	0.64	1.03	1.08	1.12
for composting	0.00	0.00	0.00	0.09	0.32	0.38	0.38
Combusion with energy recovery	0.00	0.01	0.07	0.63	0.66	0.62	0.57
Discards to landfill	2.51	3.02	3.24	3.12	2.63	2.51	2.53

Source: Environmental Protection Agency, *Municipal Solid Waste Generation, Recycling, and Disposal in the United States: Facts and Figures for 2006*, tables 3 and 4.

Notes: Recovery for composting includes yard trimmings, food scraps, and other organic waste materials.
Combustion includes combustion of waste in mass-burn or refuse-derived fuel form, and combustion with energy recovery of source-separated materials.

Units: Total amount in millions of tons; per capita in pounds per person per day.

Table 12.09: Generation, Recovery, and Discarding of Materials in the Municipal Solid Waste Stream, 1960–2006

	1960	1970	1980	1990	2000	2006
Waste Generated						
Paper and paperboard	29,990	44,310	55,160	72,730	87,740	85,290
Glass	6,720	12,740	15,130	13,100	12,620	13,200
Metals	10,820	13,830	15,510	16,550	18,240	19,130
Ferrous	10,300	12,360	12,620	12,640	13,530	14,220
Aluminum	340	800	1,730	2,810	3,150	3,260
Other nonferrous	180	670	1,160	1,100	1,560	1,650
Plastics	390	2,900	6,830	17,130	25,340	29,490
Rubber and leather	1,840	2,970	4,200	5,790	6,530	6,540
Textiles	1,760	2,040	2,530	5,810	9,440	11,840
Wood	3,030	3,720	7,010	12,210	13,020	13,930
Total for Materials	*54,620*	*83,280*	*108,890*	*146,510*	*177,120*	*183,970*
Total for All Waste	*88,120*	*121,060*	*151,640*	*205,210*	*238,260*	*251,340*
Percent Recovered						
Paper and paperboard	16.9%	15.3%	21.3%	27.8%	42.8%	51.6%
Glass	1.5	1.3	5.0	20.1	22.8	21.8
Metals	0.5	3.5	7.9	24.0	35.8	36.3
Ferrous	0.5	1.2	2.9	17.6	34.1	35.7
Aluminum	0.0	1.3	17.9	35.9	27.3	21.2
Other nonferrous	0.0	47.8	46.6	66.4	67.9	71.5
Plastics	0.0	0.0	0.3	2.2	5.8	6.9
Rubber and leather	17.9	8.4	3.1	6.4	12.6	13.3
Textiles	2.8	2.9	6.3	11.4	14.0	15.3
Wood	0.0	0.0	0.0	1.1	9.5	9.4
Total for Materials	*10.3%*	*9.6%*	*13.3%*	*19.8%*	*29.8%*	*33.2%*
Total for All Waste	*6.4%*	*6.6%*	*9.6%*	*16.2%*	*29.1%*	*32.5%*

Source: Environmental Protection Agency, *Municipal Solid Waste Generation, Recycling, and Disposal in the United States: Facts and Figures for 2006 (Data Tables)*, tables 1 and 2.

Notes: 'Recovery' includes recovery of postconsumer wastes, but excludes converting/fabrication of scrap.

Units: Amount of waste generated in thousands of tons; percent of total generation recovered, by weight.

Table 12.10: Generation, Recovery, and Discarding of Products in the Municipal Solid Waste Stream, 1960–2006

	1960	1970	1980	1990	2000	2006
Waste Generated						
Total for All Waste	*88,120*	*121,060*	*151,640*	*205,210*	*238,260*	*251,340*
Non-food wastes	54,620	83,280	108,890	146,510	177,120	183,970
Durable goods	9,920	14,660	21,800	29,810	36,980	40,170
Nondurable goods	17,330	25,060	34,420	52,170	64,120	64,180
Containers and packaging	27,370	43,560	52,670	64,530	76,020	79,620
Organic waste products	33,500	37,780	42,750	58,700	61,140	67,370
Food scraps	12,200	12,800	13,000	20,800	27,110	31,250
Yard trimmings	20,000	23,200	27,500	35,000	30,530	32,400
Other organic waste	1,300	1,780	2,250	2,900	3,500	3,720
Percent recovered						
Total for All Waste	*6.4%*	*6.6%*	*9.6%*	*16.2%*	*29.1%*	*32.5%*
Non-food wastes	10.3	9.6	13.3	19.8	29.8	33.2
Durable goods	3.5	6.4	6.2	11.6	17.6	18.5
Nondurable goods	13.8	14.9	13.6	16.9	27.4	33.6
Containers and packaging	10.5	7.7	16.1	26.0	37.8	40.2
Organic waste products	0.0	0.0	0.0	7.2	26.9	30.8
Food scraps	0.0	0.0	0.0	0.0	2.5	2.2
Yard trimmings	0.0	0.0	0.0	12.0	51.7	62.0

Source: Environmental Protection Agency, *Municipal Solid Waste Generation, Recycling, and Disposal in the United States: Facts and Figures for 2006 (Data Tables)*, tables 9 and 10.

Notes: 'Recovery' includes recovery of postconsumer wastes, but excludes converting/fabrication of scrap.

Units: Amount of waste generated in thousands of tons; percent of total generation recovered, by weight.

Table 12.11: Products in the Municipal Waste Stream, by Material, 2006

	Generated	Recovered	% Recovered	Discarded
Paper and Paperboard				
Total Paper and Paperboard	*85,280*	*44,020*	*51.6%*	*41,260*
Nondurable goods	44,840	20,160	45.0	24,680
Newspapers	12,360	10,870	87.9	1,490
Books	1,130	290	25.7	840
Magazines	2,570	1,040	40.5	1,530
Office paper	6,320	4,150	65.7	2,170
Standard mail	5,890	2,280	38.7	3,610
Tissue paper and towels	3,430	0	0.0	3,430
Containers and packaging	40,440	23,860	59.0	16,580
Corrugated boxes	31,430	22,630	72.0	8,800
Milk cartons	510	0	0.0	510
Folding cartons	5,570	890	16.0	4,680
Bags and sacks	1,340	340	25.4	1,000
Glass				
Total Glass	*13,200*	*2,880*	*21.8%*	*10,320*
Durable goods	1,810	0	0.0	1,810
Containers and packaging	11,390	2,880	25.3	8,510
Beer and soft drink bottles	7,500	2,300	30.7	5,200
Wine and liquor bottles	1,670	250	15.0	1,420
Food and other bottles and jars	2,220	330	14.9	1,890
Metal				
Total Metal	*19,130*	*6,950*	*36.3%*	*12,180*
Durable goods	14,220	4,520	31.8	9,700
Ferrous	11,470	3,340	29.1	8,130
Alumunim	1,100	0	0.0	1,100
Lead	1,190	1,180	99.2	10
Other nonferrous	460	0	0.0	460
Containers and packaging	4,690	2,430	51.8	2,260
Steel	2,750	1,740	63.3	1,010
Food and other cans	2,510	1,580	62.9	930
Aluminum	1,940	690	35.6	1,250
Beer and other soft drink cans	1,440	650	45.1	790

(continued on next page)

Table 12.11: Products in the Municipal Waste Stream, by Material, 2006

	Generated	Recovered	% Recovered	Discarded
Plastic				
Total Plastic	*29,490*	*2,040*	*6.9%*	*27,450*
Durable goods	8,790	530	6.0	8,260
Nondurable goods	6,470	0	0.0	6,470
Plastic plates and cups	890	0	0.0	890
Trash bags	1,080	0	0.0	1,080
Containers and packaging	14,230	1,510	10.6	12,720
Soft drink bottles	940	290	30.9	650
Milk and water bottles	710	220	31.0	490
Bags, sacks & wraps	4,630	360	7.8	4,270
Rubber and Leather				
Total Rubber and Leather	*6,540*	*870*	*13.3%*	*5,670*
Durable goods	5,440	870	16.0	4,570
Rubber in tires	2,490	870	34.9	1,620
Nondurable goods	1,060	0	0.0	1,060
Clothing and footwear	780	0	0.0	780
Containers and packaging	40	0	0.0	40

Source: Environmental Protection Agency, *Municipal Solid Waste Generation, Recycling, and Disposal in the United States: Facts and Figures for 2006 (Data Tables)*, tables 4 to 8.

Notes: Not all subgroups are shown. Groups may not add to total.

Units: Amount of waste generated, recovered, and discarded in thousands of tons; percent recovered out of total generated.

Table 12.12: Products in the Municipal Waste Stream by Type of Goods, 2006

	Generated	Recovered	% Recovered	Discarded
Durable Goods				
Total Durable Goods	*40,170*	*7,430*	*18.5%*	*32,740*
Major appliances	3,580	2,410	67.3	1,170
Small appliances	1,020	10	1.0	1,010
Furniture and furnishings	9,100	0	0.0	9,100
Carpets and rugs	3,070	250	8.1	2,820
Rubber tires	3,900	1,360	34.9	2,540
Batteries, lead acid	2,470	2,450	99.2	20
Selected consumer electronics	2,900	330	11.4	2,570
Nondurable Goods				
Total Nondurable Goods	*64,180*	*21,590*	*33.6%*	*42,590*
Newspapers	12,360	10,870	87.9	1,490
Books	1,130	290	25.7	840
Magazines	2,570	1,040	40.5	1,530
Office paper	6,320	4,150	65.7	2,170
Standard mail	5,890	2,280	38.7	3,610
Tissue paper and towels	3,430	0	0.0	3,430
Paper plates and cups	1,180	0	0.0	1,180
Trash bags	1,080	0	0.0	1,080
Disposable diapers	3,630	0	0.0	3,630
Clothing and footwear	8,640	1,250	14.5	7,390
Towels, sheets, and pillowases	1,030	180	17.5	850

(continued on next page)

Table 12.12: Products in the Municipal Waste Stream by Type of Goods, 2006

	Generated	Recovered	% Recovered	Discarded
Containers and Packaging				
Total Containers and Packaging	*79,620*	*31,990*	*40.2%*	*47,630*
Glass	11,390	2,880	25.3	8,510
Beer and soft drink bottles	7,500	2,300	30.7	5,200
Wine and liquor bottles	1,670	250	15.0	1,420
Food and other bottles & jars	2,220	330	14.9	1,890
Steel	2,750	1,740	63.3	1,010
Food and other cans	2,510	1,580	62.9	930
Aluminum packaging	1,940	690	35.6	1,250
Beer and soft drink cans	1,440	650	45.1	790
Foil and closures	420	40	9.5	380
Paper and paperboard	40,440	23,860	59.0	16,580
Corrugated boxes	31,430	22,630	72.0	8,800
Milk cartons	510	0	0.0	510
Folding cartons	5,570	890	16.0	4,680
Bags and sacks	1,340	340	25.4	1,000
Plastics	14,230	1,510	10.6	12,720
Soft drink bottles	940	290	30.9	650
Milk bottles	710	220	31.0	490
Bags, sacks, and wraps	4,520	360	7.8	4,270
Wood	8,480	1,310	15.4	7,170

Source: Environmental Protection Agency, *Municipal Solid Waste Generation, Recycling, and Disposal in the United States: Facts and Figures for 2006 (Data Tables)*, tables 12 through 18 and 20 through 22.

Notes: Not all subgroups are shown. Groups may not add to total.

Units: Amount of waste generated, recovered, and discarded in thousands of tons; percent recovered out of total generated.

Part IV:
Special Topics

Chapter 13

Economy & Employment

Chapter 13 Highlights

Chapter 13 features information on the economic picture for and impact of all three topics: energy, transportation, and the environment. Tables 13.01 to 13.04 show consumer price estimates and spending on energy, broken down by energy source and economic sector. In 2005, energy prices (per million Btu) were highest for retail electricity and petroleum products, and for the residential and commercial sectors (tables 13.01 and 13.02). Expenditures were also highest for petroleum products and electricity, with the highest overall spending in the transportation sector (tables 13.03 and 13.04). Gasoline prices generally increased in the last 20 years, but rose drastically from 2000 to 2007 (table 13.05, also see a state-by-state breakdown in table 13.06). Fossil fuel production prices increased in general, but have shot up dramatically for crude oil and natural gas (table 13.07, with detailed breakdowns for crude oil in tables 13.08 and 13.09). Electricity retail prices have increased somewhat, but have stayed comparatively steady when adjusted for inflation (table 13.10). Most production and refining of petroleum products is still done by domestic-affiliated companies, whose net income and profits increased greatly in the period between 2000 and 2006 (tables 13.11 and 13.12). Table 13.19 presents a state-by-state breakdown of taxes on motor fuel, and future projections for energy prices are also available in table 13.22.

Transportation services (i.e., for-hire transportation) comprise approximately 3% of the US Gross Domestic Product (GDP), with most of that coming from truck or air transportation (table 13.13). Approximately 5 million people are employed in transportation and warehousing industries, with around another 3 million employed in related occupations; the major employers are truck transportation and transportation equipment manufacturing (table 13.15). A state-by-state breakdown of transportation-related employment is also available in table 13.14. In 2006, around 12% of personal expenditures went to trasnportation, almost all of that going to user-operated vehicles (table 13.16). The Consumer Expenditure Survey for 2006 estimated that around 18% of consumer spending went to transportation-related items, and presents breakdowns by age, housing tenure, region, and race or Hispanic origin (table 13.17).

For public transportation, air carriers have the highest average passenger fare, followed by Amtrak or other intercity rail services; however, airplanes have some of the lowest revenues per passenger-mile (table 13.18). After experiencing several years of diminished profits or losses, air carriers rebounded and increased their earnings and profits in 2006 and 2007 (tables 13.20 and 13.21).

Table 13.01: Consumer Price Estimates for Energy by Source, 1970–2005

	1970	1980	1990	1995	2000	2005
Total Energy	$1.65	$6.89	$8.25	$8.28	$10.34	$15.66
By Source						
Primary Energy	$1.08	$4.57	$4.46	$4.23	$5.73	$9.25
Petroleum	1.72	7.40	7.47	7.29	9.91	15.49
Coal	0.38	1.46	1.49	1.37	1.24	1.62
Natural gas	0.59	2.86	3.82	3.73	5.62	9.92
Distillate fuel oil	1.16	6.70	7.68	6.98	9.86	16.37
Jet fuel	0.73	6.36	5.68	4.00	6.64	12.86
Liquefied propane	1.46	5.64	6.77	6.56	10.20	14.65
Motor gasoline	2.85	9.84	9.12	9.22	12.01	17.83
Residual fuel oil	0.42	3.88	3.17	2.46	4.32	6.65
Nuclear	0.18	0.43	0.67	0.54	0.46	0.43
Biomass	1.29	2.26	1.32	1.40	1.58	2.63
Electric Power Sector	0.32	1.77	1.48	1.29	1.71	2.60
Retail Electricity	4.98	13.95	19.32	20.29	20.03	23.92

Source: Energy Information Administration, *Annual Energy Review 2007*, table 3.3.

Notes: 'Primary energy' refers to the consumption-weighted average for all sectors. 'Biomass' includes wood and waste-derived energy, but excludes ethanol and biodiesel.

Units: Price in current dollars per million Btu.

Table 13.02: Consumer Price Estimates for Energy by End-Use Sector, 1970–2005

	1970	1980	1990	1995	2000	2005
Residential						
Total Residential	$2.10	$7.46	$11.88	$12.63	$14.27	$19.21
Natural gas	1.06	3.60	5.63	5.89	7.64	12.34
Petroleum	1.56	7.26	8.75	7.75	11.55	17.29
Electricity (retail)	6.51	15.71	22.96	24.63	24.14	27.68
Commercial						
Total Commercial	$1.98	$7.85	$11.89	$12.64	$13.93	$18.57
Natural gas	0.75	3.32	4.70	4.94	6.56	10.96
Petroleum	0.90	5.64	5.95	4.97	8.09	13.46
Electricity (retail)	6.09	16.06	21.20	22.29	21.52	25.40
Industrial						
Total Industrial	$0.84	$4.71	$5.23	$4.97	$6.49	$10.64
Coal	0.45	1.87	1.69	1.63	1.55	2.56
Natural gas	0.38	2.52	2.95	2.80	4.61	9.07
Petroleum	0.98	5.75	5.48	5.20	7.50	11.85
Biomass	1.59	1.67	0.99	1.21	1.43	2.31
Electricity (retail)	2.99	10.81	13.92	13.68	13.60	16.77
Transportation						
Total Transportation	$2.31	$8.61	$8.28	$8.09	$10.78	$16.84
Petroleum	2.31	8.60	8.27	8.08	10.78	16.84

Source: Energy Information Administration, *Annual Energy Review 2006*, table 3.4; *2007*, table 3.4.

Notes: 'Retail electricity' refers to the prices paid by final consumers, reported by electric utilities and other energy providers.

Units: Price in current dollars per million Btu.

Table 13.03: Comsumer Expenditures for Energy
by Source, 1970–2005

	1970	1980	1990	1995	2000	2005
Total Energy	*$82,911*	*$374,346*	*$472,539*	*$514,049*	*$689,199*	*$1,042,934*
By Source						
Primary Energy	*$63,923*	*$314,278*	*$336,475*	*$347,245*	*$517,815*	*$842,849*
Petroleum	47,955	237,676	235,368	236,905	360,889	595,594
Coal	4,630	22,607	28,602	27,431	28,080	36,933
Natural gas	10,891	51,061	65,278	75,020	119,092	200,303
Distillate fuel oil	6,253	40,797	49,335	47,533	78,207	143,261
Jet fuel	1,441	13,923	17,784	12,525	23,777	44,679
Liquefied propane	2,446	10,926	13,715	16,306	29,879	39,073
Motor gasoline	31,596	124,408	126,558	136,647	193,947	311,035
Residual fuel oil	2,046	21,573	8,721	4,676	8,870	13,951
Nuclear	44	1,189	4,104	3,810	3,628	3,477
Biomass	438	1,231	1,997	2,938	3,196	3,396
Retail Electricity	*23,345*	*98,095*	*176,691*	*205,876*	*231,577*	*295,789*

Source: Energy Information Administration, *Annual Energy Review 2007*, table 3.5.

Notes: 'Primary energy' refers to the consumption-weighted average for all sectors.
'Biomass' includes wood and waste-derived energy, but excludes ethanol and biodiesel.

Units: Expenditures in millions of current dollars.

Table 13.04: Consumer Expenditures for Energy by End-Use Sector, 1970–2005

	1970	1980	1990	1995	2000	2005
Residential						
Total Residential	*$20,213*	*$69,418*	*$111,097*	*$128,388*	*$156,089*	*$216,046*
Natural gas	5,272	17,497	25,439	29,362	38,959	61,196
Petroleum	4,286	12,695	12,308	10,715	18,051	25,150
Electricity (retail)	10,352	38,458	72,378	87,610	98,209	128,393
Commercial						
Total Commercial	*$10,628*	*$46,932*	*$79,284*	*$91,788*	*$112,870*	*$154,576*
Natural gas	1,844	8,858	12,681	15,383	21,339	33,838
Petroleum	1,391	7,267	5,669	3,638	6,121	9,724
Electricity (retail)	7,319	30,611	60,627	72,481	85,129	110,522
Industrial						
Total Industrial	*$16,691*	*$94,316*	*$102,402*	*$107,060*	*$141,533*	*$205,975*
Coal	2,082	5,888	4,636	4,068	3,507	5,004
Natural gas	2,625	16,350	19,348	21,487	34,624	55,247
Petroleum	6,069	42,765	34,132	34,170	53,509	87,679
Biomass	366	529	906	1,699	1,888	1,183
Electricity (retail)	5,624	28,863	43,358	45,402	47,859	56,229
Transportation						
Total Transportation	*$35,379*	*$163,680*	*$179,857*	*$186,813*	*$278,846*	*$466,337*
Petroleum	35,327	163,517	178,852	186,411	278,398	465,476

Source: Energy Information Administration, *Annual Energy Review 2007*, table 3.6.

Notes: 'Retail electricity' refers to the prices paid by final consumers, reported by electric utilities and other energy providers.

Units: Expenditures in millions of current dollars.

Table 13.05: Sales Price of Transportation Fuel
by Type of Fuel, 1980–2007

	1980	1985	1990	1995	2000	2007
Aviation Fuel						
Gasoline	$1.08	$1.20	$1.12	$1.01	$1.31	$2.85
Kerosene	0.87	0.80	0.77	0.54	0.90	2.17
Highway Fuel						
All Gasoline	*$1.22*	*$1.20*	*$1.22*	*$1.21*	*$1.56*	*$2.85*
Premium gasoline	NA	1.34	1.35	1.34	1.69	3.04
Regular gasoline	1.25	1.20	1.16	1.15	1.51	2.80
Diesel	0.82	0.79	0.73	0.56	0.94	2.27
Railroad Fuel						
Diesel	$0.83	$0.78	$0.69	$0.60	$0.88	NA

Source: Bureau of Transportation Statistics, *National Transportation Statistics 2008*, table 3-8.

Notes: Aviation gasoline, kerosene, and highway diesel refer to sales to end-users. Prices for highway gasoline refer to the average retail price.

Units: Price in current dollars per gallon.

Table 13.06: Gasoline Prices by State, 1995, 2000, 2006, and 2007

	1995	2000	2006	2007
United States	*$0.761*	*$1.091*	*$2.121*	*$2.337*
Alabama	0.763	1.047	2.071	2.269
Alaska	1.097	1.326	2.399	2.550
Arizona	0.827	1.141	2.182	2.345
Arkansas	0.712	1.026	2.031	2.301
California	0.779	1.187	2.282	2.488
Colorado	0.818	1.128	2.150	2.405
Connecticut	0.802	1.159	2.200	2.380
Delaware	0.785	1.097	2.151	2.270
District of Columbia	0.724	1.062	2.186	2.278
Florida	0.759	1.045	2.109	2.295
Georgia	0.726	1.028	2.089	2.287
Hawaii	0.985	1.231	2.525	2.587
Idaho	0.776	1.142	2.148	2.379
Illinois	0.770	1.148	2.119	2.375
Indiana	0.738	1.091	2.052	2.306
Iowa	0.711	1.073	2.069	2.356
Kansas	0.700	1.037	2.036	2.311
Kentucky	0.754	1.082	2.090	2.328
Louisiana	0.745	1.037	2.087	2.285
Maine	0.824	1.130	2.146	2.385
Maryland	0.773	1.045	2.161	2.311
Massachusetts	0.814	1.163	2.163	2.350
Michigan	0.722	1.095	2.095	2.358
Minnesota	0.780	1.139	2.114	2.375
Mississippi	0.772	1.081	2.097	2.279
Missouri	0.704	1.060	2.049	2.286
Montana	0.806	1.143	2.095	2.359
Nebraska	0.728	1.074	2.092	2.364

(continued on next page)

Table 13.06: Gasoline Prices by State, 1995, 2000, 2006, and 2007

	1995	2000	2006	2007
United States	*$0.761*	*$1.091*	*$2.121*	*$2.337*
Nevada	0.877	1.249	2.232	2.425
New Hampshire	0.817	1.155	2.170	2.351
New Jersey	0.834	1.161	2.188	2.317
New Mexico	0.800	1.122	2.207	2.452
New York	0.788	1.117	2.143	2.334
North Carolina	0.724	1.036	2.050	2.263
North Dakota	0.815	1.108	2.135	2.456
Ohio	0.733	1.095	2.045	2.315
Oklahoma	0.676	1.024	2.043	2.346
Oregon	0.822	1.192	2.224	2.478
Pennsylvania	0.774	1.055	2.083	2.281
Rhode Island	0.784	1.114	2.145	2.294
South Carolina	0.721	1.038	2.066	2.266
South Dakota	0.779	1.152	2.143	2.406
Tennessee	0.738	1.024	2.057	2.269
Texas	0.750	1.023	2.078	2.281
Utah	0.772	1.098	2.095	2.328
Vermont	0.837	1.143	2.196	2.420
Virginia	0.769	1.076	2.107	2.290
Washington	0.838	1.183	2.201	2.421
West Virginia	0.795	1.074	2.116	2.340
Wisconsin	0.757	1.096	2.119	2.360
Wyoming	0.838	1.147	2.180	2.430

Source: Energy Information Administration, 'Gasoline Prices by Formulation, Grade, Sales Type,' available at http://tonto.eia.doe.gov/dnav/pet/pet_pri_allmg_a_EPM0_PTA_cpgal_a.htm.

Notes: Figures are annual averages for retail sales to end-users for all grades of gasoline. Accessed September 15, 2008.

Units: Price in dollars per gallon.

Table 13.07: Fossil Fuel Production Prices, 1950–2007

	Coal	Natural Gas	Crude Oil	Fossil Fuel Composite
1950	$1.25	$0.38	$2.62	$1.54
1955	0.99	0.48	2.55	1.45
1960	0.92	0.60	2.36	1.35
1965	0.82	0.65	2.19	1.23
1970	0.97	0.56	1.99	1.15
1975	2.22	1.06	3.48	2.16
1980	2.04	2.68	6.89	3.78
1985	1.65	3.24	5.96	3.60
1990	1.22	1.90	4.23	2.26
1995	0.96	1.52	2.74	1.60
2000	0.80	3.32	4.61	2.60
2001	0.82	3.54	3.68	2.47
2002	0.84	2.56	3.73	2.12
2003	0.82	4.15	4.47	2.91
2004	0.89	4.51	5.79	3.30
2005	1.03	5.87	7.67	4.19
2006	1.06	4.98	8.83	4.06
2007	1.04	4.84	9.58	4.17

Source: Energy Information Administration, *Annual Energy Review 2007*, table 3.1.

Notes: Composite price is a weighted average obtained by multiplying the price per Btu of each type of fossil fuel by the total production, and dividing by the production total.
Coal prices are free-on-board rail/barge prices.
Natural gas prices are wellhead prices.
Crude oil prices are domestic first-purchase prices.
Data for 2007 is preliminary.

Units: Price in constant 2000 dollars per million Btu.

Table 13.08: Crude Oil Prices by Place of Origin, 1980–2007

	1980	1990	1995	2000	2006	2007
Domestic						
Total Domestic	*$21.59*	*$20.03*	*$14.62*	*$26.72*	*$59.69*	*$66.52*
Alaska North Slope	16.87	15.23	11.12	23.62	56.86	63.69
California	23.87	17.81	14.00	24.82	57.34	65.07
Texas	21.84	22.37	16.38	28.60	61.31	68.31
Imports						
Total Imports	*$33.67*	*$21.13*	*$16.78*	*$27.53*	*$59.11*	*$67.35*
Persian Gulf	30.59	20.55	16.78	26.77	58.92	69.14
OPEC	33.56	21.23	16.61	27.29	61.21	70.38
Kuwait	*	17.01	16.47	26.28	57.64	65.32
Nigeria	37.15	23.33	18.25	30.04	68.26	76.72
Saudi Arabia	29.80	21.82	16.84	26.58	59.19	70.24
Venezuela	25.92	20.31	14.81	26.05	57.37	65.92
Non-OPEC	33.99	20.98	16.95	27.80	57.14	63.65
Canada	30.11	20.48	16.65	26.69	53.90	60.32
Colombia	*	22.34	17.45	29.68	62.13	70.49
Mexico	31.77	19.64	16.19	26.03	53.76	62.21
Norway	36.82	21.11	18.06	30.13	64.39	73.42
United Kingdom	35.68	22.65	17.91	29.26	67.44	70.95

Source: Energy Information Administration, *Annual Energy Review 2007*, tables 5.18 and 5.19.

Notes: Domestic figures are first purchase prices, given as the first marketed sales price.
Import figures are the landed cost, which is the price of crude oil at the port of discharge, including charges associated with purchasing, transporting, and insuring a cargo from the purchase point to the port of discharge, and exdlusing charges incurred at the discharge port.
Data for 2007 is preliminary.
* Withheld to avoid disclosure of individual company data.

Units: Prices in current dollars per barrel.

Table 13.09: Crude Oil Prices by Type of Oil, 1980–2008

	1980	1985	1990	1995	2000	2005	2008
Saudi Arabian Light-34 API	$26.00	$29.00	$18.40	$16.63	$24.78	$31.86	$93.02
Iranian Light-40 API	30.37	28.00	18.20	16.18	24.63	33.84	94.96
Liberian ES Sider-37 API	34.50	30.15	20.40	16.05	25.85	38.00	96.79
Nigerian Bonny Light-37 API	29.97	28.00	21.20	16.15	25.55	38.21	98.52
Indonesian Minas-34 API	27.50	29.53	18.55	16.95	24.15	35.86	98.34
Venezuelan Tia Juana Light	25.20	27.88	24.69	16.57	24.85	35.98	93.85
Mexico Maya-22 API	28.00	25.50	17.05	13.77	20.20	26.16	82.78
United Kingdom Brent Blend-38 API	26.02	28.65	21.00	16.15	25.10	39.43	98.42

Source: Energy Information Administration, *Annual Energy Review 2007*, table 11.7.

Notes: Oil types are measured in terms of degrees API, which is an arbitrary scale of density for crude oil prepared by the American Petroleum Institute.

Prices are as of the Friday closest to January 1, and represent official government-selling prices, netback values, or spot market quotations.

For 1980, Libyan ES Sider-37 API price includes $4.72 in retroactive charges and market premiums, and Iranian Light-34 includes $1.87 in market premiums and credit charges.

Prices for Nigerian Bonny Light-37 API include 2 cents per barrel in harbor dues.

Units: Price in current (US) dollars per barrel.

Table 13.10: Retail Prices for Electricity
by End-Use Sector, 1970–2007

	Residential	Commercial	Industrial	Transportation*	Total
1970	8.0¢	7.6¢	3.6¢	NA	6.2¢
1975	9.2	9.2	5.5	NA	7.6
1980	10.0	10.2	6.9	NA	8.7
1985	10.60	10.43	7.13	NA	9.24
1990	9.60	9.00	5.81	NA	8.05
1995	9.12	8.35	5.06	NA	7.48
2000	8.24	7.43	4.64	NA	6.81
2001	8.38	7.73	4.93	NA	7.12
2002	8.10	7.57	4.68	NA	6.91
2003	8.20	7.55	4.80	7.09	6.99
2004	8.18	7.46	4.80	6.56	6.95
2005	8.36	7.67	5.07	7.58	7.20
2006	8.92	8.12	5.28	8.18	7.64
2007	8.89	8.08	5.31	8.69	7.64

Source: Energy Information Administration, *Annual Energy Review 2007*, table 8.10.

Notes: Prices include state and local taxes, energy and demand charges, environmental surcharges, and other fees charged to end-use consumers.
Category definitions were redefined in 2003, so readers should use caution when directly comparing figures from before and after 2003.
Data for 2007 is preliminary.
* Prior to 2003, transportation data was listed under 'other,' which included transportation (including railroads and railways), as well as public street and highway lighting, interdepartmental sales, other sales to public authorities, and agriculture and irrigation.

Units: Price in constant 2000 cents per kilowatt-hour.

Table 13.11: Production and Refining by Domestic and Foreign-Affiliated Energy Companies, 1980–2006

	1980	1985	1990	1995	2000	2005	2006
Major Domestic Companies							
Production							
Crude oil and natural gas liquids	5,700	5,800	5,000	4,300	3,500	3,100	2,900
% of US total	56.1%	54.9%	55.8%	51.7%	44.8%	44.5%	43.1%
Dry natural gas	9,300	7,300	7,600	8,100	8,300	7,800	7,900
% of US total	47.7%	44.6%	42.6%	43.3%	43.5%	43.1%	42.9%
Coal	142	230	282	165	35	18	NA
% of US total	17.2%	26.1%	27.4%	16.0%	3.2%	1.6%	NA
Uranium	19,000	2,100	NA	0	0	0	0
% of US total	43.5%	18.9%	NA	0%	0%	0%	0%
Refining							
Capacity	15,100	12,600	11,400	10,400	14,400	14,500	14,700
% of US total	81.0%	81.6%	72.5%	68.0%	86.9%	83.8%	84.0%
Output	12,200	10,800	11,300	10,700	14,500	15,100	14,800
% of US total	83.3%	78.9%	74.0%	66.6%	84.1%	84.9%	82.4%

(continued on next page)

Table 13.11: Production and Refining by Domestic and Foreign-Affiliated Energy Companies, 1980–2006

	1980	1985	1990	1995	2000	2005	2006
Foreign-Affiliated Companies							
Production							
Crude oil and natural gas liquids	1,280	1,455	1,481	1,103	1,027	962	NA
% of US total	12.6%	13.7%	16.5%	12.8%	12.7%	13.9%	NA
Dry natural gas	776	1,093	1,457	1,191	2,112	2,019	NA
% of US total	4.0%	6.7%	8.2%	6.4%	11.0%	11.1%	NA
Coal	31	147	254	316	284	155	NA
% of US total	3.8%	16.8%	24.7%	30.7%	26.4%	13.7%	NA
Uranium	NA	NA	NA	NA	3,443	2,147	NA
% of US total	NA	NA	NA	NA	87.0%	79.8%	NA
Refining and Gasoline Sales							
Refining capacity	2,066	2,656	4,379	4,164	4,831	4,848	NA
% of US total	11.1%	17.2%	27.9%	27.1%	29.1%	28.0%	NA
Gasoline sales	926	1,285	2,282	2,204	2,971	2,845	NA
% of US total	14.1%	18.8%	31.5%	29.0%	35.3%	31.6%	NA

Source: Energy Information Administration, *Annual Energy Review 2007*, tables 3.10 and 3.13.

Notes: 'Production' refers to net ownership figures.
Refinery capacity is as of January 1 of the following year.
Uranium figures refer to production of uranium oxide.

Units: Oil production, gasoline sales, and refinery capacity and output in thousand barrels per day; dry natural gas is billion cubic feet; coal in thousands tons; uranium in thousand pounds.

Table 13.12: Profitability and Net Income for Major US Energy Companies, 1980–2006

	1980	1990	2000	2002	2005	2006
Profitability						
Overall	15.3%	6.8%	11.4%	4.1%	19.0%	17.7%
Petroleum	19.2	9.5	13.9	6.5	23.7	20.9
United States	17.5	7.9	13.2	6.0	22.4	19.4
Crude oil and natural gas	20.9	8.5	17.7	10.5	22.5	17.5
Refining and marketing	9.8	5.1	9.6	-1.7	23.5	25.6
Rate-regulated pipelines	15.1	11.2	6.0	5.2	5.8	2.7
Foreign	23.0	12.5	15.1	7.2	25.5	22.8
Crude oil and natural gas	25.1	13.1	17.1	9.2	26.3	23.6
Refining and marketing	26.4	11.2	8.7	-1.1	20.8	18.6
International marine	2.4	11.7	6.4	-6.2	*	*
Net Income						
Overall	$31.0	$21.6	$53.2	$20.6	$119.2	$131.5
Petroleum	29.1	23.4	53.3	27.9	118.5	124.6
United States	17.9	12.9	31.8	15.4	61.9	65.8
Crude oil and natural gas	13.8	8.7	21.9	15.0	40.5	41.3
Refining and marketing	2.5	2.2	7.7	-1.4	21.0	24.3
Rate-regulated pipelines	1.7	2.1	2.3	1.7	0.5	0.2
Foreign	11.2	10.5	21.4	12.5	56.5	58.7
Crude oil and natural gas	6.9	7.4	18.5	12.9	48.7	51.2
Refining and marketing	4.3	2.8	2.9	-0.4	7.8	7.5
International marine	0.1	0.2	0.0	0.0	-8.0	-8.0

Source: Energy Information Administration, *Annual Energy Review 2007*, tables 3.11 and 3.12.

Notes: 'Major domestic companies' include the top publicly-owned, US-based crude oil and natural gas producers and petroleum refiners.
'Profitability' is a measure of return on investment, defined as the net income divided by net investment.
'Net income' is income minus expenses.
* Withheld to avoid disclosing individual company data.

Units: Profitability in percent; net income in billions of current dollars.

Table 13.13: Gross Domestic Product from For-Hire Transportation Services, 1990–2006

	1990	1995	2000	2005	2006
Total US GDP	*$7,113.0*	*$8,032.0*	*$9,817.0*	*$11,003.5*	*$11,319.4*
For-hire transportation GDP	*$187.9*	*$242.7*	*$301.6*	*$348.0*	*$366.2*
Percent of total GDP	*2.6%*	*3.0%*	*3.1%*	*3.2%*	*3.2%*
Percent of Transportation GDP by Mode					
Air	14.2%	15.7%	19.1%	23.0%	22.5%
Rail	10.5	10.4	8.5	7.4	9.0
Water	2.3	2.5	2.4	1.8	1.8
Truck	31.8	33.3	30.8	29.1	28.3
Transit and ground passenger	6.3	4.9	4.8	4.3	4.1
Pipeline	4.0	3.0	2.9	3.2	3.1
Other	24.9	23.0	23.3	23.1	22.9
Warehousing & storage	6.7	7.4	8.3	9.1	9.1

Source: Bureau of Transportation Statistics, *National Transportation Statistics 2008*, table 3-1b.

Notes: 'Gross Domestic Product' (GDP) is the market value of final goods and services produced within a country in a given period of time.
Groups may not add to total.

Units: GDP in billions of 2000 constant dollars; percent of total US GDP and transportation GDP.

Table 13.14: Transportation and Warehousing Establishments and Employment by State, 2006

	Establishments	Employees	Annual Payroll
United States	*215,117*	*4,306,405*	*$166,173,942*
Alabama	3,178	59,189	2,081,652
Alaska	1,119	18,999	1,023,936
Arizona	3,279	78,135	3,130,999
Arkansas	2,611	62,967	2,131,004
California	20,776	453,208	19,288,573
Colorado	3,389	61,166	2,520,981
Connecticut	1,688	39,581	1,547,668
Delaware	747	14,899	468,923
District of Columbia	180	3,692	133,357
Florida	13,213	222,194	8,525,328
Georgia	6,236	164,058	6,801,876
Hawaii	877	29,976	1,031,257
Idaho	1,726	16,045	488,375
Illinois	11,188	224,871	9,486,301
Indiana	5,188	113,377	3,948,600
Iowa	3,740	52,647	1,868,589
Kansas	2,626	44,373	1,528,551
Kentucky	3,185	80,529	3,377,087
Louisiana	3,755	63,047	2,752,908
Maine	1,269	14,487	498,045
Maryland	3,747	68,080	2,511,726
Massachusetts	3,729	77,550	2,970,141
Michigan	5,611	105,341	4,179,675
Minnesota	4,726	77,943	2,884,179
Mississippi	2,352	33,031	1,136,284
Missouri	5,041	88,083	3,237,061
Montana	1,249	10,339	327,580
Nebraska	2,303	29,329	1,100,251
Nevada	1,529	44,682	1,349,452

(continued on next page)

Table 13.14: Transportation and Warehousing Establishments and Employment by State, 2006

	Establishments	Employees	Annual Payroll
United States	*215,117*	*4,306,405*	*$166,173,942*
New Hampshire	835	12,497	418,644
New Jersey	7,266	170,735	6,920,582
New Mexico	1,325	15,872	559,789
New York	11,920	234,630	8,874,923
North Carolina	5,904	118,153	4,190,448
North Dakota	1,068	9,987	327,932
Ohio	7,562	174,327	6,665,712
Oklahoma	2,630	39,338	1,445,853
Oregon	3,134	54,819	2,026,664
Pennsylvania	7,958	208,113	6,899,238
Rhode Island	697	9,800	332,113
South Carolina	2,715	55,271	1,962,816
South Dakota	1,072	8,497	271,790
Tennessee	4,398	120,491	4,558,242
Texas	15,673	352,519	14,370,032
Utah	1,993	45,791	1,694,327
Vermont	539	6,157	191,498
Virginia	5,374	105,392	4,006,536
Washington	4,902	83,739	3,579,973
West Virginia	1,432	16,338	583,623
Wisconsin	5,577	103,047	3,577,654
Wyoming	886	9,074	385,194

Source: US Bureau of the Census, *County Business Patterns 2006*, accessed online at http://www.census.gov/epcd/cbp/index.html.

Notes: Data shown is for NAICS sectors 48 and 49, and does not include government establishments, railroad transportation, or self-employed people.
Accessed September 18, 2008.

Units: Number of establishments and employees; annual payroll in dollars.

Table 13.15: Transportation-Related Employment, May 2007

	Number of Employees	Mean Hourly Wage	Mean Annual Wage
Transportation and Warehousing			
Total Transportation and Warehousing	*5,306,240*	*$20.01*	*$41,620*
Air	485,870	30.24	62,890
Scheduled	440,160	30.58	63,610
Nonscheduled	45,710	26.90	55,960
Rail	212,660	27.66	57,530
Water	**61,720**	**24.75**	**51,480**
Deep sea, coastal, and Great Lakes	37,730	25.56	53,170
Inland	23,990	23.48	48,840
Truck	1,444,800	18.57	38,630
Transit & Ground Transport	**420,020**	**13.84**	**28,790**
Urban transit	39,860	16.22	33,730
Inter-urban and rural bus	18,750	15.66	32,570
Taxi and limousine	71,730	13.49	28,050
Pipeline	**38,180**	**28.21**	**58,680**
Crude oil	7,670	30.08	62,570
Natural gas	25,100	28.02	58,280
Scenic and sightseeing	27,790	15.14	31,500
Support activities	576,500	19.58	40,730
Postal service	785,900	21.84	45,420
Couriers & messengers	580,110	18.33	38,130
Related Industries			
Petroleum and Coal manufacturing	114,690	$27.03	$56,210
Transportation equipment manufacturing	1,734,870	23.56	49,000
Highway, street & bridge construction	358,500	21.08	43,850
Gasoline stations	861,790	9.76	20,310

Source: Bureau of Labor Statistics, *Occupational Employment Statistics, May 2007*, accessed online at www.bls.gov/oes/current/oessrci.htm.

Notes: Categories are according to the North American Industry Classification System (NAICS). Estimates dated May 2007.

Units: Number of people employed; mean hourly and annual wages.

Table 13.16: Personal Expenditures on Transportation, 1990–2006

	1990	1995	2000	2005	2006
Transportation Total	*$471,700*	*$594,600*	*$853,400*	*$1,049,900*	*$1,093,400*
User-operated	434,700	550,500	793,800	988,300	1,028,200
New and used car purchases	119,000	132,600	164,300	161,600	165,100
New and used truck and RV purchases	63,900	96,200	173,200	225,400	209,300
Tires, tubes, accessories, and parts	29,900	37,800	49,000	57,900	59,800
Repair and rental	84,900	125,500	183,500	198,400	208,400
Gasoline and oil	111,200	120,200	175,700	280,700	318,600
Tolls	2,300	3,700	5,100	6,500	6,900
Insurance premiums	23,500	34,500	43,000	57,800	60,100
Purchased intercity	**28,600**	**33,900**	**47,400**	**46,900**	**49,500**
Railroad	600	400	500	600	600
Intercity bus	1,300	1,800	2,400	2,200	2,200
Airplane	22,700	25,300	36,700	34,400	35,600
Other	4,000	6,400	7,800	9,800	11,000
Purchased local	**8,400**	**10,100**	**12,200**	**14,600**	**15,700**
Mass transit	5,800	7,100	9,100	10,700	11,500
Taxi	2,600	3,000	3,100	3,900	4,200
Total Expenditures	*3,839,900*	*4,975,800*	*6,739,400*	*8,707,820*	*9,224,507*
% from Transportation	*12.3%*	*11.9%*	*12.7%*	*12.1%*	*11.9%*

Source: Bureau of Transportation Statistics, *National Transportation Statistics 2008*, tables 3-12 and 3-13.

Notes: 'Repair and rental' also includes greasing, washing, parking, storage, and leasing.

Units: Personal expenditures in millions of current dollars; transportation spending as percent of total.

Table 13.17: Consumer Spending on Transportation, 2006

	Vehicle Purchases	Gasoline and Motor Oil	Other Vehicle Expenses	Public Transportation	Total
All Consumers	*$3,421*	*$2,227*	*$2,355*	*$505*	*$8,508*
% of total spending	7.1%	4.6%	4.9%	1.0%	17.6%
By Race or Hispanic Origin					
White	$3,555	$2,298	$2,435	$508	$8,796
Asian	3,823	2,191	2,519	1,189	9,722
Black	2,362	1,740	1,742	286	6,130
Hispanic	3,400	2,319	2,152	414	8,286
By Region of Residence					
Northeast	$2,894	$1,910	$2,386	$629	$7,819
Midwest	2,730	2,142	2,225	405	7,502
South	3,643	2,356	2,182	316	8,497
West	4,230	2,382	2,741	804	10,156
By Housing Tenure					
Homeowner	$4,030	$2,560	$2,778	$594	$9,961
Renter	2,164	1,542	1,483	321	5,511
By Age of Householder					
Under 25	$2,396	$1,637	$1,413	$221	$5,667
25–34	3,912	2,346	2,342	448	9,047
35–44	4,057	2,636	2,725	559	9,977
45–54	3,983	2,693	2,819	616	10,111
55–64	3,165	2,288	2,638	584	8,676
Over 65	2,301	1,359	1,584	414	5,658

Source: US Bureau of Labor Statistics, *Consumer Expenditure Survey 2006*, tables 2100, 2200, 3, 7, and 8.

Notes: Here, 'White' includes Native Hawaiian, Pacific Islander, American Indian, and Alaska Native, and those reporting more than one race.

Units: Average annual spending in dollars.

Table 13.18: Average Passenger Fares and Passenger Revenue by Mode of Transport, 1980–2006

	Air Carrier	Bus	Commuter Rail	Amtrak/ Intercity Rail	All Transit
Average Passenger Fare					
1980	$84.60	$10.57	$1.41	$17.72	$0.30
1985	92.53	11.98	2.85	26.15	0.53
1990	107.86	20.22	2.90	39.59	0.67
1995	106.66	20.10	3.13	39.92	0.88
2000	121.27	29.46	3.32	49.61	0.93
2001	111.60	30.27	3.44	51.58	0.92
2002	101.94	30.11	3.49	55.15	0.89
2003	103.75	NA	3.79	50.68	0.97
2004	103.59	NA	3.90	50.71	1.02
2005	106.27	NA	4.08	51.17	1.02
2006	113.25	NA	NA	56.45	NA
Average Revenue per Passenger-Mile					
1980	11.5¢	7.3¢	6.7¢	8.2¢	NA
1985	12.2	9.9	12.1	11.3	NA
1990	13.4	11.6	13.4	14.1	NA
1995	13.5	12.2	13.1	14.6	NA
2000	14.6	12.8	14.6	23.2	NA
2001	13.2	12.9	15.1	24.9	NA
2002	12.0	NA	15.2	26.8	NA
2003	12.3	NA	16.2	25.0	NA
2004	12.0	NA	16.6	26.0	NA
2005	12.3	NA	18.2	27.2	NA
2006	13.0	NA	NA	29.7	NA

Source: Bureau of Transportation Statistics, *National Transportation Statistics 2008*, tables 3-15a and 3-16.

Notes: 'Air carrier' includes domestic scheduled service only.
'Bus' includes Class I regular-route, intercity travel only.

Units: Average passenger fare in current dollars; average revenue in current cents per passenger-mile.

Table 13.19: Motor Fuel Taxes by State, 2006

	Net Volume	Gasoline	Diesel	Petroleum	Gasohol
United States	*177,430,707*	*18.4¢*	*24.4¢*	*13.6¢*	*13.2¢*
Alabama	3,387,449	18.0	19.0	17.0	18.0
Alaska	467,604	8.0	8.0	NA	8.0
Arizona	3,697,179	18.0	26.0	18.0	18.0
Arkansas	2,064,031	21.7	22.7	16.5	21.7
California	18,866,221	18.0	18.0	6.0	18.0
Colorado	2,649,272	22.0	20.5	20.5	22.0
Connecticut	1,836,679	25.0	26.0	NA	25.0
Delaware	514,691	23.0	22.0	22.0	23.0
District of Columbia	126,845	20.0	20.0	20.0	20.0
Florida	10,478,833	15.3	15.3	14.5	15.3
Georgia	6,549,461	7.5	7.5	7.5	7.5
Hawaii	531,530	16.0	16.0	8.1	16.0
Idaho	894,439	25.0	25.0	18.1	22.5
Illinois	6,635,856	19.0	21.5	19.0	19.0
Indiana	4,532,917	18.0	16.0	NA	18.0
Iowa	2,182,613	21.0	22.5	20.0	19.0
Kansas	1,715,094	24.0	26.0	23.0	24.0
Kentucky	3,112,165	19.7	16.7	19.7	19.7
Louisiana	3,310,495	20.0	20.0	16.0	20.0
Maine	878,982	26.8	27.9	NA	17.8
Maryland	3,258,197	23.5	24.3	24.3	23.5
Massachusetts	3,202,191	21.0	21.0	23.9	21.0
Michigan	5,731,225	19.0	15.0	15.0	NA
Minnesota	3,241,758	20.0	20.0	15.0	20.0
Mississippi	2,287,113	18.4	18.4	17.0	18.4
Missouri	4,243,843	17.0	17.0	17.0	17.0
Montana	748,853	27.8	27.8	NA	27.8
Nebraska	1,246,375	27.1	27.1	26.1	27.1
Nevada	1,562,107	24.8	27.7	22.0	24.8

(continued on next page)

Table 13.19: Motor Fuel Taxes by State, 2006

	Net Volume	Gasoline	Diesel	Petroleum	Gasohol
United States	*177,430,707*	*18.4¢*	*24.4¢*	*13.6¢*	*13.2¢*
New Hampshire	810,376	19.5	19.5	NA	NA
New Jersey	5,246,350	10.5	13.5	5.3	10.5
New Mexico	1,432,481	18.9	22.9	12.0	18.9
New York	6,788,196	24.7	22.9	8.1	NA
North Carolina	5,353,288	30.2	30.2	27.1	30.2
North Dakota	506,202	23.0	23.0	23.0	23.0
Ohio	6,623,058	28.0	28.0	28.0	28.0
Oklahoma	2,592,717	17.0	14.0	17.0	17.0
Oregon	2,122,504	24.0	24.0	18.5	24.0
Pennsylvania	6,536,511	30.0	38.1	22.8	31.2
Rhode Island	458,258	30.0	30.0	30.0	30.0
South Carolina	3,240,258	16.0	16.0	NA	16.0
South Dakota	602,786	22.0	22.0	20.0	20.0
Tennessee	4,078,225	21.4	18.4	14.0	20.0
Texas	15,739,598	20.0	20.0	15.0	20.0
Utah	1,535,732	24.5	24.5	24.5	24.5
Vermont	414,308	20.0	26.0	NA	20.0
Virginia	4,992,269	17.5	16.0	16.0	17.5
Washington	3,374,416	34.0	34.0	34.0	34.0
West Virginia	1,129,862	31.5	31.5	27.0	31.5
Wisconsin	3,216,569	30.9	30.9	22.6	30.9
Wyoming	682,725	14.0	14.0	14.0	14.0

Source: US Department of Transportation, Federal Highway Administration, *Highway Statistics 2006*, tables MF-2 and MF-121T.

Notes: Subgroups do not add to total due to some groups being omitted.

Units: Net volume taxed in thousands of gallons; tax rates in cents per gallon.

Table 13.20: Airline Industry Summary, 1995–2006

	1995	2000	2005	2006
Scheduled Service				
Passengers enplaned	547.8	666.2	738.4	744.6
Passenger-miles	540.7	692.8	778.9	797.4
Available seat-miles	807.1	957.0	1,003.2	1,006.4
Mean trip length	987	1,040	1,055	1,071
Cargo ton-miles	16,921	23,888	28,007	29,283
Aircraft departures	8,062	9,035	11,475	11,268
Finance				
Operating revenue	$95,117	$130,839	$147,504	$163,824
Passenger revenue	69,835	93,622	91,861	101,208
Charter revenue	3,742	4,913	5,637	5,562
Operating expenses	89,266	123,840	147,413	156,279
Revenue per passenger-mile	12.9	13.5	11.8	13.0
Operating profit margin	6.2%	5.3%	0.1%	4.6%
Employees				
Total employees	547.0	680.0	552.9	544.5
Average annual compensation	$59.1	$66.0	$73.1	$69.2

Source: US Bureau of the Census, *Statistical Abstract of the United States 2008*, table 1038.

Notes: Includes air carriers covered under Section 401 of the Federal Aviation Act.

Units: Passengers and cargo ton-miles in millions; passenger-miles and seat-miles in bilions; revenues and expenses in billions of dollars; mean trip length in miles; number of employees and aircraft departures in thousands; employee compensation in thousands of dollars; profit margin as percent of total revenue.

Table 13.21: Air Carrier Financial Trends, 2004–2007

	2004	2005	2006	2007
Revenues				
All Carriers	*$130.72*	*$145.48*	*$163.04*	*$169.83*
Major	116.66	129.68	148.69	155.66
National	13.13	14.72	13.50	13.01
Regional	0.94	1.08	0.85	1.16
Expenses				
All Carriers	*$130.05*	*$146.66*	*$157.48*	*$160.11*
Major	116.64	131.43	143.64	146.32
National	12.50	14.13	13.01	12.55
Regional	0.90	1.09	0.83	1.24
Profit/Loss				
All Carriers	*$0.67*	*-$1.18*	*$5.56*	*$9.72*
Major	0.02	-1.75	5.05	9.34
National	0.63	0.59	0.49	0.46
Regional	0.03	-0.02	0.02	-0.08

Source: Federal Aviation Administration, *Administrator's Fact Book, April 2007*, page 21; *July 2008*, page 21.

Notes: Major carriers are those with annual operating revenues over $1 billion.
National carriers have annual revenues between $100 million and $1 billion.
Regional carriers have annual revenues under $100 million.
Negative numbers represent losses.
Data is for the fiscal years 2004 through 2007.

Units: Revenues, Expenses, and profit/loss in billions of dollars.

Table 13.22: Projected Energy Prices and Expenditures by End-Use Sector and Source, 2006 to 2030

	2006	2010	2015	2020	2025	2030
Residential						
Liquefied petroleum gas	$23.08	$25.21	$24.15	$24.23	$24.63	$25.43
Distillate fuel oil	17.94	17.21	14.27	14.27	15.14	16.27
Natural gas	13.40	12.15	11.20	11.39	11.94	12.91
Electricity	30.52	31.37	30.04	30.20	30.33	30.63
Commercial						
Distillate fuel oil	$14.59	$15.24	$12.88	$13.24	$13.88	$15.00
Residual fuel oil	8.60	10.06	7.95	7.95	8.62	9.22
Natural gas	11.50	10.59	9.68	9.91	10.47	11.43
Electricity	27.75	27.89	25.52	25.64	25.71	26.17
Industrial						
Liquefied petroleum gas	$19.71	$17.74	$16.65	$16.79	$17.10	$17.79
Distillate fuel oil	15.33	15.72	13.95	14.62	15.10	16.26
Residual fuel oil	9.06	10.86	8.24	8.29	9.00	9.62
Natural gas	7.66	7.21	6.15	6.21	6.56	7.29
Electricity	17.97	19.21	17.22	17.27	17.30	17.63
Transportation						
Liquefied petroleum gas	$21.72	$26.03	$24.93	$24.94	$25.28	$26.03
Ethanol-85	24.81	23.58	17.61	18.15	18.50	19.62
Motor gasoline	21.19	21.23	18.80	19.64	19.67	20.37
Jet fuel	14.83	15.77	13.16	13.27	14.15	15.37
Distillate fuel oil	19.72	19.68	17.65	18.26	18.54	19.59
Residual fuel oil	7.89	10.53	8.56	8.69	9.50	10.39
Natural gas	14.28	13.60	12.34	12.15	12.28	12.83
Electricity	29.73	30.95	28.95	29.05	28.95	29.65

(continued on next page)

Table 13.22: Projected Energy Prices and Expenditures by End-Use Sector and Source, 2006 to 2030

	2006	2010	2015	2020	2025	2030
Electric Power						
Distillate fuel oil	$13.35	$13.62	$10.67	$10.69	$11.59	$12.71
Residual fuel oil	8.17	9.45	7.41	7.50	8.25	9.04
Natural gas	6.87	6.96	5.93	5.95	6.26	6.93
Steam coal	1.69	1.84	1.74	1.72	1.74	1.78
Average, All Users						
Liquefied petroleum gas	$20.35	$19.27	$18.32	$18.59	$19.03	$19.82
Ethanol-85	24.81	23.58	17.61	18.15	18.50	19.62
Motor gasoline	21.06	21.23	18.80	19.64	19.67	20.37
Jet fuel	14.83	15.77	13.16	13.27	14.15	15.37
Distillate fuel oil	18.56	18.48	16.57	17.20	17.62	18.74
Residual fuel oil	8.21	10.31	8.19	8.29	9.06	9.87
Natural gas	9.22	8.72	7.78	7.98	8.49	9.36
Electricity	26.10	26.90	25.00	25.23	25.43	25.93
Non-Renewable Energy Expenditures						
Total Non-renewable	*$1,139.66*	*$1,201.48*	*$1,118.69*	*$1,156.54*	*$1,197.22*	*$1,293.86*
Residential	225.38	241.71	232.60	243.22	256.33	274.70
Commercial	166.54	174.38	173.76	189.37	206.24	227.37
Industrial	205.11	224.65	197.41	193.16	194.97	203.93
Transportation	542.63	560.74	514.93	530.80	539.68	587.86

Source: Energy Information Administration, *Annual Energy Outlook 2008 with Projections to 2030*, table A3.

Notes: 'Ethanol-85' is a blend of 85% ethanol and 15% gasoline.
Gasoline prices are weighted averages (by sales) of all grades.
Overall prices are the averages of each sector's consumption, weighted by total amount.
Data for 2006 is from the projection model, and may differ slightly from the official 2006 estimates.

Units: Prices in 2006 dollars per million Btu.

Chapter 14

Government Funding

Chapter 14 Summary

Chapter 14 contains information on the government agencies that regulate energy, transportation, and the environment. For the federal government, these are the Department of Energy (DoE), Department of Transportation (DoT), and Environmental Protection Agency (EPA), respectively. Funding for all three departments increased from 1990 to 2006 (especially for transportation), keeping pace with an overall increase in federal spending (tables 14.01 and 14.02). However, employment at the Departments of Energy and Transportation declined by more than 15% during that period, while the EPA gained employees (table 14.03). Tables 14.04–14.06 show a state-by-state breakdown of federal government spending in the form of grants, procurement, and salaries & wages.

Tables 14.07–14.09 show the Fiscal Year 2009 budgets for the DoE, DoT, and EPA. The largest energy-related expenditures were for nuclear security and environmental management; the largest targets for transportation spending were the Federal Highway Administration, Federal Aviation Administration, and Federal Transit Administration; while the largest share of the EPA's budget went to the Operating program, followed by Superfund activity and water-quality programs. Table 14.10 shows state and local government spending on energy, transportation, or environment-related items.

Government spending on public transportation has increased since 1980, especially from state and local governments (table 14.11). Federal appropriations for public transportation also increased across a variety of programs from 2001–2007 (table 14.12).

Finally, table 14.13 shows federal government funding for the EPA's Superfund, Brownfields, ATSDR, and NIEHS programs from 1995–2005. Table 14.14 details the results of the EPA's compliance, monitoring, and enforcement efforts from 2002–2007. Readers seeking a further explanation of the EPA's efforts should contact the department's Office of Enforcement and Compliance Assurance.

Table 14.01: Federal Outlays by Agency, 1990–2007

	Department of Energy	Department of Transportation	Environmental Protection Agency	Total Outlays
1990	$12.1	$25.6	$5.1	$1,253.1
1995	17.6	35.1	6.4	1,515.9
2000	15.0	41.6	7.2	1,789.2
2003	19.4	50.8	8.0	2,160.1
2004	19.9	54.9	8.3	2,293.0
2005	21.3	56.6	7.9	2,472.2
2006	19.6	60.1	8.3	2,655.4
2007	22.0	63.8	8.0	2,784.3

Source: US Bureau of the Census, *Statistical Abstract of the United States 2007*, table 461; *2008*, table 458.

Notes: Figures for 2007 are estimates.
Groups may not add to total.

Units: Expenditures in billions of dollars.

Table 14.02: Federal Outlays by Function, 1990–2007

	1990	1995	2000	2003	2006	2007
Total Outlays	*$1,253.1*	*$1,515.9*	*$1,789.2*	*$2,160.1*	*$2,655.4*	*$2,784.3*
Energy	3.3	4.9	-0.8	-0.7	0.8	1.8
Energy supply	2.0	3.6	-1.8	-2.1	0.2	0.0
Natural resources and environment	17.1	21.9	25.0	29.7	33.1	35.2
Water	4.4	4.6	5.1	5.5	8.0	9.3
Conservation and land management	4.0	6.0	6.8	9.7	7.8	9.4
Recreational resources	1.4	2.0	2.6	2.9	3.1	3.0
Pollution control and abatement	5.2	6.5	7.4	8.2	8.6	8.3
Transportation	29.5	39.4	46.9	67.1	70.2	74.6
Ground	19.0	25.3	31.7	37.5	45.2	48.3
Air	7.2	10.0	10.6	23.3	18.0	18.3
Water	3.2	3.7	4.4	5.9	6.7	7.6

Source: US Bureau of the Census, *Statistical Abstract of the United States 2008*, table 459.

Notes: Not all categories are shown; groups may not add to total.
Figures for 2007 are estimates.

Units: Expenditures in billions of dollars.

Table 14.03: Federal Civilian Employment by Agency, 1990–2006

	Department of Transportation	Department of Energy	Environmental Protection Agency	Total Employment
1990	67,364	17,731	17,123	3,128,267
1995	63,552	19,589	17,910	2,920,277
2000	63,598	15,692	18,036	2,708,101
2004	57,748	15,265	17,975	2,714,140
2005	55,975	15,050	17,964	2,708,753
2006	53,573	14,838	18,166	2,700,007
Percent change, 1990–2006	*-20.5%*	*-16.3%*	*6.1%*	*-13.7%*

Source: US Bureau of the Census, *Statistical Abstract of the United States 2008*, table 485.

Notes: Groups may not add to total.

Units: Number of employees; percent change between 1990 and 2006.

Table 14.04: Department of Energy Expenditures to States, 2006

	Grants	Procurement Contracts	Salaries and Wages
United States	*$2,288.4*	*$22,468.3*	*$1,461.7*
Alabama	57.3	1.7	0.0
Alaska	16.3	0.7	0.2
Arizona	18.6	15.6	19.0
Arkansas	6.7	0.9	3.4
California	248.6	2,497.3	40.6
Colorado	59.3	824.1	60.4
Connecticut	36.9	2.1	0.2
Delaware	21.6	0.1	0.0
District of Columbia	24.1	108.7	423.9
Florida	28.8	41.3	0.0
Georgia	40.8	11.4	7.3
Hawaii	7.9	1.1	0.3
Idaho	14.8	1,181.0	32.4
Illinois	79.9	774.7	31.3
Indiana	44.5	1.9	0.2
Iowa	16.3	29.4	0.9
Kansas	12.2	0.0	0.0
Kentucky	13.2	80.6	3.1
Louisiana	9.3	157.9	7.2
Maine	5.1	0.0	0.0
Maryland	30.9	266.6	132.4
Massachusetts	139.6	2.6	1.4
Michigan	112.6	1.0	0.0
Minnesota	53.5	7.9	0.1
Mississippi	26.6	0.3	0.0
Missouri	27.3	478.2	9.2
Montana	17.6	9.2	11.6
Nebraska	6.6	2.7	1.5

(continued on next page)

Table 14.04: Department of Energy Expenditures to States, 2006

	Grants	Procurement Contracts	Salaries and Wages
United States	*$2,288.4*	*$22,468.3*	*$1,461.7*
Nevada	90.8	1,078.1	29.1
New Hampshire	4.5	1.5	0.2
New Jersey	36.6	82.9	1.5
New Mexico	81.2	4,307.5	101.2
New York	172.8	718.1	13.7
North Carolina	40.1	228.2	0.1
North Dakota	26.1	7.1	4.8
Ohio	104.6	908.9	12.8
Oklahoma	15.2	12.0	9.1
Oregon	21.3	3.3	123.8
Pennsylvania	161.3	566.6	32.9
Rhode Island	5.5	1.2	0.0
South Carolina	25.0	1,774.7	37.9
South Dakota	4.2	5.9	14.2
Tennessee	33.5	2,807.2	62.9
Texas	84.7	510.1	18.2
Utah	19.5	1.5	1.7
Vermont	5.7	0.0	0.0
Virginia	60.4	565.7	1.7
Washington	44.6	2,170.8	178.5
West Virginia	16.5	112.1	25.8
Wisconsin	46.6	2.9	0.0
Wyoming	8.7	5.7	5.1

Source: US Department of Commerce, *Consolidated Federal Funds Report for Fiscal Year 2006*, tables 4 to 6.

Notes: Groups may not add to total.

Units: Expenditures in millions of dollars.

Table 14.05: Department of Transportation
Expenditures to States, 2006

	Grants	Procurement Contracts	Salaries and Wages
United States	*$58,218.3*	*$5,198.0*	*$5,606.3*
Alabama	1,089.8	4.2	25.3
Alaska	708.9	53.3	111.4
Arizona	800.4	27.2	52.7
Arkansas	640.8	0.8	19.9
California	5,403.3	293.3	481.0
Colorado	1,365.2	65.8	141.0
Connecticut	629.3	7.4	18.8
Delaware	257.3	0.2	3.2
District of Columbia	530.3	432.5	722.4
Florida	3,257.9	581.1	278.2
Georgia	1,978.3	57.1	252.1
Hawaii	391.5	61.4	34.0
Idaho	373.4	2.4	11.1
Illinois	2,053.9	54.5	240.9
Indiana	1,350.5	18.3	111.3
Iowa	468.9	7.5	17.8
Kansas	496.7	18.7	99.5
Kentucky	937.3	6.5	40.4
Louisiana	1,742.5	146.3	30.8
Maine	260.5	5.4	14.6
Maryland	804.3	810.4	52.2
Massachusetts	953.8	236.5	117.8
Michigan	1,443.1	13.4	71.3
Minnesota	743.0	22.7	114.6
Mississippi	2,301.8	2.5	14.8
Missouri	944.4	26.6	99.2
Montana	474.3	27.6	13.9
Nebraska	361.6	6.8	15.0

(continued on next page)

Table 14.05: Department of Transportation Expenditures to States, 2006

	Grants	Procurement Contracts	Salaries and Wages
United States	*$58,218.3*	*$5,198.0*	*$5,606.3*
Nevada	463.2	20.3	35.0
New Hampshire	229.7	6.5	92.3
New Jersey	1,464.8	651.3	162.5
New Mexico	398.8	13.7	68.4
New York	4,006.8	79.9	292.3
North Carolina	1,144.0	60.4	47.7
North Dakota	328.3	3.8	11.1
Ohio	1,586.2	32.5	148.5
Oklahoma	948.5	119.5	265.1
Oregon	731.5	42.0	26.1
Pennsylvania	2,546.2	42.5	88.6
Rhode Island	268.3	0.3	9.5
South Carolina	985.6	35.1	23.3
South Dakota	302.3	5.1	7.0
Tennessee	1,041.8	21.4	110.7
Texas	4,198.4	219.9	432.1
Utah	398.3	8.7	71.7
Vermont	199.6	0.9	5.0
Virginia	1,152.7	575.8	244.9
Washington	1,129.3	51.4	194.0
West Virginia	592.8	1.4	12.9
Wisconsin	820.3	13.1	25.1
Wyoming	256.2	15.8	5.8

Source: US Department of Commerce, *Consolidated Federal Funds Report for Fiscal Year 2006*, tables 4 through 6.

Notes: Groups may not add to total.

Units: Expenditures in millions of dollars.

Table 14.06: Environmental Protection Agency Expenditures to States, 2006

	Grants	Procurement Contracts	Salaries and Wages
United States	$3,837.6	$1,559.2	$1,592.3
Alabama	48.3	8.1	3.1
Alaska	105.0	2.1	2.5
Arizona	77.5	1.0	0.3
Arkansas	36.7	0.3	0.0
California	290.0	64.9	82.8
Colorado	60.1	36.1	62.8
Connecticut	50.9	3.7	0.6
Delaware	29.1	16.2	0.0
District of Columbia	67.2	55.1	465.5
Florida	122.1	20.1	7.2
Georgia	80.6	69.9	94.6
Hawaii	28.6	0.0	0.5
Idaho	44.2	0.3	2.1
Illinois	129.2	28.2	110.9
Indiana	61.6	2.5	0.2
Iowa	30.7	2.2	0.3
Kansas	38.7	18.6	43.6
Kentucky	57.6	11.5	0.3
Louisiana	72.7	3.7	0.9
Maine	39.5	1.9	0.0
Maryland	83.6	113.0	8.1
Massachusetts	93.1	79.4	63.7
Michigan	130.0	29.1	28.2
Minnesota	67.4	7.5	7.0
Mississippi	45.5	1.1	2.2
Missouri	80.6	13.6	1.0
Montana	49.1	0.4	2.9
Nebraska	39.6	6.3	0.0

(continued on next page)

Table 14.06: Environmental Protection Agency Expenditures to States, 2006

	Grants	Procurement Contracts	Salaries and Wages
United States	*$3,837.6*	*$1,559.2*	*$1,592.3*
Nevada	40.9	7.9	13.3
New Hampshire	36.3	2.5	0.0
New Jersey	88.1	83.2	18.8
New Mexico	45.2	2.0	0.2
New York	235.2	29.0	64.8
North Carolina	89.2	67.3	110.3
North Dakota	33.1	0.8	0.0
Ohio	87.6	220.2	51.5
Oklahoma	69.2	10.7	4.8
Oregon	54.9	9.8	9.9
Pennsylvania	129.4	131.2	74.6
Rhode Island	29.7	9.2	6.3
South Carolina	38.4	0.7	0.0
South Dakota	31.0	0.0	0.1
Tennessee	47.6	1.2	0.6
Texas	221.2	63.0	76.5
Utah	36.0	2.1	0.2
Vermont	33.3	1.3	0.0
Virginia	85.9	214.3	116.6
Washington	112.3	31.5	45.7
West Virginia	60.5	0.7	2.0
Wisconsin	91.9	37.3	0.2
Wyoming	21.7	0.2	0.0

Source: US Department of Commerce, *Consolidated Federal Funds Report for Fiscal Year 2006*, tables 4 through 6.

Notes: Groups may not add to total.

Units: Expenditures in millions of dollars.

Table 14.07: Department of Energy Spending and Credit Activity, 2007 and Estimates for 2008 and 2009

	2007	2008	2009
Spending			
Total Outlays	$21,108	$24,501	$24,725
Discretionary Budget Authority	$23,609	$23,884	$25,012
National defense			
National Nuclear Security Administration	$9,076	$8,811	$9,097
Other defense activity	636	754	1,313
Energy resources	3,237	4,066	3,652
Science and technology	3,837	3,973	4,722
Environmental management	6,186	5,695	5,528
Nuclear waste disposal	446	386	495
Corporate management	191	194	207
Title XVII Innovative Technology Loan Guarantee Program	0	5	0
Mandatory outlays	-$1,881	-$692	-$1,280
Existing law	-1,881	-692	-1,310
Legislative proposal	0	0	30
Credit Activity			
Guaranteed loan disbursements			
Title XVII Innovative Technology Loan Guarantee Program	$0	$300	$943

Source: US Office of Management and Budget, *Budget of the United States Government, Fiscal Year 2009*, page 62.

Notes: Figures for 2007 are actual spending. Figures for 2008 and 2009 are estimates.
For an explanation of the line items, readers are referred to the Office of Budget and Management or the Department of Energy.
Items may not add to total.

Units: Spending and credit activity in millions of dollars.

Table 14.08: Department of Transportation Spending and Credit Activity, 2007 and Estimates for 2008 and 2009

	2007	2008	2009
Spending			
Total Outlays	*$61,699*	*$68,662*	*$71,104*
Discretionary Outlays	*$60,826*	*$67,671*	*$69,921*
Federal Aviation Administration	14,537	14,916	14,644
Federal Highway Administration	38,013	41,241	35,514
Federal Motor Carrier Safety Administration	517	530	541
National Highway Traffic Safety Administration	821	838	852
Federal Railroad Administration	1,478	1,561	1,091
Federal Transit Administration	9,952	9,491	10,136
Federal Maritime Administration	215	306	314
Pipeline and Hazardous Materials Safety Administration	120	126	139
Research and Innovative Technology Administration	8	12	12
Other programs	250	208	147
From enacted supplementals	906	195	0
Mandatory Outlays	*$873*	*$991*	*$1,183*
Federal Aviation Administration	-256	-157	-14
Federal Highway Administration	979	1,103	1,044
Federal Railroad Administration	-1	15	-4
Federal Maritime Administration	221	155	175
Pipeline and Hazardous Materials Safety Administration	13	25	29
Other programs	-83	-150	-47
Credit Activity			
Direct Loan Disbursements	*$367*	*$1,989*	*$1,786*
Transportation Infrastructure Finance and Innovation Program	267	1,389	1,186
Railroad Rehabilitation and Improvement Program	100	600	600
Guaranteed Loan Disbursements	*$33*	*$233*	*$273*
Trans. Infrastructure Finance and Innovation Program	0	40	80
Railroad Rehabilitation and Improvement Program	0	100	100
Maritime Guaranteed Loans (Title XI)	30	75	75
Minority Business Resource Center	3	18	18

Source: US Office of Management and Budget, *Budget of the United States Government, Fiscal Year 2009*, pages 100 and 101.

Notes: Figures for 2007 are actual spending. Figures for 2008 and 2009 are estimates. For an explanation of the line items, readers are referred to the Office of Budget and Management or the Department of Transportation.

Units: Spending in millions of dollars.

Energy, Transportation & the Environment 2009

Table 14.09: Environmental Protection Agency Budget, 2007 and Estimates for 2008 and 2009

	2007	2008	2009
Total Outlays	*$8,259*	*$7,541*	*$7,999*
Discretionary Outlays	*$8,509*	*$7,636*	*$8,143*
Discretionary Budget Authority	7,726	7,472	7,142
Operating program	4,298	4,270	4,251
Clean water state revolving fund	1,084	689	555
Drinking water state revolving fund	837	829	842
Brownfields assessment and cleanup	89	94	94
Clean diesel grants	7	49	49
California diesel emission reduction grants	0	10	0
Targeted water infrastructure funding	84	177	26
Requested	84	44	26
Unrequested	0	133	0
Superfund	1,255	1,254	1,264
Leaking underground storage tanks	72	106	72
Cancellation of unobligated balances	0	-5	-10
Mandatory Outlays	*-250*	*-95*	*-144*

Source: US Office of Management and Budget, *Budget of the United States Government, Fiscal Year 2009*, page 120.

Notes: Figures for 2007 are actual spending. Figures for 2008 and 2009 are estimates.
For an explanation of the line items, readers are referred to the Office of Budget and Management or the Environmental Protection Agency.
Items may not add to total.

Units: Spending in millions of dollars.

Table 14.10: State and Local Government Spending, 2005-06

	State & Local	State	Local
Total Expenditures	*$2,507,086*	*$1,551,555*	*$1,390,867*
Transportation			
Highways	$135,412	$84,289	$51,123
Capital outlay	76,371	57,025	19,346
Air transportation	18,393	1,432	16,961
Parking facilities	1,372	9	1,363
Sea and inland port facilities	4,286	1,327	2,958
Environment and Housing			
Natural resources	$25,482	$18,146	$7,336
Capital outlay	4,473	2,588	1,885
Parks and recreation	34,769	4,876	29,893
Capital outlay	9,267	1,146	8,122
Sewers	39,220	1,266	37,955
Capital outlay	15,336	650	14,687
Solid waste management	22,679	3,254	19,425
Capital outlay	2,101	341	1,760
Utilities			
Total Utilities	*$169,451*	*$24,904*	*$144,547*
Capital outlay	36,795	5,907	30,888
Water supply	47,752	337	47,415
Electric power	66,308	14,621	51,687
Gas supply	9,064	12	9,052
Transit	46,327	9,934	36,393

Source: US Bureau of the Census, Governments Division, 'State and Local Government Finances, 2005-06,' accessed online at www.census.gov/govs/www/estimate.html.

Notes: Data is collected by the Census Bureau for each state and summed to obtain the total state and local government spending.
Groups may not add to total.

Units: Expenditures in millions of dollars.

Table 14.11: Transportation-Related Government Spending, 1980–2002

	State and Local, Excluding Federal Grants	Federal, Excluding Grants	Federal Grants	Total
1980	$47,715	$19,429	$28,286	$95,431
1985	75,555	15,400	27,648	118,603
1990	90,180	14,919	26,172	131,270
1991	94,531	15,832	25,906	136,269
1992	97,551	17,386	26,552	141,489
1993	95,061	17,078	27,516	139,654
1994	100,866	19,044	26,956	146,867
1995	102,233	17,699	27,966	147,898
1996	103,202	17,278	27,482	147,963
1997	105,665	16,868	27,984	150,518
1998	112,282	17,178	26,660	156,120
1999	115,986	16,401	28,766	161,153
2000	117,916	16,459	32,984	167,360
2001	123,069	17,035	36,105	176,209
2002	NA	18,085	39,654	NA

Source: Bureau of Transportation Statistics, *National Transportation Statistics 2007*, table 3-25b.

Notes: 'Federal' and 'State & local spending' exclude federal grants.

Units: Spending in millions of constant 2000 dollars.

Table 14.12: Federal Appropriations for Public Transportation, 2001–2008

	2001	2003	2005	2007	2008
Total Appropriations	*$6,260.6*	*$7,179.0*	*$7,646.3*	*$8,974.8*	*$9,491.7*
Formula Programs	3,392.3	5,806.7	6/076.6	7,262.8	7,767.9
Urbanized areas	2,935.1	3,423.5	3,593.2	3,606.2	3,910.8
Growing and high-density states	NA	NA	NA	404.0	438.0
Nonurbanized areas	205.0	239.0	250.9	404.0	438.0
Elderly and disabled	77.2	90.1	94.5	117.0	127.0
New freedom	NA	NA	NA	81.0	87.5
Over-the-road bus	4.7	7.0	6.9	7.6	8.3
Fixed-guideway modernization	1,056.1	1,206.5	1,204.7	1,448.0	1,570.0
Bus and bus facilities	578.4	652.9	719.2	900.5	872.1
Planning	62.9	72.5	72.4	99.0	107.0
Job access and reverse commute	99.8	104.3	124.0	144.0	156.0
Alternative transportation in parks	NA	NA	NA	23.0	25.0
National Transit Database	NA	NA	NA	3.5	3.5
Alternatives analysis	NA	NA	NA	25.0	24.7
Other	70.5	10.8	10.8	NA	NA
Major Capital Investment	1,060.1	1,251.2	1,437.8	1,566.0	1,569.1
Research total	46.9	48.7	54.6	61.0	65.4
Federal Transit Administration	63.9	72.5	77.4	85.0	89.3

Source: American Public Transportation Association, *Public Transportation Fact Book, 58th ed*, table 41; *59th ed*, table 41.

Notes: Data shown is for fiscal years.

Units: Appropriations in millions of dollars.

Table 14.13: Federal Funding for Superfund, Brownfields, and Related Environmental Programs, 1995–2005

	Total	Superfund	Brownfields	ATSDR	NIEHS
1995	$1,589	$1,437	$2	$81	$69
1996	1,514	1,377	9	68	60
1997	1,578	1,403	42	72	61
1998	1,682	1,431	100	83	68
1999	1,660	1,406	100	84	70
2000	1,519	1,275	100	76	68
2001	1,489	1,247	96	79	67
2002	1,473	1,220	99	81	73
2003	1,622	1,290	170	84	78
2004	1,579	1,258	170	73	78
2005	1,537	1,223	161	75	78

Source: US Bureau of the Census, *Statistical Abstract of the United States 2007*, table 369.

Notes: Superfund values are the appropriated funding minus amounts designated for Brownfields, ATSDR, and NIEHS programs.
ATSDR = Agency for Toxic Substances and Disease Registry.
NIEHS = National Institute for Environmental Health Sciences.

Units: Funding in millions of constant 2004 dollars.

Table 14.14: Results of Compliance and Enforcement Actions by the Environmental Protection Agency, 2002–2007

	2002	2003	2004	2005	2006	2007
Criminal Enforcement Results						
Criminal cases initiated	484	471	425	372	305	340
Defendants charged	325	247	293	320	278	226
Years of incarceration	215	146	77	186	154	64
Fines and restitution	$62	$71	$47	$100	$43	$63
Judicially-mandated projects	NA	NA	$6	$26	$29	$135
Civil Penalties						
All Cases	*$90*	*$96*	*$149*	*$154*	*$124*	*$71*
Judicial cases	$64	$72	$121	$127	$82	$40
Administrative cases	$26	$24	$28	$27	$42	$31
Private Party Commitments for Superfund Site Study and Cleanup						
Site study and cleanup	$501	$896	$569	$753	$391	$688
Oversight	$40	$55	$45	$53	$47	$62
Cost recovery	$126	$223	$142	$218	$164	$252
Voluntary Disclosure Programs						
Disclosures Initiated						
Companies	500	379	491	627	541	448
Facilities	927	614	1,223	1,487	1,032	1,021
Disclosures Resolved						
Companies	252	511	460	512	551	491
Facilities	1,467	848	969	1,002	1,475	728
Case Counts						
Referrals to Justice Department	252	268	265	259	286	278
Cases concluded	216	195	176	157	173	180
Number of facilities	NA	453	450	402	268	416
Penalty order complaints	1,533	1,888	2,122	2,229	4,647	NA
Administrative penalty orders	1,417	1,707	2,248	2,273	4,624	2,255
Administrative compliance orders	1,250	1,582	1,807	1,916	1,438	1,247
Number of inspections/evaluations	18,000	19,000	21,000	21,000	23,000	22,000

Source: US Environmental Protection Agency, Office of Enforcement and Compliance Assurance, *EPA FY2006 Compliance & Enforcement Annual Results*, released November 15, 2006; *FY2007*, released November 13, 2007.

Notes: Data may have been revised since its original publication.

Units: Number of cases opened and resolved; total years of incarceration; value of fines and penalties in millions of dollars.

Guide to Sources

Note: All URLs are valid and accessible, as of November 1, 2008. Whenever possible, we have provided a general web address that should still be available when the data sources update, but some sources may move, and the URLs given below may be inaccessible at a later date.

Part I: Energy

Alternative Fueling Stations by State and Type. **US Department of Energy, Office of Energy Efficiency and Renewable Energy, Alternative Fuels Data Center.**

The Alternative Fuels Data Center (AFDC) contains a wealth of information on alternative fuels and vehicles, including biodiesel, electricity, ethanol, hydrogen, natural gas, and propane. The AFDC also provides a frequently-updated list and count of the alternative fueling stations in each state, and a locator to help people find the station nearest to them. The AFDC also provides the list of federal and state incentives for alternative energy and fuel efficiency that was used to create the list of incentives in the Transportation Energy Data Book. Accessible at www.eere.energy.gov/afdc/fuels/stations_counts. html, or through the AFDC's website at www.eere.energy.gov/afdc

Alternative Fuel and Hybrid Vehicles Made Available 2006. **US Department of Energy, Energy Information Administration.**

The results of an annual survey of automobile suppliers of the number of vehicles made available in that year, with projections for the next year. With detailed information on supplier (original manufacturer vs. converter) and vehicle type. Accessible at www.eia.doe.gov/cneaf/alternate/page/atftables/ atf14-20_05.html

American Housing Survey for the United States: 2007. **US Department of Housing and Urban Development.**

The biennial *American Housing Survey (AHS)* is the most comprehensive government source on many topics relating to housing characteristics. Of particular interest for the purposes of this book is information on the fuels used in housing units presented by characteristics of the householder. The AHS also contains detailed information on people who commute to and from work. The main AHS site can be found at www.census.gov/hhes/www/housing/ahs/ahs.html, and the 2007 survey is at www.census. gov/prod/2008pubs/h150-07.pdf.

Annual Energy Outlook 2008, with Projections to 2030. **US Department of Energy, Energy Information Administration.**

This publication contains the EIA's projections from the present day to 2030 for many of the areas discussed in the *Annual Energy Review*, including energy production, consumption, prices, supplies, and environmental impact. The publication also includes a detailed description of the methodology used in generating the projections, and compares the model used to other models using different parameters. Accessible at www.eia.doe.gov/oiaf/aeo/

Annual Energy Review 2007. **US Department of Energy, Energy Information Administration.**

By far the most comprehensive source for energy data, this is the EIA's major annual publication. It contains over 400 pages, integrating information from many other publications (from the EIA and elsewhere), with detailed information on energy production and consumption, prices and economic data, environmental impact, petroleum, natural gas, nuclear power, coal, international energy, renewable energy, as well as historical data (in many cases stretching back 50 years or more). The results of most of the US government's energy publications are excerpted here. However, due to varying publication dates, the data used from other reports may not be from the most current version available. Readers are urged to check the source report to see if a more recent edition is available. Accessible at www.eia.doe.gov/emeu/aer/

Guide to Sources

Biomass Energy Data Book, 1ˢᵗ ed, September 2006. Oak Ridge National Laboratory.

A joint project of the Oak Ridge National Laboratory and the Department of Energy, this new publication provides a wide range of information on the production of energy from biological fuels such as ethanol and biodiesel. Aside from the usual measures of production, consumption, and prices, the *Biomass Energy Data Book* provides detailed descriptions of the processes involved in the production of ethanol and biodiesel fuel, including agricultural supplies and refineries. Accessible at http://cta.ornl.gov/bedb/index.shtml

BP Statistical Review of World Energy: June 2008. BP.

The oil and gas company BP has been producing its own world energy review for over 50 years. This report contains many of the same topics as the EIA's *International Energy Annual*, with a special emphasis on reserves, production, consumption, and trade for oil and petroleum proucts, natural gas, and coal. The report contains data on most available countries in the world, and detail on organizations like the Organization for Petroleum Exporting Countries (OPEC) and the Organization for Economic Cooperation & Development (OECD). The printed version contains a small cross-section of the years available, but the full data set is available for download. Accessible at www.bp.com/productlanding.do?categoryId=6929&contentId=7044622

Clean Cities Alternative Price Report: July 2008. US Department of Energy, Office of Energy Efficiency and Renewable Energy, Clean Cities Program.

This joint project between the US Department of Energy and industry groups seeks to reduce petroleum consumption. The Clean Cities program produces a quarterly report on the prices of several alternative fuels, including ethanol, propane, natural gas, and several grades of biodiesel. The report gives the average fuel prices, as well as their gasoline gallon equivalents, for several regions. The Clean Cities program is accessible at www.eere.energy.gov/cleancities, and the report can be found at www.eere.energy.gov/afdc/price_report.html

Consumer Views on Transportation and Energy, 3ʳᵈ ed, January 2006. US Department of Energy, National Renewable Energy Laboratory.

This report, released in January 2006, contains the results of public opinion surveys on a variety of issues relating to energy, transportation, and the environment, including gas prices, alternative energy and energy efficiency, and environmental issues. Accessible at http://cta.ornl.gov/bedb/index.shtml. (Data in this table is used in Parts I through III, but the source is only listed for Part I.)

International Energy Annual 2005. US Department of Energy, Energy Information Administration.

The EIA's major publication on International Energy contains much of the same information as other reports (energy production, consumption, prices, supplies, and emissions) for most countries in the world with available data. In many ways, this report is the world energy companion to the *Annual Energy Review*. Accessible at www.eia.doe.gov/iea/

Renewable Energy Consumption and Electricity: Preliminary 2007 Statistics. US Department of Energy, Energy Information Administration.

This is the EIA's annual report on renewable energy, encompassing biomass energy (including ethanol, biodiesel, wood, and waste energy), geothermal, hydroelectric, wind, and solar energy. Includes state-by-state breakdowns of the energy consumption and electricity generation for each source. The figures contained in this report are preliminary, but are more current than the data contained in the *Annual Energy Review*. Accessible at www.eia.doe.gov/cneaf/alternate/page/renew_energy_consump/rea_prereport.html

State Energy Consumption, Price, and Expenditure Estimates (SEDS), Data for 2005. **US Department of Energy, Energy Information Administration.**

This report gives state-by-state data on several key energy topics, including consumption, prices, and expenditures, broken down by end-use sector and source for each state. It contains much of the data available in the *Annual Energy Review*, but for each state. Accessible at www.eia.doe.gov/emeu/states/_seds.html

Part II: Transportation

The 2007 Urban Mobility Report. **Texas Transportation Institute.**

This report, from Texas Transportation Institute (part of the Texas A&M University system) and sponsored by the Department of Transportation, provides data on traffic congestion for 437 urban areas across the US. The report estimates the cost of traffic congestion in cities of different sizes (in terms of wasted time, fuel, and money), and the possible impact of proposed solutions, including increasing public transportation and improving traffic networks. Accessible at http://mobility.tamu.edu/ums/report

Adminstrator's Fact Book, July 2008. **Federal Aviation Administration.**

This publication gives a useful overview of the airline industry in the United States, including flights, pilots, airports, and financial trends. Previous versions of the *Fact Book* are also available for readers interested in older data. Accessible at www.faa.gov/about/office_org/headquarters_offices/aba/admin_factbook

Air Carrier Summary Data, **US Department of Transportation, Research and InnvoativeTechnology Administration, Bureau of Transportation Statistics.**

The Bureau of Transportation Statistics provides a searchable online database containing information on all manner of topics relating to aviaton, including major air carriers, airports, flights, hours flown, and aircraft type. The data used here lists the activity for the 50 busiest airports in the US. The database can be accessed at www.transtats.bts.gov/DataIndex.asp under 'Air Carrier Summary Data.'

American Community Survey 2007. **US Bureau of the Census.**

The American Community Survey is a monthly sample of the US population. The ACS is beginning to track much of the information previously only measured by the long form of the Decennial Census, and is expected to replace the long form by the 2010 census. The ACS provides data at the national and state level, as well as for cities and counties with populations in excess of 65,000, and three-year averages for places over 20,000 population. While the ACS collects data on nearly every facet of people's lives, of interest for this book is the information on people's commutes to and from work. Accessible through www.census.gov/acs/www/

Aviation Accident Statistics. **National Transportation Safety Board.**

The National Transportation Safety Board is an independent federal agency that investigates aviation accidents. The aviation safety statistics are updated regularly; the most recent release presents the number and rate of accidents, injuries, and fatalities in airplane travel from 1987 to 2007. The statistics used in this book are dated April 18, 2008. Accessible at www.ntsb.gov/aviation/Stats.htm

Boating Statistics 2007. **US Department of Homeland Security, United States Coast Guard.**

The Coast Guard's annual report on boating safety in the United States contains information on the number of boats, and number and rate of accidents, injuries, and fatalities (including breakdowns by state), and data on accidents in which alcohol was a factor. Accessible at www.uscgboating.org/statistics/accident_stats.htm

Guide to Sources

***Commodity Flow Survey*. US Bureau of the Census, 2002 Economic Census.**

This report from the Departments of Transportation and Commerce contains information on the amount, value, and distance of materials that were shipped in the United States, including breakdowns by mode of transport and type of material. The Commodity Flow Survey is part of the Economic Census, one of the federal government's largest data-collection projects, which is conducted every 5 years. Accessible at www.census.gov/svsd/www/cfsdat/2002cfs.html

***Commodity Flow Survey: Hazardous Materials*. US Bureau of the Census, 2002 Economic Census.**

This report contains information similar to that in the standard *Commodity Flow Survey*, but for hazardous materials. It contains information on the amount, value, and shipping distance of materials that were shipped in the United States, including breakdowns by mode of transport and type of hazardous material (according to several classification schemes), and interstate shipment totals for several states. The Hazardous Materials report is a subset of the *Commodity Flow Survey*, which in turn is part of the Economic Census, one of the federal government's largest data-collection projects, conducted every 5 years. Accessible at www.census.gov/svsd/www/cfsdat/2002cfs.html

***General Aviation and Air Taxi Activity and Avionics Surveys (GAATAA) CY2006*. Federal Aviation Administration.**

This FAA report presents information on the number and types of planes, flights, fuel, and equipment used in general aviation. Of particular interest here is the data on the types of aircraft used. Accessible at www.faa.gov/data_statistics/aviation_data_statistics/general_aviation

***Highway Statistics 2006*. US Department of Transportation, Federal Highway Administration.**

The FHWA's annual report is the most comprehensive annual source for highway data, including drivers and vehicles, fuel used, lane-miles of road, and types of highways, with several breakdowns by state. *Highway Statistics* provides the most complete data for each year, but readers should note that the larger *National Transportation Statistics* contains time series data excerpted from several years of *Highway Statistics*. Accessible at www.fhwa.dot.gov/policy/ohim/hs06/index.htm

***National Summaries of Domstic and Foreign Waterborne Commerce, Calendar Year 2006*, US Army Corps of Engineers, Institute for Water Resources, Navigation Data Center.**

The US Army Corps of Engineers' Institute for Water Resources engages in long-range planning to improve the Corps' Civil Works program. Their Navigation Data Center provides information on a range of of topics relating to waterborne transportation, including commerce, vehicles, ports, and locks. The *Waterborne Commerce Report* summarizes the relevant commercial and industry topics. Accessible at www.iwr.usace.army.mil/NDC/publications.htm

***National Transit Summaries and Trends for the 2006 National Transit Database Report Year*. Federal Transit Administration, National Transit Database.**

This annual publication is the government's major report on public transportation, with detailed information on riders, vehicles, infrastructure, routes, revenues and expenses, fuel usage, and environmental impact. Agencies receiving referal funding are required to submit reports to the Federal Transit Administration, and the National Transit Database forms the basis of most of the public transit data. Accessible at www.ntdprogram.gov/ntdprogram/data.htm

***National Transportation Statistics 2008*. US Department of Transportation, Research and Innovative Technology Administration.**

By far the largest and most comprehensive source for transportation data, this report contains over 500 pages of information on all aspects of transportation: vehicles, travel, shipping, infrastructure, safety, economy, energy consumption, and emissions. *National Transportation Statistics* excerpts data from dozens of other sources (including many not readily available elsewhere), and brings together information from different domains, often in a single table. This should be the first stop for further research into any area relating to transportation. While much of the information presented in the report is not the most current available, each table contains citations that can point the reader to the original source, which in many cases has been updated in the meantime. Accessible at www.bts.gov/publications/national_transportation_statistics

Public Transportation Fact Book 2007, 59th ed. Amercian Public Transportation Association.

The APTA is a nonprofit association of over 1,500 public transportation organizations, covering transit outfits used by over 90% of the public transit riders in the US and Canada. Their annual report, along with the Federal Transit Administration's *National Transit Database*, serves as a clearinghouse for information on public transportation, and presents a complete profile – passengers and passenger-miles, trips, vehicles, power sources and consumption, fares, employees, revenues, and expenses. Accessible at www.apta.com/research/stats/factbook/index.cfm

State Transportation Statistics 2007. US Department of Transportation, Research and Innovative Technology Administration, Bureau of Transportation Statistics.

This annual report contains much of the key transportation data from *National Transportation Statisitcs*, such as vehicle data, roads, safety, travel, shipping and commerce, energy use, and environmental impact, broken down by state. Accessible at www.bts.gov/publications/state_transportation_statistics. The index page also contains links to more detailed reports about each state in the US.

Traffic Safety Facts 2006. US Department of Transportation, National Highway Transportation Safety Administration, National Center for Statistics & Analysis.

Traffic Safety Facts is the annual report from the NHTSA, the organization responsible for keeping track of transportation safety and accident data. The NTHSA's accident database is the basis for most reports on traffic accidents and safety. The 2006 report contains comprehensive information on a variety of topics. including accident breakdowns by type of accident, vehicle, driver characteristics, state, time of day, and alcohol involvement. At press time, the full 2007 report was not available, but several short previews present advance excerpts from the forthcoming report. This book uses preview publications on fatalities, alcohol involvement, seat belt use, and motorcycle accidents, broken down by state. Accessible at www-nrd.nhtsa.dot.gov/Pubs/tsf2006fr.pdf. The more recent preview reports can be found at www-nrd.nhtsa.dot.gov/CMSWeb/listpublications.aspx?Id=F&ShowBy=DocType

Transportation Energy Data Book, 27th ed. Oak Ridge National Laboratory.

This joint project from the Oak Ridge National Laboratory and the Department of Energy is the most comprehensive source for the data on the intersection between energy and transportation. Containing over 300 pages of tables, the *Transportation Energy Data Book* collects data from a wide range of sources, including information not readily available elsewhere. For the purposes of this book, it was especially useful in finding data on the automotive industry and energy-efficiency standards. Accessible at http://cta.ornl.gov/data/index.shtml

Transportation Statistics Annual Report, December 2006. US Departent of Transportation, Research and Innovative Technology Administration, Bureau of Transportation Statistics.

The *Transportation Statistics Annual Report* is a smaller, less exhaustive version of the *National Transportation Statistics* report, covering much of the same ground. Of interest for this book is the data on long-distance travel in the US, and the performance of major air carriers, which is more current than the analagous data in the larger report. Accessible at www.bts.gov/publications/transportation_statistics_annual_report/2006

Part III: Environment

2006 TRI Public Data Release eReport. Environmental Protection Agency, Toxics Release Inventory Program.

The Toxics Release Inventory (TRI) program measures the amount of toxic materials produced as waste products in industrial and other processes, and the treatment and disposal of those chemicals. The TRI's major report provides a wealth of data on toxic chemical releases, including the industry releasing the material, and treatment methods for the chemicals. It also provides breakdowns by state, and for certain chemicals such as lead, mercury, and dioxin. The most recent edition of the report was released in February 2008. Accessible at www.epa.gov/tri/tridata/tri06/index.htm

Air Pollutant Emissions Trends Data, 1970-2007 Average Annual Emissions. Environmental Protection Agency, Technology Transfer Network, Clearinghouse for Inventories & Emissions Factors, National Emissions Inventory.

The EPA's air pollution-tracking program measures the concentrations of certain pollutants as a measure of air quality in accordance with the Clean Air Act. The complete data set can be downloaded at http://www.epa.gov/ttn/chief/trends/index.html

Blood Lead Data–Reported from 2002 through 2005 CDC, NIOSH's Adult Blood Lead Epidemiology and Surveillance (ABLES) Program. US Department of Health and Human Services, Centers for Disease Control, National Institute for Occupational Safety and Health, Adult Blood Lead Epidemiology and Surveillance (ABLES).

The ABLES program tracks exposure to lead through the blood levels of lead in adults. The data used here shows the prevalence of adults with high lead levels (defined as greater than 25 micrograms per deciliter of blood), and those with very high levels (greater than 40 micrograms/deciliter). Accessible at www.cdc.gov/niosh/topics/ABLES/ables.html

CEPs at Hazardous Waste Sites and CERCLA Priority List of Hazardous Substances, 2007 editions. US Department of Health and Human Services, Centers for Disease Control, Agency for Toxic Substances & Disease Registry (ATSDR).

The ATSDR produces two lists of hazardous chemicals that pose a risk to human health: the Completed Exposure Pathway (CEP) and the Comprehensive Environmental Response, Compensation, and Liability Act (CERCLA) Priority List. Both use slightly different methodologies (see glossary or program website for details) to rank the chemicals in order of the greatest potential threat. CEP information can be found at http://www.atsdr.cdc.gov/cep/index.html, while CERCLA information is at http://www.atsdr.cdc.gov/cercla/index.html

Cumulative Data and Graphics for Oil Spills 1973-2004. US Department of Homeland Security, United States Coast Guard.

This report lists the number of oil spills by volume and total spill volume for the years indicated, as well as breakdowns by water body, location, spill source, type of oil, and Coast Guard district. Unfortunately, due to a recent website redesign, the report is no longer accessible online.

Factoids: Drinking Water and Ground Water Statistics for 2007. Environmental Protection Agency, Office of Water.

The EPA's drinking water report lists the drinking water systems (and population served by them) for each state, as well as the number and type of violations of EPA or state standards. Accessible at www.epa.gov/safewater/data/getdata.html

Inventory of Greenhouse Gas Emissions and Sinks: 1990–2006. **Environmental Protection Agency.**
The EPA's greenhouse gas report is the government's comprehensive source for greenhouse gas emissions data. The 450+ page report contains exhaustive data on the amount of carbon dioxide and other greenhouse gases emitted through energy production and fuel combustion, industrial proceses, and other sources. The report also provides good explanations of many of the terms, issues, and processes involved, and is very useful in understanding greenhouse gases and climate change issues. Accessible at www.epa.gov/climatechange/emissions/usinventoryreport.html

Municipal Solid Waste in the United States: 2006 Facts and Figures. **Environmental Protection Agency, Office of Solid Waste.**
The annual report on the nation's municipal solid waste gives the amount of waste generated, used in energy recovery (either recycling, composting, or combustion for waste energy), and discarded to landfills. The report gives breakdowns by product and type of material used, as well as time series comparisons from 1960 to 2006. Accessible at www.epa.gov/epawaste/nonhaz/municipal/msw99.htm

National Priorities List (NPL), Environmental Protection Agency, Superfund Division.
The NPL is a list of the highest-priority Superfund sites in terms of known releases or threatened releases of hazardous substances, pollutants, or contaminants. The list, intended primarily to guide the EPA in determining which sites warrant further investigation, is available online, through a searchable database accessible at www.epa.gov/superfund/sites/query/basic.htm, and is updated frequently. It is possible to search by a specified state or EPA region, type of site, contaminant, contaminated medium, or zip code, with detailed information available on most of the sites.

The National Biennial RCRA Hazardous Waste Report (Based on 2005 Data). **Environmental Protection Agency, Office of Solid Waste.**
The EPA's biennial report on hazardous waste and waste management tracks all materials designated under the Resource Conservation and Recovery Act (RCRA), including the amount of waste generated, managed, shipped, and received for each state, as well as breakdowns by the industry producing the waste (using NAICS codes), and the different methods used to manage the waste. Accessible at www.epa.gov/epaoswer/hazwaste/data/biennialreport

National Resources Inventory 2003 Annual NRI–Land Use. **US Department of Agriculture, Natural Resources Conservation Service.**
The NRI is a statistical survey of natural resource conditions and trends on non-federal land in the United States. The land use portion of the survey lists the amount of different types of land, such as crop land, pasture land, range land, forest land, developed land, and water areas. The report lists the area of each type for the United States, with further breakdowns for states, and for major river basins. Accessible at www.nrcs.usda.gov/technical/land/nri03/nri03landuse-mrb.html

National Resources Inventory 2003 Annual NRI–Soil Erosion. **US Department of Agriculture, Natural Resources Conservation Service.**
The NRI is a statistical survey of natural resource conditions and trends on non-federal land in the United States. The soil erosion portion of the survey lists the amount of soil lost to wind and water erosion, for regular and highly-erodable cropland, with breakdowns by state and by major river basin. Accessible at www.nrcs.usda.gov/technical/land/nri03/nri03eros-mrb.html

Number of Days with with Air Quality Index Values Greater than 100 at Trend Sites, 1990–2007, and All Sites in 2007. **Environmental Protection Agency, Air & Radiation, Air Trends, Air Quality Index Information.**
The EPA's Air Quality standards for several pollutants form the basis for its Air Quality Index. For any pollutant, an AQI value over 100 indicates a pollutant level that exceeds standards and makes the air in

a certain area unsafe. This report gives the number of days in which at least one pollutant was at unsafe levels for several major metropolitan areas. Accessible at www.epa.gov/air/airtrends/aqi_info.html

Summary for Policymakers. In: Climate Change 2007: The Physical Science Basis. Contribution of Working Group I to the Fourth Assessment Report of the Intergovernmental Panel on Climate Change. [Solomon, S., D. Qin, M. Manning, Z. Chen, M. Marquis, K.B. Averyt, M.Tignor and H.L. Miller (eds.)]. Cambridge University Press, Cambridge, United Kingdom and New York, NY, USA.

The Intergovernmental Panel on Climate Change (IPCC) was established in 1988 by the World Meteorological Organization (WMO) and the United Nations Environment Programme (UNEP) to assess the scientific, technical, and socio-economic information relevant to understanding the scientific basis of risk of human-induced climate change, its potential impacts, and options for adaptation and mitigation. The IPCC's *Fourth Assessment Report*, published in 2007, contains a huge amount of scientific data, along with a less technical summary for policymakers and supplementary materials. This topic is extremely complex and far-reaching, and the IPCC should be the first stop for further information into the massive amount of research that has been conducted on climate change. The IPCC's home page is found at www.ipcc.ch. Information appearing in this volume comes from Working Group I (studying the physical science basis of climate change): the full AR4 report from Working Group 1 can be found at http://ipcc-wg1.ucar.edu/wg1/wg1-report.html

Status and Trends of Wetlands in the Coterminous United States 1998 to 2004. US Department of the Interior, Fish & Wildlife Service.

The Fish & Wildlife Service's report details changes in the amount and type of wetlands in the United States from 1998 to 2004. The report is notable for showing a net gain in the total amount of wetland area for the first time. Accessible at http://wetlandsfws.er.usgs.gov/status_trends/national_reports/trends_2005_report.pdf

Third National Report on Human Exposure to Environmental Chemicals, 2005. US Department of Health and Human Services, Centers for Disease Control, National Center for Environmental Health.

The CDC's major report on human exposure to chemicals presents over 450 pages of data on over 100 potentially hazardous chemicals, measuring concentrations of the chemcials of their byproducts in the blood, urine, or fatty tissues of a representative sample. For readers interested in the most commonly listed chemicals, or who do not need as much raw technical information, a short executive summary is also available. Accessible at www.cdc.gov/exposurereport/report.htm

Threatened and Endangered Species System (TESS) database. US Department of the Interior, Fish & Wildlife Service, Endangered Species Program.

The US Fish & Wildlife System's TESS database provides a frequently-updated list of species designated 'endangered' or 'threatened.' The database is searchable by species type, region or state, listing status, and can be grouped along several dimensions. It can be accessed at http://ecos.fws.gov/tess_public/StartTESS.do

Wadeable Streams Assessment: A Collaborative Survey of the Nation's Streams. Environmental Protection Agency, Office of Water.

This report, the first to present comprehensive data on the small streams and rivers in the US, lists data on several environmental factors, including the streams' biological condition, levels of phosphorous, nitrogen, salt, acid, sediment, fish habitats, and plant cover. The information is also broken down by region of the US. Accessible at www.epa.gov/owow/streamsurvey

Part IV: Special Topics

Budget of the United States Government, Fiscal Year 2009. **White House Office of Management and Budget.**

The federal budget for FY 2009 includes detailed data on the budgets for the Departments of Energy and Transportation, and the Environmental Protection Agency. Accessible at www.whitehouse.gov/omb/budget/fy2009

Consolidated Federal Funds Report for Fiscal Year 2006. **US Census Bureau.**

The major report on federal government grants and other spending to the states, the CFFR is notable here for its data on the amount of money granted to each state by the Departments of Energy and Transportation, and the Environmental Protection Agency. Accessible at www.census.gov/govs/www/cffr06.html

Consumer Expenditures in 2006. **US Department of Labor, Bureau of Labor Statistics.**

The Consumer Expenditure Survey tracks spending on a variety of goods and services. Of interest for the purposes of this book are the amounts spent on different facets of transportation, broken down by characteristics of the consumer. Accessible at www.bls.gov/cex/

County Business Patterns 2006. **US Bureau of the Census.**

County Business Patterns is an annual Census program measuring economic activity of industries between Economic Censuses (which are taken every 5 years). The survey gives estimates for establishments, employees, and payrolls for several industries by NAICS code. It covers several classes of small areas (states, counties, metropolitan areas, and zip codes), and covers most of the country's economic activity, excluding self-employed individuals, employees of private households, railroad employees, agricultural production employees, and most government employees. Accessible online at www.census.gov/epcd/cbp/view/cbpview.html)

EPA FY2007 Compliance & Enforcement Annual Results. **Environmental Protection Agency, Office of Enforcement and Compliance Assurance.**

This annual report summarizes the results of the EPA's various monitoring and enforcement efforts, including a breakdown of the civil and criminal cases by agency referral and statute, as well as case outcomes. Accessible at www.epa.gov/compliance/data/results/annual/index.html (the report itself is located at www.epa.gov/compliance/data/results/annual/fy2007.html

Gasoline Prices by Formulation, Grade, and Sales Type. **US Department of Energy, Energy Information Administration.**

The Petroleum section of the EIA's website contains frequently-updated price information, including gasoline prices. Data is available for periods of weeks, months, or years, often on state-by-state or metropolitan area basis. The information used in this book was accessed at http://tonto.eia.doe.gov/dnav/pet/pet_pri_allmg_a_EPM0_PTA_cpgal_a.htm, but more recent (weekly) price data can be found at http://tonto.eia.doe.gov/dnav/pet/pet_pri_top.asp

Occupational Employment Statistics, May 2007. **US Deptartment of Labor, Bureau of Labor Statistics.**

The BLS' Occupational Employment Statistics is one of the primary sources of employment data broken down across a variety of industries and occupations. Here, the relevant figures are for employment in transportation-related industries and occupations. Accessible at www.bls.gov/oes/current/oessrci.htm

Guide to Sources

State & Local Government Finances: US Summary, 2005-06. **US Bureau of the Census, Governments Division.**

The Census Bureau's Governments Division reports the finances for state and local governments for several spending and revenue categories, including several that are relevant to energy, transportation, and the environment. Data is given for state governments, local governments, and a combination of both. Data is available for each of the 50 states and the District of Columbia, but only the US total is shown here. Accessible at www.census.gov/govs/www/estimate06.html

Statistical Abstract of the United States, 2008. **US Bureau of the Census.**

The *Statistical Abstract* is the summary publication for all the data collected by the Census Bureau, as well as the government's other programs, and collectively presents a thorough profile of the United States and its population, economy, and government. The *Abstract* contains information on just about every possible topic, and is a useful place to start any research project. The *Abstract* is available online at www.census.gov/prod/www/statistical-abstract.html

Glossary

14 CFR 121

Title 14, part 121 of the Code of Federal Regulations, prescribing rules governing the operation of domestic, flag, and supplemental air carriers and commercial operators of large aircraft. Applies to planes containing 10 or more seats; prior to 1997, it included only planes with at least 30 seats or a payload capacity of at least 7,500 pounds.

14 CFR 135

Title 14, part 135 of the Code of Federal Regulations, prescribing rules governing the operations of commuter air carriers (scheduled) and on-demand air taxi (unscheduled). Includes planes with fewer than 10 seats; prior to 1997, it also included planes with fewer than 30 seats and a payload capacity under 7,500 pounds. Generally, regulations for this category are not as strict as those for **14 CFR 121** aircraft.

ACCESSIBILITY

Vehicles that do not restrict access, are usable, and provide allocated space and/or priority seating for individuals who use wheelchairs. For public transit, a vehicle's availability for use by people with disabilities, in compliance with the Americans with Disabilities Act (ADA). Here, accessible vehicles are those that provide access through a lift, ramp, or at a transit station.

ACCIDENT

Although the definition varies by mode of transportation, generally an accident is an occurrence resulting in a serious or fatal injury, or property damage in excess of a certain threshold. For vehicles, accidents usually involve collisions between a vehicle, any another vehicle, a non-occupant, or a stationary object. For the transport of natural gas, oil, or hazardous materials, accidents can also include the loss or release of the material.

Air carriers classify accidents according to the following scheme:

Major: an accident in which either an aircraft was destroyed, there were miltiple fatalities, or there was one fatality and an aircraft was substantially damaged.

Serious: an accident in which either there was one fatality without serious damage to an aircraft, or there was at least one serious injury and an aircraft was seriously damaged.

Injury: an accident in which there was at least one serious injury (but no fatalities) and no substantial damage to an aircraft.

Damage: an accident in which no one was killed or seriously injured, but an aircraft was substantially damaged.

A **serious injury** is defined as one requiring hospitalization for more than 48 hours, commencing within 7 days of the injury; results in a bone fracture (except simple fractures of fingers, toes, or nose); involves lacerations that cause severe hemorrhages, nerve, muscle, or tendon damage; involves injury to any internal organ; or involves second or third-degree burns or any burns affecting more than 5% of the body's surface.

ACIDIFICATION

The process of streams and rivers becoming acidic through the effects of acid deposition (e.g., acid rain) or acid mine drainage, particularly from coal mining.

Glossary

AIR CARRIER

A person who undertakes directly, by lease or other arrangement, to engage in air transportation. More specifically, the commercial system of air transportation comprising large certificated air carriers, small certificated air carriers, commuter air carriers, on-demand air taxis, supplemental air carriers, and air travel clubs.

AIR QUALITY INDEX (AQI)

EPA system for measuring air quality on a given day, based on levels of six major pollutants (**particulate matter, sulfur dioxide, carbon monoxide, ozone, lead,** and **nitrogen dioxide**), which provides a single number that represents the worst daily air quality experienced in a particular area.

AIR TAXI

An aircraft operator who conducts operations for hire or compensation in accordance with **14 CFR 135** (for safety purposes) or **FAR Part 135** (for economic regulations/reporting purposes). An air taxi operates on an on-demand basis and does not meet the flight scheduling qualifications of a **commuter air carrier**.

ALTERNATIVE FUELS

The Energy Policy Act of 1992 defines alternative fuels as methanol, denatured ethanol, and other alcohol; mixtures containing 85% or more (or other level, not less than 70%, as determined by the Secretary of Energy) by volume of methanol, denatured ethanol, and other alcohols with gasoline or other fuels. Includes compressed natural gas, liquid petroleum gas, hydrogen, coal-derived liquid fuels, fuels other than alcohols derived from biological materials, electricity, or any other fuel the Secretary of Energy determines by rule is substantially not petroleum and would yield substantial energy security and environmental benefits.

ALTERNATIVE-FUELED VEHICLE

Either a vehicle designed and manufactured by an original equipment manufacturer, or a converted vehicle designed to operate in either dual-fuel, flexible-fuel, or dedicated modes on fuels other than motor gasoline or diesel fuel. This does not include a conventional vehicle that is limited to operation on blended or reformulated motor gasoline fuels.

AMMONIA (NH_3)

A colorless gas that can be toxic to humans. It occurs naturally, but is also released and tracked as a pollutant.

AMTRAK

A public rail system operated by the National Railroad Passenger Corporation of Washington, D.C., and created by the Rail Passenger Service Act of 1970 (P.L. 91-518, 84 Stat. 1327). It is responsible for the operation of intercity (as distinct from suburban) passenger trains between points designated by the Secretary of Transportation.

API GRAVITY

A measure of specific gravity of crude oil or condensate in degrees, calculated by the American Petroleum Institute, based on an arbitrary scale expressing the gravity or density of liquid petroleum products. The measuring scale is calibrated in terms of degrees API, calculated as follows: degrees API = (141.5/specific gravity at 60 °F) – 131.5.

APPROPRIATIONS

The provision of funds, through an annual appropriations act or a permanent law, for federal agencies to make payments out of the treasury for specified purposes. *See also* **outlays**.

ARTERIAL HIGHWAY

A major highway used primarily for through traffic.

ARTICULATED BUS

An extra-long bus (54 to 60 feet) with two connected passenger compartments, in which the rear body section is connected to the main body by a joint mechanism that allows the vehicle to bend for sharp turns and curves, and yet have a continuous interior.

B2-B5

A mixture of 2–5% **biodiesel** fuel blended with 95–98% **diesel**.

B20

A mixture of 20% **biodiesel** fuel blended with 80% **diesel**.

B99-100

A mixture of 99–100% **biodiesel** fuel blended with 0–1% **diesel**.

BAC *see* **BLOOD ALCOHOL LEVEL**

BARREL

A unit of volume used to measure oil; equal to 42 US gallons.

BIODIESEL

Any liquid **biofuel** suitable as a diesel fuel substitute or diesel fuel additive or extender. Biodiesel can be made from oils from vegetables (soybeans, rapeseed, or sunflowers), animal tallow, or from agricultural byproducts such as rice hulls.

BIOFUELS

Liquid fuels and blending components produced from biomass (plant) feedstocks, used primarily for transportation. *See also* **biodiesel, ethanol**.

BIOMASS

Organic nonfossil material of biological origin constituting a renewable energy source. *See also* **ethanol, wood energy,** and **waste energy**.

BLACK LIQUOR

Also known as alkaline spent liquor, a byproduct of the paper production process that can be used as a source of energy. Often included in estimates of **wood energy**.

BLOOD ALCOHOL CONCENTRATION

A measurement of the percentage of alcohol in the blood by grams per deciliter. A level of .08 is generally considered the standard for legal impairment. Abbreviated as **BAC**.

BRITISH THERMAL UNIT

The quantity of heat needed to raise the temperature of 1 pound of water by 1 °F at or near 39.2 °F. Used as a standard unit in measuring energy. Abbreviated as **Btu**.

BROWNFIELDS

Property whose expansion, redevelopment, or reuse may be complicated by the presence or potential presence of a hazardous substance, pollutant, or contaminant.

Btu *see* **BRITISH THERMAL UNIT**

BUNKER FUELS

Fuel supplied to ships and aircraft, both domestic and foreign, consisting primarily of **residual fuel oil** and **distillate fuel oil** for ships and kerosene-type jet fuel for aircraft. For the purposes of greenhouse gas emissions inventories, data on emissions from combustion of international bunker fuels is subtracted from national emissions totals. Historically, bunker fuels have meant only ship fuel.

BUS

A large motor vehicle used to carry more than 10 passengers:, including school buses, intercity buses, and transit buses.

CAFE *see* **CORPORATE AVERAGE FUEL ECONOMY**

CANCELLED FLIGHT

A flight that is listed within a carrier's reservation system within 7 days of the scheduled departure and does not take off.

CAPACITY

The maximum output of generating equipment (commonly expressed in megawatts) adjusted for ambient conditions.

CAPACITY FACTOR

The ratio of the electric energy produced by a generating unit for a given period of time to the electric energy that could have been produced at continuous full-power operation during the same period.

CAPITAL EMPLOYEE

A public transportation employee whose labor hour cost is reimbursed under a capital grant or is otherwise capitalized. Generally, only large transit agencies have such employees.

CAPITAL EXPENSES

Expenses incurred by public transit agencies related to the purchase of equipment.

CAPITAL FUNDING

Any funding source used to pay capital expenses. Includes government funding and **directly generated funds**, which include passenger fares, advertising revenue, donations, bond proceeds, and taxes imposed by the transit agency.

CARBON DIOXIDE (CO_2)

A colorless, odorless, non-poisonous gas (CO_2) that is a normal part of Earth's atmosphere. Carbon dioxide is a product of fossil-fuel combustion as well as other processes. It is considered a **greenhouse gas**, as it traps heat (infrared energy) radiated by the Earth into the atmosphere and thereby contributes to the potential for **global warming**. The global warming potential of other greenhouse gases is measured in relation to that of carbon dioxide, which by international scientific convention is assigned a reference value of 1.

CARBON DIOXIDE EQUIVALENT (CO_2 eq)

The amount of **carbon dioxide** by weight emitted into the atmosphere that would produce the same estimated radiative forcing as a given weight of another radiatively active gas. Carbon dioxide equivalents are computed by multiplying the weight of the gas being measured (for example, methane) by its estimated **global warming potential** (which is 21 for methane). 'Carbon equivalent units' are defined as carbon dioxide equivalents multiplied by the carbon content (by weight) of carbon dioxide (i.e., 12/44).

CARBON INTENSITY

A measure of the amount of carbon emitted per unit of energy output in an energy-generating process (such as the combustion of fossil fuels). A measure of the efficiency and relative environmental impact of an energy source.

CARBON MONOXIDE (CO)

A highly toxic gas produced by the incomplete combustion of carbon-containing fuels. Carbon monoxide is also an **indirect greenhouse gas,** and a pollutant tracked as part of the **Air Quality Index (AQI)**.

CARBON SINK

Anything with the ability to store carbon, removing it from the air. Natural carbon sinks include trees and other plants. *See also* **sequestration**.

CARCINOGEN

Any substance that is known to cause cancer.

CAR-MILE

The movement of a railroad car a distance of 1 mile. For example, a 10-car train traveling 2 miles travels 20 car-miles.

CEP *see COMPLETED EXPOSURE PATHWAY*

CERCLA *see COMPREHENSIVE ENVIRONMENTAL RESPONSE, COMPENSATION, AND LIABILITY ACT*

CH_4 *see METHANE*

CHAINED DOLLARS

A measure used to express real prices, defined as prices that are adjusted to remove the effect of changes in the purchasing power of the dollar (i.e., inflation). Real prices usually reflect buying power relative to a reference year. The "chained-dollar" measure is based on the average weights of goods and services in successive pairs of years. It is "chained" because the second year in each pair, with its weights, becomes the first year of the next pair.

Glossary

Prior to 1996, real prices were expressed in constant dollars, a weighted measure of goods and services in a single year. *See also* **constant dollars**, **current dollars**.

CHLOROFLUOROCARBONS (CFCs)

Compounds consisting of carbon, hydrogen, chlorine, and flourine used as refrigerants. CFCs are harmful to the Earth's atmosphere and are considered **greenhouse gases**.

CLASS I RAILROAD

A carrier that has an annual operating revenue of $250 million in 1991 dollars (the reference year). Currently the inflation-adjusted figure is around $350 million in 2006 dollars.

CLEARINGHOUSE FOR INVENTORIES & EMISSIONS FACTORS (CHIEF)

The EPA's system for tracking air pollutants, using the **National Emissions Inventory (NEI)**. The **NEI** measures emissions of **carbon monoxide, nitrogen oxides, sulfur dioxide, particulate matter, volatile organic compounds (VOCs)**, and **ammonia**.

CLIMATE CHANGE

A term used to refer to all forms of climatic inconsistency, but especially to significant change from one prevailing climatic condition to another. In some cases, "climate change" has been used synonymously with the term "**global warming**." However, scientists tend to use the term in a wider sense to include natural changes in climate as well as climatic cooling.

The **Intergovernmental Panel on Climate Change IPCC** has created climate projections for the end of the 21st century, using several scenarios according to their projected concentrations of CO_2 **equivalents**.

A1 assumes a very rapid economic growth, with a population that peaks in mid-century and declines after that, and the rapid introduction of new and more efficient technologies. The scenario is further split into 3 paths, according to the emphasis on technological development: fossil-fuel intensive (**A1FI**, 1,550 parts per million CO_2 equivalent), alternative sources (**A1T**, 700 ppm CO_2 eq), and balanced (**A1B**, 850 ppm CO_2 eq).

A2 assumes a more heterogenous, locally-determined world in which population continues to increase continuously throughout the 21st century. It uses a CO_2 equivalent concentration of 1,250 ppm.

B1 assumes a population similar to the **A1** scenario, but with a rapid shift towards a service- and information-based economy, with an emphasis on "clean" technologies and sustainability, and changes at a global level. It assumes a CO_2 equivalent concentration of 600 ppm.

B2 assumes a population simiar to the **A2** scenario, but with slower population growth. There is technological change, but slower than the **A1** and **B1** scenarios, and environmental protection efforts are focused on local and regional levels. It assumes a CO_2 equivalent concentration of 800 ppm.

For more information on these scenarios, and details on the methodology behind climate change projections, readers are directed to the IPCC.

CO *see* **CARBON MONOXIDE**

CO₂ *see* **CARBON DIOXIDE**

COLIFORM

The amount of microorganisms in a sample. Levels of certain coliform (such as *E. coli*), along with **turbidity**, can be used to suggest bacterial contamination.

COLLECTOR

In rural areas, routes that serve intracounty rather than statewide travel. In urban areas, streets that provide direct access to neighborhoods and arterials.

COAL

A readily-combustible black or brownish-black rock whose composition, including inherent moisture, consists of more than 50% by weight and more than 70% by volume of carbonaceous material (carbon-rich). It is formed from plant remains that have been compacted, hardened, chemically altered, and metamorphosed by heat and pressure over geologic time. Coal is divided into categories called **ranks**, which are presented below from highest rank to lowest rank:

Anthracite: Used primarily for residential and commercial space heating. Often referred to as hard coal, it is a hard, brittle, and black lustrous coal, with a high percentage of fixed carbon and a low percentage of volatile matter, a moisture content generally less than 15%, and heat content ranging from 22 to 28 million Btu per short ton on a moist, mineral-matter-free basis.

Bituminous Coal: Dense, usually black, sometimes dark brown, often with well-defined bands of bright and dull material, used primarily as fuel in steam-electric power generation, with substantial quantities also used for heat and power applications in manufacturing and making coke. The most abundant coal in active US mining regions, with a moisture content usually less than 20%, and a heat content ranging from 21 to 30 million Btu per short ton on a moist, mineral-matter-free basis.

Subbituminous Coal: Properties range from those of lignite coal to those of bituminous coal. Used primarily as fuel for steam-electric power generation. Lower quality subbituminous coal ranges from a dull, dark brown to black, soft, and crumbly. Higher quality subbituminous coal is bright, jet black, hard, and relatively strong. Subbituminous coal contains 20% to 30% inherent moisture by weight, with a heat content ranging from 17 to 24 million Btu per short ton on a moist, mineral matter-free basis.

Lignite: Often referred to as brown coal, used almost exclusively as fuel for steam-electric power generation. It is brownish-black, with a high inherent moisture content (as high as 45%), and a heat content ranging from 9 to 17 million Btu per short ton on a moist, mineral-matter-free basis.

COMMERCIAL SECTOR

An energy-consuming sector that consists of service-providing facilities and equipment for businesses; federal, state, and local governments; and other private and public organizations, such as religious, social, or fraternal groups. The commercial sector also includes institutional living quarters, and sewage treatment facilities. Common uses of energy associated with this sector include space heating, water heating, air conditioning, lighting, refrigeration, cooking, and running a wide variety of other equipment. *See also **end-use sector**.*

Glossary

COMMERCIAL SERVICE AIRPORT

An airport receiving scheduled passenger service and having 2,500 or more enplaned passengers per year.

COMMUNITY WATER SYSTEM (CWS)

Public water systems that supply water to the same population year-round.

COMMUTER AIR CARRIER

For safety analysis, commuter carriers are defined as air carriers operating under **14 CFR 135** that carry passengers for hire or compensation on at least five round trips per week on at least one route between two or more points according to published flight schedules, as well as helicopters carrying passengers or cargo, regardless of their size. For economic regulations and reporting requirements, commuter air carriers are those carriers that operate aircraft with fewer than 60 seats or a maximum payload capacity of less than 18,000 pounds. Safety requirements are generally less stringent for commuter air carriers than for the larger carriers regulated under **14 CFR 121**.

COMMUTER RAIL

Urban passenger train service for short-distance travel between a central city and adjacent suburb. Does not include rapid rail transit or **light rail service**.

COMMUTING

The process of traveling between a place of residence and a place of work.

COMPENSATION

The total renumeration given to employees. Compensation is divided into two categories: **salaries and wages** (the pay and allowances due directly to employees in exchange for labor services), and **fringe benefits** (payments or accruals to others, such as insurance companies, governments, etc., on behalf of an employee, or payments directly to an employee arising from something other than their of work).

COMPLETED EXPOSURE PATHWAY (CEP)

A ranking of toxic chemical exposure, compiled by the Agency for Toxic Substances & Disease Registry (ATSDR). Completed Exposure Pathways are cases in which a contaminant found in the population is linked to a specific source. The CEP ranks chemicals based on the number of exposure sites. The CEP differs from the **CERCLA** list in that it only considers the possible exposure to a chemical, but does not take toxicity into acount, while the CERCLA list uses an algorithm based on toxicity, frequency of occurrence, and possibility for human exposure. Also, the CEP receives reports from all waste sites, while the CERCLA reports only on sites designated on the National Priority List (NPL). Thus, the two rankings are frequently similar, but may differ at times. *See also Comprehensive Environmental Response, Compensation, and Liability Act.*

COMPREHENSIVE ENVIRONMENTAL RESPONSE, COMPENSATION, AND LIABILITY ACT (CERCLA)

A ranking of chemicals with the greatest health and environmental risks, compiled by the Agency for Toxic Substances & Disease Registry (ATSDR), the CERCLA list determines which chemicals represent the greatest potential threat to human health using an algorithm based on toxicity, frequency of occurrence, and possibility for human exposure, looking at only at those sites designated on the National Priority List (NPL), the EPA's list of the most serious uncontrolled or abandoned hazardous waste sites in the United States. The CERCLA list is similar to the **CEP** list. However, the **CEP** list does not consider toxicity, only the possiblity of exposure, and receives reports from all waste sites, not just those on the National Priority List. Thus, the two rankings are likely to be similar, but may differ at times. *See also **Completed Exposure Pathway**.*

COMPRESSED NATURAL GAS

Natural gas compressed to a volume and density that is practical as a portable fuel supply. It is used as a fuel for natural gas-powered vehicles.

COMPOSITE FOSSIL FUEL PRICE

A weighted average price for **fossil fuels**, derived by multiplying the price per Btu of each fuel by the total Btu content of the production, and then dividing this accumulated value of total fossil fuel production by the accumulated Btu content of total fossil fuel production.

CONDENSIBLES

Gases that condense to form liquid or solid **particulate matter**. They are sometimes (but not always) included in particulate matter data. When they do condense, they are almost always classified as **fine particles**.

CONGESTION COST

A measure of the amount of money wasted by traffic congestion in terms of time and fuel wasted. It is calculated by estimating the value of travel time delay at $14.60 per hour of person travel, $77.10 per hour of truck time, and excess fuel consumption (using the state average cost per gallon).

CONSERVATION RESERVE PROGRAM

A federal program established under the Food Security Act of 1985 to help private landowners convert highly erodible cropland to vegetative cover for 10 years. Abbreviated as **CRP**.

CONSTANT DOLLAR

Dollar value adjusted for changes in the average price level by dividing a current dollar amount by a price index. *See also **chained dollar**, **current dollar**.*

CONSUMER PRICE ESTIMATE

A monthly program that tracks changes in the prices paid by urban consumers for a representative group of goods and services.

CONTINE

A by-product in the breakdown of nicotine. Contine is currently regarded as the best indicator of exposure to environmental tobacco smoke in active smokers and in nonsmokers (measures of **secondary smoke**), because it remains in the blood longer than nicotine.

CONVENTIONAL DEPOSITS

Discrete subsurface accumulations of crude oil or natural gas with well-defined hydrocarbon/water contacts.

CORPORATE AVERAGE FUEL ECONOMY STANDARDS (CAFE)

Under CAFE, automobile manufacturers are required by law to produce vehicle fleets with a composite sales-weighted fuel economy not lower than the CAFE standards in a given year. CAFE was originally established by Congress for new automobiles and later for light trucks. For every vehicle that does not meet the standard, a fine is paid for every one-tenth of a mile per gallon that vehicle falls below the standard.

CROPLAND

Areas used for the production of adapted crops for harvest. Two subcategories of cropland are recognized: **cultivated cropland** and **non-cultivated cropland. Cultivated cropland** includes land in row crops or close-grown crops and also other cultivated cropland. (For example, hay land or pastureland that is in a rotation with row or close-grown crops.) **Non-cultivated cropland** includes permanent hay land and horticultural cropland.

CRUDE OIL

A mixture of hydrocarbons that exists in liquid phase in natural underground reservoirs and remains liquid at atmospheric pressure after passing through surface separating facilities. Depending upon the characteristics of the crude stream, it may also include: 1) small amounts of hydrocarbons that exist in gaseous phase in natural underground reservoirs but are liquid at atmospheric pressure after being recovered, or **lease condensate** recovered as a liquid from natural gas wells in lease or field separation facilities and later mixed into the crude stream; 2) small amounts of nonhydrocarbons produced with the oil, such as sulfur and various metals; and 3) drip gases and liquid hydrocarbons produced from tar sands, oil sands, gilsonite, and oil shale. Liquids produced at natural gas processing plants are excluded. Crude oil is refined to produce a wide array of **petroleum products**, including heating oils, **gasoline, diesel fuel** and **jet fuels**, lubricants, asphalt, ethane, **propane**, butane; and many other products used for their energy or chemical content.

CRUDE OIL DOMESTIC FIRST PURCHASE PRICE

The marketed first sales price of domestic crude oil, consistent with the removal price defined by the provisions of the Windfall Profits Tax on Domestic Crude Oil.

CRUDE OIL LANDED COST

The price of crude oil at the port of discharge, including charges associated with purchasing, transporting, and insuring a cargo from the purchase point to the port of discharge. The cost does not include charges incurred at the discharge port (e.g., import tariffs or fees, wharfage charges, and demurrage).

CRUDE OIL REFINERY INPUT

The total crude oil put into processing units at **refineries**.

CRUDE OIL STOCKS

Stocks of **crude oil** and **lease condensate** held at refineries, in petroleum pipelines, at pipeline terminals, and on lease.

CUBIC FOOT

The amount of natural gas contained at standard temperature and pressure (60 degrees Fahrenheit and 14.73 pounds of standard pressure per square inch) in a cube whose edges are one foot long. Used as a standard unit for **natural gas**.

CULTIVATED CROPLAND *see* **CROPLAND**

CURRENT DOLLAR

Dollar value of a good or service in terms of current prices at the time the good or service is sold (i.e., not adjusted for inflation). *See also* **chained dollar**, **current dollar**.

DEADWEIGHT TON

The carrying capacity of a vessel in metric tons (2,240 pounds), measured as the difference between the number of tons of water a vessel displaces when unloaded and the number of tons it displaces when submerged to the load line.

DEEPWATER HABITAT

Permanently flooded land lying below the deepwater boundary of **wetlands**. Deepwater habitats include environments where surface water is permanent and often deep, so that water, rather than air, is the principal medium in which the dominant organisms live, whether or not they are attached to the substrate. Deepwater habitats are not considered wetlands. Deepwater habitats can be classified as:

Estuarine: Deepwater tidal habitats and adjacent tidal wetlands that are usually semi-enclosed by land but have open, partly obstructed, or sporadic access to the open ocean. Ocean water is at least occasionally diluted by freshwater runoff from the land, but evaporation may sometimes cause the salinity level to be higher than that of the open ocean.

Lacustrine: Deepwater habitats with all of the following characteristics: 1) situated in a topographic depression or a dammed river channel; 2) lacking trees, shrubs, persistent emergents, emergent mosses or lichens with greater than 30 percent coverage; 3) total area exceeds 20 acres.

Riverine: Deepwater habitats contained within a channel, with the exception of habitats with water containing ocean-derived salts in excess of 0.5 parts per thousand.

see also **wetlands**.

DEEPWELL INJECTION

A process of disposing of liquid waste in which treated or untreated liquid waste is pumped underground into storage that has no potential to allow chemicals to contaminate local water supplies or other resources. Also known as **underground injection**.

DELAYED FLIGHT

A departure or arrival more than 15 minutes later than its scheduled time.

DEMAND-RESPONSIVE VEHICLE

A nonfixed-route, nonfixed-schedule vehicle that operates in response to calls from passengers or their agents to the transit operator or dispatcher. *Also known as* **paratransit**.

DEVELOPMENT WELL

A well drilled within the proved area of a crude oil or natural gas reservoir to the depth of a stratigraphic horizon known to be productive. *See also **exploratory well**.*

DIESEL FUEL

A fuel composed of **distillate fuel oils** obtained in petroleum refining operations, or blends of such distillate fuel oils with **residual fuel oil** used in motor vehicles. The boiling point and specific gravity are higher for diesel fuels than for gasoline. Diesel is used primarily by heavy-duty road vehicles, construction equipment, locomotives, and by marine and stationary engines.

DIESEL GALLON EQUIVALENT

The amount of a fuel that produces the same amount of energy when consumed as a gallon of diesel fuel.

DIOXIN

One of a family of compounds, known as **polychlorinated dibenzodioxins (PCDDs)**, that are known to cause cancer, reproductive and developmental disorders, and immune system problems, and are known to build up in fatty tissues over time.

DIRECT EMISSIONS

Greenhouse gases that are emitted as a direct result of a process, (e.g., industrial processes or fuel combustion), and not as a by-product of producing the electricity used in that process.

DIRECT USE

Use of electricity that is 1) self-generated, 2) produced by either the same entity that consumes the power or an affiliate, and 3) is used in direct support of a service or industrial process located within the same facility or group of facilities that house the generating equipment. Direct use excludes station use.

DIRECTLY GENERATED FUNDS *see CAPITAL FUNDING*

DISCRETIONARY SPENDING

Spending (budget authority and outlays) controlled in annual appropriations acts. The opposite of **mandatory spending**.

DISTILLATE FUEL OIL

A general classification for one of the petroleum fractions produced in conventional distillation operations, used primarily for space heating, on- and off-highway diesel engine fuel (including railroad engine fuel and fuel for agricultural machinery), and electric power generation. *See also **residual fuel oil**.*

DIVERTED FLIGHT

A flight that takes off from the scheduled airport, but lands at a different airport than was scheduled.

DRY NATURAL GAS

Natural gas which remains after the liquefiable hydrocarbon portion has been removed from the gas stream, and any volumes of nonhydrocarbon gases have been removed where they occur in sufficient quantity to render the gas unmarketable. Also known as consumer-grade natural gas. The parameters for measurement are cubic feet at 60 °F and 14.73 pounds per square inch absolute.

E85

A mixture of 85% **ethanol** and 15% **gasoline**.

E95

A mixture of 95% **ethanol** and 5% **gasoline**.

ELECTRIC POWER PLANT

A station containing prime movers, electric generators, and auxiliary equipment for converting mechanical, chemical, and/or fission energy into electricity.

ELECTRIC POWER SECTOR

An energy-consuming sector that consists of electricity-only and combined heat and power (CHP) plants whose primary business is to sell electricity, or electricity and heat, to the public. Includes electric utilities and independent power producers. *See also **energy-use sectors**.*

ELECTRIC UTILITY

Any firm that generates, transmits, or distributes electricity and that recovers the cost of its generation, transmission or distribution assets and operations (either directly or indirectly) through cost-based rates set by a separate regulatory authority (e.g., state public service commissions), or is owned by a governmental unit or the consumers that the entity serves. Examples include investor-owned entities, public power districts, public utility districts, municipalities, rural electric cooperatives, state and federal agencies, and associations that are part of the aforementioned groups. *See also **electric power sector**.*

ELECTRICAL SYSTEM ENERGY LOSSES

The amount of energy lost during generation, transmission, and distribution of electricity, including plant uses and uses that are unaccounted for.

ELECTRICITY

A form of energy characterized by the presence and motion of elementary charged particles generated by friction, induction, or chemical change. Electric energy is measured in **kilowatt-hours**.

EMERGENT WETLANDS *see **WETLANDS***

EMISSIONS

Gases and particles released into the air as by-products of a natural or artificial process. Of particular interest are emissions of **greenhouse gases** and pollutants by artificial processes such as energy generation.

ENDANGERED SPECIES

An animal or plant species in danger of extinction throughout all or a significant portion of its range. *See also **threatened species**.*

Glossary

END-USE SECTORS

The residential, commercial, industrial, and transportation sectors of the economy. *See also* **energy-use sectors**.

ENERGY

The capacity for doing work as measured by the capability to do work (potential energy) or the conversion of this capability to motion (kinetic energy). Energy has several forms, some of which are easily convertible and can be changed to another form useful for work. Most of the world's convertible energy comes from **fossil fuels** that are burned to produce heat that is then used as a transfer medium to mechanical or other means in order to accomplish tasks. Electric energy is usually measured in **kilowatt-hours**, while heat energy is usually measured in **British thermal units** (abbreviated as **Btu**).

ENERGY CONSUMPTION

The use of energy as a source of heat, power, or as an input in a manufacturing process.

ENERGY EFFICIENCY

The ratio of energy inputs to the outputs from a process; for example, miles traveled per gallon of fuel (mpg). *See also* **energy intensity**.

ENERGY EXPENDITURES

Money spent directly by consumers to purchase energy. Expenditures equal the amount of energy used by the consumer multiplied by the price per unit paid by the consumer.

ENERGY INTENSITY

The ratio of energy inputs to a process to the useful outputs from that process; for example, gallons of fuel per passenger-mile or Btu per ton-mile. *See also* **energy efficiency**.

ENERGY SOURCE

Any substance or natural phenomenon that can be consumed or transformed to supply heat or power. Examples include **petroleum, coal, natural gas, nuclear power, wood, waste, electricity, wind, geothermal power,** sunlight (**solar energy**), water movement (**hydroelectric power**), and hydrogen in fuel cells.

ENERGY-USE SECTORS

A group of major energy-consuming components of US society developed to measure and analyze energy use. The sectors most commonly referred to by the EIA are: **residential, commercial, industrial, transportation,** and **electric power**. (Note: various EIA programs differ in sectoral coverage. For more information see http://www.eia.doe.gov/neic/datadefinitions/Guideforwebcom.htm.)

ENPLANED PASSENGERS

The total number of passengers boarding aircraft, including both originating and connecting passengers.

ENVIRONMENTAL PROTECTION AGENCY (EPA)

The federal government agency in charge of protecting the environment and human health.

EROSION

The wearing away of land surface by running water, waves, moving ice and wind, or by such processes as mass wasting and corrosion. The term "geologic erosion" refers to natural erosion processes occurring over long (geologic) time spans. "Accelerated erosion" refers to erosion that exceeds what is presumed or estimated to be naturally-occurring levels, and which is a direct result of human activities (e.g., cultivation or logging).

ESTUARINE *see* **DEEPWATER HABITATS, WETLANDS**

ETHANOL

A clear, colorless, flammable oxygenated **hydrocarbon** with a boiling point of 78.5 °C in the anhydrous (waterless) state. It is typically produced chemically from ethylene, or biologically from the fermentation of various sugars from carbohydrates found in agricultural crops and cellulosic residues from used crops or wood. Used in the United States as an **alternative fuel**, a gasoline octane enhancer, and an **oxygenate** (10% concentration), ethanol can be used in high concentrations in vehicles optimized for its use. Ethanol is also known as ethyl alcohol, alcohol, or grain-spirit.

EXPLORATORY WELL

A well drilled to find and produce **crude oil** or **natural gas** in an area previously considered unproductive, to find a new reservoir in a known field (i.e., one previously producing crude oil or natural gas in another reservoir), or to extend the limit of a known crude oil or natural gas reservoir. Often drilled as a prelimiary to a **development well**.

EXPORTS

Shipments of goods from within the 50 States and the District of Columbia to US possessions, US territories, or to foreign countries.

FATALITY

Any death caused by and occuring within 30 days of a crash, accident, or transport incident.

FEEDSTOCKS

Generally, a substance used as the raw material in a manufacturing process. For example, feedstocks for the production of **ethanol** include corn and other **biomass** material. Ethanol feedstocks are calculated as fuel ethanol production multiplied by the approximate heat content of the corn and other biomass inputs to the production of fuel ethanol.

FERRY BOAT

A vessel that carries passengers and/or vehicles over a body of water: generally steam or diesel-powered, but may also be a hovercraft, hydrofoil, or other highspeed vessel.

FINANCIAL REPORTING SYSTEM (FRS)

The Energy Information Administration's method of collecting financial and operating information from major energy companies. Companies are selected if they are within the top 50 publicly-owned US crude oil producers that have at least 1% of either production or reserves of crude oil, natural gas, coal, or uranium in the United States, or 1% of either refining capacity or petroleum product sales in the United States.

FINE PARTICLES *see PARTICULATE MATTER*

FIRST PHASE OF OPERATION

In the case of air carrier accidents, the phase of a flight when the problem that eventually caused the accident first appears, regardless of when the accident actually occurred.

FISCAL YEAR

Generally speaking, an accounting system in which the "year" begins and ends on a date other than January 1. The US government's fiscal year runs from October 1 through September 30. The fiscal year is designated by the calendar year in which it ends (e.g., fiscal year 2004 began on October 1, 2003, and ended on September 30, 2004).

FIXED-WING AIRCRAFT

Any aircraft with wings that do not move to generate lift, including piston, turboprop, and turbojet planes, but excluding helicopters and lighter-than-air craft.

FOREST LAND

Land that is at least 10% stocked by single-stemmed woody species of any size that will be at least 4 meters (13 feet) tall at maturity. Also includes land bearing evidence of natural regeneration of tree cover (cut over forest or abandoned farmland) and not currently developed for nonforest use.

FORESTED WETLANDS *see WETLANDS*

FORWARD COSTS

For **uranium**, the operating and capital costs that will be incurred in any future production from in-place reserves. Includes costs for labor, materials, power and fuel, royalties, payroll taxes, insurance, and general administrative costs that are dependent upon the quantity of production and are therefore applicable as variable costs of production. Excludes prior expenditures incurred for property acquisition, exploration, mine development, and mill construction, as well as income taxes and profit. By use of forward costing, estimates of reserves for uranium ore deposits in differing geological settings can be aggregated and reported as the maximum amount that can theoretically be extracted to recover the specified costs of **uranium oxide** production under the listed forward cost categories.

FOSSIL FUEL

Any naturally-occurring fuel formed from decayed organic material in the Earth's crust, such as **petroleum**, **coal**, and **natural gas**.

FREE ON BOARD (FOB) PRICE

Price from the point of first sale, in a sales transaction in which the seller makes the product available for pickup at a specified port or terminal at a specified price and the buyer pays for the subsequent transportation and insurance.

FRINGE BENEFITS *see COMPENSATION*

FUGITIVE AIR EMISSIONS

All releases to air that are not released through a confined air stream (or **stack**), including equipment leaks, evaporative losses from surface impoundments and spills, and releases from building ventilation systems.

FUNCTIONALLY OBSOLETE

Functional obsolescence occurs as a result of differences in design requirements and traffic demands from the time a bridge was built to the present day. Note that a bridge can be structurally sound and still functionally obsolete. *See also **structurally deficient**.*

GASOHOL

A blend of finished **motor gasoline** (leaded or unleaded) and alcohol (generally **ethanol** but sometimes **methanol**) between 5.7% and 10% by volume of alcohol.

GASOLINE

A complex mixture of relatively volatile **hydrocarbons**, with or without small quantities of additives that have been blended to produce a fuel suitable for use in spark ignition engines. Includes both leaded or unleaded grades of finished motor gasoline, blending components, and gasohol. Leaded gasoline is no longer used in highway motor vehicles in the US. *See also **motor gasoline**.*

GASOLINE GALLON-EQUIVALENT (GGE)

The amount of a fuel that produces the same amount of energy when consumed as a gallon of gasoline.

GDP *see **GROSS DOMESTIC PRODUCT***

GENERAL AVIATION

All civil aviation activity except that of air carriers governed under Federal Aviation Regulations (FAR) Parts 121, 123, 127, and 135. Many types of aircraft are used in general aviation, including corporate multiengine jet aircraft piloted by professional crews, amateur-built single-engine acrobatic planes, and balloons and dirigibles.

GEOTHERMAL ENERGY

Hot water or steam extracted from geothermal reservoirs in the Earth's crust and used for geothermal heat pumps, water heating, or electricity generation.

GLOBAL WARMING

An increase in the near-surface temperature of the Earth. Global warming has occurred in the distant past as the result of natural influences, but the term today is most often used to refer to the warming many scientists predict will occur as a result of increased anthropogenic (caused by humans) emissions of **greenhouse gases**. *See also **climate change**.*

GLOBAL WARMING POTENTIAL *see **CARBON DIOXIDE EQUIVALENT***

GRAZING LAND

The combined total of **range land**, **pasture land**, and **forest land** that is used for grazing.

GREENHOUSE EFFECT *see **GREENHOUSE GASES***

GREENHOUSE GASES

Those gases, such as water vapor, **carbon dioxide, nitrous oxide, methane, hydrofluorocarbons (HFCs), perfluorocarbons (PFCs)**, and **sulfur hexafluoride (SF$_6$)**, that are transparent to solar (short-wave) radiation but opaque to long-wave radiation, thus preventing long-wave radiant energy from leaving the Earth's atmosphere. The net effect is a trapping of absorbed radiation and a tendency to warm the planet's surface, and is known as the **greenhouse effect**.

GRID-INTERACTIVE

Power sources that are connected to the electrical distribution system ("the grid"). Sources that are not connected to the grid (such isolated residential sites or mobile homes) are known as **remote**.

GROSS VEHICLE WEIGHT RATING (GWVR)

The maximum rated capacity of a truck, including the weight of the base vehicle, all added equipment, the driver, passengers, and all cargo.

GROSS DOMESTIC PRODUCT

The total output of goods and services produced by labor and property located in the US, valued at market prices. As long as the labor and property are located in the US, the suppliers (workers and owners) may be either US residents or residents of foreign countries. Abbreviated as **GDP**.

HAZARDOUS MATERIAL

Any toxic substance or explosive, corrosive, combustible, poisonous, or radioactive material that poses a risk to the public's health, safety, or property, particularly when transported in commerce. *See also **hazardous waste**.*

HAZARDOUS WASTE

Any waste product with properties that make it dangerous or capable of having a harmful effect on human health or the environment. *See also **hazardous material**.*

HEAVY RAIL

A mode of public transit consisting of an electric railway with the capacity to transport a heavy volume of passenger traffic and characterized by exclusive rights-of-way, multicar trains, high speed, rapid acceleration, sophisticated signaling, and highplatform loading. Also known as a "subway," "elevated (railway)," or "metropolitan railway (metro)."

HIGHLY ERODABLE CROPLAND

Land that is determined to be especially vulnerable to erosion, based on the physical and chemical properties of the soil and climatic conditions where it is located.

HIGHWAY-RAIL GRADE CROSSING

A location at which one or more railroad tracks are crossed by a public highway, public road, public street, or private roadway at grade, including sidewalks and pathways at or associated with the crossing.

HOUSEHOLD

A family, individual, or group of up to nine unrelated persons occupying the same housing unit. In order to be said to "occupy" a housing unit, that unit must be the person's usual or permanent place of residence.

HOUSING UNIT

A house, apartment, group of rooms, or single room if it is either occupied or intended for occupancy as separate living quarters by a family, an individual, or a group of one to nine unrelated persons. In order for a space to constitute seperate living quarters, the occupants must 1) live and eat separately from other persons in the house or apartment, and 2) have direct access from the outside of the buildings or through a common hall (that is, they can get to it without going through someone else's living quarters). Housing units do not include group quarters such as prisons or nursing homes where ten or more unrelated persons live. A common dining area used by residents is an indication of group quarters. Hotel and motel rooms are considered housing units if occupied as the usual or permanent place of residence.

HYDROCARBON

An organic chemical compound of hydrogen and carbon in the gaseous, liquid, or solid phase. The molecular structure of hydrocarbon compounds range from simple (**methane**, a constituent of natural gas) to very heavy and very complex.

HYDROELECTRIC POWER

Production of electricity from the kinetic energy of falling water. Hydroelectric power is classified as **pumped storage** if it is generated during peak load periods by using water previously pumped into an elevated storage, or **conventional hydroelectric power** otherwise.

HYDROFLUOROCARBONS (HFC$_s$)

A group of man-made chemicals composed of one or two carbon atoms and varying numbers of hydrogen and fluorine atoms. Most HFCs have high **global warming potentials**.

IMPORTS

Receipts of goods into the 50 States and the District of Columbia from US possessions, US territories, or from foreign countries.

INCIDENT

Generally, any event involving a collision, derailment, personal casualty, fires, and property damage in excess of $1,000 associated with transit vehicles, trains, or other vehicles. For vehicles transporting hazardous materials, also includes any unintentional release of hazardous material while in transit or storage.

INDIRECT GREENHOUSE GASES

Gases, including **carbon monoxide**, **nitrogen oxides**, **non-methane volatile organic compounds (NMVOCs)**, and **sulfur dioxide**, which do not have a direct global warming effect, but indirectly affect terrestrial radiation absorption by influencing the formation or destruction of ozone.

INDUSTRIAL SECTOR

An energy-consuming sector that consists of all facilities and equipment used for producing, processing, or assembling goods. The industrial sector encompasses manufacturing; agriculture, forestry, fishing and hunting; mining, including oil and gas extraction; and construction. Overall energy use in this sector is largely for process heat and cooling and powering machinery, with lesser amounts used for facility heating, air conditioning, and lighting. **Fossil fuels** are also used as raw material inputs to manufactured products. Note: This sector includes generators that produce electricity and/or useful thermal output primarily to support the above-mentioned industrial activities. *See also **end-use sectors** and **energy-use sectors**.*

INHALABLE COARSE PARTICLES *see PARTICULATE MATTER*

INJURY

Generally, any incident that requires medical attention beyond first aid. The definition and classification of injuries differs based on the type of transportation.

Police-reported highway injuries are classified as follows:

Fatal Injury: Any injury resulting from an accident or crash leading to a death within 30 days.

Incapacitating Injury: Any non-fatal injury that prevents the injured person from walking, driving, or normally continuing the activities the person was capable of performing before. Includes severe lacerations, broken or distorted limbs, skull or chest injuries, abdominal injuries, unconsciousness at or when taken from the accident scene, and inability to leave the accident scene without assistance. Excludes momentary unconsciousness.

Nonincapacitating Evident Injury: Any injury, other than a fatal injury or an incapacitating injury, evident to observers at the scene of the accident. Includes lumps on head, abrasions, bruises, minor lacerations, and others. Excludes limping.

Possible Injury: Any injury reported or claimed that is not evident. Includes momentary unconsciousness, claim of injuries not obvious, limping, complaints of pain, nausea, hysteria, and others.

INTERGOVERNMENTAL PANEL ON CLIMATE CHANGE (IPCC)

A group affiliated with the United Nations comprised by a group of scientists studying the causes, extent, and effects of climate change. The IPCC is the foremost international group studying climate change, creating future projections based on current trends, and making plans for mitigating the effects of increased global temperatures. *See also **climate change**.*

INTERNATIONAL ROUGHNESS INDEX (IRI)

A measurement system used by the Federal Highway Administration to evaluate the condion of pavement. The IRI measures the cumulative deviation from a smooth surface in inches per mile. The IRI is preferred over the **Persent Servicability Rating (PER)** because is is more objective and more accepted worldwide, but is not collected in all cases, so reported data is often a mixture of IRI and PER data.

INTERSTATE HIGHWAY

A limited-access, divided highway of at least four lanes designated by the Federal Highway Administration as part of the Interstate System.

INTERTIDAL WETLANDS *see WETLANDS*

JET FUEL

The term includes kerosene-type jet fuel and naphtha-type jet fuel. **Kerosene-type jet fuel** is used primarily for commercial turbojet and turboprop aircraft engines. **Naphtha-type jet fuel** is used primarily for military turbojet and turboprop aircraft engines.

JITNEY

A transit mode comprised of passenger cars or vans operating on fixed routes (sometimes with minor deviations) as demand warrants without fixed schedules or fixed stops.

KEROSENE

A light petroleum distillate that is used in space heaters, cook stoves, and water heaters and is suitable for use as a light source when burned in wick-fed lamps.

KILOWATT

A unit of electrical power equal to 1,000 **watts**.

KILOWATT-HOUR (KWH)

A measure of electricity defined as a unit of work or energy, measured as 1 **kilowatt** of power expended for 1 hour. One kilowatt-hour is equivalent to 3,412 **Btu**.

LACUSTRINE *see **DEEPWATER HABITATS***

LANE-MILE

The total traveling length of roads, calculated by multiplying the length of a road by the number of lanes.

LARGE REGIONAL AIR CARRIER

An air carrier group with annual operating revenues between $20 million and $100 million.

LARGE TRUCK

Trucks with a **gross vehicle weight rating** over 10,000 pounds. Includes single-unit trucks and truck tractors.

LEASE CONDENSATE

A mixture consisting primarily of pentanes and heavier **hydrocarbons**, which are recovered as a liquid from **natural gas** in lease or field separation facilities. Does not include natural gas liquids, such as butane and propane, which are recovered at natural gas processing plants or facilities.

LIGHT RAIL

A streetcar-type vehicle operated on city streets, exclusive rights-of-way, or semi-exclusive rights-of-way. Service may be provided by step-entry vehicles or by level boarding.

LIGHT TRUCK

Trucks with a **gross vehicle weight rating** of less than10,000 pounds. Includes pickups, vans, truck-based station wagons, and sport utility vehicles.

LIPID LEVELS

A measure of chemical exposure. Many chemicals (including pollutants like DDT) are stored in fatty tissues, and exposure is measured by the amount found in people's fatty tissues (as opposed to the amount found in the blood). *See also **serum***.

LIQUEFIED NATURAL GAS

Natural gas, primarily **methane**, that has been converted to liquid by reducing its temperature to -260 °F at atmospheric pressure.

LIQUEFIED PETROLEUM GAS

Propane, propylene, normal butane, butylene, isobutane, and isobutylene produced at refineries or natural gas processing plants, including plants that fractionate new **natural gas plant liquids**.

LONG TON *see* **METRIC TON**

LOSSES AND COPRODUCTS

Energy lost in a manufacturing process. For example, **ethanol** losses and coproducts are calculated as ethanol **feedstocks** minus fuel ethanol production.

M85

A mixture of 85% **methanol** and 15% **gasoline**.

M100

A fuel consisting of pure **methanol**.

MACROINVERTEBRATE INDEX

An index created to evaluate the biological health of streams using several indicators: taxonomic richness, composition, biological diversity, and sensitivity to human influence and pollution.

MAJOR AIR CARRIER

An air carrier group with annual operating revenues exceeding $1 billion.

MAJOR US ENERGY COMPANIES

Top publicly-owned, US-based crude oil and natural gas producers and petroleum refiners that form the **Financial Reporting System**.

MANDATORY SPENDING

Spending (budget authority and outlays) controlled by laws other than annual appropriations acts. The opposite of **discretionary spending**.

MARINE WETLANDS *see* **WETLANDS**

MASS TRANSIT *see* **PUBLIC TRANSPORTATION**

MAXIMUM CONTAMINANT LEVEL (MCL)

The highest level of a contaminant that is allowed in drinking water. MCL standards are set and enforced by the **EPA**.

MEDIUM REGIONAL AIR CARRIER

An air carrier group with annual operating revenues less than $20 million.

MEGAWATT

A common measurement of electric power, equal to one million **watts**.

METHANE

A colorless, flammable, odorless hydrocarbon gas (CH_4), which is the major component of **natural gas**. It is also an important source of hydrogen in various industrial processes.

METHANOL

A light, volatile alcohol (CH_3OH) produced commercially by the catalyzed reaction of hydrogen and **carbon monoxide**. It is blended with gasoline to improve its operational efficiency. *See also* **oxygenates**.

METHYL TERTIARY BUTYL ETHER

A colorless, flammable, liquid oxygenated hydrocarbon that contains 18.15% oxygen. It is a fuel **oxygenate** produced by reacting methanol with isobutylene.

METRIC TON

A unit of weight cooresponding to approximately 2,200 pounds (1,000 kilograms). Also called a **long ton**.

METROPOLITAN AREA

In general, a population concentration of at least 50,000 inhabitants, generally consisting of a central city with a dense population and a surrounding area whose economy is closely linked to the city. The US Office of Budget and Management (OMB) designates which areas are considered metropolitan. The definitions are frequently altered and updated to reflect changes in the population. The most recent definition, **Core-Based Statistical Area (CBSA)**, was adopted in June of 2003. Past categories used the the OMB are **Metropolitan and Micropolitan area, Consolidated Metropolitan Statistical Area (CMSA), Metropolitan Statistical Area (MSA), Primary Metropolitan Statistical Area (PMSA)**, and **Standard Metropolitan Statistical Area (SMSA)**. Data referring to metropolitan or non-metropolitan areas uses the definition that was in effect at the time the data was published.

MINOR ARTERIAL

A street or highway linking cities and larger towns in rural areas, and distributing trips to small geographic areas in urban areas (but not penetrating identifiable neighborhoods).

MONITORING/REPORTING

The process of monitoring drinking water's contaminant levels, and reporting any violations to the EPA.

MOTOR GASOLINE

A complex mixture of relatively volatile hydrocarbons with or without small quantities of additives, blended to form a fuel suitable for use in spark ignition. Motor gasoline is characterized as having a boiling range from 122–158 °F at the 10% recovery point to 365–374 °F at the 90% recovery point. Includes conventional motor gasoline, all types of **oxygenated** gasoline including **gasohol**, and reformulated gasoline, but excludes aviation gasoline.

Gasoline is classified in to several different grades, according to **octane rating** (also known as the **anti-knock index**). **Regular gasoline** has an octane rating greater than or equal to 85 and less than 88. **Midgrade gasoline** has an octane rating greater than or equal to 88 and less than 90. **Premium gasoline** has an octane rating greater than 90. Note that octane requirements can be lower at high altitudes, so in some regions (such as the Rocky Mountain states), octane rating requirements may be 2 or more octane points lower.

Gasoline can also be **oxygenated** or **reformulated**. **Oxygenated** gasoline contains at least 2.7% oxygen by weight, and is required by the EPA to be sold in areas designated as **carbon monoxide (CO)** nonattainment areas. **Reformulated** gasoline includes Oxygenated Fuels Program Reformulated Gasoline (OPRG), but excludes Reformulated Gasoline Blendstock for Oxygenate Blending (RBOB). Both can be formulated in regular, midgrade, and premium grades.

MOTOR GASOLINE BLENDING

Mechanical mixing of motor gasoline blending components and **oxygenates** as required, to produce finished motor gasoline. Finished motor gasoline may be further mixed with other motor gasoline blending components or oxygenates, resulting in increased volumes of finished motor gasoline and/or changes in the formulation of finished motor gasoline (e.g., conventional motor gasoline is mixed with **MTBE** to produce oxygenated motor gasoline).

MOTORCYCLE

A two or three-wheeled motor vehicle designed to transport one or two people, including motor scooters, minibikes, and mopeds.

MTBE *see METHYL TERTIARY BUTYL ETHER*

MUNICIPAL SOLID WASTE (MSW)

Total waste from residential, commercial, institutional, and industrial sources, excluding industrial waste, agricultural waste, and sewage sludge. MSW is divided into catrgories of durable goods, non-durable goods, containers and packaging, food wastes, yard wastes, and miscellaneous inorganic wastes. Examples include appliances, newspapers, clothing, food scraps, and boxes. Municipal solid waste is often used in the generation of **waste energy**. Also known as "trash" or "garbage."

MUNICIPAL SOLID WASTE ENERGY

Energy derived from recovery of **municipal solid waste** products, which can include paper and paper board, wood, food, leather, textiles and yard trimmings.

N$_2$O *see NITROUS OXIDE*

NAICS *see NORTH AMERICAN INDUSTRY CLASSIFICATION SYSTEM*

NAPHTHA

A generic term applied to a **petroleum** fraction with an approximate boiling range between 122 and 400 °F.

NATIONAL AIR CARRIER

An air carrier group with annual operating revenues between $100 million and $1 billion.

NATIONAL EMISSIONS INVENTORY (NEI) *see CLEARINGHOUSE FOR INVENTORIES & EMISSIONS FACTORS*

NATIONAL PRIORITIES LIST (NPL)

A list of known or threatened releases of hazardous substances, pollutants, or contaminants throughout the United States and its territories, intended primarily to guide the EPA in determining which sites warrant further investigation. *See also* **Superfund**.

NATURAL GAS

A naturally-occurring mixture of hydrocarbon and nonhydrocarbon gases found in porous geologic formations beneath the Earth's surface, often in association with **petroleum**. The principal constituent is **methane**.

NATURAL GAS LIQUIDS

A general term for all liquid products separated from natural gas in gas processing or cycling plants. They include **natural gas plant liquids** and **lease condensate**.

NATURAL GAS PLANT LIQUIDS

Liquids recovered from **natural gas** in processing plants or field facilities, or extracted by fractionators. They include ethane, propane, normal butane, isobutane, pentanes plus, and other products, such as finished motor gasoline, finished aviation gasoline, special naphthas, kerosene, and distillate fuel oil produced at natural gas processing plants.

NATURAL GAS PIPELINE

A continuous pipe conduit, complete with such equipment as valves, compressor stations, communications systems, and meters, for transporting natural gas and/or supplemental gaseous fuels from one point to another, usually from a point in or beyond the producing field or processing plant to another pipeline or to points of utilization. Also refers to a company operating such facilities.

NAVIGABLE CHANNELS

An estimate of all domestic waterways, including rivers, bays, channels, and the inner route of the Southeast Alaskan Islands, but excluding the Great Lakes or deep ocean traffic, originating from a 1950s US Army Corps of Engineers estimate. The Corps estimated that there were approximately 25,000 miles of commercially important navigable channels in the United States.

NET GENERATION

The amount of gross electricity generation minus station use (the electric energy consumed at generating stations for station service or auxiliaries).

NET IMPORTS

Total imports minus total exports.

NET INCOME

Revenues minus expenses.

NET SUMMER CAPACITY

The maximum output, commonly expressed in **megawatts (MW)**, that generating equipment can supply to system load, as demonstrated by a multi-hour test, at the time of summer peak demand (from June 1 through September 30). This output reflects a reduction in capacity due to electricity use for station service or auxiliaries.

NHTSA – *NATIONAL HIGHWAY TRANSPORTATION SAFETY ADMINISTRATION* (abbreviation)

NITROGEN OXIDES (NO$_x$)

Compounds of nitrogen and oxygen produced by the burning of fossil fuels. Most NO$_x$ gas occurs as nitrogen dioxide (NO$_2$). Nitrogen oxides are **indirect greenhouse gases**.

NITROUS OXIDE (N$_2$O)

A naturally occurring greenhouse gas produced by biological processes that occur in soil and water and by a variety of agricultural, energy-related, industrial, and waste management activities. While emissions are much lower than **carbon dioxide**, N$_2$O is approximately 300 times more powerful than CO$_2$ at trapping heat in the atmosphere.

NON-METHANE VOLATILE ORGANIC COMPUNDS (NMVOCS)

Chemicals from the group of **volatile organic compounds**, excluding **methane (CH$_3$)**.

NONSCHEDULED SERVICE

For air carriers, flights not operated as regular scheduled service, such as charter flights.

NON-TRANSIENT NON-COMMUNITY WATER SYSTEM (NTNCWS)

Public water systems that regularly supply water to at least 25 of the same people at least 6 months of the year, but not year-round. Examples include schools, factories, and office buildings.

NORTH AMERICAN INDUSTRY CLASSIFICATION SYSTEM (NAICS)

A coding system developed jointly by the United States, Canada, and Mexico to classify businesses and industries according to the type of economic activity in which they are engaged, replacing the Standard Industrial Classification (SIC) codes.

NOS – NOT OTHERWISE SPECIFIED (abbreviation)

NUCLEAR ELECTRIC POWER

Electricity generated by the use of the thermal energy released from the fission of nuclear fuel in a reactor.

NUCLEAR ELECTRIC POWER PLANT

A single-unit or multi-unit facility in which heat produced in one or more reactors by the fissioning of nuclear fuel is used to drive one or more steam turbines.

NUCLEAR REACTOR

An apparatus in which a nuclear fission chain reaction can be initiated, controlled, and sustained at a specific rate. A reactor includes fuel (fissionable material), moderating material to control the rate of fission, a heavy-walled pressure vessel to house reactor components, shielding to protect personnel, a system to conduct heat away from the reactor, and instruments to monitor and control the reactor's systems.

OCTANE RATING

A rating of a gasoline's autoignition reistance, measured in terms of the ratio of octane to other materials, and used to determine the grade of a gasoline. Also known as the **anti-knock index**.

OECD *see ORGANIZATION FOR ECONOMIC COOPERATION AND DEVELOPMENT*

OFFSHORE

The geographic area that lies seaward of the coastline. In general, the coastline is the line of ordinary low water along with the portion of the coast that is in direct contact with the open sea or the line marking the seaward limit of inland water. If a state agency uses a different basis for classifying onshore and offshore areas, the state classification is used (e.g., Cook Inlet in Alaska is classified as offshore and in Louisiana, the coastline is defined as the Chapman Line, as modified by subsequent adjudication).

OIL SANDS

A mixture of sand or clay, water, and extremely heavy **crude oil**. Also known as **tar sands**.

OPEC *see ORGANIZATION OF THE PETROLEUM EXPORTING COUNTRIES*

OPERABLE NUCLEAR UNIT

In the United States, a nuclear generating unit that has completed low-power testing and possesses a full-power operating license issued by the Nuclear Regulatory Commission.

OPERABLE REFINERIES

Refineries that were in one of the following three categories at the beginning of a given year: 1) in operation; 2) not in operation and not under active repair, but capable of being placed into operation within 30 days; or 3) not in operation, but under active repair that can be completed within 90 days.

OPERATING EMPLOYEE

An employee engaged directly in the operation of a public transit system.

OPERATING EXPENSES

The total expenses associated with operation of an individual transit carrier. Although the definition differs slightly according to the mode of transit, operating expenses generally include expenditures for equipment maintenance, supervision, wages, fuel, equipment rental, terminal operations, insurance, safety, and administrative and general functions.

OPERATING FUNIDING

Any source of funds used to pay for **operating expenses**.

OPERATING INCOME

Operating revenues minus operating expenses. Excludes items of other revenue and expense, such as equity in earnings of unconsolidated affiliates, dividends, interest income and expense, income taxes, extraordinary items, and the cumulative effect of accounting changes.

ORGANIZATION FOR ECONOMIC COOPERATION AND DEVELOPMENT (OECD)

An international organization that assists governments in dealing with the economic, social and governance challenges that may arrise as a result of a globalized economy. Its membership comprises about 30 member countries, with active relationships with some 70 other countries, and many nongovernmental organizations (NGOs). For details about the organization, see www.oecd.org.

Glossary

ORGANIZATION OF THE PETROLEUM EXPORTING COUNTRIES (OPEC)

An organization founded in Baghdad, Iraq, in September 1960, to unify and coordinate member nations' petroleum policies. OPEC members' national oil ministers meet regularly to discuss prices and, since 1982, to set crude oil production quotas. Original OPEC members include Iran, Iraq, Kuwait, Saudi Arabia, and Venezuela. Between 1960 and 1975, the organization expanded to include Qatar (1961), Indonesia (1962), Libya (1962), the United Arab Emirates (1967), Algeria (1969), Nigeria (1971), Ecuador (1973), and Gabon (1975). Gabon withdrew in January 1995. Angola joined OPEC on January 1, 2007, and so is not yet included in some data for OPEC countries. Ecquador suspended its membership from December 1992 to October 2007, so some data may not include it. Although Iraq remains a member of OPEC, Iraqi production has not been a part of any OPEC quota agreements since March 1998. Abbreviated as **OPEC**. For more information, go to OPEC's website at: http://www.opec.org/aboutus/history/history.htm.

OUTLAYS

Outlays are payments made (in this case, by a government agency) to liquidate obligations. Outlays during a fiscal year may be for payment of obligations incurred in prior years or in the same year. *See also* **appropriations**.

OXYGENATE

Any substance that, when added to **motor gasoline**, increases the amount of oxygen in that gasoline blend. Includes oxygen-bearing compounds such as **ethanol, methanol,** and **methyl tertiary butyl ether**. Oxygenated fuel tends to give a more complete combustion of carbon into **carbon dioxide** (rather than **carbon monoxide**), thereby reducing air pollution from exhaust emissions.

PARATRANSIT *see DEMAND-RESPONSIVE VEHICLE*

PARTICULATE MATTER

A mixture of extremely small particles and liquid droplets, tracked as a pollutant by the EPA, and made up of a number of components, including acids (such as nitrates and sulfates), organic chemicals, metals, and soil or dust particles. The EPA is concerned about particles that are 10 micrometers in diameter or smaller because those are the particles that generally pass through the throat and nose and enter the lungs, and can then cause serious problems with the heart and lungs. Particulate matter is divided into two categories:

Inhalable coarse particles (also called PM-10), such as those found near roadways and dusty industries, are larger than 2.5 micrometers and smaller than 10 micrometers in diameter.

Fine particles (also called PM-2.5), such as those found in smoke and haze, are 2.5 micrometers in diameter and smaller. These particles can be directly emitted from sources such as forest fires, or they can form when gases emitted from power plants, industries and automobiles react in the air. Most **condensibles** fall into this category.

PASSENGER-MILE

Total distance traveled obtained by multiplying the number of passengers in a vehicle by the distance traveled by the vehicle. For example, a car containing 4 passengers and traveling 5 miles results in 20 total passenger-miles.

PASSENGER REVENUE

Revenue from the sale of tickets and other spending by passengers (e.g., transfer, zone, and park-and-ride parking charges paid by transit passengers).

PASTURE LAND

Land managed primarily for the production of introduced forage plants for livestock grazing, including land that has a vegetative cover of grasses, legumes, and/or forbs, regardless of whether or not it is being grazed by livestock.

PEAK PERIOD

The times of day when traffic volume is the highest and congestion is heaviest, usually from 6:00–9:00 AM and 4:00–7:00 PM.

PEAK WATT

A manufacturer's unit indicating the amount of power a **photovoltaic cell** or **module** will produce at standard test conditions (normally 1,000 watts of solar energy input per square meter and 25 degrees Celsius). A **peak kilowatt** is 1,000 peak watts.

PERFLUOROCARBONS (PFCs)

A group of manufactured chemicals composed of one or two carbon atoms and four to six flourine atoms, containing no chlorine. PFCs have no commercial uses and are emitted as a by-product of aluminum smelting and semiconductor manufacturing. PFCs have high **global warming potentials** and are very long-lived in the atmosphere.

PETROLEUM

A generic term applied to **oil** and oil products in all forms, such as **crude oil, lease condensate, unfinished oils, petroleum products, natural gas plant liquids**, and nonhydrocarbon compounds blended into finished petroleum products.

PETROLEUM PIPELINE

Crude oil and product pipelines used to transport **crude oil** and **petroleum products**, respectively (including interstate, intrastate, and intracompany pipelines), within the 50 States and the District of Columbia.

PHOTOVOLTAIC CELL *see PHOTOVOLTAIC MODULE*

PHOTOVOLTAIC ENERGY

Direct-current electricity generated from sunlight through solid-state semiconductor devices that have no moving parts.

PHOTOVOLTAIC MODULE

An integrated assembly of interconnected **photovoltaic cells** designed to deliver a selected level of working voltage and current at its output terminals, packaged for protection against environmental degradation, and suited for incorporation in photovoltaic power systems.

PIPELINE

A pipe through which goods, most commonly liquids and gases, are sent. Most pipeline transport involves **crude oil**, other **petroleum products**, or **natural gas**.

PM-2.5 *see* **PARTICULATE MATTER**

PM-10 *see* **PARTICULATE MATTER**

POST-CONSUMER WASTE

Material that has been used for its intended purpose and then separated from solid waste, usually for the purpose of recycling.

POTW

Publicly Owned Treatment Works for the processing of waste metals.

PRESENT SERVICABILITY RATING (PER)

A measurement system used by the Federal Highway Administration to evaluate the condion of pavement, based on a subjective scale ranging from 1 to 5. In many cases, the **International Roughness Index (IRI)** is preferred over the PER, but is not always collected, so data reported is often a mixture of IRI and PER data.

PREVALENCE

The proportion of the total population with a specified condition.

PRIMARY ENERGY CONSUMPTION

Coal consumption; coal coke net imports; petroleum consumption (petroleum products supplied, including natural gas plant liquids and crude oil burned as fuel, but excluding ethanol blended into motor gasoline); natural gas consumption (excluding supplemental gaseous fuels); nuclear electricity net generation (converted to Btu using the nuclear plants heat rate); conventional hydroelectricity net generation (converted to Btu using the fossil-fueled plants heat rate); geothermal electricity net generation (converted to Btu using the geothermal plants heat rate), and geothermal heat pump and geothermal direct-use energy; solar thermal and photovoltaic electricity net generation (converted to Btu using the fossil-fueled plants heat rate), and solar thermal direct-use energy; wind electricity net generation (converted to Btu using the fossil-fueled plants heat rate); wood and wood-derived fuels consumption; biomass waste (municipal solid waste from biogenic sources, landfill gas, sludge waste, agricultural byproducts, and other biomass) consumption; fuel ethanol and biodiesel consumption; losses and co-products from the production of fuel ethanol and biodiesel; and electricity net imports (converted to Btu using the electricity heat content of 3,412 Btu per kilowatt-hour). *See also **conventional hydroelectric power, geothermal gnergy, nuclear electric power, photovoltaic energy, solar thermal energy, waste wnergy, wind energy, wood energy.***

PRIMARY ENERGY PRODUCTION

Coal production, waste coal supplied, and coal refuse recovery; crude oil and lease condensate production; natural gas plant liquids production; natural gas (dry) production; nuclear electricity net generation (converted to Btu using the nuclear plants heat rate); conventional hydroelectricity net generation (converted to Btu using the fossil-fueled plants heat rate); geothermal electricity net generation (converted to Btu using the geothermal plants heat rate), geothermal heat pump energy, and geothermal direct-use energy; solar thermal and photovoltaic electricity net generation (converted to Btu using the fossil-fueled plants heat rate), and solar thermal direct-use energy; wind electricity net generation (converted to Btu using the fossil-fueled plants heat rate); wood and wood-derived fuels consumption; biomass waste (municipal solid waste from biogenic sources, landfill gas, sludge waste, agricultural byproducts, and other biomass) consumption; and biofuels feedstock (biomass inputs to the production of fuel ethanol and biodiesel). *See also* **conventional hydroelectric power, geothermal energy, nuclear electric power, photovoltaic energy, solar thermal energy, waste energy, wind energy, wood energy.**

PRIMARY PETROLEUM STOCKS

For individual petroleum products, quantities that are held at refineries, in petroleum pipelines, and at bulk terminals that have a capacity of 50,000 barrels or more, or that are in transit thereto. Stocks held by product retailers and resellers, as well as tertiary stocks held at the point of consumption, are excluded. Stocks of individual products held at gas processing plants are excluded from individual product estimates, but are included in other oil estimates and totals.

PROPERTY DAMAGE

For transit vehicles, the dollar amount required to repair or replace transit property (including stations, right of way, bus stops, and maintenance facilities) damaged during an incident.

PROFITABILITY

The return on investment in a company, measured as net income divided by the net investment in place.

PROPANE

A normally gaseous straight-chain hydrocarbon (C_3H_8). It is a colorless paraffinic gas that boils at a temperature of -43.67 °F. It is extracted from natural gas or refinery gas streams.

PROVED RESERVES

The estimated quantities of **crude oil** or **natural gas** that geological and engineering data demonstrate with reasonable certainty to be recoverable in future years from known reservoirs under existing economic and operating conditions.

PUBLIC TRANSPORTATION

Any transportation system in which the passengers do not travel in their own vehicles, including **buses, subways, rail, trolleys, ferryboats, paratransit, vanpools,** and taxi services operated under contract to a public transportation agency.

RADIONUCLIDES

Atoms with unstable nuclei, which undergo radioactive decay and emit radiation.

RECOVERY

The removal of materials from the total amount of municipal solid waste generated, usually for the purposes of **recycling** or combustion.

RANGE LAND

Land on which the potential plant cover is composed principally of native grasses, grasslike plants, forbs, or shrubs suitable for grazing and browsing, and introduced forage species that are managed like rangeland. Includes areas where introduced hardy and persistent grasses are planted and such practices as deferred grazing, burning, chaining, and rotational grazing are used, with very little fertilizer or other chemicals applied.

RECOVERABLE RESOURCES

Resources that are producible using current technology without reference to the economic viability of doing so.

REFINERY

An installation that manufactures finished **petroleum products** from **crude oil**, unfinished oils, **natural gas liquids**, other hydrocarbons, and alcohol.

REGIONAL AIR CARRIER

An air carrier group with annual revenues under $100 million.

RENEWABLE ENERGY

Energy obtained from sources that are essentially inexhaustible (unlike, for example, **fossil fuels**, which are in finite supply). Renewable sources of energy include **conventional hydroelectric power, wood energy, waste energy, alcohol fuels, geothermal energy, solar energy,** and **windenergy**.

RESIDENTIAL SECTOR

An energy-consuming sector that consists of living quarters for private households. Common uses of energy associated with this sector include space heating, water heating, air conditioning, lighting, refrigeration, cooking, and running a variety of other appliances. The residential sector excludes institutional living quarters. *See also **end-use sectors** and **energy-use sectors**.*

RESIDUAL FUEL OIL

The heavier oils that remain after the **distillate fuel oils** and lighter hydrocarbons are distilled away in refinery operations. Includes Navy Special oil used in steam-powered vessels in government service and No. 6 oil used to power ships. Imports of residual fuel oil include imported crude oil burned as fuel.

RESOURCE CONSERVATION AND RECOVERY ACT (RCRA)

Waste management program, run by the EPA, created to protect human health and the environment from the potential hazards of waste disposal, conserve energy and natural resources, reduce the amount of waste generated, and ensure that wastes are managed in an environmentally sound manner.

RETAIL SALES (ELECTRICITY)

The amount of electricity sold by **electric utilities** and other energy service providers to customers purchasing electricity for their own use and not for resale. These sales are usually grouped by classes of service, such as **residential, commercial, industrial,** and "other," which includes sales for public street and highway lighting and other sales to public authorities and railways, as well as interdepartmental sales.

REVENUE

Remuneration received by carriers for transportation activities.

REVENUE VEHICLE-MILES

Total mileage traveled by transit vehicles while revenue passengers are on board, in scheduled or unscheduled revenue-producing services.

RESEARCH OCTANE NUMBER *see OCTANE RATING*

RIPARIAN DISTURBANCE

A measure of the evidence of human activities in and alongside streams, such as dams, roadways, pastureland, and trash.

RIPARIAN VEGETATIVE COVER

Vegetation corridor alongside streams and rivers. Intact riparian vegetative cover reduces pollution runoff, prevents streambank erosion, and provides shade, lower temperatures, food, and habitat for fish and other aquatic organisms.

RIVERINE *see DEEPWATER HABITATS*

RURAL HIGHWAY

Any highway that is not an **urban highway**.

SALARIES AND WAGES *see COMPENSATION*

SCHEDULED SERVICE

Air transport service operated pursuant to published flight schedules.

SECONDHAND SMOKING

The exposure of nonsmokers to the dangerous chemicals contained in tobacco smoke. Also known as **passive smoking**.

SEQUESTRATION

The net removal (storage) of carbon by a **carbon sink**.

SERUM LEVELS

In the context of exposure to chemicals, "serum" refers to concentrations found in the blood. *See also lipid levels*.

SF$_6$ *see SULFUR HEXAFLUORIDE*

SHALE OIL

A synthetic petroleum dervied from oil shale, a fine-grained sedimentary rock from which liquid hydrocarbons can be manufactured. Deposits of oil shale are located around the world, with major deposits in the United States.

SHORT TON *see TON*

SHRUB WETLANDS *see WETLANDS*

SINK *see CARBON SINK, SEQUESTRATION*

SO$_2$ *see SULFUR DIOXIDE*

SOIL LOSS TOLERANCE FACTOR

The maximum rate of annual soil loss that will permit crop productivity to be sustained economically and indefinitely on a given soil.

Glossary

SOLAR THERMAL COLLECTOR

A device designed to receive solar radiation and convert it to thermal energy. Normally, a solar thermal collector includes a frame, glazing, and an absorber, together with appropriate insulation. The heat collected by the solar thermal collector may be used immediately or stored for later use. Solar collectors are used for space heating, domestic hot water heating, and heating swimming pools, hot tubs, or spas.

SOLAR THERMAL ENERGY

The radiant energy of the sun that can be converted into other forms of energy, such as heat or electricity.

SPACE HEATING

The use of energy to generate heat for warmth in housing units using space-heating equipment. Does not include the use of energy to operate appliances (such as lights, televisions, and refrigerators) that give off heat as a by-product.

STACK AIR EMISSIONS

Emissions through confined air streams such as stack, vents, ducts, or pipes. Also called **point source** emissions. All other air emissions are **fugitive air emissions**.

STAGE I DISINFECTANTS

Disinfectants containing chlorine dioxide (ClO_2) used in surface water systems. The by-products of these disinfectants can be toxic.

STOCKS

Inventories of fuel stored for future use.

STRATEGIC PETROLEUM RESERVE

Petroleum stocks maintained by the Federal Government for use during periods of major supply interruption.

STREAMBED SEDIMENTS

Fine sediments and silt on the streambed. In excess quantities, they can fill the habitat spaces between stream pebbles, cobbles, and boulders, and suffocate macroinvertebrates and fish eggs.

STRUCTURALLY DEFICIENT

Bridges are considered structurally deficient if significant load-carrying elements are in poor or worse condition due to deterioration and/or damage, or the adequacy of the waterway opening provided by the bridge is determined to be extremely insufficient to the point of causing intolerable traffic interruptions. Determinations of deficiency are based on condition ratings and structural assessments, and differ from determinations of **functional obsolescence**.

SUBTIDAL WETLANDS *see* **WETLANDS**

SULFUR DIOXIDE (SO$_2$)

A toxic, irritating, colorless gas soluble in water, alcohol, and ether. Used as a chemical intermediate, in paper pulping and ore refining, and as a solvent. Sulfur dioxide is an **indirect**

greenhouse gas, has also been implicated in the formation of acid rain, and is one of the pollutants tracked in the **Air Quality Index (AQI)**.

SULFUR HEXAFLUORIDE (SF₆)

A colorless gas soluble in alcohol and ether, and slightly less soluble in water. It is used in electronics and possesses the highest **global warming potential** of any gas (23,900).

SUPERFUND

An environmental program established to address abandoned hazardous waste sites.

SURFACE WATER TREATMENT RULE

Law effective December 31, 1990, applying to all systems that use surface water or groundwater under the direct influence of surface water. The Rule established drinking water **treatment techniques** in lieu of **maximum contaminant levels** for Giardia lamblia, viruses, heterotrophic plate count bacteria, Legionella, and **turbidity**.

TANKER

An oceangoing ship designed to haul liquid bulk cargo in world trade.

TAR SANDS *see OIL SANDS*

THIRD RAIL

A method of powering **public transportation** vehicles with electricity.

THREATENED SPECIES

An animal or plant species likely to become **endangered** within the foreseeable future throughout all or a significant portion of its range.

THROUGHPUT

The output of a refinery (or, more generally, of a process).

TON

A unit of weight corresponding to 2,000 pounds. Also called a **short ton**.

TON-MILE

The movement of one ton of cargo the distance of one mile. Ton-miles are calculated by multiplying the weight in tons of each shipment transported by the miles hauled.

TOTAL COLIFORM RULE *see COLIFORM*

TOXICS RELEASE INVENTORY (TRI)

An EPA program, established in 1972, that collects information on the disposal or other releases and other waste management activities for over 650 chemicals from industrial sources in all 50 states, the District of Columbia, and US territories.

TRANSIENT NON-COMMUNITY WATER SYSTEMS (TNCWS)

Public water systems that provide water to places such as gas stations or campgrounds where people do not remain for long periods of time.

TRANSPORTATION SECTOR

An energy-consuming sector that consists of all vehicles whose primary purpose is transporting people and/or goods from one physical location to another. Included are automobiles; trucks; buses; motorcycles; trains, subways, and other rail vehicles; aircraft; and ships, barges, and other waterborne vehicles. Vehicles whose primary purpose is not transportation (e.g., construction cranes and bulldozers, farming vehicles, and warehouse tractors and forklifts) are classified in the sector of their primary use. *See also **end-use sectors** and **energy-use sectors**.*

TRAVEL TIME INDEX

The ratio of travel time during the **peak period** to travel time under free-flowing (normal) conditions. Used as a measure of traffic congestion.

TREATMENT TECHNIQUE

A required process intended to reduce the level of a contaminant in drinking water. For EPA violations, this indicates that some sort of treatment must be carried out to reduce a contaminant level.

TREND SITE

An air quality monitoring site that has provided complete data for at least eight of the last ten years. Used in tracking the **Air Quality Index (AQI)**.

TROLLEY BUS

Rubber-tired electric transit vehicle, manually steered and propelled by a motor drawing current, normally through overhead wires, from a central power source.

TURBIDITY

A measure of the cloudiness of water. Along with **coliform** information, turbidity can be used to indicate possible bacterial contamination.

UNCONVENTIONAL DEPOSITS

Oil deposits that are geographically extensive and generally lack well-defined hydrocarbon/water contacts.

UNCULTIVATED CROPLAND *see* **CROPLAND**

UNDERGROUND INJECTION *see* **DEEPWELL INJECTION**

UNLINKED PASSENGER TRIPS

The number of passengers who board public transportation vehicles. A passenger is counted each time he or she boards a vehicle even if on the same journey from origin to destination.

URANIUM

A heavy, naturally-radioactive, metallic element, with atomic number 92. Its two principally-occurring isotopes are uranium-235 and uranium-238. Uranium-235 is indispensable to the nuclear industry because it is the only naturally-occurring isotope that is fissionable to any appreciable extent by thermal neutrons. Uranium-238 is also important because it absorbs neutrons to produce a radioactive isotope that subsequently decays to the isotope plutonium-239, which also is fissionable by thermal neutrons.

Uranium is a key element in the generation of **nuclear power**, and is found in several forms:

Uranium Ore: Rock containing uranium mineralization in concentrations that can be mined economically, typically one to four pounds of U_3O_8 per ton or 0.05% to 0.2% U_3O_8. Can be refined into **uranium oxide**.

Uranium Oxide: A yellow or brown powder obtained by the milling of uranium ore, processing of in situ leach mining solutions, or as a byproduct of phosphoric acid production. Also called **uranium concentrate**, and abbreviated as U_3O_8.

Yellowcake: A natural uranium concentrate that takes its name from its color and texture. Yellowcake typically contains 70 to 90 percent U_3O_8 (uranium oxide) by weight. It is used as feedstock for uranium fuel enrichment and fuel pellet fabrication.

URBAN HIGHWAY

Any road or street within the boundaries of an urban area. An urban area is an area including and adjacent to a municipality or urban place with a population of 50,000 or more. The boundaries of urban areas are fixed by state highway departments, subject to the approval of the Federal Highway Administration, for purposes of the Federal-Aid Highway Program. *See also* **highway, rural highway.**

UTILIZATION

The ratio of a refinery's gross distillation input to its annual average capacity.

VANPOOL

Public transit service operating under prearranged schedules for previously-formed groups of riders in 8 to 18-seat vehicles. Drivers are also commuters who receive little or no compensation besides the free ride.

VEHICLE MAINTENANCE

All activities associated with revenue and nonrevenue (service) vehicle maintenance, including administration, inspection and maintenance, and servicing (cleaning, fueling, etc.) of vehicles. In addition, it includes repairs due to vandalism or to revenue vehicle accidents.

VEHICLE-MILES

Miles of travel by all types of motor vehicles on highways, as determined by states on the basis of actual traffic counts and established estimating procedures.

VOLATILE ORGANIC COMPOUNDS

Organic (carbon-containing) compounds that are often found as gases (or are easily converted to gases) under normal conditions, and can be toxic in high concentrations.

WADEABLE STREAMS

Streams that are small and shallow enough to adequately sample by wading, without a boat.

WASTE ENERGY

Energy obtained from using waste products as fuel, including **municipal solid waste**, landfill gas, **methane**, digester gas, liquid acetonitrile waste, tall oil, waste alcohol, medical waste, paper pellets, sludge waste, solid byproducts, tires, agricultural byproducts, closed loop biomass, fish oil, and straw.

WATT (W)

The unit of electrical power equal to one ampere under a pressure of one volt. A watt is equal to 1/746 horsepower. A **kilowatt** equals 1,000 watts. A **megawatt** equals 1 million watts.

WELLHEAD PRICE

Price of natural gas calculated by dividing the total reported value at the wellhead by the total quantity produced as reported by the appropriate agencies of individual producing states and the US Mineral Management Service. The price includes all costs prior to shipment from the lease, including gathering and compression costs, in addition to state production, severance, and similar charges.

WETLANDS

Lands where saturation with water is the dominant factor determining the nature of soil development and the types of plant and animal communities living in the soil and on its surface. The single feature that most wetlands share is soil or substrate that is at least periodically saturated with or covered by water. Wetlands can be classified in the following categories: (not all possible categories are shown)

Emergent: wetlands that are usually dominated by perennial plants such as erect, rooted, herbaceous hydrophytes, excluding mosses and lichens.

Estuarine: deepwater tidal habitats and adjacent tidal wetlands that are usually semi-enclosed by land but have open, partly obstructed, or sporadic access to the open ocean. Ocean water is at least occasionally diluted by freshwater runoff from the land, but evaporation may occasionally make the salinity level higher than that of the open ocean.

Forested: wetlands characterized by woody vegetation that is 20 feet (6 meters) tall or taller.

Intertidal: areas that are exposed and flooded by tides. Intertidal includes the splash zone of coastal waters.

Marine: open ocean overlying the continental shelf and its associated high energy coastline. Marine habitats are exposed to the waves and currents of the open ocean, with high salt concentrations (over 30 parts per thousand).

Shrub: wetlands that are dominated by woody vegetation less than 20 feet (6 meters) tall, such as true shrubs, young trees, and trees or shrubs that are small or stunted because of environmental conditions.

Subtidal: areas where the land is continuously submerged by marine or estuarine waters.

see also **deepwater habitats.**

WIND ENERGY

Energy present in wind motion that can be converted to mechanical energy for driving pumps, mills, and electric power generators. Wind pushes against sails, vanes, or blades radiating from a central rotating shaft.

WOOD ENERGY

Wood and wood products used as fuel, including round wood (cord wood), limb wood, wood chips, bark, sawdust, forest residues, charcoal, pulp waste, and spent pulping liquor.

YELLOWCAKE *see* **URANIUM**

Index

Index

ORDER FORM

S=ETE09 Book

Title	Qty	Edition	Price	ISBN Number	Standing Order	
State & Municipal Profiles Series					YES	NO
Almanac of the 50 States 2009		Hardcover	$95	978-0-929960-53-1	☐	☐
		Paperback	$85	978-0-929960-52-4	☐	☐
California Cities, Towns & Counties 2009		Paperback	$129	978-0-911273-48-9	☐	☐
		CD	$129	978-0-911273-49-6	☐	☐
Connecticut Municipal Profiles 2009		Paperback	$89	978-0-941391-32-0	☐	☐
		CD	$89	978-0-941391-33-7	☐	☐
Florida Cities, Towns & Counties 2009		Paperback	$129	978-0-941391-34-4	☐	☐
		CD	$129	978-0-941391-35-1	☐	☐
Massachusetts Municipal Profiles 2009		Paperback	$119	978-0-911273-44-1	☐	☐
		CD	$119	978-0-911273-45-8	☐	☐
The New Jersey Municipal Data Book 2009		Paperback	$129	978-0-911273-46-5	☐	☐
		CD	$129	978-0-911273-47-2	☐	☐
North Carolina Cities, Towns & Counties 2009		Paperback	$129	978-0-941391-36-8	☐	☐
		CD	$129	978-0-941391-37-5	☐	☐
Essential Topics Series						
Energy, Transportation & the Environment: A Statistical Sourcebook and Guide to Government Data 2009		Paperback	$85	978-0-929960-57-9	☐	☐
		CD	$85	978-0-929960-61-0	☐	☐
American Profiles Series						
Black Americans: A Statistical Sourcebook and Guide to Government Data 2009		Paperback	$85	978-0-929960-55-5	☐	☐
		CD	$85	978-0-929960-59-3	☐	☐
Hispanic Americans: A Statistical Sourcebook and Guide to Government Data 2009		Paperback	$85	978-0-929960-56-2	☐	☐
		CD	$85	978-0-929960-60-9	☐	☐
Asian Americans: A Statistical Sourcebook and Guide to Government Data 2009		Paperback	$85	978-0-929960-54-8	☐	☐
		CD	$85	978-0-929960-58-6	☐	☐

Offer and prices valid until 12/31/09

Purchase orders accepted from libraries, government agencies, and educational institutions.
Prepayment required from all other organizations.

Order Subtotal	
(Required ONLY for shipments to California) CA Sales Tax	
Shipping & Handling	
Total	

Please complete the following shipping and billing information. If paying by credit card or PO please call **(877)544-4636** or fax your completed order form to **(877)544-4635**. To pay by check, please mail this form and your payment to the address below.

Information Publications, Inc.
2995 Woodside Rd., Suite 400-182
Woodside, CA 94062

U.S. Ground Shipping Rates

Order Subtotal	Shipping & Handling
$0-129	$9
$130-260	$15
$261-400	$19
$401-500	$22
>$500	Call

Call for Int'l or Express Shipping Rates

Shipping Information (UPS/FedEx tracking number sent via email)

Organization Name	
Shipping Contact	
Address (No PO Boxes, please)	

City	State	Zip
Email Address (req'd if want tracking #)	Phone #	

Payment Information (mark choice)	☐ **Check**	☐ **Credit Card** ☐ Visa ☐ MC ☐ AMEX	☐ **Purchase Order** (attach PO to this form)
	Check #	CC#	PO #
		Exp Date	

Credit Card Billing Information   ☐ Check if same as Shipping Address

Name on Credit Card		
Billing Address of Credit Card		
City	State	Zip
Signature		

[ip] information
publications

ORDER FORM

Title	Qty	Edition	Price	ISBN Number	Standing Order YES	NO
State & Municipal Profiles Series						
Almanac of the 50 States 2009		Hardcover	$95	978-0-929960-53-1	☐	☐
Almanac of the 50 States 2009		Paperback	$85	978-0-929960-52-4	☐	☐
California Cities, Towns & Counties 2009		Paperback	$129	978-0-911273-48-9	☐	☐
California Cities, Towns & Counties 2009		CD	$129	978-0-911273-49-6	☐	☐
Connecticut Municipal Profiles 2009		Paperback	$89	978-0-941391-32-0	☐	☐
Connecticut Municipal Profiles 2009		CD	$89	978-0-941391-33-7	☐	☐
Florida Cities, Towns & Counties 2009		Paperback	$129	978-0-941391-34-4	☐	☐
Florida Cities, Towns & Counties 2009		CD	$129	978-0-941391-35-1	☐	☐
Massachusetts Municipal Profiles 2009		Paperback	$119	978-0-911273-44-1	☐	☐
Massachusetts Municipal Profiles 2009		CD	$119	978-0-911273-45-8	☐	☐
The New Jersey Municipal Data Book 2009		Paperback	$129	978-0-911273-46-5	☐	☐
The New Jersey Municipal Data Book 2009		CD	$129	978-0-911273-47-2	☐	☐
North Carolina Cities, Towns & Counties 2009		Paperback	$129	978-0-941391-36-8	☐	☐
North Carolina Cities, Towns & Counties 2009		CD	$129	978-0-941391-37-5	☐	☐
Essential Topics Series						
Energy, Transportation & the Environment: A Statistical Sourcebook and Guide to Government Data 2009		Paperback	$85	978-0-929960-57-9	☐	☐
Energy, Transportation & the Environment: A Statistical Sourcebook and Guide to Government Data 2009		CD	$85	978-0-929960-61-0	☐	☐
American Profiles Series						
Black Americans: A Statistical Sourcebook and Guide to Government Data 2009		Paperback	$85	978-0-929960-55-5	☐	☐
Black Americans: A Statistical Sourcebook and Guide to Government Data 2009		CD	$85	978-0-929960-59-3	☐	☐
Hispanic Americans: A Statistical Sourcebook and Guide to Government Data 2009		Paperback	$85	978-0-929960-56-2	☐	☐
Hispanic Americans: A Statistical Sourcebook and Guide to Government Data 2009		CD	$85	978-0-929960-60-9	☐	☐
Asian Americans: A Statistical Sourcebook and Guide to Government Data 2009		Paperback	$85	978-0-929960-54-8	☐	☐
Asian Americans: A Statistical Sourcebook and Guide to Government Data 2009		CD	$85	978-0-929960-58-6	☐	☐

Offer and prices valid until 12/31/09

Purchase orders accepted from libraries, government agencies, and educational institutions.

Prepayment required from all other organizations.

Order Subtotal _____

(Required ONLY for shipments to California) CA Sales Tax _____

Shipping & Handling _____

Total _____

Please complete the following shipping and billing information. If paying by credit card or PO please call **(877)544-4636** or fax your completed order form to **(877)544-4635**. To pay by check, please mail this form and your payment to the address below.

Information Publications, Inc.
2995 Woodside Rd., Suite 400-182
Woodside, CA 94062

U.S. Ground Shipping Rates	
Order Subtotal	Shipping & Handling
$0-129	$9
$130-260	$15
$261-400	$19
$401-500	$22
>$500	Call

Call for Int'l or Express Shipping Rates

Shipping Information (UPS/FedEx tracking number sent via email)

Organization Name		
Shipping Contact		
Address (No PO Boxes, please)		
City	State	Zip
Email Address (req'd if want tracking #)	Phone #	

Payment Information (mark choice)	☐ Check	☐ Credit Card ☐ Visa ☐ MC ☐ AMEX	☐ Purchase Order (attach PO to this form)
	Check #	CC#	PO #
		Exp Date	

Credit Card Billing Information   ☐ Check if same as Shipping Address

Name on Credit Card		
Billing Address of Credit Card		
City	State	Zip
Signature		

2995 WOODSIDE RD., SUITE 400-182
WOODSIDE, CA 94062   **WWW.INFORMATIONPUBLICATIONS.COM**
TOLL FREE PHONE 877-544-INFO (4636)
TOLL FREE FAX 877-544-4635

• Since 1980, A Trusted Ready Reference Resource for Easy-To-Use Federal, State and Local Information •